Social Studies for the Preschool-Primary Child

Fifth Edition

Carol Seefeldt
Institute for Child Study
University of Maryland

Merrill,
an imprint of Prentice Hall
Upper Saddle River, New Jersey   Columbus, Ohio

Library of Congress Cataloging-in-Publication Data

Seefeldt, Carol.
     Social studies for the preschool-primary child/Carol Seefeldt.—5th ed.
       p. cm.
     Includes bibliographical references and index.
     ISBN 0-13-457045-6 (pbk.)
     1. Social sciences—Study and teaching (Primary)—United States. 2. Social
     sciences—Study and teaching (Preschool)—United States.   I. Title.
    LB1530.S37 1997
    372.83'044—dc20

96-573
CIP

Cover art/photo: © Melanie Carr/Zephyr Pictures
Editor: Bradley J. Potthoff
Production Editor: Louise N. Sette
Copy Editor: Norma Nelson
Photo Researcher: Dawn Garrott
Design Coordinator: Jill E. Bonar
Text Designer: Ed Horcharik
Cover Designer: Jill E. Bonar
Production Manager: Patricia A. Tonneman
Electronic Text Management: Marilyn Wilson Phelps, Matthew Williams, Karen L. Bretz,
    Tracey Ward

This book was set in Zapf Calligraphic by Prentice Hall and was printed and bound by Quebecor Printing/Book Press. The cover was printed by Phoenix Color Corp.

© 1997 by Prentice-Hall, Inc.
Simon & Schuster/A Viacom Company
Upper Saddle River, New Jersey 07458

Earlier editions © 1993 by Macmillan Publishing Company and © 1989, 1984, 1977 by Merrill Publishing Company.

Photo credits: Andy Brunk/Merrill/Prentice Hall, p. 212; Scott Cunningham/Merrill/Prentice Hall, pp. 57, 144; Richard Farkas, pp. 75, 85, 120, 184, 194, 203, 220, 233, 245; Brad Feinknopf/Merrill/Prentice Hall, pp. 110; Linda Peterson/Merrill/Prentice Hall, p. 99; Barbara Schwartz/Merrill/Prentice Hall, pp. 61, 101, 121, 172, 275; Anne Vega/Merrill/Prentice Hall, pp. 1, 5, 10, 15, 34, 45, 50, 66, 68, 81, 104, 125, 135, 142, 158, 160, 170, 181, 204, 248, 255, 262, 279, 288, 290; Tom Watson/Merrill/Prentice Hall, pp. 24, 127, 239; Todd Yarrington/Merrill/Prentice Hall, pp. 71, 93, 150, 280, 284.

Printed in the United States of America

10 9 8 7 6 5

ISBN: 0-13-457045-6

Prentice-Hall International (UK) Limited, *London*
Prentice-Hall of Australia Pty. Limited, *Sydney*
Prentice-Hall of Canada, Inc., *Toronto*
Prentice-Hall Hispanoamericana, S. A., *Mexico*
Prentice-Hall of India Private Limited, *New Delhi*
Prentice-Hall of Japan, Inc., *Tokyo*
Simon & Schuster Asia Pte. Ltd., *Singapore*
Editora Prentice-Hall do Brasil, Ltda., *Rio de Janeiro*

To Hennessee, our friend who made so many things possible

Preface

Preparing this fifth edition of *Social Studies for the Preschool-Primary Child*, designed as a textbook for early childhood pre-service teachers and a resource for inservice teachers, has been a stimulating and exciting experience. In the years since it was first published, much has changed, but even more has remained the same. Each edition is based on knowledge of children, their growth and development; the idea that learning takes place through play in enriching environments; and the belief that learning is an integrated activity.

CHILD GROWTH, DEVELOPMENT, AND LEARNING

This fifth edition continues to be based on children. Although the world has changed, children have not. Today's children grow, develop, and learn in the same ways they always have. This newest edition of *Social Studies for the Preschool-Primary Child* is based on a solid theoretical and research foundation of child growth, development, and learning. Each chapter incorporates information on children's growth and development, including a section for children with special needs, and suggestions and ideas for working with these children and their families. Working with children from diverse cultural and ethnic backgrounds is also featured.

LEARNING TAKES PLACE THROUGH PLAY IN ENRICHING ENVIRONMENTS

This text assumes that all young children will be educated in enriching, stimulating educational environments that foster and promote their play, activity, and learning. Young children learn best through play with things, play with others, and play with ideas. Because play is the integrator of the curriculum and viewed as the basic mode for children's learning, it is featured in each chapter. Specific suggestions for teaching social studies content through children's play and activity are given throughout.

AN INTEGRATED APPROACH

The wholeness of the child is honored by advocating an integrated social studies curriculum. The wholeness of learning, the intimate relationship between children's cognitive growth and their social, physical, and emotional growth, is recognized and respected.

Social studies is approached as an integrated experience, one that involves the school, parents, and community. The social studies are also presented as a continual experience, one that builds as children move from a child-care setting or preschool to kindergarten and the primary grades.

Even though the text presents separate chapters for teaching social studies content, it is based on the theory that learning is an integrated activity. Thus teaching social studies involves all curriculum areas. Integrated throughout this fifth edition of *Social Studies for the Preschool-Primary Child* are suggestions for incorporating content from the visual arts, music, movement, science, health, and the language arts.

SOME CHANGES

While children and the way they learn have not changed since the first edition of *Social Studies for the Preschool-Primary Child,* the world has changed—dramatically so. Wars have come and gone, and the "Velvet Revolutions" in Eastern Europe have changed the climate in which we live. Recognizing the need to prepare children to become effective, fully functioning citizens in a rapidly changing world, authorities have called for reforms in social studies education. Position papers and national standards developed by the Office of Research and Improvement in the U.S. Department of Education in history, geography, and civics education suggest new directions for social studies education. The content of the position papers, including those of the California State Department of Education, the National Commission on Social Studies in the Schools, the National Council for the Social Studies, and the national standards, forms another basis of this text.

These position papers and standards all lead to the conclusion that social studies has been a neglected topic in schools for young children. *Social Studies for the Preschool-Primary Child* can remedy this neglect. Structured around the concepts considered key to the social science disciplines—the attitudes, values, and skills believed essential for citizens of a democratic society—it presents a multitude of ideas for introducing young children to social studies content. These suggestions will give young children an opportunity to build a foundation of knowledge of history, geography, economics, global education, and other social science disciplines, skills, and attitudes that will enable them to learn in the future.

The changes in the field of early childhood education itself are a final underpinning for *Social Studies for the Preschool-Primary Child*. As the field enters the future, it does so with a new sense of professionalism and newly established standards. The National Association for the Education of Young Children has set new standards for quality in programs serving children from birth through age 8, standards for appropriate curricula, and standards for the professional preparation of early childhood teachers.

The assumption that all children will be taught by professional, highly intelligent, and qualified early childhood teachers continues in this edition. Teachers are needed who take their cues from children, who understand children, and who know how to follow their leads. This text offers a multitude of practical ideas, suggestions, and guides for teaching social studies based on current research and theory, but the most important component of any social studies program will be a reflective, thoughtful, highly educated teacher who will plan, implement, and assess the social studies concepts, skills and attitudes, and learning experiences found herein.

ACKNOWLEDGMENTS

As always, I acknowledge those I live and work with. Even though living with someone who is continually preoccupied with completing a textbook has to be unpleasant, my family, Eugene Seefeldt, Paul and Kelcey Seefeldt, and Andrea Seefeldt-Knight, and my colleagues, Alice Galper, Kristin Denton, and Tonja Rucker are constantly supportive, cheerful, and patient. I do thank them.

There are many others who must be thanked. Brad Potthoff has offered invaluable advice that has strengthened this fifth edition of *Social Studies for the Preschool-Primary Child*. The insights and talents of Louise Sette, production editor, are deeply appreciated.

Special thanks are given to Dr. Fran Favretto, director of the Center for Young Children, and the faculty of the Center for always permitting me to visit and learn. The innovative, child-centered curriculum and practices of the Center for Young Children are reflected in this text. Likewise, working with Ms. Nancy Goldsmith, Ms. Juanita Green and the staff of the Montgomery County Head Start—Public School Transition Demonstration has been inspiring.

The thoughtful insights and comments of the reviewers Dr. JoAnne Buggey, University of Minnesota; Janice K. Ewing, University of Alabama at Birmingham; Dr. Blythe Hinitz, Trenton State College; Suzanne Krogh, Western Washington University; and Dr. Louise Swiniarski, Salem State College, are greatly appreciated.

Brief Contents

PART ONE
Planning for the Social Studies 1

Chapter 1   These Are the Social Studies   2
Chapter 2   Planning to Teach   21
Chapter 3   Resources for Learning   55

PART TWO
The Processes of Social Studies 99

Chapter 4   Social Skills   100
Chapter 5   Attitudes and Values   133
Chapter 6   Thinking and Concept Formation   155

PART THREE
The Content of the Social Studies   181

Chapter 7   History   182
Chapter 8   Geography   208
Chapter 9   Economics   237
Chapter 10   Multicultural Education   251
Chapter 11   Current Topics   272

References   291

Index   301

Contents

PART ONE
Planning for the Social Studies   1

Chapter 1
These Are the Social Studies   2

Past Approaches to the Social Studies   3
    Here-and-Now Curriculum   3
    Social-Living Curriculum   5
    Holiday Curriculum   7
More Recent Approaches   7
    Sputnik's Challenge   8
    Civil Rights   8
    Piaget   9
    Vygotsky   10
Social Studies Today   12
    Integrated   12
    Meaningful   13
    Of High Interest   14
    Skills, Attitudes and Knowledge   15
Summary   16
Projects   16
Resources   18
References   19

Chapter 2
Planning to Teach   21

Knowledge of Children   22
    All Children Are Alike   23
    So Alike—So Different   25
    Special Needs   26
Knowledge of the Community   30
    The Child's Physical World   31
    Cultural Knowledge and Values   31
    Knowledge of the Social Studies   32

Short- and Long-Term Planning   33
    Involving the Children   34
    Planning for the Spontaneous   35
Lesson Plans   37
    Day-to-Day Lesson Plans   37
    Preparation   37
    Long-Term Units, Projects, and Thematic Learning   40
Evaluation   47
    Observation   47
    Portfolios   48
    Informal Interviews   49
    Performance Interviews   50
    Checklists   51
    Standardized Tests   51
Summary   52
Resources   52
References   53

Chapter 3
Resources for Learning   55
The Children   56
The Family   56
    Informal Involvement   56
    Formal Involvement   59
The School   59
The Classroom   60
    Deciding on Centers of Interest   61
    Introducing Centers of Interest   61
    Types of Centers of Interest   63
    Vicarious Materials in the Classroom   77
Resources Within the Community: Field Trips   89
    Types of Field Trips   90
    Planning the Trip   91
    After the Trip   94
Summary   95
Projects   95
Resources   96
References   96

PART TWO
The Processes of Social Studies   99

Chapter 4
Social Skills   100
Social Skills   101

Theories of Socialization   102
Factors Affecting Social Development   106
The Self-Concept   109
Prosocial Skills   115
Making and Having Friends   126
Summary   129
Projects   129
Resources   130
References   130

Chapter 5
Attitudes and Values   133

How Children Learn Attitudes and Values   134
Values and Attitudes Are Modeled   134
Values and Attitudes Are Reinforced   135
Values and Attitudes Are Learned   136
Which Theory?   137
What Values Should Be Taught?   140
Democratic Values   141
Participation in a Democratic Society   145
Summary   152
Projects   152
Resources   153
References   153

Chapter 6
Thinking and Concept Formation   155

Role of the Teacher   156
Planning Experiences   156
Fostering Thinking Processes   159
Questioning and Sensing Problems   159
Locating Information   160
Organizing and Interpreting Information   163
Seeing Relationships and Beginning to Generalize   167
Interpreting, Reflecting, and Reaching Conclusions   168
Concept Formation   170
Key Concepts   171
Concept Development   173
Nurturing Concept Formation   174
Guidelines for Concept Formation   176
Summary   179
Projects   179
Resources   179
References   180

PART THREE
The Content of the Social Studies   181

Chapter 7
History   182
Key Concepts   183
Time   184
    Development of Time Concepts   184
    Routines That Teach Time   186
    Measuring Time   187
    The Passage of Time   188
Change   189
    In School   189
    In the Neighborhood   189
    In Nature   190
    In Children   190
The Continuity of Human Life   193
    The Family   193
    Intergenerational Contacts   193
    Holiday Celebrations   196
The Past   200
    People   200
    Objects   201
Methods of the Historian   203
Summary   205
Projects   205
Resources   205
References   206

Chapter 8
Geography   208
Key Concepts   209
The Earth is the Place in Which We Live   210
    Environment in Which We Live   211
    Land and Water   213
    A Nearly Round Sphere in a Solar System   214
Direction and Location   217
    Movement Exploration   217
    Directional Terms   219
    Relative Position   221
    Location   221
    Distance and Measurement   222
    Maps and Globes   223
Relationships Within Places   229

Spatial Interactions   232
Regions   234
Summary   234
Resources   235
References   235

Chapter 9
Economics   237
Development of Economic Concepts   238
Key Concepts   240
    Scarcity   240
    Economic Production   244
Summary   249
Projects   249
Resources   249
References   250

Chapter 10
Multicultural Education   251
How Children Learn of Others   251
    What Are Your Attitudes?   253
Key Concepts   254
Interdependency   255
    Similarities   256
    Resources for Learning About Others   259
Conflict Resolution   263
    Minimizing Conflicts   265
    Understanding War—Teaching Peace   266
Summary   268
Projects   268
Resources   269
References   270

Chapter 11
Current Topics   272
Current Events   273
    Making News   273
    Understanding News   274
Environmental Education   276
    Observation Skills   276
    Interdependency   278
    Aesthetic Awareness   278
    Social Consciousness   279
Career Education   282

Attitudes and Values   283
Essential Skills   285
Summary   288
Projects   289
Resources   289
References   290

References   291

Index   301

PART ONE

Planning for the Social Studies

❑ **Chapter 1:** These Are the Social Studies
❑ **Chapter 2:** Planning to Teach
❑ **Chapter 3:** Resources for Learning

These Are the Social Studies

After you read this chapter, you should be prepared to respond to the following questions:

- ❑ Can you give a definition of social studies?
- ❑ How was social studies taught in the past?
- ❑ Which theories have most influenced social studies today?
- ❑ What characterizes social studies today?

The goal of all education in our nation is to prepare children to become citizens of a democratic society. The field of social studies is uniquely suited to prepare children with the knowledge, skills, and attitudes they need to participate in, and contribute to, the small democracies of their homes, their preschool or primary groups, and their immediate neighborhoods today, as well as to become functioning citizens of society in general in the future. As defined by the National Council for the Social Studies, Social Studies is

> the integrated study of the social sciences and humanities to promote civic competence . . . social studies provides coordinated, systematic study drawing upon such disciplines as anthropology, archaeology, economics, geography, history, philosophy, political science, psychology, religion and sociology, as well as appropriate content from the humanities, mathematics, and natural sciences. (National Council for the Social Studies [NCSS], 1992 p. 5)

It seems overwhelming. The field of social studies is enormous, and children are so young. Children are too new to this earth to be expected to learn all about economics, history, and geography, much less the attitudes and skills involved in promoting equality for all and participation in democracy. Yet it is because children are so young that the subject of social studies is believed critical during early childhood. It is during these early years that the "foundation for later and increasingly mature understanding" (NCSS, 1989, p. 19) is constructed.

Realizing that children have a long time in which to grow and learn makes teaching social studies in the preschool-primary classroom less overwhelming. During their early years, children need to develop only anticipatory, intuitive ideas and interests that will serve as a foundation for the elaboration of the more complex understandings, attitudes, and skills of adults (Bredekamp & Rosegrant, 1995).

Then too, social studies learning takes place naturally as children participate in an early childhood classroom, which is itself a small democratic society. Within an early childhood program, children experience respect for the individual, the valuing of diversity, and the sharing of control. In this setting, the rights of the individual are constantly balanced with those of the group, and children naturally learn and utilize the knowledge, skills, processes, dispositions, and attitudes that will serve as a foundation for later social studies learning.

Looking to the past helps today's educators understand how social studies and young children can be brought together in meaningful, appropriate ways. Over the years, a number of approaches to social studies education for young children have been developed and implemented. Each of these approaches—(a) Lucy Sprague Mitchell's "here and now" expanding communities approach, (b) the social-living curriculum, (c) the holiday approach, and (d) more recent approaches stemming from social forces or research and theory—has contributed to current conceptions of social studies curriculum.

PAST APPROACHES TO THE SOCIAL STUDIES

Here-and-Now Curriculum

Prior to the 1930s, social studies was concerned with an unchanging body of facts—facts to be memorized. Appalled by this dry memorization of things children knew nothing of and had no experience with, Lucy Sprague Mitchell (1934) developed a practical and detailed account of the ways in which teachers of young children could enlarge and enrich children's understanding of the world around them and their place in it. Encouraged and influenced by the child development theory and progressive education movement of John Dewey (1944), Mitchell created a curriculum that was a direct attack on the elementary school's concentration of facts totally unrelated to children's lives.

Mitchell's basic educational concept was that children need to experience things for themselves. She believed that the social studies curriculum should be based on children's experiences and on their discovery of the world around them—on "the here and now."

Anything that was given to the children before they had an opportunity to experience it for themselves was considered dangerous by Mitchell. "It was never expected that the teacher could 'pour in' information, but that she would provide experiences that would enable the child to absorb information through firsthand manipulation and encounter" (Weber, 1969, p. 1920).

Even today, the dominant organizational pattern for social studies teaching is based on Mitchell's work (Brophy, 1990). For example, the typical social studies curriculum begins with the child in the neighborhood and then expands so that the child is introduced gradually to societies farther away in time and space.

Grade	Emphasis
K	The home and neighborhood
1	The community-community helpers
2	The United States
3	People in other lands

Unfortunately, many misinterpreted Mitchell's theories and ideas. Although convinced that social studies for young children should be solidly based on the here and now of children's lives, teachers ignored the complexities of the environment. Instead of focusing on the relationships of things in the environment, on the web of interdependency within it, social studies instruction revolved around the trite. Kindergarten children learned that they live in a family, first graders that the fire fighter helps them, and third graders that they live in a neighborhood. In the end, Mitchell's strong concern for relationship thinking and intellectual development was ignored.

Mitchell, however, saw the curriculum as complex, complicated, and full of opportunities to enhance children's knowledge and foster thinking. She wrote that at first glance, her suggestion that geography learning begin with children's explorations of their immediate environment seems preposterous because the environment is too complex. "Modern children are born into an appallingly complicated world. The complications of their surrounding culture, however, instead of making this attack impossible, make it imperative" (Mitchell, 1934, p. 8). By enlarging and enriching children's understanding of their immediate environment and world and their place in it, Mitchell aimed to develop children's intellectual capabilities in terms of "relationship thinking, generalization from experience, and the re-creation of concrete experience through symbolic, dramatic play" (p. 11).

Mitchell's insights into the intellectual processes of young children, in terms of relationship thinking, generalizing from experience, and re-creating concrete experience through symbolic or dramatic play, are consistent with current theories. Piaget (1969) and Vygotsky (1986), as well as Mitchell, agreed that:

❑ the younger the child, the greater the need for first-hand sensory experiences.

❑ one experience, fact, or idea needs to be connected in some way to another; two facts and a relation joining them are and should be an invitation to generalize, extrapolate, and make a tentative intuitive leap, even to build a theory.

❑ what a child learns must be useful in some way, related to daily life.

❑ play and active learning are necessary.

Certainly nothing can be more potent for fostering intellectual development than real experiences, and the here and now of children's lives can provide a foundation for social studies experiences, that is, if the total of children's here-and-now lives is considered.

Today, children's here-and-now world has expanded. "Bad whale, bad whale," said 3-year-old Jack to his mother, who was reading to him from a book

The younger the child the greater the need for first-hand, sensory experiences.

of nursery rhymes. "What whale?" asked his mother. Jack pointed to a tiny picture of a whale nearly hidden in an illustration and explained, "Bad whale didn't go home on time and got stuck in the ice." Jack identified with the three whales caught in the ice off Point Barrow, Alaska, demonstrating that the here-and-now world of young children extends beyond their immediate neighborhood. This doesn't mean that 3-year-olds should study maps to locate Alaska or trace the migration pattern of whales, but it does mean that today's teachers should recognize the complexities and totality of children's here-and-now environment. Building on children's interests and fostering their understandings of both their immediate world and what is far away in space and time are part of teaching social studies to young children.

Social-Living Curriculum

As Mitchell was formulating her theories, Patty Smith Hill, in an attempt to apply "the principles of democracy to school organization" (Hill, 1923), initiated a curriculum with the goal of habit and social skill development. Training children in the skills and habits necessary to function in a democratic society would prepare them to participate in a democracy. *A Conduct Curriculum for the Kindergarten and First Grade* (Burke, 1923) contained an inventory of habits stated in measurable form, primarily in the realm of moral and social conduct. This book specified all the social skills and habits children were to learn when in school.

This curriculum grew from child development and psychoanalytic theories as well as from the growing concern during the 1930s for education for citizenship. The social-living approach maintained that young children were developmentally ready to learn skills required for them to live with a group. Having learned in infancy and early childhood who they were and how they fitted into their family unit, children were then ready to develop the social skills necessary for nursery school and kindergarten.

Psychoanalytic theory, with its strong emphasis on the psychosocial segment of life, lent support to the social-living curriculum. The concepts that children should learn to express feelings and to find emotional and social support in the school situation were readily translated into the social-living curriculum.

Many of the early nursery schools established in our nation were based on the social-living curriculum. The primary goal of these schools was to support and foster the social and emotional growth of young children. Some were established by faculty wives at universities to provide socializing experiences for their young children, and others were set up for children of immigrants or poverty-stricken parents. Some of the goals of these schools were to lead children to

- ❑ learn to share materials and ideas.
- ❑ develop happy, healthy relationships with others.
- ❑ become self-reliant.
- ❑ feel responsibility for their own behavior.
- ❑ develop interest and attention span.
- ❑ cooperate with others in a friendly, willing spirit.
- ❑ appreciate the worth and contribution of others.
- ❑ develop self-concept and respect.

Implementation of these goals led to social studies programs that included large blocks of time for free play with others, discussions of feelings, emphasis on sharing and cooperating behaviors, and rule learning. Rather than becoming a strong, interdisciplinary, interrelated curriculum based on an individual's relationship with others and the environment, and rather than focusing on such complex social studies concepts as interaction, cooperation, and interdependency, the social studies curriculum called "social living" became a curriculum of benign neglect. Children were given a rich environment of toys and materials and left alone to learn to live with themselves and others. Even worse, in some programs elaborate plans and procedures were developed and implemented to teach children how to share, hang up their coats, take care of materials, blow their noses, and cooperate, with little concern for the intellectual development of the child.

If today's report cards are any indication, the social studies curriculum continues to revolve around the promotion of social skills. An analysis of report cards from Ohio indicates that over 80% of school systems include social skills items on their kindergarten and primary report cards, and 100% of all report cards include items categorized as work habits or social skills (Freeman & Hatch, 1989).

The social-living approach to the social studies curriculum has been criticized as much as the expanding communities approach. To focus the curriculum on the development of habits and skills is not only simplistic but even silly.

Perhaps the real failure of the social-living approach in social studies was the inability to view the child holistically. Failing to relate the social living of young children to their cognitive growth, the social-living curriculum proved to be inadequate. Many teachers failed to understand that learning to relate to others, to see another's point of view, and to understand the complex social rule system are cognitive as well as social tasks. Relating to others demands communication—a facility with language. The ability to express ideas, to share thoughts with others, to listen, and to speak are cognitive skills. Nevertheless, fostering children's language development, enhancing their cognitive growth, or even developing concepts of rules, moral values, and understandings, which should have been an integral part of the curriculum designed to foster social living, were neglected or ignored.

Holiday Curriculum

Another common approach to social studies in early childhood education—though a total embarrassment to those teachers who do guide children through valuable learning episodes—is the "holiday" curriculum.

Holidays, predictable and familiar, enjoyable diversions from the regular school routine, of interest to children and teachers, have become the basis for teaching social studies in some classrooms. Year after year, the same holiday celebrations are repeated without much concern for the knowledge, skills, attitudes, or values gained from them.

Commercial companies have fostered the holiday approach with unit plans, posters, and entire curriculum packages—all centering around the celebration of holidays. Children make Pilgrim hats following a pattern, cut a pumpkin at Halloween, sing songs, and listen to contrived stories that are more myth and legend than fact, turning social studies teaching into a superficial, untrue, and unrealistic perpetuation of myths (Derman-Sparks, 1989).

Even though the holiday approach is trite and inappropriate, this does not mean that there is no place for the recognition of holidays in the social studies curriculum. Celebration of holidays can promote identification with family, community, and nation (Vygotsky, 1986). Further, acquaintance with the "holiday customs of many lands fosters an appreciation of other cultures" (Duffey, 1982, p. iii). The use of stories, filmstrips, role playing, music, bulletin boards, and discussions to clarify the meaning of *honest, brave,* and *kind* can lead to children's developing historical understandings (NCHS, 1994; NCSSS, 1989).

MORE RECENT APPROACHES

Children have not changed over the years, but their world has. Children still grow in the same dependable ways (Ames & Ames, 1981). Their needs for food, rest, and activity have remained the same. Only the world around them has changed.

"Hey, watch out, you almost knocked down the rocket . . . if you want to go to the moon you'll have to sit here. Close the hatch . . . 9 . . . 8 . . . 7 . . . 6 . . . BLAST OFF!"

"Why are there wars? I saw a baby killed dead on TV last night . . . why?"

"Tomorrow we're going to see my grandmother in Texas, then I'll have been in eight states . . . Texas, Louisiana, Alabama, Georgia. . . . "

Today's young children have access to a variety of experiences, both actual and vicarious. Many have traveled, moved several times, or know friends, relatives, or teachers who have lived in different places and traveled far from home. Children watch television, go to movies, read books and magazines, listen to and observe the adults around them, and question and try to understand their complex, changing world.

To help children answer their questions and adjust to their rapidly changing world, social studies education has taken a number of new directions. The challenges of *Sputnik*, the civil rights movement, and changing ideas on the nature of children's thinking, found in the work of Piaget (1969), each led to different conceptions of the social studies curriculum in the preschool and primary classroom.

Sputnik's Challenge

Other forces have directed new trends in social studies education for young children. Following the U.S.S.R.'s launching of *Sputnik*, the first satellite to circle the earth, educators began a reevaluation of their theories and practices. In 1959 the famous Woodshole Conference was held. At this conference, scientists and educators met to determine the content of any given discipline and how to present that content to children. It was after this conference that Bruner (1960) stated that the "curriculum of a subject should be determined by the most fundamental understanding that can be achieved of the underlying principles that give structure to that subject" (p. 31).

This idea, that curriculum content should emphasize the structure of a discipline, caught the imagination of curriculum planners and educators and has guided curriculum development since that time. Concepts and theories were to become the core of the curriculum, inductive thinking the method of teaching. A number of mathematics, science, and social studies curricula resulted from this theory.

In 1965, Robison and Spodek published *New Directions in the Kindergarten*, a description of a program for 5-year-old kindergarten children that focused on the structure of subject matter and included curriculum content from science, mathematics, language, and social studies. Robison and Spodek concluded that young children could successfully learn concepts that once were believed to be beyond their grasp. Spodek (1973) later reinforced this conclusion by stating that young children

❑ can begin to develop significant social science concepts.
❑ bring a background of knowledge with them to school.
❑ deal with ideas over long periods of time.
❑ gather information in many ways.
❑ use the tools of the social scientist.
❑ transfer their understandings in approaching new situations (p. 197).

Civil Rights

At the same time that the reexamination of curriculum and educational practices was taking place, a growing awareness of the inequality of educational opportunities for many in our society was developing. The recognition that large groups of people had for many years been systematically discriminated against led to organized efforts to gain full civil rights and educational opportunity for all citizens, regardless of ethnic background or race. This drive for civil rights was manifest in the Johnson administration's War on Poverty.

The War on Poverty included the Elementary-Secondary Education Act of 1965 and the Head Start Program. Using the theories of Hunt (1961) and Bloom (1963), who believed that intelligence was malleable and could be influenced by early, enriching educational experiences, the government looked to early childhood education as a means of increasing children's intelligence and as an instrument to break the poverty cycle. Preschool programs that were enriching and stimulating and involved the child's total family were thought to increase young children's intelligence, as well as change their attitudes and the attitudes of their parents toward the school experience. Thus, early childhood education was designed to increase children's motivation to learn and achieve while increasing basic cognitive skills; all of this would, in turn, lead to success in later school experiences and in a chosen career.

Of all the programs within the War on Poverty, the Head Start Program has had, and continues to have, the most influence. The program is not only popular with parents, educators, and members of the community but has demonstrated long-lasting positive effects (Lazar & Darlington, 1982; Schweinhart, Weikart, & Larner, 1986). Twenty years after participating in a model early-intervention program, children had repeated fewer grades, had been less likely to be placed in special education programs, or to be involved in delinquency, and had been more productive than those of comparable backgrounds who had not participated in such a program (Washington & Bailey, 1995).

Because it emphasizes the development of self-concepts, skills in relating with others, and multicultural understanding as well as knowledge, social studies proved an excellent vehicle for fostering the goals of Head Start. Many social studies experiences—taking field trips, exploring the environment, observing adults at work, talking to visitors to the class—helped Head Start children better understand themselves and their place in the world.

Piaget

Coupled with renewed concern for providing equality of educational opportunity for all children during the 1960s was an emerging acceptance of the work of Jean Piaget (1969). The research and theories of Piaget, a Swiss psychologist who had been exploring children's thought processes since the early 1900s, began receiving the attention of psychologists and educators in the United States. It may be that Piaget's work became well known at this time because his writings were then being translated into English. On the other hand, the interest may have arisen because his theories offered psychologists a new way of looking at children's learning.

Piaget advocated that children, like humans of any age, construct their own knowledge through maturation and interaction with the total environment. He suggested that as children mature, they pass through four stages of cognitive development: (a) the sensorimotor period, from birth through age 2; (b) the preoperational period, ages 2 through 7 or 8; (c) the concrete operational period, ages 8 to adolescence; and (d) formal thought, after adolescence. To progress through these stages requires interaction with the social and physical environment and mental activity.

The social studies curriculum was heavily influenced by knowledge of the stages of intellectual growth identified by Piaget. Piaget's work on describing young children's abilities and their conceptions of the world, time, and space offered insights for social studies curriculum planners and teachers. Teachers can use Piaget's methods to delve into children's concepts of the world, space, and time, as well as to explore children's understanding of any other concepts. Further, the Piagetian interview, the probing technique used to uncover children's concepts, also can be used as a model for evaluating the outcomes of lessons, units, and other teaching sequences.

Vygotsky

The current focus on the social and cultural influences of all aspects of children's development has promoted the ideas of another theorist, Lev Semenovich Vygotsky (Berk & Winsler, 1995). Vygotsky, a student of literature, philosophy, and esthetics, was born in the late 1800s into a middle-class Jewish family in Belorussia. He graduated from the University of Moscow in 1917, and entered the field of psychology in the 1920s. His written research, during the 1920s and 1930s was banned by the Soviet Union. Vygotsky died in 1934, before the ban was lifted. His works were translated into English in the 1960s and 1970s and gradually became

Piaget and Vygotsky described how children learn through interactions with others, whether adults or children.

popular. They are now used to support curriculum development (Kozulin, 1986), especially social studies curriculum.

Vygotsky believed that:

❑ the human's social and psychological world are connected.

❑ child-adult interaction is important for cognitive development.

❑ the capacity to use language to regulate thought and action is distinctly human, and the source of conscious mental life.

❑ social experience is of utmost importance for cognitive growth.

❑ education leads development.

❑ teaching must be geared to the zone of proximal development, and must match what is to be taught to what the child already knows and can accomplish independently as well as with the help of an adult.

Vygotsky's ideas are similar in a number of ways to those of Piaget. Both believed that learning is the result of firsthand experiences that stem from the

Date	Approach	Concept	Weakness	Strength
1920s–1930s	Social Skills	Social skills are necessary for living in a democracy.	Translated into habit training and formation. Ignored the complexities of social learning.	Social skills are required to function in a democracy. The ability to cooperate, share, negotiate, and give up some of oneself to consider the rights of others is necessary.
1934	Here and Now	Children's learning is first-hand, based on experiences in their immediate environment.	Misunderstood and translated into meaningless simplistic units of my family, community helpers, etc.	When complexities of the immediate here-and-now world are considered and used to support thinking, this approach is current and supported by both theory and research.
1930s+	The Holiday Curriculum	None	Stereotypic and sterile in content, ideas; limits thinking, problem solving.	None.

Box 1.1
Historical foundations of social studies in early childhood education

child's environment. Both regarded play as a major educative activity, and both believed that social interaction with others, whether peers or adults, was critical for learning to take place.

SOCIAL STUDIES TODAY

Today's social studies are based firmly on the past. The theories of both Piaget and Vygotsky continue to influence the field. Mitchell's work of the 1930s, because of its similarity to Piagetian and Vygotskian thought, continues to undergird today's social studies. Current learning theory and research have also led to social studies curriculum that is integrated, meaningful, and of high interest.

Integrated

"The more situated in context, and the more rooted in cultural background and personal knowledge an event is, the more readily it is understood, learned, and remembered" (Iran-Nejad, McKeachie, & Berliner, 1990, p. 511).

Social studies is not isolated bits of information or knowledge children memorize but as Vygotsky indicated, is deeply rooted in their cultural background and personal experience. Planning to teach social studies begins by build-

Social Studies must match children's interest, growth, development, and mode of learning.

ing an understanding of children, their culture, and their home and neighborhood backgrounds.

Embedded within the context of children's family, school, and neighborhood, the social studies is integrated. This text presents the social science disciplines as separate subjects to enable teachers to plan and organize their own thinking. This organization, however, does not negate that fact that no one social science discipline can be separated or segregated from another or from the development of skills, attitudes, and values.

Just as social studies is an integrated subject, so is the entire early childhood curriculum. The social studies cannot be separated from any other subject matter of the school. Try to find a key concept or a suggested activity in any of the chapters of this text that does not involve the children in the other subjects of the school. Most will involve the children in using language through listening, speaking, reading, or writing, or in expressing their ideas through art, music, or movement, and many social science concepts will overlap with those of science and mathematics.

Meaningful

To be meaningful, social studies content must match children's intellectual growth. J. McVickers Hunt wrote years ago that meaningful teaching requires matching the richness of the learning environment to the intellectual growth of the child. The richness of an environment for intellectual growth is a function of the appropriateness of this match between inner organizations and external circumstances in a child's succession of encounters with his or her environment (Hunt, 1961). Hunt did not believe this would be easy: "While it is highly unlikely that even the best of contemporary child-rearing and education comes near maximizing the potential of children, any attempt to facilitate intellectual development with improvements demands a markedly increased understanding of this matter of the match" (1961, p. 261).

Vygotsky explained the importance of matching what is to be learned with the nature of children's cognitive maturity this way. "It is a well known and empirically established fact that learning should be matched in some manner with the child's developmental level" (Vygotsky, 1978, p. 85).

Today, early childhood educators have increased their understanding of the problem of the match with the publication of the National Association for the Education of Young Children's *Developmentally Appropriate Practice in Early Childhood Programs Serving Children From Birth Through Age 8* (Bredekamp, 1987), *Reaching Potentials: Appropriate Curriculum and Assessment for Young Children, Vol. 1* (Bredekamp & Rosegrant, 1992), and *Reaching Potentials: Transforming Early Childhood and Assessment, Vol. 2* (Bredekamp & Rosegrant, 1995).

The search for matching content to the child's intellectual development continues. Organizing the social science disciplines—skills, attitudes, and values—around key concepts or principles, and then describing what we do know of how children grow in understanding these, teachers have an opportunity to plan to present children with social studies material and content that will have meaning because it will match their developmental level.

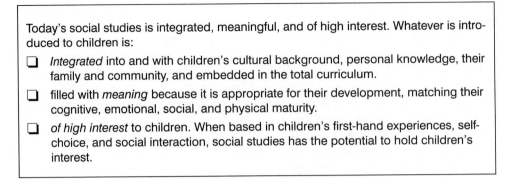

Today's social studies is integrated, meaningful, and of high interest. Whatever is intro-duced to children is:

☐   *Integrated* into and with children's cultural background, personal knowledge, their family and community, and embedded in the total curriculum.

☐   filled with *meaning* because it is appropriate for their development, matching their cognitive, emotional, social, and physical maturity.

☐   *of high interest* to children. When based in children's first-hand experiences, self-choice, and social interaction, social studies has the potential to hold children's interest.

Box 1.2
Social studies today

Then too, today's social studies is based on the concept that children are very young and do have a long time to grow. Social studies for these very young children is conceptualized as an initial foundation of social and physical knowl-edge on which later logical knowledge will be built. There is the desire to push young children to social studies concepts beyond their intellectual reach because teachers know children have a long time to grow and learn.

> Learning is a much more complex and drawn out process than generally acknowl-edged. The type of complex, meaningful learning that occurs in school and through-out the life span occurs over a period of weeks, months, and years, and there is good reason to believe that the nature of the learning process changes as the tasks of mas-tering a complex body of knowledge unfolds. (Shuell, 1990, p. 531)

Of High Interest

Interested children are learning children. Interest leads to "meaningful learning, promotes long-term storage of knowledge, and provides motivation for further learning" (Hidi, 1990, p. 549).

Whether studying history, geography, economics, current events, or cul-tures, children must find the material of high interest. All this knowledge satisfies their curiosity about themselves and the world in which they live, promoting a sense of competence. Competent children feel a sense of accomplishment, mas-tery, and success, which in turn motivates them to continue to want to learn.

At least three other factors stimulate children's interest in social studies—firsthand learning, self-choice, and social interaction. All the social studies in this text begin with children's firsthand interactions with their world. Because chil-dren, as all humans, learn through direct experience, the foundation for all social studies is in children's firsthand experiences, play, and spontaneous activity.

Child choice is encouraged throughout this text. Through centers of inter-est, children are able to select their own learning experiences and activities. Chil-dren who are given choices—who initiate their own learning experiences and activities, choose the centers in which they will work, and then make choices within the centers—are more likely to be successful, for the problem of match is at least partially solved.

As social beings, children are interested in being with others and learning to relate ever-more effectively with them. Relating with others, children are exposed to different ways of thinking, knowing, and valuing, all of which lead to expanding cognitive powers. Feeling competent socially and cognitively, children are fully motivated to want to continue to learn more about themselves, others, and the world in which they live (Barclay & Breheny, 1994).

Through the social studies, children continually become more successful learners. Successful learners are those who want to see and hear more, motivated not only to learn throughout their years in school, but throughout their entire lifetime.

Skills, Attitudes and Knowledge

Using the recommendations of the National Council for the Social Studies and the national standards, today's social studies revolves around introducing children to the skills, attitudes, and knowledge required of citizens of a democracy.

Focus on Skills

Within the small democracy of the preschool and primary classrooms, children begin to develop the social and participatory skills required of citizens in a

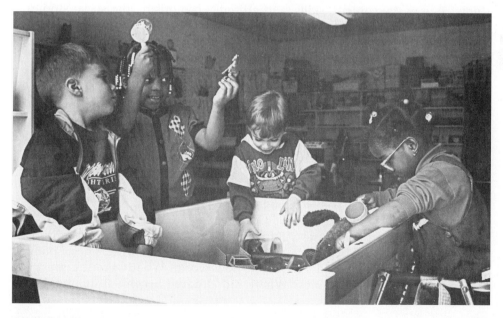

The development of skills, attitudes, and social studies content form an integrated whole and have their foundation in children's play.

democracy. They will be taught and gain the skills necessary to cooperate and share, and begin to assume responsibility for themselves as the total group. Because "good citizenship is not just a matter of the observance of outward forms, transmitted from the old to the young, but also a matter of reasoned conviction, the end result of people thinking for themselves" (NCSS, 1989, p. xi), thinking skills are fostered throughout the social studies curriculum.

Focus on Attitudes

There can be no doubt that children need to develop the attitudes and values congruent with the democratic way of life if democracy is to continue. The attitudes and values of respect for each individual, freedom of speech, setting and following rules, learning to make choices, and participating in the democracy of the classroom are fostered through the social studies.

Focus on Knowledge

More than ever before children need knowledge and a basic understanding of the world in which they live. Without knowledge of history, geography, economics, current events, and global interrelationships, children will be ill-prepared to assume responsible citizenship in the future.

SUMMARY

Knowledge of the content, skills, and attitudes comprising the social studies is necessary if children are to be prepared to take their place as fully productive members of a democratic society. Only when social studies is integrated, meaningful, and of interest to children, however, will it fulfill its purpose.

Built on the solid foundation of theorists, and based on knowledge of social studies education of the past, today's social studies is also grounded in current thinking about social studies education. Using the recommendations of the National Council for the Social Studies, the National Commission on Social Studies in the Schools, and the California State Department of Education, social studies is an exciting field.

PROJECTS

1. Observe a group of young children at play. As you observe, make a list of all the topics the children discuss or even mention. Then write a description of the nature of the child's here-and-now world. What were the most frequently mentioned topics? Where did children become acquainted with these topics?

2. Interview a teacher of young children. Ask him or her to define the social studies. What is included in this definition? How does the teacher decide

Charting a Course: Social Studies for the 21st Century (NCSSS, 1989)

The commission strongly recommends that the social studies curriculum revolve around the following:

- ❑ the history and culture of the people of the United States
- ❑ the history and culture of other people in the world
- ❑ geographic knowledge, national and worldwide, to provide a sense of place and relationship in time to historical and current events
- ❑ U.S. democratic traditions and political institutions, ideals, and values, and a comparison and contrast of them with other political systems
- ❑ the U.S. economic system and a comparison and contrast of it with other economic systems
- ❑ knowledge of other social sciences, such as anthropology, sociology, and psychology, where feasible and appropriate
- ❑ humane values and human achievements in religion, literature, philosophy, and the arts
- ❑ a social studies curriculum for the elementary schools based on the core curriculum
- ❑ the ability to think critically and to speak and write clearly and intelligently

History-Social Science Framework (CSDE, 1987)

This framework represents an effort to strengthen education in the history-social science curriculum. Among other ideas, this framework:

- ❑ is centered in the chronological study of history.
- ❑ proposes an integrated, sequential, and correlated approach.
- ❑ emphasizes the importance of history as a story well-told.
- ❑ emphasizes in-depth study as opposed to superficial skimming of enormous amounts of material.
- ❑ incorporates a multicultural perspective.
- ❑ includes ethical understanding and civic virtue.
- ❑ encourages development of civic and democratic values.
- ❑ proposes that critical thinking be included at every grade level.

Social Studies for Early Childhood and Elementary School Children: Preparing for the 21st Century (NCSS, 1989)

This report identifies three traditional standards as the social studies:

1. knowledge
2. attitudes
3. skills

Box 1.3
Social studies position papers and standards

what to include in the social studies curriculum? You may be able to interview a number of teachers, asking the same or similar questions. The goal is to determine how teachers define the social studies and make decisions about what to teach.

3. Describe your own experiences with the social studies. What was your first experience with social studies? Which memories are based on your feelings, which on knowledge? Interview a group of your peers and ask the same questions. What conclusions do you reach about your own experiences with social studies education as a child?

4. Obtain copies of the commissions' reports on the social studies. These are *Social Studies for Early Childhood and Elementary School Children: Preparing for the 21st Century,* from the National Council for the Social Studies; *Charting a Course: Social Studies for the 21st Century,* from the National Commission on Social Studies in the Schools; and *History-Social Science Framework,* from the California State Department of Education. Read and discuss these with other students. Which of the ideas presented in these reports will affect how you teach the social studies?

RESOURCES

Successful teachers identify and use the resources that are available to them. There are a number of organizations concerned with social studies education and with the education of young children. These associations offer publications, educational materials, services, and other resources for teachers. Why not write and request information about these services?

Association for Childhood Education International
11501 Georgia Avenue, Suite 315
Wheaton, MD 20902

Administration for Children, Youth, and Families
Box 1182
Washington, DC 20013

National Association for the Education of Young Children
1509 16th Street, NW
Washington, DC 20036-1426

National Council of Social Studies
3501 Newark St., NW
Washington, DC 20016

Your local school system, state department of education, and local affiliates of national associations have excellent resources that can be used in teaching the social studies.

REFERENCES

Ames, L., & Ames, J. (1981). *Don't push your preschooler.* New York: Harper.

Barclay, K. H., & Breheny, C. (1994). Letting the children take over more of their own learning: Collaborative research in the kindergarten classroom. *Young Children, 49*(6), 33–40.

Berk, L. E., & Winsler, A. (1995). *Scaffolding children's learning: Vygotsky and early childhood education.* Washington, DC: National Association for the Education of Young Children.

Bloom, B. (1963). *Stability and change in human characteristics.* New York: Wiley.

Bredekamp, S. (1987). *Developmentally appropriate practice in early childhood programs serving children from birth through age 8.* Washington, DC: National Association for the Education of Young Children.

Bredekamp, S., & Rosegrant, T. (1992). *Reaching potentials: Appropriate curriculum and assessment for young children, 1.* Washington, DC: National Association for the Education of Young Children.

Bredekamp, S. & Rosegrant, T. (1995). *Reaching potentials: Transforming early childhood and assessment, 2.* Washington, DC: National Association for the Education of Young Children.

Brophy, J. (1990). Teaching social studies for understanding and higher-order applications. *The Elementary School Journal, 90,* 351–419.

Bruner, J. (1960). *The process of education.* Cambridge, MA: Harvard University Press.

Burke, A. (1923). *A conduct curriculum for the kindergarten and first-grade.* New York: Scribner's.

California State Department of Education. (1987). *History-social science framework.* Sacramento, CA: Author.

Derman-Sparks, L. (1989). *Anti-bias curriculum: Tools for empowering young children.* Washington, DC: National Association for the Education of Young Children.

Dewey, J. (1944). *Democracy and education.* New York: Free Press.

Duffey, R. (1982). *Special days for special people.* Washington, DC: National Geographic Society.

Freeman, E. B., & Hatch, J. A. (1989). What schools expect young children to know and do: An analysis of kindergarten report cards. *The Elementary School Journal, 89,* 595–607.

Hidi, S. (1990). Interest and its contribution as a mental resource for learning. *Review of Educational Research, 60,* 549–573.

Hill, P. S., (1923). Introduction. In A. Burke, *A conduct curriculum for the kindergarten and first grade* (pp. x-xix). New York: Scribner's.

Hunt, J. (1961). *Intelligence and experience.* New York: Ronald Press.

Iran-Nejad, A., McKeachie, W. J., & Berliner, D. C. (1990). The multisource nature of learning: An introduction. *Review of Educational Research, 60*(4), 509–517.

Kozulin, A. (1986). *Vygotsky in context.* Introduction to L. Vygotsky, *Thought and Language.* Cambridge, MA: MIT Press.

Lazar, I., & Darlington, R. (1982). Lasting effects of early education: A report from the consortium for longitudinal studies. *Monographs of the Society for Research in Child Development, 47* (2–3, Serial No. 195).

Mitchell, L. S. (1934). *Young geographers.* New York: Bank Street College.

National Commission on Social Studies in the Schools. (1989). *Charting a course: Social studies for the 21st century.* Washington, DC: Author.

National Council for the Social Studies. (1989). *Social studies for early childhood and elementary school children: Preparing for the 21st century.* Washington, DC: Author.

Piaget, J. (1969). *The psychology of the child.* New York: Basic Books.

Robison, H., & Spodek, B. (1965). *New directions in the kindergarten.* New York: Teachers College Press.

Schweinhart, L. J., Weikart, D. P., & Larner, M. B. (1986). Consequences of three preschool curriculum models through age 15. *Early Childhood Research Quarterly, 1,* 15–45.

Shuell, T. J. (1990). Phases of meaningful learning. *Review of Educational Research, 60,* 531–549.

Spodek, B., (1973). Needed: A new view of kindergarten education. *Young Children, 49,* 191–197.

Vygotsky, L. (1978).*Thought and language.* Cambridge, MA: MIT Press.

Vygotsky, L. (1986). *Thought and language* (rev. ed.). Cambridge, MA: MIT Press.

Washington, V., & Bailey, V. J. (1995). *Project Head Start.* New York: Garland Press.

Weber, E. (1969). *The kindergarten: Its encounter with educational thought in America.* New York: Teachers College Press.

Chapter 2

Planning to Teach

Each school will make its own curriculum for small children.

L. S. Mitchell, 1934, p. 12

After you read this chapter, you should be prepared to respond to the following questions:

❑ Why is knowledge of children's growth, development, and learning necessary for planning the social studies?
❑ How does the nature of the community in which children live affect planning? How does social studies content affect planning?
❑ What short term plans will you set for social studies learning? Long range plans?
❑ What are the benefits of planning to teach through themes, units, or projects?
❑ How will you know if children have learned what you have planned to teach them?

B ut what do I teach?" asked one student after a discussion of the scope of the social studies. "I know social studies is a large, complex field, but isn't there a workbook, or something we can use that tells what to teach?"

Even if there were a set of guidelines telling exactly what social studies content, skills, and attitudes to teach young children, teachers would still have the responsibility of deciding what to teach and how. If social studies is to be meaningful and totally integrated into children's culture, background of experiences, and social interactions—and be of high interest—the teacher must, based on her knowledge of the children, the community in which they live, and the social studies, "make her own curriculum for small children" (Mitchell, 1934, p. 12).

Throughout the years, reflective teachers have followed Lucy Sprague Mitchell's (1934) guidelines for planning the social studies. Those teachers understand that in order to bring children and the social studies together, curriculum must first hold meaning and interest for each child (Hidi, 1990) and be based on children's firsthand interactions (Iran-Nejad, McKeachie, & Berliner, 1990) with their immediate environment.

Even when given mandated curriculum plans, national standards, or a curriculum designed by a local school district or state department of education, teachers still must make decisions about what they will teach. The decisions teachers will make include the following:

❑ What short- and long-term goals and objectives will guide the curriculum?
❑ How will these goals and objectives be achieved?
❑ How can children's interactions with their environment and community be used to achieve these goals?
❑ What place will mandated curriculum plans hold in the curriculum? How can the goals and objectives of mandated plans be achieved in meaningful ways?
❑ How will the curriculum be evaluated?

As in the past, these decisions cannot be made without (a) knowledge of children, (b) knowledge of the community in which the children live, and (c) knowledge of social studies content.

KNOWLEDGE OF CHILDREN

"I am advising you to retain Judy in kindergarten for another year," the teacher said to 6-year-old Judy's parents. "She doesn't know which day comes before or after another, nor can she tell you the name of the month or the months that came before or after. She just won't make it in first grade until she can do so."

If Judy's teacher had based her social studies instruction on knowledge of child growth, and development, she would have known that isolated facts, such as the names of the days of the week or month, have no meaning to children. Further, she would have known that children will learn these automatically as they progress through the primary grades.

Without knowledge of children, teachers are unable to match the curriculum or its goals and expectations for children's learning to the developmental capabilities of children. Without this match, social studies is without meaning and is of no interest to children. As a result, they will fail. Once children have experienced failure, research shows they continue to think of themselves as failures.

Basing curriculum on knowledge of children's growth and development, social studies can be both age appropriate and appropriate for each individual.

1. *Age appropriateness.* Knowledge of the predictable changes that occur in all domains of development—physical, emotional, social, and cognitive—is the framework from which teachers prepare the learning environment and plan appropriate experiences.

2. *Individual appropriateness.* Each child is a unique individual with an individual pattern and timing of growth and an individual personality, learning style,

Each child is unique.

and family background. Both the curriculum and adults' interactions with children should be responsive to these individual differences (Bredekamp, 1987, p. 2).

Basing curriculum on the universal characteristics of children (i.e., those characteristics that make all children alike) and on the unique characteristics of each child (i.e., those things that make each an individual) is one way to ensure that children will be living fully each day and will be prepared to take their place in a democratic society in the future.

All Children Are Alike

Regardless of where children live, their ethnic background, or the structure of their family, they all have the same needs and share similar characteristics.

All Children Have Similar Needs

Young children share certain characteristics. For instance, all young children need

- ❑ love, security, and the attention of a friendly, interested, sympathetic adult they can trust.
- ❑ to have their physical needs met for shelter, food, warmth, and clothing.

All children have the same need for love, friendship, security, and safety.

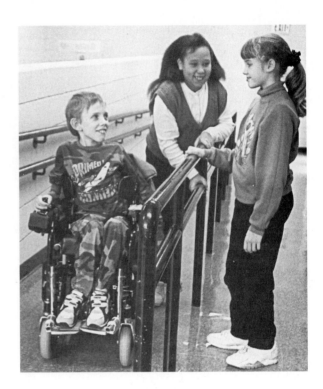

❑   to feel good about themselves and to have the opportunity to learn to relate to others, to make friends, and to be a friend to others.

All Children Are Active Learners

All young children are active socially, physically, and mentally. Their growing bodies demand that they move about physically and interact with one another. Children need to talk, to question, to take things apart in their attempts to find out about, and make sense of, their world.

If children's basic needs for security and love have been met, they are curious, interested in their environment, and filled with the desire to learn more about themselves and the world in which they live.

All Children Pass Through the Same Stages of Thought

All young children are in the stage of preoperational thought. "An operation is a thought—what Piaget called an internalized action. In this sense, it is a mental action, or more precisely, an operation performed on ideas according to a certain rule of logic" (Lefrancois, 1989, p. 364). Between the ages of 2 and around 7 or 8, children's thinking is preoperational. This means that these young children are beginning to think and use symbols, to represent their actions mentally, to anticipate consequences before an action actually occurs, and to develop some idea of causes, but they are not yet capable of thinking abstractly. Their thinking is pre-operational—done before they can think about ideas or perform operations on them.

A child in the stage of preoperational thought relies heavily on the way things look. Perception dominates thought; the way things look is the way they are. Thus a child under age 7 or 8 says there is more juice in a tall, skinny glass because it *looks* bigger than a short, squat one, or there are more candies in a long, spread-out row because it *looks* like more pieces than candies in a bunched group.

At around age 7 or 8, children's thinking changes, and they begin to think operationally. They can tell you that the amount of juice poured into two containers of different shapes stays the same because no juice has been added or taken away. Even though children after age 7 or 8 can reason this way, their thinking is still tied to the concrete. They cannot think about the hypothetical and cannot go from the real to the merely possible, or from the possible to the real. Their thought is bound to the real world, the concrete—hence the term *concrete operations*. It is not until around the age of 11 or 12 that children enter the last stage of thought, in which they can think formally and have the ability to manipulate abstract ideas.

Because children cannot think abstractly until nearly age 11 or 12, most of the goals and objectives planned for early social studies learning will be informal and introductory. During the preschool and primary grades, children only need to develop a base of firsthand experiences from which to learn later abstract concepts, and an interest in learning.

So Alike—So Different

Young children who are so alike are, as individuals, very different. Each child is unique. Understanding the basic characteristics of all children, teachers recognize that each one brings to school a different background of experiences, interests, and motivations. Each grows and learns according to an individual internal plan. Successful social studies is based on teachers' understanding of the experiences children have had before coming to school, the interests of each child, individual abilities, special needs, and the culture in which children live (Winter, 1994/1995).

Experiences

For the most part, children entering school have a full, rich background of experience. Many children have had opportunities to explore their immediate neighborhoods, to become familiar with traffic systems and community helpers, to discuss their experiences with adults, and to recognize the relationships among their experiences. Teachers can determine the children's background of experience by

❑ visiting their homes and talking with their parents about the things the children have done.

❑ walking around the children's neighborhoods to see what the community offers in the way of experiences.

❑ interviewing the children, asking them to tell about the things they do, places they have been, and things they would like to do.

Whatever the children's backgrounds, they are important indicators of objectives and goals for the social studies program. Teachers plan objectives to support past experiences of children; to introduce new experiences that can be incorporated into the children's previous experiences; and to extend, clarify, and expand all experiences.

Interests

As anyone who has contact with young children knows, they are interested in learning about everything. They enter preschool interested in learning about "ants, worms, cars, boats, water, air, space, foreign countries, letters, machines, trees, colors, families, seeds, rocks, love, hate, birth, death, friendship, war, peace, cosmic forces, good and evil" (Martin, 1985, p. 396). To plan a social studies curriculum, some understanding of what the group, and each individual child within the group, is interested in will be necessary. You could begin by

❑ talking with them informally, asking them what they would like to know more about, what they would like to do, or what they know a lot about.
❑ observing them at play, noting the things they play with, how they use materials, what they play, and which books they select.
❑ discussing the children's interests with their parents, asking what the children like to do at home.

Abilities

Not only do children bring a wide range of experiences and interests to the classroom, they also bring great differences in social, emotional, physical, and intellectual abilities. These differences in abilities form the basis of other goals and objectives of the social studies for the group and individual children.
To determine the abilities of children, you might

❑ review past records of health and physical growth.
❑ observe them at play to note social skills and how they interact with others.
❑ structure some task for them to complete, observing how successful each child is.
❑ review results of standardized measures.

Special Needs

All children are special, and each has individual needs, strengths, and weaknesses. Some children, however, have needs and individual characteristics that require special planning and care. Public laws have been passed to ensure that the special needs of these children will be met. PL 94-142, The Education of All Handicapped Children Act of 1975, protects children with special needs by requiring that every child, regardless of handicapping condition, have access to free and appropriate educational experiences in the least restrictive environment.

PL 99-457, The Federal Preschool Program and Early Intervention Program Act of 1986, extends rights and services to handicapped infants, toddlers, and preschoolers. Until 1986, children between ages 3 and 5 received services only at each state's discretion. PL 99-457 requires appropriate public education for those children. From birth through age 2, the law provides for services to children who show signs of developmental delay, have identifiable physical or mental conditions, or are at risk because of medical or environmental problems. (Diamond, Hestenes, & O'Connor, 1994).

Teaching children with special needs is not new to early childhood education. The needs of exceptional children in the regular preschool or primary classroom have been recognized for decades by teachers in early childhood education.

What is new is that PL 94-142 and PL 99-457 protect children with special needs by requiring educational experiences in the least restrictive environment. The preschool or primary classroom is often determined to be the least restrictive environment, for it gives children with special needs the opportunity to enter the mainstream of living and learning with other children their age. (Wolery & Wilbers, 1994).

As a teacher of special children you need to (a) familiarize yourself with the complete text of PL 94-142; (b) ask your director, principal, or supervisor for your child-care or school system's guidelines for implementation of PL 94-142; (c) obtain resources and special assistance when mainstreaming children with special needs; and (d) perhaps request an aide in the classroom—a teacher of a specific skill such as sign language—or assistance in helping you acquire specialized skills.

- ❑ Explain terminology. Professionals may use terms or names that have little or no meaning to others.
- ❑ Acknowledge and then try to develop an understanding of the parents' feelings.
- ❑ Listen to parents' agenda and wishes concerning their child.
- ❑ Keep parents informed.
- ❑ Be accountable. If you say you're going to be responsible for a task, make certain parents can depend on you.
- ❑ Recognize that diverse family structures and parenting styles will influence parent participation.

Box 2.1
Communicating with Parents of Children with Special Needs
From "Parental Feelings: The Forgotten Component When Working with Parents of Handicapped Preschool Children" by R.M. Gargiulo and S.B. Graves, 1991, *Childhood Education, 67*(3), pp. 176–179.

Special-needs children who benefit from being in the mainstream preschool or primary classroom are those who are visually or hearing-impaired, who have physical disabilities or mental retardation, emotional problems, speech or language impairments, or who are gifted. While labeling of individual children is discouraged, it does help to know something of the specific conditions children may bring to the classroom.

Visual Impairments.   Visually impaired children are frequently able to work and learn effectively in the regular classroom. They are able to participate in many of the activities without special assistance. Reynolds and Birch (1986) offer a commonsense approach to teachers working with visually impaired children by saying, "These children cannot see!"

Remember that the visually impaired child does not learn by looking, or through imitating others. Visually impaired children will need systematic and deliberate introduction to the physical environment of the room, school, and playground, as well as to the activities of the school. You will need to maintain consistency in the physical environment, to provide tactile guides in the room, and to communicate by touching as well as speaking.

Hearing Impairments.   Children who are hearing impaired also find the mainstream preschool and primary classroom suited to their needs. You will want to learn how to communicate with the hearing-impaired child, using the method the child uses, and learn the care of hearing aids and how to assist the child with the aid.

Children come to school with a variety of visual skills.

Hearing-impaired children can participate in nearly all school activities. As with the visually impaired, you need to communicate with hearing-impaired children in special ways. They learn by seeing, and they respond to touch.

Physical Disabilities.   The physical environment may need to be adjusted for children with physical disabilities and for those who use orthopedic aids. Ask specialists for assistance in adapting the physical plant to the needs of the child, both indoors and outdoors. Special chairs, tables, and play equipment can be purchased or made for children with physical disabilities, enabling them to participate in school activities.

As with any child, you will want to learn all you can about the physically disabled child's condition. You will need to know the child's limitations and potentials, as well as how to care for orthopedic equipment and assist the child with the equipment.

Mental Retardation.   Children who differ markedly from average/normal intelligence are also frequently mainstreamed in the preschool and primary classroom. The open schedule, free activity times, and emphasis on concrete learning, as well as on social, emotional, and language development, are well suited for children who are retarded.

You will need to analyze each task so that you can present it to the child in small steps. Specific experiences and instruction in listening and speaking, social skills, and self-help skills will enable children who are retarded to achieve success.

Emotional Problems.   Nearly everyone has lost control, felt afraid, or had difficulty interacting with others. At one time or another all children experience difficulty handling strong emotions. Children who have more difficulty than most in handling their emotions find a preschool experience very beneficial. Here they can learn techniques for channeling emotions appropriately and strengthening their ability to control behavior.

Probably all preschool activities will benefit children who need to learn to handle emotions, and the primary classroom environment can be modified to permit more activities designed for this purpose. When you have a child who is totally out of control—hitting, kicking, hurting self and others—it will be helpful to assign an aide or a volunteer to stay with the child for a while, offering the child support and guidance in learning to gain control over strong emotions.

Speech and Language Impairments.   Specific diagnoses and planned activities in listening and speaking can be arranged for children with language impairments. Speech and hearing specialists can assist you as you plan for these children, and volunteers or aides may help you implement specific lessons.

Remember too that all of the language activities of the preschool-primary classroom will benefit children with speech and language impairments. The stories, poems, creative dramatics, and dramatic play will be of great benefit.

Gifted Children.   Children who demonstrate intelligence higher than the norm, or who have specific gifts and talents, deserve to have their special needs met.

Typically, the needs of the gifted have been met by acceleration, enrichment, placement in special schools, or advancement to a higher grade. The social studies offer the gifted child the opportunity to explore special interests and develop talents.

A Program of Inclusion.   While public laws protect all children's rights to appropriate education, teaching special-needs children requires much more than just being together in a classroom. Children with special needs require "acceptance for who they are and an environment that fosters their autonomy and the development of alternative modes of interaction with the world" (Derman-Sparks & A.B.C. Task Force, 1989, p. 40).

Derman-Sparks and the ABC Task Force (1989) suggest that early childhood programs

- ❏ develop an "inclusive" educational environment in which all children can succeed.
- ❏ enable children with disabilities to develop autonomy, independence, competency, confidence, and pride.
- ❏ provide all children with accurate, developmentally appropriate information about their own and others' disabilities, and foster understanding that a person with a disability is different in one respect but similar in many others.
- ❏ enable all children to develop the ability to interact knowledgeably, comfortably, and fairly with people having various disabilities.
- ❏ teach children with disabilities how to handle and challenge name calling, stereotypic attitudes, and physical barriers.
- ❏ teach nondisabled children how to resist and challenge stereotyping, name calling, and physical barriers directed against people with disabilities.
- ❏ encourage children to ask about their own and others' physical characteristics.
- ❏ provide children with accurate, developmentally appropriate information.
- ❏ enable children to feel pride, but not superiority, about their racial identity.
- ❏ enable children to develop ease with, and respect for, physical differences.
- ❏ help children become aware of our shared physical characteristics—what makes us all human beings.

KNOWLEDGE OF THE COMMUNITY

"I found four signs with words, and seven without," exclaimed an excited first-grader returning from a walk around the block. The teacher explained, "There's so much available for children to learn in the environment, that I rarely use a social studies book."

Knowledge of child growth and development is not the only foundation on which social studies curriculum is planned (Bredekamp, 1991). Just, as Mitchell (1934) suggested, teachers must become aware of the nature of the here-and-now world in which children live. Then they must develop knowledge of the culture and values of the community. Just as teachers cannot plan social studies curriculum without knowledge of child growth and development, they cannot successfully implement it without knowledge of the community.

The Child's Physical World

"The practical tasks for each school are to study the relations in the environment into which their children are born and to watch the children's behavior in their environment, to note when they first discover relations and what they are" (Mitchell, 1934, p. 12). To do this, you might drive or walk through children's neighborhoods. One teacher asked a parent to guide her through the school's neighborhood. As they walked and talked together, they noted the following:

- ❏ the physical nature of the area
- ❏ places children enjoyed going
- ❏ the history of the neighborhood
- ❏ neighbors who had special skills or resources
- ❏ places of business
- ❏ other resources for learning

One day after school, the teacher walked through the neighborhood again. This time she noted where children played, the pathways they took on their way home from school, and most importantly, the way they interacted with peers, adults, and their parents. She also noted how people functioned in the neighborhood. The insights into the children's community and here-and-now world led to the teacher's decisions about the overall goals and objectives for the social studies curriculum.

Cultural Knowledge and Values

Less concrete than knowledge of the physical environment, but perhaps even more important, is the knowledge of the culture and values of the community. Early in the school year, teachers try to become acquainted with each child's ethnic and subcultural group backgrounds, as well as the culture and values of the community as a whole. This can be done through various sources:

- ❏ Informal conversations. Early in the school year, teachers can talk informally with parents and children. Teachers can ask them what the family does on weekends, in the evenings, before school starts, or on vacations. They can note the traditions, customs, language, special foods, items of dress, and types of celebrations mentioned by the children or their parents during these conversations (Lee, 1995).
- ❏ Resource persons. A resource person might be able to inform teachers about the traditions, history, and meaning of a group's practices.

❑ Formal inservice activities. Teachers and administrators can initiate a variety of activities and programs designed to acquaint them with different cultures and values. One school enrolled a large number of children from Cambodia. A resource person knowledgeable about the Cambodian culture and its demands on children and their families was invited to talk with the teachers. In a short period of time, she was able to build a base of knowledge useful for understanding and teaching these children. (Newman, 1995).

Other meetings might be sponsored by community organizations or local businesses and might involve parents and other community residents. Slides, videos, and photographs of the community are helpful in illustrating the culture of a community.

Knowledge of the Social Studies

"I have to take *two* more courses from the social sciences if I want to teach young children? What in the world does my taking geography, history, and economics have to do with young children?" an undergraduate student complained to her advisor.

Yet, without complete, in-depth knowledge of the social sciences, and the skills and values considered a part of social studies, teachers will not be effective. Most teachers have taken undergraduate courses in history, geography, economics, and the other social sciences. Most teachers continue to expand their knowledge of content by participating in inservice courses and summer workshops or by taking advantage of community-sponsored courses. Local museums, associations, and businesses all offer a variety of seminars and activities designed to promote knowledge of geography, history, and other social science disciplines.

The social science disciplines embody a great deal of knowledge. To make this vast, even overwhelming amount of information accessible to both teacher and child, key concepts have been identified. In each of the social science disciplines, ideas, overriding principles, or generalizations considered key to that discipline have been identified. Social studies curriculum can be based on these key concepts.

In *The Process of Education* (1960), Bruner described how key concepts could be used as a base for curriculum planning. By thinking in terms of key concepts, teachers can organize the curriculum in a spiral fashion. Once a broad idea or concept has been identified, such as the idea that people establish laws, teachers of young children can then decide the most effective and appropriate way to introduce this idea to children in an intellectual, honest way. Bruner (1960) was adamant that concepts be taught with scrupulous intellectual honesty, as well as with an emphasis on children's intuitive grasp of ideas. Thus, knowledge of both child development and content is required. If a concept key to politics is setting and keeping rules, then 4-year-olds might decide on rules for using the woodworking bench, 5-year-olds could dictate a list of rules they will follow in their group for the coming year, and 6- and 7-year-olds might draw up rules for their class. Children in the middle grades might study the rules of their school, and those in junior high school and high school could study the lawmaking bodies of the community, state, and nation.

Teachers also need to be knowledgeable of the nature of social studies skills, attitudes, and values. Teaching skills is a part of both the social studies and other areas of the curriculum. Some skills, however—thinking skills and the social skills, such as map reading and decision making—are believed to be best fostered within the context of the social studies.

Skill development begins at birth and continues throughout life. To gain proficiency, to be able to do something well, means that children will have the opportunity to practice thinking skills and social skills throughout their preschool and primary experiences.

Attitudes and values constitute the third major area of the social studies. Those included in the social studies are those necessary for the perpetuation and continuation of our society. Teachers select goals and objectives for children's learning of content and skills congruent with the values of a democracy. The entire early childhood program will be arranged around the goals and objectives that will foster

❑ each child's own worth and dignity.
❑ respect for self and others.
❑ participation in, and responsibility for, the group.
❑ the disposition of learning to learn.

SHORT- AND LONG-TERM PLANNING

With an understanding of the children, their culture, and the social studies, you have a base from which to answer the questions, "What can the children do tomorrow?" and "What am I trying to help the children learn, understand, and experience?"

Before you begin to answer these questions, consider some other factors:

❑ the reality of your situation
❑ available resources
❑ any constraints with which you must work
❑ how to provide for a balanced program

1. *Reality.*   The reality of a situation influences how a teacher plans to meet objectives. The size of the group of children, their ages and abilities, and the school's physical plant all affect your plans, as do the adult-child ratio, special grouping practices, teaching arrangements, and mandated plans. Many teachers take a less-than-ideal situation and—by changing or rearranging furniture, using outside spaces, or involving parent volunteers—create a more suitable situation in which to teach.

2. *Resources.*   Thinking about the type of resources available for children's social studies learning is a part of planning. Every area and each school has unique resources for children's learning. Using the ideas of Lucy Sprague

Mitchell, you can base some of your plans on the resources unique to your school and community.

3. *Constraints.*   In addition to the school's physical plant, other factors can constrain your plans. These might be in the form of mandates from the school system or state department of education. Reviewing such mandates before you begin planning enables you to build on them rather than be restricted by them.

4. *Balance.*   Balance is important when making any plans. For social studies, teachers need to achieve a balance among objectives fostering skills, attitudes and values, and knowledge, and a balance in the ways these objectives will be achieved. You need a balance between large-group, small-group, and individual activities; free play and more structured activities; concrete and vicarious experiences; and activities for divergent and convergent thinking.

Then too, before planning for specific lessons, units, or projects, it's necessary to think about involving the children in planning and to make plans for spontaneous and incidental learning.

Involving the Children

Everyone benefits when children and teachers plan together. Teachers benefit because children who have been involved in planning their own learning are more highly motivated to learn and less likely to disrupt the group. Children benefit because they know they belong. They feel in control.

Teacher-child planning implies cooperation between teacher and child. It doesn't mean that children take over. Young children would feel insecure if that were the case; they do want and need an adult to make decisions and to protect and guide them. On the other hand, teacher-child planning doesn't mean that a

Everyone benefits when children
and teachers plan together.

teacher decides ahead of time, then fishes until the children give the responses she had in mind. "What should we make today?" asked a teacher. "I'm going to build a garage," answered one child, and another said, "I'll make a painting." The teacher continued questioning until a child asked, "Are we going to make valentines?" "Yes, that's it. Today we're making valentines," said the teacher. Later, when asked why she proceeded this way, the teacher explained, "It's very important to involve the children in making plans."

Much teacher-child planning is informal and takes place when 3- and 4-year-olds are asked to plan what they will do next or during the morning. Five-year-olds may be able to make plans for a party next week or at the end of the month, and primary-age children can develop even more extended plans.

All children should be asked to take part in making plans. Those who may be too shy to speak in front of a group or not quick enough to take their turn may need other opportunities besides group discussions to contribute their ideas. Some planning can be done by talking with individuals or small groups of children as they play and work.

Children plan

❑ with what they will begin to work and play.
❑ with whom they will play and work.
❑ the materials they need to complete a project.
❑ what things they would like to learn more about.
❑ how they will celebrate a birthday or holiday.
❑ places they would like to visit to learn more about a specific topic.

More formal ways of planning with children have been developed. Many teachers ask children to tell them what they Know about a specific topic, what they Want to learn, and after the lesson, what they have Learned (Ogle, 1986) as a means of involving children in planning (see Box 2.2).

A teacher from the University of Maryland's Center for Young Children sent a letter to each kindergarten child before school started. She asked each to return the enclosed self-addressed postcard to her with the things they thought they wanted to learn in the coming year.

After the children had settled into the kindergarten routine, the teacher organized their postcards into a graph. The children discussed the graph, counting the cards in a given area. Most of the children responded that they wanted to learn to read and do math, but many other topics were included which were incorporated into the teacher's plans.

Planning for the Spontaneous

Teaching young children is never predictable. Their curiosity, interests, and creativity can jump from one exciting event to an equally thrilling moment, none of which may have been planned by a teacher or curriculum guide. Being able to

Box 2.2
A K–W–L Chart
(D. Ogle, 1986)

K   *What do we **K**now about fire fighters?*
They put out fires.
Only men can be fire fighters, girls can't.
Firemen are big.

W   *What do we **W**ant to learn about fire fighters?*
Where do they sleep?
How do they slide down the pole?
What do they eat?
Do they like to ride on the truck?

L   *What have we **L**earned about fire fighters?*
Men and women can be fire fighters.
They sleep and eat at the fire station, but they have a home too.
A computer tells them where there is a fire.
Fire fighters put on boots, fireproof clothing, and helmets.
They carry air with them.
The truck has another computer, hoses, and equipment.
Fire fighters go to school and learn everything.
They know how to stop, drop, and roll.
Fire fighters are daddies and mommies too. They have children.
Fire fighter Bob's little boy is named Daniel, and his girl is
   Catlain.
They're nice.

respond to children's spontaneous interests and to incidental events, whether it be a bird that flies against the window, a dead fish in the aquarium, snow, or the need for a repair person, is a part of being an effective teacher. When teachers ignore the changing interests, immediate needs, or incidental experiences of children, they miss too many opportunities for teaching, and children miss opportunities to follow their curiosity and have their needs for knowledge met.

Although you cannot ignore the opportunities for social studies teaching and learning that arise spontaneously, planning is still critical. You could keep in mind the broad goals and objectives of social studies, as well as specific objectives for individual children, and then use the spontaneous and incidental as a means of fostering the achievement of these. With goals in mind, any number of spontaneous happenings become a lesson.

Then too, you can keep complete lesson plans or even unit plans handy. A lot of things seem to happen spontaneously or incidentally, yet they are really very predictable. For instance, the apple tree outside the window will bloom one day, it will rain or be windy one of these days, and children will fight and argue over a toy. Aware of the many things that happen throughout the year, some teachers keep "concept boxes" on hand. These boxes contain props and equipment—perhaps a complete lesson plan with poems and books—on a variety of topics. They may focus on the weather, interpersonal disputes, recognition and safe release of feelings, the functions of school personnel, or mainstreaming children with special needs.

One day when an unpredicted wind came up, a teacher went to the storeroom and picked out a box labeled WIND. Using the small parachutes, kites, scarves, and poems about the wind in the box, she led the children through a series of lessons that, although they seemed spontaneous, were in reality very carefully and thoughtfully planned to meet children's interests.

LESSON PLANS

Teachers make plans for day-to-day experiences and activities as well as long-range plans. Lesson plans are made for short-term, day-to-day learning experiences, and units or projects are planned for learning experiences that extend over time.

Day-to-Day Lesson Plans

Lesson plans are one useful tool for short-term planning. They enable a teacher to plan meaningful activities for the present—for today and perhaps tomorrow or even next week. Once you get into the habit of making lesson plans, planning becomes second nature, like driving a car. Once internalized, planning lessons enables teachers to focus on the broader aspects of teaching, to meet individual differences, relax, and take advantage of the spontaneous.

Lesson plans can revolve around an individual child, a small group, or the total group. They include such things as

❑ arranging the room to provide different opportunities for children's play.
❑ presenting new materials or demonstrating possibilities with materials familiar to the children.
❑ providing opportunities for open-ended outcomes and creativity.
❑ giving teacher guidance in the form of feedback, listening to children, talking with them and asking questions.

There are many types of lesson plans and formats. It isn't important which format is used, but every lesson plan includes the following:

❑ preparation
❑ a statement of goals and objectives
❑ procedures to obtain the stated goals and objectives
❑ some way to evaluate the lesson

Preparation

"Is Jefferson City north or south of where we live?" a teacher asked a group of 5-year-olds. When no one answered, the teacher said, "I told you yesterday. Now listen, Jefferson city is north of us; north is always up," pointing to a globe she was holding.

If this teacher had been prepared, she would have known that concepts of north and south are meaningless to children until nearly 11 or 12 years of age. Then too, she would not have given children inaccurate information, that north is always up.

Before planning, you must be fully certain that you understand the concept, attitude, or skill you want to present. You can obtain references from the library, or discuss the topic with an authority on the subject. If you are planning experiences in geography, you might attend a lecture at the local library, community center, or university. Teachers need to understand content for two important reasons: (a) translating subject matter into experiences for children demands knowledge of the scope and structure of the discipline; and (b) facts (the names of countries, for example, or the number of chemical elements) change so rapidly in today's world that continually updating knowledge is required to ensure accuracy.

It is also useful to observe children as they work and play and to interview them to find out what they already know about a topic and would like to know. Some teachers simply ask children to "tell me everything you know about _____." The answers to this type of question provide valuable insights about children's ideas on any given topic. Others teachers ask children to make books about a topic, for example, having children make a booklet about dogs to discover their level of knowledge about the subject (Bredekamp & Rosegrant, 1992).

Your final preparation for planning involves locating resources for children's use, obtaining materials, arranging the room, or contacting experts who might visit the class. Outstanding resources in the community may lead you to select a goal you had not thought about; limited resources may cause you to eliminate an experience you were considering.

Objectives

The song "Happy Talk," from the musical *South Pacific,* expresses the idea that you must first have a dream before you can make it come true. This same idea can be applied to teaching. How do you know when you have achieved your goals if you have never established any? Thus, the first and perhaps the most essential part of planning is deciding upon your objectives.

State the lesson's major purpose, either specifically or generally. One or two carefully thought-out objectives stated in specific behavioral terms are more effective and realistic for a lesson plan than many, less specific goals. Teachers decide on objectives based on their knowledge of the children, the content of social studies, and their knowledge of the environment.

Today, nearly every educator is familiar with behavioral objectives. Although writing objectives behaviorally is somewhat tedious, stating them behaviorally is not at all mysterious or difficult. A behavioral objective, unlike the more general objective mentioned earlier, is a precise statement of behavior that will be accepted as evidence of the child's having achieved what was set out to be accomplished. A behavioral objective answers the following questions:

1. What will we teach?
2. How will we know when we've taught it?

3. What materials and procedures will work best to teach what we wish to teach? (Mager, 1962)

In writing behavioral objectives, you will want to pay particular attention to your use of language. Since behavioral objectives are specific, the language you use must be specific. Mager (1962) suggests looking at the following words and deciding just how well each of them communicates what will be taught and learned:

General	*Specific*
to know	to name
understand	identify
appreciate	construct
enjoy	compare
believe	solve (p. 11)

1. Identify the terminal behavior you desire by name. (Name four ways to travel on land.)
2. Try to define the desired behavior further by describing the conditions under which the behavior will be expected to occur. (When given a set of pictures of vehicles, the children will be able to identify and name those that travel on land.)
3. Specify the criteria of acceptable performance by describing how well the learner must perform. (The child will select three out of the five vehicles that travel on land.)

Goals stated in these terms—specific student behaviors related to lesson content—facilitate the teaching-learning process as well as its evaluation. Once you determine the lesson's behavioral objectives, you need to teach only those behaviors identified in the objective and, after the teaching, check each child's performance only in regard to the specified behavior.

Behavioral objectives have been in use for a number of years, and while they enable teachers to plan more precisely, they are not without problems. Because they always specify the outcome, they can limit children's learning by leading teachers to ignore children's behaviors or outcomes not prespecified by an objective. Assuming only one correct response leaves little room for divergent thinking, choice, or selection of materials. Then too, behavioral objectives are very specific, breaking learning into isolated steps without considering the entire experience. A child can learn the 22 steps in shoe tying, yet never be able to put them together to actually tie a shoelace.

Procedures

It is not necessary to excite or stimulate young children; however every lesson plan includes some means to initially involve children and hold their interest.

Some teachers find that an interesting picture, a photograph, a book, an object, or even a finger play captures children's interest in a lesson.

Learning activities are then specified. These describe what the teacher and children will do to achieve the stated goals and objectives.

Evaluation

The beauty of stating objectives behaviorally is that once stated, evaluation is nearly complete. The teacher has only to check the children's behavior against the statement, and the lesson is evaluated. If the objectives are not stated behaviorally, the teacher can evaluate the success of the lesson by (a) observing the children as they play, (b) interviewing children informally to see if misconceptions have been corrected and concepts gained, and (c) structuring some informal task for children to complete, for example, asking each to follow a map of the room to find a hidden treasure, to describe the things happening in a picture, to tell the story of something, or to select the pictures showing the objective taught.

Long-Term Units, Projects, and Thematic Learning

The unit or project provides for integrated, continual learning experiences organized around a unifying theme over a period of time. Since the early 1900s, when the unit plan was first introduced, social studies have been presented to children in the form of a unit. Planning social studies curriculum around a theme or unit is congruent with the belief that children are active and learn through their interactions with their social and physical environment and that children are whole. "The learning experiences in a unit of study allow children the opportunity to learn concepts as parts of an integrated whole, rather than isolated bits and pieces of information under a particular content area" (Raines & Canady, 1990, p. 120).

Units and projects organized around a theme accomplish a number of things:

1. They offer opportunities for a group of children to build a sense of community by working together around a common interest.

When children work together on a common theme or project, they have the chance to relate to one another. They check one another, spontaneously offering criticism and information as they exchange ideas and prior knowledge in a cooperative effort. Vygotsky saw this type of social activity as the generator of thought. He believed that individual consciousness is built from outside through relations with others. "The mechanism of social behavior and of consciousness is the same" (1986, p. ii).

2. They give relevance to the curriculum. When content is a part of an organized whole, children see it as useful and relevant to their daily lives.

"Conceptual organizers such as themes, units, or projects, give children something meaningful and substantive to engage their minds. It is difficult for children to make sense of abstract concepts such as colors, mathematical symbols, or letter sounds when they are presented at random or devoid of any meaningful context" (National Association for the Education of Young Children, 1991, p. 30).

3. They provide for flexibility of teaching and learning, following children's interests and building on their experiences. Because units and projects are flexible, they are planned for varying lengths of time. Some seem to end as quickly as they begin if children satisfy their interests immediately. Others extend for several weeks, or even a semester, as children expand their interests and seek other information.

In one kindergarten, a police officer permitted children to sit in a police car. Following the visit, the children began building a police car in the classroom out of large blocks. A posted sign let others know what the block structure represented and that it was not to be disturbed. The teacher added a steering wheel, a piece that looked like an instrument panel, and some boards. The block structure expanded and became a more permanent "car" with seats, a dashboard, a horn, and a gearshift.

The children did research as they strove to make the car more and more realistic. Finally, the teacher added wires, bulbs, and batteries. With the help of a volunteer who guided and directed them in their discovery, the children made the right connections and were able to turn the lights in their car on and off. They consulted books, compared different types of cars and trucks, and held discussions. Videos of police cars in action were shared when the police officer visited the class again. The entire unit lasted for over 6 weeks.

4. They can meet individual children's needs through the variety of learning experiences and opportunities offered over time. Children can pace themselves, staying with a specific activity for a long period of time in order to satisfy their interests or needs, or selecting tasks that permit them to practice skills or gain mastery over new skills.

Planning a Unit

Planning a unit involves selecting a topic, specifying goals and objectives, and identifying content. Each part of a unit or project plan includes specific plans for individual children.

Additional plans are made for children with disabilities so they can participate freely and fully. A teacher who wanted the class to experience a field trip to a fast-food restaurant made special arrangements so Sally, a child in a wheelchair, could take part.

Plans are also made for children who are disinterested in the topic. In one second-grade class, a unit on fruits and where they come from bored two of the children. Observing them, the teacher noted their curiosity about an apple that was beginning to mold. She directed their attention to molds, and the two children completed an entire unit on that subject, concluding by presenting their findings to the class, while the others studied fruit.

Topics.   The theme or topic of the unit or project can stem from a number of sources. In the child-care programs in Reggio Emilia (a city in northern Italy), the selection of a project topic is a complicated process, and the genesis may take a number of forms:

1. The teacher may observe something of interest and importance to the children and introduce it for a topic.

2. A topic may stem from the teacher's interest or professional curiosity.

3. The topic might stem from some serendipity that redirects the attention of the children and teacher to another focus (New, 1993).

Some topics may be selected by the school system, the state department of education, or even the parents. The general goals of the total program and of the experiences are all considered in topic selection.

Objectives.   Objectives direct the unit. They tell what the unit is to accomplish, describe how the children will change following the unit experience, and lead to evaluation of the unit. Here again, your careful selection of a few well-thought-out objectives will be more effective than listing numerous, general objectives. Focusing objectives on each area of the social studies—knowledge, skills, attitudes, and values—helps provide for a balance of learning experiences.

Objectives are flexible, however. At all times, teachers remain alert to children's interests, continually looking for new objectives and ways to extend rather than dampen children's enthusiasm and curiosity for the theme or topic.

Content.   The unit content lists the major points to be covered. You will want to organize and specify the facts, information, and knowledge that will be presented. A list of available materials and possible field trips should be included.

❑ Is the project developed in response to children's questions?

❑ Does it give rise to children's independent, creative thinking?

❑ Will it be managed in ways that enable diverse levels of involvement and diverse cognitive challenges so that no child is forced to see himself or herself as a failure?

❑ Are there features within the scope of the unit or project that invite (necessitate) the use of basic academic skills?

❑ Is there room for all participants to experience both social cooperation and moral responsibility in order to ensure successful completion of the project?

❑ Will participation provide possibilities for children to increase their knowledge and appreciation of the "stuff of the world"—materials, objects, people, events?

❑ Does the unit or project reflect children's attempts to construct their own understanding and interpretations?

Box 2.3
Before Deciding on a Unit or Project, Ask Yourself Some Questions
From "Projects as Curriculum: Under What Conditions?" by T. Webster, 1990, *Childhood Education*, 67(1), pp. 2–4.

Here too, flexibility is the key. Guided by the overall goals and objectives of the program, teachers select content that meets children's developmental and learning needs (Fromberg, 1995).

Procedures

The introduction to a unit is followed by learning experiences—the core of the unit—and a summary activity.

Introduction.   Almost anything that serves to motivate and stimulate the children's interest can be used to introduce a unit. The purpose of the introduction is to arouse the children's curiosity by stimulating their interest in the topic. This could be done by any of the following:

❑ A teacher-initiated discussion. You might ask the children some questions to stimulate their thinking or interest, or you could make a direct statement: "We all have to ride the school bus, so today we're going to begin learning the safety rules for riding the bus." This could begin a unit on safety.

❑ An incidental experience. Sometimes a unit arises from an unplanned experience. A child getting sick in school could be the beginning of a unit on health. Some happening in the local community—fire prevention week, elections, construction—might be the initiator for a unit. A kitten wandering into the classroom could stimulate interest in a unit on animals.

❑ An audiovisual resource. A television show, a filmstrip, a record, or slides could serve to stimulate interest. You can make use of other media as well, such as newspapers or news magazines.

❑ Some ongoing activities. Units can lead to other units. A study of the grocery store might lead into a unit on food, purchasers, consumers, or transportation. A unit on seashells can lead directly into a study of life in the sea and then to life on land.

❑ An arranged environment. You might display objects from some other country, place, or time; exhibit a poster or an open book; or prepare a bulletin board, any of which would call children's attention to a topic and stimulate questions and interest. A branding iron on the library table, with a few books opened to pictures of cowhands at branding time, can be used successfully to introduce a unit on this type of work.

Learning Experiences.   The learning experiences are the heart of the unit. Rather than a listing of isolated activities, these experiences are planned to foster the goals and objectives of the unit. You can plan some activities for individual children, others for small groups, and still others for the total group.

Since the purpose of a unit is to build a strong relationship between learning experiences and content, you will want to design the learning experiences to work together as a whole. You can plan a sequential presentation of learning experiences around the objectives of the unit. Analysis of each objective will sug-

Box 2.4
Social Studies: An Integrated
Web

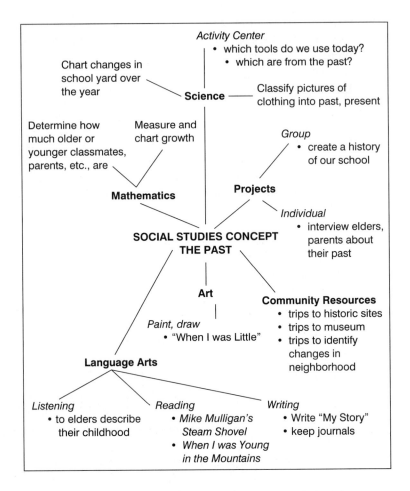

gest activities to you that would foster children's attainment of the objective.
Teachers can ask themselves, "What experience will foster this goal?" "Which
experiences should come first and provide a base for further experiences?" "What
will extend and clarify children's understanding?"

Learning experiences may come from any of the following:

❑ Language experiences. Oral discussion, listening to records, recording ideas
in writing, dictating to a teacher or tape recorder, reporting to a group, and
dictating or writing letters, booklets, or stories are all examples of language
experiences you could plan to foster children's attainment of unit goals.

❑ Community resources. Field trips in the school neighborhood or in the community are considered part of a unit plan. You could ask individuals from the
community to visit and share information with the class.

❑ Audiovisual experiences. Films, filmstrips, slides, models, graphs, and murals
are classified as audiovisual experiences. Children could make their own
graphs or murals or illustrate some topic by taking their own photographs.

❑ Arts and crafts. Painting, constructing, drawing, modeling with clay, paper weaving, and many other art activities can be coordinated with other learning experiences.

❑ Music and physical activities. Songs, games, making and playing musical instruments, creative rhythms, and dance foster children's active involvement with a unit's stated objectives.

❑ Mathematics activities. Any unit presents opportunities to use mathematics. Children might measure, weigh, count, add, or classify objects as part of the unit. One unit, stimulated by the discovery of parsley caterpillars in the class garden, led to the children's determining how many days the caterpillars spent eating, how long the caterpillars were, how many days it took for the chrysalises to form, and the number of days it took for the butterflies to emerge.

❑ Social skills. Social skills are an integral part of the unit as children participate together in the planning of the unit or work together on some part of the unit. Children's interests might dictate that they work together to investigate some subtopic; later, they could report to the group. Young children can also better their social skills by working together on a mural, painting, scrapbook, or construction project.

Learning experiences are the heart of any teaching unit.

Regardless of the number and type of learning experiences selected, continuity between experiences is planned. One experience builds on another. A thread of meaning runs through several experiences. Experiences and activities are juxtaposed to enable children to see the connections between past and present, among and between people, and between objects in their world.

Summary.   The concluding activity is time spent for review and summing up the unit; it provides closure for teacher and children. A concluding activity gives the teacher a chance to observe the children and learn what concepts they have formed about the topic; it gives the children an opportunity to tie the pieces together. Units could end simply with the children singing songs, acting out stories they have learned, or listening to the poetry they have enjoyed. Dictating experience charts or thank-you letters, compiling a booklet, or sharing experiences are other summary activities.

Anne Daniels, a teacher of 5-year-olds at the Center for Young Children, University of Maryland, concludes a unit on Winnie the Pooh with a trip to the university apiary to collect honey for a snack. This activity, in turn, leads to a new theme—that of studying and identifying different types of insects, where and how they live, and what they contribute to our lives.

Evaluation

No unit is complete without an evaluation. The behavioral objectives offer a built-in evaluation; other types of evaluation might include asking the children to evaluate the unit themselves: "What did you like best about the topic? What did you learn? What can you do now that you couldn't do before? What would you like to do again? What could you do differently next time?" Children could dictate or write booklets reporting the *Things I've Learned.* You can evaluate the success of the unit informally as you observe children at play or work; or you can structure the evaluations by asking each child to tell about a topic, demonstrate a task, or respond to some questions. Informal checklists, developed around the goals of the unit and the specified content, might be used.

In addition to evaluating the children, teachers will want to evaluate their planning and teaching. A well-planned unit should include

- ❑ clear, realistic, obtainable goals and objectives.
- ❑ material of high interest to the children.
- ❑ activities that provide for different abilities, interests, and backgrounds of the children.
- ❑ involvement of the children in planning the goals and activities of the unit.
- ❑ active experiences that fully involve the children.
- ❑ opportunities for children to work and play together.

Following a unit, teachers could ask themselves if it did include these factors, how it could have been improved, what parts were highly successful and why, and what they would do differently next time.

EVALUATION

Evaluation is a necessary and important part of teaching. When evaluation is authentic, it can only benefit children, teachers, and parents. Authentic evaluation takes place as a part of the curriculum. The tasks used to evaluate children's learning in the social studies are real, and they connect to children's daily experiences, rather than detract from them (Kirst, 1991).

Authentic evaluation

❑ gives evidence for teachers that can lead to improvement of the quality of instruction for individual children as well as for groups of children.

❑ offers clarification of goals and objectives that may help determine the extent to which the children are learning, growing, and developing in desired ways.

❑ is a system of quality control that permits teachers to determine which parts of the teaching-learning process have been effective and which have not.

❑ stimulates ideas for alternative procedures that may be effective in enabling the teacher to achieve a set of educational goals.

❑ gives feedback for parents. Some evaluation communicates to parents something about children's growth and learning, the program, and the quality of your teaching.

A broad and complex process, evaluation is not to be confused with tests and measurements. Authentic evaluation is ongoing, comprehensive, and an integral part of social studies instruction. Evaluation procedures can include

❑ observation
❑ portfolios
❑ informal interviews
❑ performance interviews
❑ checklists
❑ standardized tests

Observation

Observing children's behavior in a systematic fashion, teachers see indications of their achievement of social studies goals. Teachers look for behaviors that demonstrate children's skills, attitudes, values, or knowledge. Behavior observation is a valid way to evaluate social studies goals relating to social skills, problem solving, decision making, and acceptance of the values of others.

Observing means noting only the behavior that is occurring, without making inferences. Teachers observe and record children's behavior in the following situations:

1. at free play
2. on the playground
3. during the routines of dressing, eating, resting
4. during group activity time
5. at discussion time

In recording repeated behaviors of children, you are compiling a record of children's progress. You could structure your observations around the specific and general goals of the social studies program. You could observe and record children's behavior in applying knowledge, solving a problem, taking responsibility, or working with others; or you might structure your observations around more specific goals. Children's use of maps during block building and their drawing of maps for use with wheel toys give real indications of their mapping concepts; shopping at the play store, children reveal economic concepts through their behavior. As children play, you might note when they (a) use new vocabulary correctly; (b) demonstrate their understanding of making change, purchasing, or producing; and (c) follow social rules and procedures.

Portfolios

Collecting samples of children's work in portfolios illustrates children's progress over time. Each child has an individual portfolio; whatever work or records are placed in the portfolio are dated, and often something about when, how, and under what conditions the work was completed is included. Growth charts, photos of children completing skills, and tape recordings of their speech can also be collected.

Several times a year, teachers go over the portfolios and note the changing form of children's concepts, new vocabulary, expansion of ideas, and children's

---

Some things that might be included in the portfolio are:

- ❏ samples of children's drawings, maps, or other work
- ❏ logs of books read to or by the children
- ❏ photos of children working on a unit project or of a special product
- ❏ notes and comments from interviews with the child
- ❏ copies of pages of journals with invented spelling preserved
- ❏ tape recordings of children telling or reading a story, reciting a poem, or recording some special event
- ❏ videos of children on a field trip or during some other special event
- ❏ dictated or written stories about social studies

Box 2.5
The Portfolio

increasing ability to express their ideas. This analysis offers a base on which to evaluate both children's learning in the social studies and your teaching.

Children, teachers, and parents all contribute to a portfolio. The child, as well as teachers and parents, should have the opportunity to select work samples to place in the portfolio. Teachers can guide children when asking children to contribute work samples to the portfolio. Teachers might ask children to select something that was difficult to do, that illustrates a special accomplishment, or has special meaning and merit (Meisels & Stelle, 1991).

When the work in the portfolios is an accurate representation of children's growth and achievement, teachers can use the portfolio to evaluate their progress. The work is not to be compared with the work of other children, but rather each child's work should be analyzed and evaluated for progress toward a standard or performance consistent with the child's development and growth (Grace & Shores, 1992).

Informal Interviews

Another, more specific form of evaluation of children's progress in social studies is the informal interview method. You could conduct interviews during free play, or anytime you and individual children can get together. Darrow (1964) suggests that teachers look for the following as they interview children:

1. *Consistency.*   Does the child have a stable set of responses? Does the child reply in the same way to the same type of question?
2. *Accuracy.*   Are the answers correct? The child may not include all of the possibilities, but is the response somewhat accurate?
3. *Clarity.*   Is the response clear and acceptable?
4. *Fullness.*   How complete was the response? How many aspects of the concept were covered by the response?
5. *Extensiveness.*   How many illustrations of the concept were given?

As they conduct interviews to discover children's thinking on a social studies topic, teachers sometimes use pictures or objects for the children to manipulate to demonstrate or illustrate the concepts. Not all concepts can be expressed by children verbally; you could ask them to act out a concept, show it, draw all the things they know about it, or find an example of the concept in the pictures.

The work of Piaget (1969) provides other guidelines for interviewing young children. The questions Piaget asks and the way he builds his questions on the child's responses to the first question offer examples of the type of interview technique that reveals children's thinking.

An example of an interview is given by McAulay (1961), who wanted to determine second graders' concepts of time. He asked individual children to respond to the following questions: "Who do you think has lived longer, your mother or your grandmother?" "Which comes first, Christmas or Easter?" "Who lived first, Lincoln or Washington?" This technique could be used to evaluate children's thinking on any topic.

Informal interviews are one form of evaluation that can be conducted casually during free play or anytime.

In administering Piagetian kinds of interviews, you must establish an atmosphere of security and trust by communicating to the child that he or she is in a safe, nonthreatening position. When a child responds to your question, accept the answer without judgment. You might use a small tape recorder to record the answer, or write the answer in a type of shorthand. Children's responses are often short, and the major ideas are not difficult to record by hand.

When the child responds, continue questioning by asking for justification. Do not assume if a child gives a correct answer he has done the proper thinking (Sund, 1976). Several questions may be necessary to understand the child's perceptions and thinking processes. You might ask the child, "Could you show me?" "Would you tell me more?" or, "What if . . . ?" You could ask the child to act it out, or challenge a child's answer by saying, "Well, another person said. . . . " In this way you will be able to uncover more of the child's thinking and ideas.

You will need to give the child plenty of time to answer. In many testing situations time is limited; when conducting an individual interview, you will want to allow the child all the time necessary to think and answer.

Performance Interviews

Structuring tasks for children to demonstrate concepts and skills is another kind of informal evaluation. You might ask children to draw a map of the room, show on a graph which bus has the most riders, complete a puzzle, or sort pictures into categories. One teacher used a set of pictures to assess children's awareness of selected concepts in physical geography by asking them to select the four pictures that represented the concept and the four that did not.

Checklists

Some teachers find that checklists of behaviors or skills are a convenient way to evaluate children's progress. You can construct a checklist for yourself, one designed around the specific concepts, goals, and objectives of the social studies unit or lesson plan. Other checklists are often provided by the school, or by the county or state department of education, and might be based on the general goals of social studies. Publishers of textbooks and instructional kits sometimes prepare checklists. Figure 2–1 shows a checklist developed by a teacher for use with a group of 5-year-old children.

Standardized Tests

Standardized tests are based on goals and objectives decided by someone other than the classroom teacher and meet the criteria for serving as a tool of summative evaluation. Thus, the content of standardized tests may have little to do with the goals of the classroom teacher or the experiences or activities of the children.

No one type of evaluation can be considered adequate in a field as broad as social studies. For this reason, you will want to consider a combination of evaluation techniques. Keeping records of the children's work, systematically observing their behavior, or using informal interviews might be most helpful in reporting progress to parents; in giving insights on how to improve your teaching methods; or in indicating which experiences, activities, goals, and objectives would be appropriate to introduce at a given point in time. This type of evaluation, conducted by the teacher for the purpose of evaluating the teaching, and the attainment of specific goals, is often called formative. It is the type of evaluation that enables you to formulate your program; to set goals; and to know when the goals

NAME	DATE		
Behavior	Always	Sometimes	Never
completes a task			
works with others			
assumes responsibility			
cooperates in group work			
listens to others			

Figure 2.1
Example of a Checklist

have been reached, what new goals should be set, and what modification of set goals should be made (Genishi, 1992; Gullo, 1992).

SUMMARY

Planning is essential for successful teaching and learning. Having a clear idea of what children are like, the goals of society and education, and content knowledge of the social studies, you are prepared to plan. In planning you must consider the reality of your situation, provide balance throughout the program, involve the children, and allow for spontaneity.

Long-term planning of social studies units and short-term planning of the daily lessons involve designing appropriate learning objectives. In setting specific goals for your teaching and children's learning, evaluation follows naturally as you assess the degree to which the goals have been reached.

RESOURCES

Often, curriculum guides are developed by local school systems or state departments of education. Inquire in your school system or state department of education about curriculum guides. The guides offer suggestions for objectives for many subject areas, including the social studies. They also contain abundant information and ideas for lesson planning and things to do with children.

The ERIC organization produces and disseminates information on every aspect of early childhood education. It offers publications about growth characteristics of young children, objectives for programs, curriculum guides, and other information for teachers.

> ERIC Clearinghouse on Early Childhood Education
> College of Education
> University of Illinois
> 805 W. Pennsylvania Ave.
> Urbana, IL 61801-4897

Other useful resources include the following:

Reaching potentials: Appropriate curriculum and assessment for young children. Vol. I. (1992) and *Vol. II* (1995). Edited by Sue Bredekamp and Terri Rosegrant; published by the National Association for the Education of Young Children, Washington DC. Offers a complete guide to planning developmentally appropriate curricula.

Ways of assessing children and curriculum: Stories of early childhood practice. (1992). By Celia Genishi, published by Teachers College Press, New York. Provides many ideas for evaluating young children, as does Dom Gullo's *Understanding assessment and evaluation in early childhood education* (1992), also by Teachers College Press.

Even though Doris Fromberg's *The full day kindergarten program (2nd ed.)* (1995) by Teachers College Press seems to be only about kindergarten, it offers excellent ideas for planning curriculum in any early childhood program.

REFERENCES

Bredekamp, S. (1987). *Developmentally appropriate practice in early childhood programs serving children from birth through age 8.* Washington, DC: National Association for the Education of Young Children.

Bredekamp, S. (1991). Redeveloping early childhood education: A response to Kessler. *Early Childhood Research Quarterly, 6*(2), 199–211.

Bredekamp, S., & Rosegrant, T. (Eds.) (1992). *Reaching potentials: Appropriate curriculum and assessment for young children. Vol. I.* Washington, DC: National Association for the Education of Young Children.

Bruner, J. (1960). *The process of education.* Cambridge, MA: Harvard University Press.

Darrow, H. (1964). *Research: Children's concepts.* Washington, DC: Association for Childhood Education International.

Derman-Sparks, L., & The A.B.C. Task Force (1989). Anti-bias curriculum: Tools for empowerment. Washington, DC: National Association for the Education of Young Children.

Fromberg, D. (1995). *The full day kindergarten program* (2nd ed.). New York: Teachers College Press.

Gargiulo, R. M., & Graves, S. B. (1991). Parental feelings: The forgotten component when working with parents of handicapped preschool children. *Childhood Education, 67*(3), 176–179.

Genishi, C. (1992). *Ways of assessing children and curriculum: Stories of early childhood practice.* New York: Teachers College Press.

Grace, F., & Shores, E. F. (1992). *The portfolio and its use: Developmental appropriate assessment of young children.* Little Rock, AR: Southern Association for the Education of Young Children.

Gullo, D. F. (1992). *Understanding assessment and evaluation in early childhood education.* New York: Teachers College Press.

Hidi, S. (1990). Interest and its contribution as a mental resource for learning. *Review of Educational Research, 80*(4), 549–573.

Iran-Nejad, A., McKeachie, W. J., & Berliner, D. C. (1990). The multisource nature of learning: An introduction. *Review of Educational Research, 60(4),* 509–517.

Kirst, M. W. (1991). Interview on assessment issues with Lorrie Shepard. *Educational Researcher, 20,* 21–24.

Lee, F. Y. (1995). Asian parents as partners. *Young Children, 50*(3), 1–10.

Lefrancois, G. R. (1989). *Of children: An introduction to child development* (6th ed.). Belmont, CA: Wadsworth.

Mager, R. (1962). *Preparing instructional objectives.* Palo Alto, CA: Fearon.

Martin, A. (1985). About teaching and teachers. *Harvard Educational Review, 55,* 396–420.

McAulay, J. (1961). What understanding do second grade children have of time relationships? *Journal of Educational Research, 54,* 312–314.

Meisels, S., & Stelle, D. (1991). *The early childhood portfolio collection process.* Ann Arbor, MI: Center for Human Growth and Development, University of Michigan.

Mitchell, L. S. (1934). *Young geographers.* New York: Bank Street College.

National Association for the Education of Young Children. (1991). Position statement: Guidelines for appropriate curriculum content and assessment in programs serving children ages 3–8. *Young Children, 46*(3), 21–40.

New, R. (1993). The integrated curriculum. In C. Seefeldt (Ed.), *The early childhood curriculum: A review of current research*. New York: Teachers College Press.

Newman, R. (1995). For parents particularly: The home-school connection. *Childhood Education, 71,* 296–298.

Ogle, D. M. (1986). K-W-L: A teaching model that develops active reading of expository text. *The Reading Teacher, 39,* 564–570.

Piaget, J. (1969). *Science of education and the psychology of the child.* New York: Viking Press.

Raines, S., & Canady, R. (1990). *The whole language kindergarten.* New York: Teachers College Press.

Reynolds, M. C., & Birch, J. W. (1986). *Teaching exceptional children in all America's schools* (2nd ed.). Reston, VA: Council for Exceptional Children.

Sund, R. B. (1976). *Piaget for educators: A multimedia program.* Upper Saddle River, NJ: Merrill/Prentice Hall

Vygotsky, L. (1986). *Thought and language.* Cambridge, MA: Harvard University Press.

Webster, T. (1990). Projects as curriculum: Under what conditions? *Childhood Education, 67*(1), 2–4.

Winter, S. M. (1994/1995). Special challenges in education-diversity: A program for all children. *Childhood Education, 71,* 91–96.

Wolery, M., & Wilbers, J. S. (1994). *Including children with special needs in early childhood programs.* Washington, DC: National Association for the Education of Young Children.

Chapter 3

Resources for Learning

After you read this chapter, you should be prepared to respond to the following questions:

- ❑ How can each child's family be used as a resource for teaching social studies?
- ❑ What resources in and around the school are useful in fostering the goals of the social studies?
- ❑ Why are centers of interest necessary? What is the role of the teacher in establishing centers of interest, and in supervising and teaching through centers?
- ❑ Can you plan a field trip to fully utilize the resources in the community?

Suppose you wanted to learn how to swim. Would you read books about swimming and listen to people telling you how to swim? Or would you jump in a pool and, with the guidance of an expert swimmer, learn by doing?

Since the beginning of time, people have known that humans, whether adults or children, learn best by doing. This is why the preschool-primary classroom is rich with resources for children's social studies learning. In any developmentally appropriate classroom, children can find water and sand, rocks and mud, woodworking tools, computers, art materials, blocks, books, other children and adults, boxes, foil, animals, and many, many other resources for learning.

But the careful selection of resources for social studies learning is not enough. Teachers must know how and when to present them to children. "Clearly, manipulatives alone have no great educational value unless the teacher knows the materials and can instruct children in their productive use" (Elkind, 1981, p. 435).

Anyone can present children with materials, but good teachers use those materials to lead children to meaningful activity and thinking, and to the fulfillment of their educational goals. Good teachers know

- ❑ what materials to select, and how and when to present these to children.
- ❑ when and how to interact with children as they use the materials.
- ❑ how to extend children's activity and expand their thinking.

❑   when to remove resources, add new materials, or end activities.

THE CHILDREN

Children themselves serve as resources for social studies learning by

❑   sharing their backgrounds of experiences—telling others about things they have done and the way they do things in their families.
❑   bringing things from home—objects, photographs, cultural foods, stories—to share with classmates.
❑   demonstrating how to make a bridge of blocks, how to paint, or how to model with clay.
❑   teaching one another how to complete a puzzle, read a map, or sing a song from their culture.

THE FAMILY

The family—a world of resources for the social studies! Think about it: Probably all of the content, attitudes and values, and the skills included in the social studies could be fostered through study of the family.

Families have a history: Where did each family come from? What stories are told of how they got here and where they first settled? Do children's parents tell them about their own childhood? What about family celebrations?

Geography can also be found in study of the family. Find out where each family came from and locate the country on a map. How did the family travel here? Families move, even within the same city. Make a map and locate places each family once lived.

What jobs do parents hold? How are tasks divided within the family? What about budgeting? Children find economic concepts meaningful when these are related to their own experiences within the family unit.

Involving parents in their children's preschool or primary experience is a goal of education. Parent involvement benefits children, parents, and the school. But for social studies learning, involvement is important because parents are an important resource for children's learning—actually a necessity. Today teachers live far from the family and may be from a different culture or ethnic group; parents work and are unable to take a day off to visit their child's school; it is important for parents and teachers to feel comfortable with and know one another.

Informal Involvement

Some simple things that you might do to involve parents in the social studies program include

Where did your family come from? How did they travel here?

❑ establishing an open-door policy. Rather than asking parents to visit only during American Education Week, or on special days when parents may not be able to take time off from work, encourage them to visit the school anytime they can. Often, parents may find themselves with an afternoon off, an hour or two at lunch, or a few hours free during the morning. Be certain the parents know that they are welcome to spend this unexpected free time in school with their children.

❑ sending home a questionnaire at the beginning of the year, inviting parents to indicate the kinds of things they would like their children to learn in social studies. It might be a good idea to list several choices, asking the parents to check the ones they wish as well as leaving space for their suggestions. Other questionnaires could request suggestions for field trips or visitors to the class.

❑ sending home a brief outline of each unit plan. A page of simple statements ("For the next few days we're going to be studying the concept of production. We will visit a store, and . . . ") would tell parents something about their children's activities.

❑ writing a class newsletter using several stories written or dictated by the children. In the letter, you can include plans for parties or field trips, reviews of movies or books the children have enjoyed, or the things they have learned.

❑ forwarding a booklet of the children's favorite poems and songs.

❑ sending home individual notes with the children telling parents of their progress—a new skill learned or how the child has used new knowledge to solve a problem. Single sentences on the back of a picture, or attached to some work of the child—"Please notice how Aletha completed this; it's a wonderful job," "This is the first time John included a base line in his painting; it means . . . ," or "Toni's ideas are exciting; her story shows imagination and thought"—do much to inform parents about the progress their children are making and the things that happen during the school day.

Involving parents in the school's program implies respect for each child and every family. You can communicate the school's respect by

❑ referring frequently to the children's parents during the day: "I wonder what your mother is having for lunch." "Do you think your father would like this?" "We'll have to tell your parents how well you worked today."

❑ involving parents in the teaching-learning process. Letters telling the parents about the concepts being taught and asking them to extend these concepts at home are useful: "We're learning about traffic safety. The next time you go for a drive could you point out the traffic signs and explain their meanings to the children?" Parents can also take part in children's homework, not the dreary pencil-and-paper kind, but the "homework" involved in looking for all the tools in the home, counting the number of jobs family members have, drawing a map of their block, or watching a certain television program together. Many preschool programs foster children's cognitive growth by involving parents as teachers of their own children. You could send toys, books, games, puzzles, and other equipment home with the children, permitting parents to take an active part in their child's education.

❑ being aware that attitudes are communicated subtly through language use. The terms *broken home* or *he doesn't have a father* imply stereotypical attitudes. Families who have experienced divorce may be more whole after the divorce than broken by the divorce, and each child does in fact have a father, who may or may not be present in the home (Clay, 1980).

❑ structuring school activities for the parent in general, not specifying the mother or father. This shows your respect for the family unit as it may exist in many children's homes.

❑ offering real support in your recognition of time limitations of working parents, and scheduling conferences at times parents are free to attend.

Informal parent-involvement activities often lead to more structured involvement of parents in the social studies program. At first, parents and teachers are comfortable communicating at the day-by-day informal level. As trust develops, parents find they are interested in more structured involvement. Attending group meetings, working with children, and making decisions about the social studies program then take place.

Formal Involvement

Group Meetings

Parents are interested in seeing slides and videos of their children at school, and these could serve as the focus of a group meeting. One teacher continuously took slides of the children participating in social studies activities. At the end of the year, she held a parent meeting and showed slides taken at the beginning, middle, and end of the year that illustrated the children's growth in skills and their progression in attitudes and knowledge.

Working With Children

Parent volunteers are needed for field trips, as well as on a daily basis. Parents may be able to work with individual children or assist as groups carry out projects. Some parents may serve as resources as children study various topics and themes.

Decision Making

Parent involvement should lead to parents making decisions about the social studies program. They may help in setting some of the goals and objectives of the program or in deciding on topics or themes.

THE SCHOOL

If you want to be a teacher of young children you must be able to look at the world through the eyes of a child. Take a walk inside the school and on the play yard and consider what would interest a child of 3-, 5-, or 8 years of age? Look at the play yard and pretend you are that child filled with wonder and curiosity. What do you see?

Following the theories of Mitchell, Piaget, and Vygotsky, you can ground a great deal of your social studies in the here-and-now world of the school. Some experiences might stem from:

- ❑ identification of building materials, how they got to the building, and who used them
- ❑ study of communication systems—mail, typewriters, duplicating machines, and telephones
- ❑ concern for care of the school grounds
- ❑ examination of various delivery systems for food, materials, and supplies

The people in the school also serve as resources for children's learning. Every member of the school staff has some special skill or background to share with the children. Just observing the staff at work—art, music, and physical education teachers, media specialists, lunchroom personnel, office workers, custodians— puts children back in touch with real-world learning. Some of the school staff might demonstrate a specific skill used in their jobs, or they could invite small groups to observe them complete a specific task. Just as the parents do, the staff might share something from their background with the children—a song, favorite food, game, or custom enjoyed by their family (Bennett, 1995).

The teacher is a resource for social studies learning. Your experiences, the different places you have worked, the things you did in college, the places you have visited—all can be used to enrich children's learning by giving them vicarious experiences on which to build concepts.

Then, too, the skills, knowledge, and information you bring to your job are potent factors for children's learning. Regardless of the extent of materials available, the teacher's creativity is the most important learning resource in the classroom.

THE CLASSROOM

"The classroom is greater than the sum of its parts. The classroom is more than one child plus one child. It is a community" (Loughlin & Martin, 1987, p. xiii).

Even though an artificial setting, the room can, through careful planning and arranging, become a world for social studies learning. Re-creating the real world, the room becomes a community for learning. Through creation of centers of interest, the room is arranged to provide as many opportunities for learning as the home, community, or world. Clearly defined spaces within the room, where children can find equipment, materials, and furniture grouped together for specific purposes and goals, are arranged (Vergeront, 1996).

Taking on the appearance of a workshop, these interest centers, or learning areas, permit children to make choices about how and what they will learn. The areas of interest enable individualization of instruction to take place as children themselves select the materials to use, decide how to use them, and determine the purposes for their use.

The idea is for children to be actively engaged in meaningful learning, either alone or with others. As children work in these interest centers, they learn social skills, especially cooperation and sharing, and they run head-on into the ideas, attitudes, and values of others (Lanser & McDonnell, 1991).

1. An abundant and accessible supply of specific materials adaptable to many uses and ideas
2. A large, open space that invites a child to take the initiative
3. A teacher who encourages each child to develop independently in her or his own way

Box 3.1
The Classroom Features Three Things
From "Creating Quality Curriculum Yet Not Buying Out the Store." by S. Lanser and L. McDonnell, 1991, *Young Children, 47*(3), 4–11.

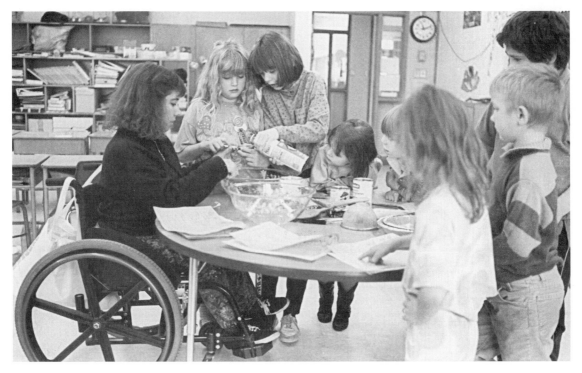

The classroom is greater than the sum of its parts.

Any number of centers of interest could be located within one room. Decisions about the number and type of centers depend on the goals of the program, interests of the children, and space available.

Deciding on Centers of Interest

Typically, every preschool and primary room should include areas of interest for sociodramatic play, blocks, mathematics, art, library, manipulative play, music, writing, sand and water play, and woodworking. For the social studies curriculum, other areas are planned. These depend on the children's interests and the curriculum.

Depending on characteristics of the community you oberserved, you might want to create a post office, a gas station, a grocery store, a doctor's office, an airport, or other area to promote sociodramatic play. Or you could set up learning centers of books and slides on children living in a different country. These areas can be rotated and changed, with areas added as needed and removed when no longer in use.

Introducing Centers of Interest

Just setting up centers of interest does not ensure that learning will take place. You need to allow children large blocks of time and the freedom to explore and

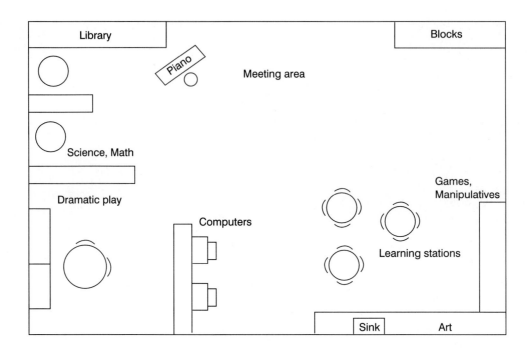

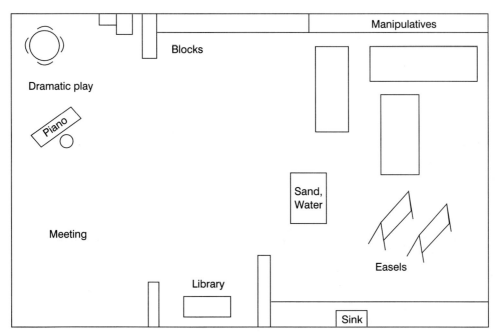

Box 3.2
Centers of Interest

experiment, and you need to be actively involved with the children as they work in the centers.

Introduce the centers by describing some of the possibilities, limitations, and rules of each. "Always put the books back here," "The blocks are used this way and placed back on the shelf," "Here are the paints, brushes, and paper; this is how you wash the brushes" are examples of the types of statements that give children the security of adult guidance necessary for them to feel free to assume responsibility and begin to be self-directing.

As children use the interest centers, you can suggest problems for them to solve and interest them in different learning opportunities. As 4-year-olds enter the classroom, the teacher might talk with each child, discussing the possible choices available in the centers and asking each what things she or he might want to do that day. A group of 5-year-olds can listen to a description of the learning areas, materials, and problems and make a selection of the area in which they wish to begin working. Children in primary grades can place their names on a chart indicating the center or centers they will work in that morning.

Sometimes, you might suggest a choice of areas for individual children— "John, you've worked with blocks for the past several weeks. Can you think of some other things you might like to try today?" "Look in the building area, Robin. There's a piece of cardboard you might find useful in completing your truck." Or, "Susan, John, and Alicia, begin your work with me today at this table."

Types of Centers of Interest

A Place of Their Own

In open classrooms filled with interest centers, it is imperative that children have some place to call their own. Young children seem to feel more comfortable when there is a territory of which they are sure. This does not mean that children need a desk of their own or even a cubicle or locker—discarded shoe boxes, empty ice cream cartons, or other boxes for their treasures give children the feeling of having their own territory.

Sand and Water

Sand and water areas are a must for social studies learning. As children play with natural materials, they are constructing physical knowledge. Sand and water centers may not be available every day, but they should be frequent and regular centers. It is not necessary to purchase commercial sand tables; large cardboard boxes, leaky plastic bathtubs, or discarded plastic wading pools make excellent substitutes. Partially filled, flat cardboard containers (12" × 18" × 3") can become miniature sand environments for children's explorations.

In the sand, children can construct roads, tunnels, bridges, cities, farms, airports—anything they have seen and want to re-create. A clean squirt bottle can be filled with water so that the children can keep the sand moist enough for building.

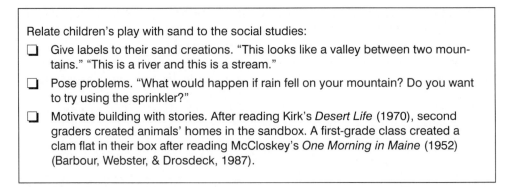

Relate children's play with sand to the social studies:

❑   Give labels to their sand creations. "This looks like a valley between two mountains." "This is a river and this is a stream."

❑   Pose problems. "What would happen if rain fell on your mountain? Do you want
to try using the sprinkler?"

❑   Motivate building with stories. After reading Kirk's *Desert Life* (1970), second
graders created animals' homes in the sandbox. A first-grade class created a
clam flat in their box after reading McCloskey's *One Morning in Maine* (1952)
(Barbour, Webster, & Drosdeck, 1987).

Box 3.3
Sand and the Social Studies

Props that might be added to the sand include toy animals, people, shops, cars
and airplanes, and shells, sticks, feathers, marbles, rocks, or even live land crabs
and beetles. Children will not be ready to construct sand environments until they
have had opportunities for manipulation and exploration of sand. For this, children need buckets, plastic containers, sieves, bottles, sponges, funnels, and sticks.

A water center gives children the opportunity to learn more about their
earth. You can easily provide water for children's use; small plastic dishpans
placed on a plastic or newspaper-covered table are adequate. Other containers
might be plastic tubs or buckets, commercial water tables, or plastic wading pools.
Children can cover themselves with plastic aprons, and teachers can keep an
extra set of clothing handy in case children do become too wet (Crosser, 1994).

Adding objects to water play gives children new ideas and materials with
which to experiment. Sieves, funnels, squirt bottles, a piece of hose, plastic spoons,
cups, and dishes are all appropriate additions. If children lose interest in water
play, adding dishes, pots, pans, and doll clothes to wash renews their motivation.

When using water with primary children, you can introduce the ideas of

❑   floating and sinking. Provide a large number of objects—a piece of crumpled-
up foil, a flat square of foil, toy boats, blocks, rocks, wood scraps, feathers—
and ask the children to find out which will float and which will sink. Ask
them to predict by holding and looking at the object, and then to test their
predictions. Children can also find other things in the room or on the playground with which to experiment.

❑   dissolving. Bring in paper cups, sticks for stirring, water pitchers, and a variety
of materials for testing, such as sand, gravel, coffee, tea leaves, salt, sugar, and
beads. Have children try small amounts of the material in cups of water to see
which will dissolve and which will not. Children can record their findings.

❑   properties of water. Children's exploration with water can help them to discover
that water takes on the shape of the container it is in and to practice with the idea
that the amount of water remains the same, even when poured into containers

of different shapes. Children can count and record the number of cups of water it takes to fill a large container. Ask them to pour a cup of water into another container and to predict whether or not the amount of water has stayed the same. They can test their hypothesis by pouring the water back into the first container.

Blocks

Blocks are one of the most valuable learning resources in the social studies. Block building invites children to work together. Rather than relying on suggestions from the teacher, the discipline of construction itself asks for cooperative effort. They seek each other's help, working together as they build.

First introduced by Froebel, unit blocks were used by Caroline Pratt in the early 1930s as a primary tool for social studies learning in her New York City nursery school. Unit blocks—smooth, solid, and increasing in size in one dimension only, length—allow children the comfort of repeating forms and predicting results. Although initially expensive, unit blocks are indestructible and are a good investment.

A variety of blocks might be used in addition to unit blocks. Large, wooden, hollow blocks, cardboard blocks, blocks made from wood scraps that have been sanded and smoothed, or blocks made from paper milk cartons stuffed solidly with newspaper and covered with paper are all useful. Storage of blocks is easiest

---

The role of the teacher includes:

❑ providing firsthand experiences to be represented through block building. Ask children to observe the school building, the fire station, or a shopping center and speculate on how it was built.

❑ recognizing children's representations. Pay attention to the block configurations with comments and questions such as "How will the truck get in and out?" "Where can the street go?" "Did you see the warehouse?" "This block will balance the others."

❑ encouraging children with a smile, nod, or comment to let them know you support their building.

❑ adding vocabulary. "Shaneka, use the arch." "Put the double block here."

❑ posing problems. "What will happen if you . . . ?"

❑ adding props. Based on firsthand experiences, add wood animals, people, street signs, cars, boats, planes, trains, and ladders to the block area. Natural materials, pieces of shrubs, stones, wood, plants, shells, and human-made materials such as wire, cables, and ropes motivate block building.

❑ evaluating their block play. Observe children's buildings, noting their progress and movement from laying blocks out flat on the floor to constructing vertical buildings.

❑ providing resources.

Box 3.4
Blocks—The Teacher's Role

All kinds of blocks are available for children to express social studies experiences.

on open shelves, with a place on the shelf for each shape and size. When blocks are stored in this manner, children can see all of the possibilities for constructing and can find the right block for the right job. Symbols on each shelf, representing the shape of the block to be stored there, help children remember where to return the blocks when they have finished working with them.

A smooth, hard surface is best for constructing. If possible, allow the buildings to stand as long as the children's interest lasts. Encourage the children to add to or rebuild them, thereby extending their original concept and using it in play. If this is not possible, some place in the room away from traffic, and with a measure of privacy, can be set aside for block play.

Children's first block buildings are explorative. Young children begin to build by placing the blocks in rows, making lines across the floor. Later, they start putting one block on top of another, knocking them down, then beginning again. Simple construction is next, with square and rectangular buildings of one level appearing (Hirsch, 1984). As children mature and their backgrounds of experience increase, they begin to create the things they have observed in the community—the zoo, the airport, an apartment house, a mobile-home park, and the neighborhood. They begin cooperative play, with plans, goals, and purposes; their block play and its resulting structures become increasingly complex, based on group effort and individual ideas (Cartwright, 1990).

Housekeeping/Dramatic Play

Dramatic play—that is, play that encourages children to take on the role of another and use symbolic thought—has been called "a unifying force by which the child's social and physical experiences with the external world are integrated with his internal mental and emotional processes to produce novel transformations which are then projected outward in symbolic form" (Curry, 1974, p. 72). Sociodramatic play, with children acting as if they were astronauts, mothers, fathers, doctors, or teachers, is important in the development of learning strategies and the skills involved in thinking. In the housekeeping area, children can develop the skills of (a) maintaining a planned sequence of activities, (b) abstracting and embodying the salient features of a situation or role, and (c) focusing their attention, over a period of time, on the capacity for objectivity and empathy.

Keeping in mind the social studies experiences the children have had, you can add other props that would encourage children to try out still different roles. A trip to the dentist's office might be followed by the addition of a mirror, chair, and white shirt; a trip to the airport, by the addition of suitcases and a ticket desk; and a visit from the postal clerk, by the addition of a shoulder bag and hat (Vukelich, 1990).

Every area of the social sciences can be reinforced with props in the housekeeping area:

❑ economics—play money for purses and wallets, scales for weighing groceries, cash registers, blank receipt books

❑ history—sunbonnets, long skirts, ranch-hand hats

Seek donations for:

❑ used but safety-proofed kitchen utensils.

❑ doll and baby clothes and furniture.

❑ an assortment of clothes for dress up. A lace curtain or panel becomes a king's gown or queen's skirt. Ordinary boots and galoshes become those of a lumberjack, an astronaut, or a fire fighter.

❑ tool kits, lunch boxes, briefcases, and other items representing the work of parents.

❑ an assortment of scarves and jewelry.

❑ all kinds of hats.

❑ papers, pencils, old receipt books and checkbooks, plastic creditlike cards, and notepads for writing and notetaking.

❑ old telephones.

❑ books and magazines

❑ paper, envelopes, and stamps (those found in mail soliciting for donations or magazine subscriptions).

❑ play money, both coins and bills.

Box 3.5
Equipping the Dramatic Play Area

Through dramatic play, children can take on the roles of others.

☐ geography—road maps, dress-up clothes for travelling, wheel toys, steering wheel

☐ international education—clothing, games, or other objects used in other countries

Although teachers do not interfere in children's housekeeping play, they do reinforce the play by pretending, "This birthday cake is delicious," by facilitating, "Knock on the door. They'll let you in," and by extending, "You could take the baby to the doctor."

You can settle disputes before the children become frustrated and aggressive: "Use the hat now, Christian; then Joe can have it." You can redirect the play: "I think the supper's burning," or, "Why don't you sell the cookies?"

Special Centers

A number of special areas are also required from time to time to foster social studies concepts. The usual grocery store is well known in kindergarten and first-grade classrooms. Other shops may come and go as children's interests and experiences suggest. Children could use a large packing crate, with a change of signs and the addition of curtains and a few appropriate props, to portray the post office, card shop, beauty or barber shop, hardware store, gasoline station, drugstore, toy shop, laundromat, or bank. These are the kinds of shops that are useful only if the children have experienced them and are interested in re-creating the experience. Even if space would permit, there is no need for them to become permanent additions to the room.

The Nuffield Mathematics Project (1967) uses many different shops to foster children's economics concepts and has identified the stages through which children progress in shop play:

Stage One—imitative play by the very young child, often with a mother or father, and imaginary goods being used; usually there is no concern for purchasing, or for exchange of money.

Stage Two—beginning of creative play; children improvise play materials, use buttons for money, and play at purchasing items.

Stage Three—children appear to desire more representative goods; empty cartons, canned goods, and play money are useful at this stage.

Stage Four—children construct the store and goods, build counters, cut money out of paper, make signs, and take parts in purchasing and in exchanging money.

Stage Five—a continuation of free play leading to more involved projects and teacher-contrived explorations of children's interests; chil-

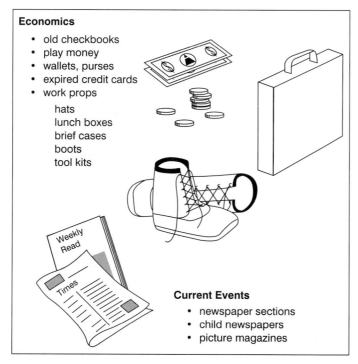

Economics
- old checkbooks
- play money
- wallets, purses
- expired credit cards
- work props

    hats
    lunch boxes
    brief cases
    boots
    tool kits

Current Events
- newspaper sections
- child newspapers
- picture magazines

Box 3.6
Social Materials for the Dramatic Play Area

Box 3.7

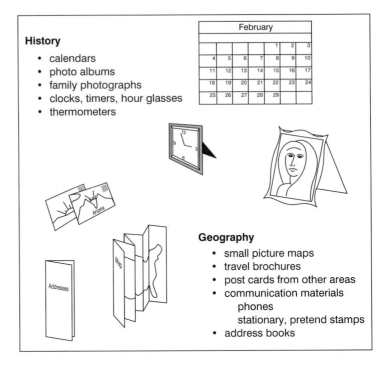

dren use signs, prices, graphs, and scales and hold sales with reduced merchandise or actually sell small boxes of raisins, cookies baked by the class, or plants grown from seeds.

As with other play, children need time to develop complex responses and to become involved in store play. To obtain the full potential from shop play, children need the opportunity to progress from the imitative stage to the creative and complex stage. Thus, shop play should continue through the primary grades rather than stopping at kindergarten or first grade.

Library

A library area is more than a place to read books. It should be filled with color and beauty—growing plants, a dried-flower arrangement, a terrarium, prints, children's art. Here, children can read by themselves or with a friend; they can curl up in a big, overstuffed chair or use a pillow on the floor.

To reinforce children's social studies experiences, you need to offer all types of books at reading levels appropriate for children's use. Simple reference books, picture dictionaries and encyclopedias, books on various topics studied by the children—all are useful resources for children's social studies learning. There is also a place for other books that show the beauty of language, humor, security, suspense, and excitement.

With young children, it is best if you rotate the books, selecting those relevant to children's interests or experiences. Too many books at one time can be confusing.

Display the books on a table or arrange them on shelves so children can see the choices available. You can help children sharpen their thinking skills by providing several different books on the same topic (compare and contrast), two different versions of the same story (find similarities and differences), or two identical books (discuss and play riddles: "I see a picture of . . . ." "What page am I on . . . ?").

The best loved and most frequently read books in the library are those the children dictate or write themselves. Class booklets, with children in the class contributing an illustration or a dictated or written story about a class trip, an experience, or a unit topic, give them the pleasure of cooperating in a group project while expressing and recording their ideas. Individually written booklets are also valuable additions to the library corner. The authors of these books grow in self-esteem as others read their books or as the teacher reads them to the class. Class scrapbooks, with photos of the children on a field trip, at work, or at play, are also useful library resources.

Books can be shelved in other areas of the classroom as well. In both the library area and other places in the room, some teachers separate books in plastic buckets according to type. Biographies, nonfiction, fiction, concepts, and poetry are stored in separate containers. Some books are arranged in other centers. For example, Lynn Cohen, a teacher in New York, places a plastic container of books about building in the block area, spring books with art supplies to provide chil-

An array of materials is available for children's learning.

dren with ideas for their construction, or Mother Goose and baby poem books in the housekeeping area to use to "read babies to sleep."

Writing

Social studies provides a point of departure for children to write and record their experiences and ideas. Children can share their writings with others in the library area, with their parents, or with another class in the school (Schickedanz, 1986). Sometimes, if children's interest in writing lags, you might suggest that they dictate or write the story of how they think it would feel to go to the moon, what they saw on the latest field trip, how they would feel without a friend or about their friend, or some other topic.

In the kindergarten and primary grades, a writing area is successful in fostering children's written expression and in recording their ideas about social studies learning. A shelf set aside for writing materials in the library or art area is all the space that is required. You can provide a can of sharpened pencils, soft-tipped pens in a variety of colors, blank booklets (several sheets of paper stapled together), and an assortment of different sizes, shapes, and colors of paper. These supplies can be available to children who have a story to dictate, write, or draw. You might provide box dictionaries (holding cards with words that children can read), chart dictionaries (listing words that might be needed during a special season or unit of study), and commercial dictionaries (Bakst & Essa, 1990).

Art

Every social studies experience can be enhanced by re-creating it, giving it expression through an art activity.

As children create, they share materials, sometimes work together in a group, take the responsibility for cleanup, and help prepare the materials needed; they are learning and practicing social skills. The very act of creating is emotionally satisfying, for it lets children know they have power and control over materi-

---

Teachers can either make a journal for each child by stapling some paper together between cardboard covers or purchase a loose-leaf notebook for each child. Labeling these with children's names and storing them in plastic bins, with pencils and markers nearby, encourages children to write something in their journal each day.

While this practice is recommended for children in the kindergarten and primary grades, teachers of 3– and 4–year-old children may also offer them journals to write in each day. Younger children draw pictures, scribble words, and begin writing stories using combinations of scribbles, drawings, and letters, which leads to invented spelling.

Box 3.8
Journal Writing

als and things. It is a safe, acceptable way of releasing feelings and expressing ideas (Fromberg, 1995).

Through art, children become acquainted with cultures other than their own. Observing paintings from Japan, touching pottery from Mexico, or examining a woven mat from the Philippines, children gain understanding of other cultures. "Who made this?" "How did they do it?" "Why did they make it?" "What does it mean to them?" are questions that might be asked (Schuman, 1981).

An art center is really many different areas containing a variety of materials through which children can symbolize their knowledge and understanding as well as their values and attitudes. Every day, children need to find something with which to draw, paint, cut and paste, model, construct, sew and weave, or build. In addition to all of the materials readily available for children's use, one additional ingredient is required—experience. The secret ingredient in stimulating children's art production, in making it relevant as a learning tool for social studies, is experience. Without experience, children have no ideas to express through art. All of the social studies experiences—field trips, observations, interactions with others—stimulate children's art (Dixon & Chalmers, 1990; Seefeldt, 1995).

Another type of art experience is possible. By sharing an object of art with children, you stimulate ideas for art while introducing children to the cultures of others. You might share a Mexican bark painting with the children, examining how it was made, who made it, and why. Children could then make their own bark paintings on brown wrapping paper or wood planks. There are many other ideas:

❑ A piece of Inca or Pueblo pottery can lead children to finding out who made it and how these people lived, and to trying pottery making for themselves.

❑ An Oriental brush painting can give children ideas for using their brushes in different ways to achieve different effects.

❑ Puppets can be constructed to portray the first Thanksgiving, the discovery of America, or other historic events.

❑ A unit on Indian life can lead to replication of Indian designs and sign writing.

❑ A model of a farm, a factory, or an airport can be constructed with blocks or boxes.

❑ At Halloween, a story about masks can lead to making masks.

❑ Costumes, made of brown paper bags, and decorations can be constructed for plays and creative dramatics when children act out some historic event.

❑ Jewelry made of ceramic clay might replicate jewelry made by Mexicans, Spaniards, or American Indians.

❑ Hats and clothing, similar to those worn in another country or time, can be constructed.

❑ Rhythm instruments such as drums, bamboo sticks, and shakers can be constructed to duplicate those used by other peoples.

Drawing and Painting.   Because drawing and painting are symbolic processes, they are uniquely related to the social studies. As children draw and paint, they have the opportunity to clarify relationships among their social studies experiences and to bring their own interpretation and imagination to them. Drawing and painting activities contribute to children's social skills by permitting them to communicate ideas, feelings, and experiences and to solve problems.

You can provide a variety of drawing tools. None require much space, but the organization of the materials should remind children of their availability. A shelf, a tabletop, or even a windowsill can hold drawing materials. For ease of cleanup, each type of drawing tool should be kept in a separate container, either a clear type or one that is labeled with a symbol of the tool.

Easels, already set up, with cans of paint, brushes, and large newsprint stored nearby, are typical but not the only possible arrangement. If easels are not available in the classroom, any type, size, and color of paper, a can of brushes, and a six-pack of paints can serve as painting tools. Children can pick up their materials and paint anywhere in the room they wish or even in the hallway.

Commercial tempera paints are usually best suited for children's painting, for they provide a smooth, bright medium, thick enough not to run or drip. An assortment of brushes—wide, rounded and fine pointed—can be provided.

Murals are often outcomes of children's social studies experiences. Kindergarten and preschool children do not understand the purpose of working together to create a group project, and even primary children require some introduction to murals. The value of having children work together to create a project enjoyed by the entire class is worth any effort needed. In some fashion, divide the large brown paper used for murals, giving each child a section to paint. This permits children to work by themselves and with a group. After the class has enjoyed the mural, it can be cut apart, and children can take home their own paintings. You might suggest mural themes depicting some social studies topic—transportation, the firehouse, the farm—and each child can do something connected with the general theme.

Constructing.   An assortment of odd pieces of junk, such as berry baskets, toilet-paper tubes, cookie containers, and other types of boxes, ribbons, string, foil pie pans, foam meat trays—anything that is going to be discarded—fosters a wide range of creative responses to social studies concepts. Masking tape, hole punches, plastic-coated wires, and pipe cleaners are also helpful additions.

Once the children have joined boxes together with masking tape or wire, they can paint them with tempera that has had detergent or liquid starch added to it to allow it to adhere to a variety of surfaces. Or the entire structure can be covered with a thin layer of papier-mâché and left to dry. Once it's dry, the children can paint the piece with any type of paint.

Sewing/Weaving.   Using sewing and weaving, people have expressed their cultures throughout the years. Once children have mastered the techniques of sewing and weaving, they can create banners, flags, mats, and clothing representative of many cultures.

Large, blunt needles and brightly colored yarns are ideal for beginning stitchery experiences. You will need to show children how to thread the yarn through the eye of the needle and how to make a knot in the end of the yarn. Usually one or two of the children catch on very quickly and can help the other children with the threading and knotting task. The stitchery experience is much more successful if the sewing material is loosely woven. Plastic screening or berry baskets, net potato or onion bags, or burlap with a border of masking tape to stiffen it are useful materials for beginning sewers, since the large needles and thick yarn slip easily through the mesh. A tightly woven material does not permit the large needle, threaded with thick yarn, to pass through it easily. Mounting the material to be stitched on an embroidery hoop or stiffening it in some other way is very helpful for young children, enabling them to hold the material more securely.

An old-fashioned sewing box is useful. This box could contain spools of thread, blunt scissors, buttons, fancy lace, patches, and a large sewing needle. Before using the sewing box, children should know how to use needles and scissors safely. This sewing kit allows children to make clothes for puppets and dolls, or to mend other items.

Weaving is possible with a large variety of materials. First, children can begin the weaving process with paper. Later, you might provide the cut paper and let the children weave with materials they have found during a field trip or nature walk. Once children learn the over-and-under pattern of weaving, they can use it to make decorations, wall hangings, mats, or items of clothing.

Woodworking. Children have always delighted in the power and sensory pleasure working with wood brings. Wood is solid, has weight, takes up space, and real products can be created with it. A woodworking bench is not necessary in order for children to have experiences with wood; any discarded stand, table, shelf, or solid wooden chair can become a woodworking bench with the addition of C-clamps, which hold the wood while children are working.

Tools, strong, sturdy, and real, can be mounted on a pegboard hanging on the wall or stored in a box if space is a problem. You can get soft wood scraps

Working with wood can reinforce a number of social studies concepts

from the local cabinet shop, from high school or college industrial arts programs, or from builders. As with other art materials, there are definite developmental levels children progress through when working with wood. The first experiences with wood are exploratory, with children pounding nails into pieces of wood, not joining anything, but enjoying the power and thrill of working with real materials. The next stage involves children's joining two pieces of wood together with no definite plan in mind; sometimes after the pieces have been joined, children will give names to their creations. The last stage involves the children making plans, deciding on materials to use, and completing the construction.

Many social studies concepts are reinforced as children work with wood. They can work together in committees to build a product the class can use—a rabbit hutch, shelf, record-player stand, or playhouse—or they can re-create their observations of construction workers, cabinetmakers, or builders. If involved in purchasing the wood and wood supplies, they become consumers as well as producers. Woodworking might also stimulate interest in this type of career or in finding out how things are made and who makes them.

Cutting/Pasting.   Even the youngest children, who only cut, cut, and cut, enjoy cutting and pasting and making collages. Scissors that do cut, stored point down in a box, an assortment of things to cut—paper, fabric, ribbons, yarns, gummed papers, felt, feathers—and glue and paste give children unlimited possibilities for re-creating their experiences.

Collage materials are more useful when they are stored by category. Keeping all of the feathers, sticks, pebbles, shells, ribbons, upholstery scraps, and toothpicks in their own boxes enables children to select the materials needed. Returning from a trip to the zoo, one group of kindergartners went directly to the box of rough-textured upholstery scraps and began creating the animals they had seen, with the exception of one child. He ignored the upholstery scraps, picked up the box of toothpicks, and re-created, with all the intricacies of spans and wires, the bridge they had crossed on the way.

Modeling.   Modeling activities are excellent for making objects, folk art, pottery, jewelry, or a character—animal or human—from a well-loved story. Preschool or primary children, without a background of experience with modeling materials, will need time to experiment with clay before actually creating any objects. Teachers may also need to introduce children to techniques of working with clay—such as slipping two pieces together—for children to make objects. When children examine clay products from other cultures or times, you might ask, "How do you think they made this point?" "Feel this seam. They must have joined it here," or, "What tools do you think they used to make this rough part?" These kinds of questions help children see possibilities for their own modeling work.

Water-based clay can be stored in any airtight container. If it dries, you can add water, and in a day or two it will have returned to its original pliable texture. Storing clay in fist-sized pieces and keeping it pliable and soft encourages children to use it. Plasticine, because of its oil base, will never completely dry out; however, it is not as pliable as other materials and may be more difficult for young children to handle. A set of oilcloth-covered boards, stored next to the clay container, allows children to take a piece of clay or dough and a board and work in any area of the room.

Vicarious Materials in the Classroom

Vicarious experiences cannot replace children's concrete experiences. Learning that results from vicarious experience is often inaccurate and incomplete. Nevertheless, until the time that children can actually walk on the moon or go to a foreign country, they can learn something about these places from others. Looking at photographs, reading, or watching a movie about the moon, children learn something about the moon's nature. The wise use of audiovisual materials, bulletin boards, books, and pictures can help children (a) clarify concrete experiences, (b) refine their perceptions of these experiences, and (c) extend their meanings. A movie filmed on a trip to the bottle factory can be a useful tool for children's learning. Shown after their trip, it enables children to

- ❑ recall. "Do you remember what that was used for?" "What was the purpose of this tool?" "Let's watch the movie again to find out."
- ❑ focus. "When we see the movie this time, be sure to look for the way the bottles got into the box."
- ❑ clarify. "Let's check that idea when we watch the movie."

Then, too, concrete experiences seem to happen so quickly—the moth emerges from the cocoon, the snake sheds its skin, the lights are fixed, the telephone wires are spliced and back in their casing—children have little opportunity to make accurate observations. Vicarious experiences—a book on electricity, photographs of the telephone system, a movie showing in slow motion a moth emerging from a cocoon—help to enrich and extend children's actual experiences.

Careful selection of resources for vicarious experience is necessary. Deciding on the resources to use depends on the goals and objectives of social studies. You will want to choose whatever experiences help foster the children's attainment of your goals. Having determined that a specific resource might aid in fostering your goals and objectives, you can ask the following:

- ❑ How available is the resource? Materials that require mailing time or that are not handy when children's interests demand them are not useful.
- ❑ How costly is it? Can a natural material or real experience serve the same purpose less expensively?
- ❑ How easily can it be used? The problem of finding space for projectors or changing rooms to see a movie, especially with young children, may require more time and effort than it is worth.
- ❑ How does it fit in with the children's background of experiences? Does it fit logically into their previous experiences and provide information on which to base future experiences?

❑ How will it be used to meet the needs of individual children? Not all resources are necessary for the total group; some might be selected for use with individual children or small groups.

Children's Literature

In today's whole language classroom, children's books are everywhere. For children to give genuine, honest, personal, rich, and deep responses to literature, the books they find in the library, dramatic play areas, science and math corners, and throughout the room must be of the highest quality possible. Only then will children be able to identify and become involved with the major characters of books, learning of people and places far from them (Noori, 1995). Libraries are most willing to lend teachers armloads of books for a month to 6 weeks at a time. There are beautifully illustrated books on all reading levels to meet children's interest on any social studies topic.

The power of children's literature depends on the responses children bring to it. Having enjoyed listening to a story read by the teacher or another child, or having read special books themselves, children can follow up on this pleasurable experience. They might report on the books they have read or listened to by

❑ drawing or painting a picture of the parts that they enjoyed most, that frightened them the most, or that were the most exciting.
❑ making clay models of an animal, a character, or some object in the story.
❑ constructing something that was made in the book or that the book was about.
❑ acting out the story with puppets or with other children.

Social studies textbooks may be useful as well. Instead of ordering one textbook for each child, it may be more valuable for you to have a few copies from each of several different textbook series. When textbooks from various series are available, children can select the book they need and find information on a particular topic or problem of interest to them.

Reference Materials

Feet propped up against the table and with newspaper open, the 5-year-old boy clearly was trying on the role of father. Young children, intrigued by anything that appears to be adultlike, find something appealing about using newspapers, news magazines, and other reference materials. It makes them feel grown-up. Taking advantage of this natural interest, teachers can use newspapers and news magazines as social resources.

You can gradually introduce the local newspaper to young children. Besides being a useful prop in the housekeeping area, it also contains information that children can use. Certain sections of the newspaper—the picture magazine, sports, or feature sections—are manageable by children.

Some newspapers or news magazines are produced especially for children. You can subscribe to these for individual children or obtain a few copies for use by small groups of children. The value of these newspapers depends on how they are used. It is inappropriate to give an entire group of kindergarten or primary children the same paper and make them listen to an adult read it, for any reason. If you make these papers available as they pertain to topics of interest, and as incidental resources, they might be useful. In the housekeeping area or on the library table, they can be used independently.

Audiovisual Resources

Movies and Videos.   There are many readily available movies and videos about places, people, and things of interest to children. Movies and videos offer an effective way to present information to young children. Just as with other resources, you will need to select these carefully and use them with a specific purpose and objective in mind. Short movies or portions of longer movies work best since young children cannot sit for long periods of time. If the content of a particular video or movie is of interest to the children, but the narration is too complex, you might show it with the sound off, letting the children tell the story in their own words, letting the pictures tell the story, or having the children make up the narration as they view the movie or video.

   1. Before viewing: You will want to preview any movie or video you select before showing it to the children. You can then give the children a focus for viewing, asking questions or identifying things to look for or things to support their "I thought so's." You can ask the children to predict what they will see. Before the presentation is the time to clarify unfamiliar vocabulary and prepare children for viewing.

   2. During viewing: Children should be encouraged to talk with one another, ask questions, or make points while the video or movie is being shown. You may want to show it twice, the first time for viewing, the second for discussing; or once for listening and looking, and another time for looking and children's telling the story in their own words. The single-loop film, which can be shown by preschool-primary children without the help of an adult, is useful for individualizing movies and for fostering development of a single concept.

   3. After viewing: A number of experiences can follow a movie or video. Children might not want or need to follow it with any activity; on the other hand, films often are used to stimulate discussion, ideas, or activities on the part of the children. Follow-up experiences could include

❑ dramatic play, with props added to the play areas reflecting the theme of the movie or video.

❑ books to read about the topic covered.

❑ art, music, and rhythm activities based on something seen in the video or movie.

❑ a further study of the topic, by observing the environment and by interviewing others.

Filmstrips/Slides.   Filmstrips and slides are sometimes more practical than movies. Preschool and primary children can learn to use the filmstrip and slide projectors themselves and can view slides or strips individually if the machines can be set up in a corner of the room. Filmstrips are also easier for young children to follow than movies. They can be stopped for discussion, started over in order to answer a question, and used to stimulate children's language by letting them supply the narrative.

An interesting way to discuss relationships or to solve problems of living with one another in a group is to use slides taken of the children while working and playing. Some slides might be used to illustrate the rules that are necessary when using wheel toys, the swing, or the slide; others could be used to discuss how to settle arguments or to illustrate cooperative use of materials. All children enjoy seeing themselves, and slides will stimulate language use as well as help children see solutions to problems.

Record Players/Tape Recorders/Television.   Records, used with or without a listening jack, are also available to reinforce children's social studies concepts. Some records offer children the opportunity to listen to the music of children far from them. They might listen to folktales recorded by Native Americans, songs and music from Hawaii, the sound of African musical instruments, or the music of Appalachia. The value of this type of listening lies in children's responses of singing, dancing, making instruments, or recording their own folk songs.

Singing the folk songs of a culture, especially singing them in the language in which they are written, children are transported in spirit to this culture, and in the process feel a kinship with its people. Listening to music recorded in a particular culture serves the same purpose.

> After the Communists overtook Hungary in the 1950s, Kodaly, a Hungarian philosopher and musician, created a national music curriculum. He believed that if the Hungarian people could sing and share the experience of their music, they would continue to be united and connected with their culture until the time that they would once again experience freedom. During the "Velvet Revolutions" in Eastern Europe as the Soviet Union was breaking up, a news program showed the Hungarian people in Freedom Square celebrating their freedom by singing the folk songs of their country. Listening to their national anthem and songs, one could only conclude that music can transmit a culture and hold people together. (Seefeldt, 1993)

Tape recorders have become readily available, are inexpensive, and are nearly childproof. Children can tape reports or interview school personnel or their parents. You might even tape the sounds of the children. A tape of the sounds of a factory, recorded during a field trip, lets children review and remember the trip. Taping stories the children love allows them to listen to these again and again. Some teachers use the tape recorder to leave messages for the children, such as a news item, a surprise that will happen during the day, or some directions to follow. Children can develop strong listening skills through use of a tape recorder.

Every culture has music that unites its children.

Occasionally, a television program or news show can be useful as a resource for children's listening. When some event is going to be televised—the visit of a king, the arrival of a new animal at the zoo, a space launch—the television could be placed in the classroom and turned on to allow the children to witness the event. Young children will want to listen and watch for only a brief time, just long enough to satisfy their curiosity.

Few television shows in their entirety are appropriate for viewing by young children. Investing 20 or 30 minutes in the vicarious experience of a television program is not an efficient use of time. However, children can be guided to view specific shows at home with their families in order to gain information on a specific topic, to find out the meaning of a term, or just to enjoy a program related to their interests.

Computers

Computers are now a part of nearly every early childhood program. They are useful for developing computer literacy and introducing content. (Wright & Shade, 1995).

Developing Computer Literacy.   Children are becoming competent in the use of the computer. Just as they are learning to use tools such as the telephone, typewriter, or television, preschool and primary children learn to use the computer. The two skills needed to develop computer literacy are learning how to turn the computer on and off and learning to type. Children can master these skills easily as they play with computers. "Children mastered keyboard letter-matching tasks after a few weeks. Within 2 months, most children were easily able to select options from menus and read prompts related to the operation of particular programs. Even among different programs, the framework for using the computer is often similar. Within this meaningful context, children became adept at reading the language they needed to control a new environment" (Anselmo & Zinck, 1987).

Teaching Content.   Computer-assisted instruction is another use for the computer. Educational Testing Company studied how computer-assisted instruction could reinforce classroom work by helping the students learn basic skills and providing drill and practice. Children in the study demonstrated impressive math scores, and ETC concluded that "for school systems that are concerned with basic skills, these curricula are available. If similarly implemented in other schools, comparable results should come from their use" (Ragasto, 1982).

Selecting Programs.   Software must be evaluated in the context of developmentally appropriate curriculum goals. In selecting computer programs, ask yourself the following:

1. Can more than one child use the program at a time?
2. How can I arrange the computer area to promote child/child interactions?
3. Will the program be used only for computer-assisted instruction of the practice or rote learning type? How does the program differ from typical workbooks or worksheets?
4. Is the program designed to develop high-order thinking skills such as judging, evaluating, analyzing, or synthesizing information?
5. Does the program require some action on the part of the child such as drawing, moving things, or writing?

Additionally, you will want to examine the program for accuracy, as well as for the values it presents. An emphasis on war and violence, and the absence of women and minorities in visual representations have been found in some computer programs. You will want to consider the quality of the program in terms of color, sound or voice quality, animation, and other technical elements (Wright & Shade, 1995).

Packages are becoming available touching on every subject, including the social studies. Teachers also have found they can adapt some computer games for classroom use. These programs have been integrated into the classroom in several ways:

❑   to introduce a new unit
❑   to offer enrichment
❑   as a reward
❑   for regulating the pace of individualized work
❑   to foster thinking skills (Noori, 1995)

Pictures

Pictures mounted on a bulletin board or for children to handle, sort out, feel, or carry with them as they play are a valuable social studies resource. You can use them to begin a discussion, as a takeoff for role or dramatic play, or to give information about people, places, or things far from the child's immediate environment. But the primary purpose of picture reading is to develop thinking skills. For pictures to be of value, they must be read as thoughtfully as the printed page is read. When problem solving provides the motivation for reading pictures, children use them to discover clues about land forms and climate, economic development of an area, relationships of work to environment, cultural likenesses and differences, density of populations, characteristics of historical periods, and so on.

Children do not automatically develop the skills of using pictures to solve problems in the manner just described. Young children should not even be asked to read pictures until their experiential background indicates readiness. Although most young children have had these experiences, it is important to begin with real objects and events before asking children to interpret the symbols of a picture or photograph. Pictures are symbols that stand for some object or event, and children require many experiences in classifying, comparing, and contrasting real objects and events before they are able to interpret a picture representing them.

The first stage in picture reading involves naming the objects that appear. At the beginning level, ask questions that require children to name, list, or tell what they see in the picture. Unless children have had a great deal of experience with oral language and obtaining meaning from symbols, they cannot be expected to do more than simply name the objects that appear in a picture.

The next stage in picture reading is interpretive. Having mastered the ability to describe or name what is in the picture, children can then begin to interpret or discuss what is happening. This is followed by the ability to predict what might occur. Only after repeated experiences, increased maturity, language development, and a background of experience in creative thinking can young children use their imaginations to create a story when given a picture as a stimulus.

Teachers can ask questions to stimulate picture reading. Beginning questions revolve around knowledge—"What do you see?" Next, comprehension questions—"Why did this happen?"—seek to elicit a response that indicates an understanding of the conditions or trends included in the picture. Application questions are those that demonstrate the use of an abstraction in a concrete situation— "What will he do?" These questions seek to elicit responses that demonstrate the children's ability to identify the elements, relationships, or organizational principles, or the ability to put together elements and parts to form a whole, not clearly identified in the picture—"Do you think he did the right thing?"

Not all children will see the same thing in a picture, nor will they interpret the picture the same way. These differences in perception can lead to small group discussions and later to critical, analytical thinking. Picture reading is not easy for children, and teachers sometimes become discouraged with the process and look for other methods that seem easier for both children and teacher. Work, effort, and repeated experiences with picture reading are required before the process is entirely successful. You do need to encourage children in their development of picture-reading skills, accepting the level of skill children bring to the task and continuing to use pictures as a resource for learning.

Realia

"What is it?" "What is it made of?" "How does it feel?" No picture, movie, or film-strip can compare to real objects, to things that children can see, hear, touch, smell, or even taste for themselves. Real objects help children understand the past and life far from them, and see significant relationships within their own neighborhood. Real objects might be obtained from families, local museums, or historical societies. Any object you can use to foster social studies knowledge is appropriate. Some examples are

- ❑ plants. "How is this plant like the ones we know? How is it different? Where does it grow? What does it need to live?"
- ❑ foods. "Taste them. Where were they grown? Who grew them? How did they get here?"
- ❑ old tools. "Who used these? How were they used? For what purpose? What tools do we use today?"
- ❑ clothing. "Who wore this? Why? Who made it? What is it like?"
- ❑ models. "How is this car (train, boat) like a real one? How is it different?"
- ❑ furniture. "How was it made? When was it used? Who made it?"
- ❑ old photographs. With old photographs of their school, neighborhood, or community, or of the children's families, their parents, and even themselves, children are able to compare and contrast past and present. You might ask, "What is the same? Do you wear the same kind of clothing? What is different today?"

Objects alone stimulate children's language and thinking without adult questioning or interference. A spinning wheel, a model ship, an old-fashioned coffee mill, or a photograph from the past provides sufficient motivation for children to begin asking questions and seeking information.

Bulletin Boards and Displays

Bulletin boards and displays are one way for children to organize their thoughts and reflect on a social studies experience. By arranging materials on a table or creating a bulletin board, children have the opportunity to classify information, to find some way to record their ideas and experiences and label these.

Set the stage for involving preschool and kindergarten children in constructing a display or bulletin board by asking each to make a contribution to the display. Popular topics might include a bulletin board titled. "We Are in Kindergarten." Each child draws a self-portrait for the board, which is later labeled with the child's name and other information. Other boards might be "Ways We Travel." "Machines in School," "Clothes We Do Not Wear," or "Our Friends."

Who wore this dress? Nothing can compare with real objects that children can touch and experience for themselves.

Primary-age children may take more responsibility for the boards and displays and will be better able to begin coordinating their work as members of small groups. They are able to select a theme and decide on what will be included and how things will be displayed. Displays and boards might be created around themes of "Fire Fighters," "The Supermarket," and "Recycling in Our Neighborhood" to illustrate and explain content of interest or things the children learned through some social studies experience.

Commercial Materials

There are commercial kits and materials available for teaching social studies concepts. Before investing in commercial kits, you will want to evaluate them by

- ❑ observing children using similar materials to get an accurate idea of how appropriate they will be.
- ❑ talking with teachers who have used the materials to obtain other information on children's reactions to them and asking if the children were able to use the materials independently, how interested they were, if they held their interest, how many ways they could be used, and if they helped to accomplish stated goals.

Box 3.9
Iinteractive Bulletin Boards

How Many Ladybugs Can You Find?

A kindergarten class released 1,000 ladybugs in their garden.
Two children painted pictures of the garden with hidden ladybugs.

A Survey Bulletin Board
What Should We Do About Trash in Our Neighborhood? Vote for one.

Send a Letter To the Paper	Tell the Police	Get More Trash Cans	Put Up Signs
	✗	✗	✗
✓	✓	✗	✗
✗	✓	✗	
	✓	✓	
		✓	

❑ answering the question, "What else is available that would accomplish the same purpose for less money?"

Learning Stations

Learning stations are not to be confused with interest centers. Centers of interest, or areas for learning, are broadly based areas set aside for a particular type of play, exploration, or work. Learning stations are much more specific in nature and are designed to reinforce, clarify, and extend specific concepts or skills. Arising from the thrust for accountability and the emphasis on individualizing the curriculum, learning stations are designed to permit children to work and proceed at their own pace, without help from an adult.

Generally, learning stations should be

Box 3.9
Iinteractive Bulletin Boards *(continued)*

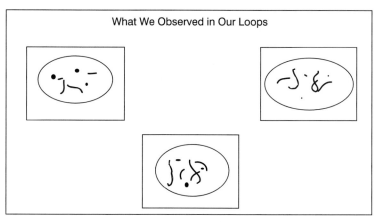

A class took yarn loops outside and observed what they found inside the loops when they placed them in different areas on the playyard.

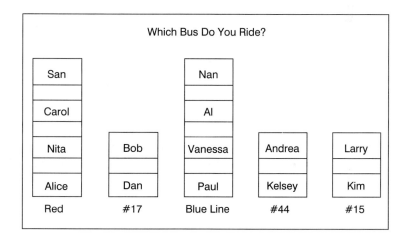

- ❑ self-directing. The directions should be so obvious that the children will need no help from an adult. Teachers have to be very creative when designing learning stations for children who do not have reading skills.
- ❑ self-correcting. Children should be able to tell, by the way they have completed the station, whether the task has been completed correctly.
- ❑ activity oriented. Learning stations should be based on children's active manipulation of materials and should not be paper-and-pencil tasks.

Although learning stations are designed for individual children, there should be time for interaction with others. When children and teacher have an opportunity to talk over the completed learning station, children become aware of patterns and relationships intuitively observed, but not clearly defined.

There are as many possibilities for learning stations as there are topics in social studies. Learning stations could be designed to reflect the basic skills of thinking: observing, classifying, interpreting, and summarizing.

Observing.   Learning to observe is a basic skill. Learning stations can reinforce skills of looking and touching.

1. Match the object: To develop the understanding that a picture represents an object and to strengthen observation skills, *Match the Object* contains a basket of objects—toy cars, boats, furniture, items of clothing—related to a social studies topic and a set of pictures representing the objects. Children can match the objects with the pictures of the objects. Objects and pictures can be color or symbol coded, to allow children to check their responses. You can talk to children about the functions of the objects, who uses them, why, and where.

2. See and find: Take two identical posters or pictures of a street, a farm, an airport scene, or whatever reflects the social studies interest at the time. Cover one of the pictures with clear plastic paper and mount it on a cardboard. Use the other picture to cut out details, such as a stop sign, a red light, or yellow lines of the crosswalk. Mount these on stiff paper and cover them with clear plastic paper. Children can find the details on the large picture and place the cut-out items on it.

3. Touch and tell: To strengthen observation through touch, *Touch and Tell* also uses objects and pictures. In this station, the objects are enclosed in a box, with a place for children to reach in, but they are not able to see the contents. Contents can reflect any current lesson or unit plan; for example, miniature replicas of animals, vehicles, or clothing can be used. Children select a picture from the stack, then reach into the box to try to find the object represented by the picture.

Classifying.   Classification provides a base for many different types of social studies learning stations. Stations should be based on children's ability to classify; real objects or replicas are inherently more valuable than pictures, but not always available or feasible to use in a learning station. You can cut out pictures, mount them, and cover them with clear paper; objects can be put into boxes or baskets, ready to be classified. Providing some type of sorting tray, such as empty plastic egg cartons, clear plastic containers mounted on a board, empty box tops, or trays, encourages children to keep their categories separate. The skill of classification involves noting similarities and differences, so all of the stations should provide for this activity.

Examples of classifying stations include the following:

❑ Transportation—Use pictures of objects or things that travel on the street, in the air, or in the water. Children can sort the pictures into three categories using a sorting tray.

❑ History—Have two sets of pictures, one of clothing items and transportation tools of the past, and another of similar things used today. Children can sort the pictures into two categories—past and present.

❑ Geography—Obtain pictures of the earth's surfaces: streams, rivers, lakes, valleys, hills, mountains, and plains. Select those that are alike.

❑ Economics—Pictures of work and play, of producers and consumers, tools used at home, in the factory, or at school, and so forth, can be sorted into similar groups.

To vary the stations, you can provide different types of sorting trays. Some can be flannel boards, and the pictures or things to be sorted can be backed with sandpaper so they will stick to the board. Other sorting trays can be boards with hooks attached. The pictures would have holes punched in them or loops of yarn attached for hanging them on the appropriate hooks.

Interpreting.   Interpreting means gaining meaning from the objects or pictures. Children could use the process of matching to learn to interpret. Matching stations, in which children match pictures of objects or events that go together, can be developed around numerous concepts:

❑ workers and the tools they use
❑ clothes and weather conditions
❑ hats and the workers they belong to
❑ houses and the people or animals that live in them
❑ the product and a picture of the region it came from
❑ the product and the raw, unprocessed first stage
❑ signs that say the same thing
❑ money and the numeral designating the amount

Whenever real objects can be used, it adds to the fun of a learning station. Even so, children do enjoy sorting and matching pictures, and the process of gaining meaning from the picture or object is a valuable learning experience.

Summarizing.   Some stations might be built around the skill of summarizing information. Children can place things in sequence on a flannel board, on hooks on a board, or in a sorting tray. Pictures children can place in sequence are the time of day, seasons of the year, days of the week, or months of the year; for older children, pictures of before, during, and after holiday celebrations, making or constructing something, or historic events can be placed in order.

RESOURCES WITHIN THE COMMUNITY: FIELD TRIPS

In the lovely, northern Italian city of Reggio Emilia, children in the city-run child-care centers leave their centers frequently, taking trips into their community. They run in the poppy fields, sit on the stone lions guarding one of the buildings, go to the supermarket, and walk in the rain. Just as the teachers in Reggio Emilia, teachers in America have always valued taking children on excursions into the community. Field trips and social studies seem to go together. A field trip can

- ❑ extend children's knowledge of their environment, providing them with first-hand experiences that would not be possible to implement within a classroom.
- ❑ help to acquaint the children with their immediate environment and to orient them in the environment. Concepts of direction, maps, and spaces are developed.
- ❑ provide contact with adult models in the social world, increasing children's knowledge of the world of work.
- ❑ allow children to use the scientific methods as they gather information, observe the environment, and draw conclusions.
- ❑ serve as a unifying agent for the children, providing a common core of experience for them to play out, problem-solve, share, and discuss.
- ❑ promote parent involvement by taking children to visit one another's homes or the places their parents work, or by going to the same places they go with their parents. A field trip also involves parents as participants.
- ❑ stimulate new ideas and new learning by enlivening children's interests and posing new questions that demand answers.

Types of Field Trips

"There can be no general list of trips recommended for kindergarten or first grade. Each environment furnishes its own particular trips. Each school, each teacher, must find trips within his own environment which fit each group of children. Each year the trips fit into an integrated program" (Mitchell, 1934, p. 23).

It is up to the teacher to identify, locate, and evaluate the possibilities for field trips within a community and to decide what type of trip is best suited for the children. Lucy Sprague Mitchell would probably have chosen walking trips through children's immediate environment of the school and neighborhood. Other types—split-group, repeated, those for a specific purpose, and WOW trips—can be taken as well.

Walking Trips

Perhaps the most valuable are walking field trips that can be taken once or twice a week within the school building, school yard, or neighborhood. There is much to see and learn within walking distance. These trips can be planned ahead by you or the children or can arise spontaneously as the children's interests dictate.

Split-Group Trips

Some trips will involve the total classroom, with the entire group visiting the library, firehouse, or florist. Other trips might involve a committee or a small group of children vitally interested in some specific place. Once children become accustomed to waiting their turn to go on a trip, and the trips are frequent, there is no difficulty in planning committee trips.

With a volunteer adult, a committee can be sent to purchase a goldfish for the class or a soup bone to make "stone soup." Or the three children interested in engines can be allowed to go to the corner garage to observe a mechanic at work. On some total-group trips, the class can be divided into committees, with each having a specific purpose or goal to fulfill. One group might be asked to investigate where the fire fighters sleep, another what they eat, and another to find out the answer to a question about fighting fires. On purchasing trips, each group of children can purchase a separate item.

Repeated Trips

Why not return to a place? Children can gain from visiting the same place again, learning something new from each trip. Young children, excited about being away from their familiar classroom, often do not see everything or focus on the specific idea or purpose of the trip. Returning to the same place gives children a sense of mastery; being familiar with the place, they feel secure, competent, and safe to risk new learning.

Specific-Purpose Trips

You can plan trips to fulfill specific purposes. A trip can be taken to observe all of the round things inside and outside the classroom, to record the sound that feet make on different materials in the building, or to find out the name of the street on which the school is located.

WOW Trips

Once or twice a year, perhaps as a culminating activity or perhaps as a traditional school trip, you might plan a WOW-type experience, with all of the parents involved. Trips to the zoo or circus and end-of-the-year picnics are of this type. These trips are relatively unimportant for children's learning; their value lies in involving parents and in providing the excitement of doing something new and different within the school.

Planning the Trip

The longest part of the trip will be the hours the teacher spends getting ready for it. Just the thought of dealing with a group of young children away from the confines of the classroom can be terrifying to the inexperienced teacher; yet once the teacher knows the group, this problem seems minor compared to the difficulty of planning meaningful trips, trips that provide a continuity of experiences for the children. In planning for valuable field trips, you must do the following:

1. Survey the community to learn what is available, where places of interests are, who to contact, and what places welcome children. One teacher discovered a broom factory, one of only a few still in existence in the country, just a block from the school. Another teacher made a card file of places of interest in the community, recording the telephone number, contact person, safety factors, and special things of interest for children.

2. Have a clear idea of the purpose of each trip. Writing a list of objectives for the trip helps you clarify the purpose for the trip and internalize your goals.

3. Attempt to provide a continuity among and between trips. Education is a continuous experience, and field trips should ensure the continuity of that experience rather than interrupt it.

4. Think in terms of a simple field trip. The world is so confusing to the young child that a simple trip to help the children understand their world might be more valuable than a complicated one.

5. Use the children's play to direct your planning. Observing the children at play, you can note their interests as well as their misconceptions that might be clarified with a trip. If children are interested in transportation, a trip to visit a gas station might be more appropriate than a trip to a zoo. A teacher can also observe what ideas of the children need to be extended or enriched, and can plan trips accordingly.

6. Make a survey of the children and their parents to find out places the children have already visited, things the parents would like their children to see and do, or places the children would like to know more about.

7. Consider the time of the day, week, and year the trip will be taken. It is wise to take walking trips when the children are fresh—early in the day or following a nap. You can plan returns to coincide with snacktime, lunchtime, or rest periods. The weather and seasonal conditions will also affect the type of trip planned.

Before the Trip

Establish the goals and objectives for a trip and assure yourself that the trip will provide the children with a continuity of experience that is built on their backgrounds of interest and experience. You then begin the actual planning for the trip.

Some of the things you will need to do in planning a trip are as follows:

1. Visit the place first, checking for safety hazards, noting special needs for clothing or supervision, checking bathroom facilities, and confirming the arrangements with the contact person.

2. Notify the parents that their children are leaving the school building. A blanket statement, given at the beginning of the year in a handbook or at a parents' meeting, can inform parents that their children will be going on many walking trips. Notices can still be sent home informing the parents about the exact nature of the trip; however, the parents need to know that some trips will be spontaneous—walking in the rain, finding ice puddles, or looking for the rainbow. For more involved trips, permission slips prepared according to the dictates of the school board will need to be sent home, signed, and returned.

3. Discuss the trip with the children. You might speculate with the children about where they are going, what they will do, and what they will see. The children might want to list the questions they want answered during the trip.

4. Provide the children with a background of experiences. Stories, props for play, filmstrips, pictures, or slides of the place to be visited give children a foundation on which to build their new experiences.

5. Review simple safety rules with the children. Definite standards of behavior can be established for field trips. It is important to review these standards with the children as well as with the adults going on the trip. When adults and children are certain about what is expected of them, trips are safer. Some rules might be recorded on a chart.

6. The teacher will want to involve as many adults as necessary for a safe trip, plan for emergencies, and include supplies such as tissues, adhesive bandages, and a thermos of water.

During the Trip

Skillful and tactful guidance will be required of the teacher during the trip. The interest of the group will be somewhat restricted by the trip's location and activities, yet you may still need to focus the children's attention on the goals of the trip and keep them together as a group.

During the trip you can do the following:

Children conduct research prior to taking a field trip.

1. Encourage singing of marching songs to keep children together.
2. Repeat some of the safety rules: "Remember to stop at the corner," "Always stay on the sidewalk."
3. Follow a map, showing the children their present location, where they will turn, and how they will return to the school.
4. Tell the children again what they will see.
5. Let the children take their own time, observing the things that are of interest to them, making discoveries, asking questions, and discussing the things they see.
6. Help the children to observe, identify, and recognize different things in the environment. Empty paper-towel or toilet-paper tubes were given to one group of children on a nature field trip to use as field glasses or tele-scopes, which helped them focus on specific things in the environment.
7. Take pictures of the children or make tape recordings to use in the class-room for recall and discussion.

After the Trip

For very young children, the time immediately following a trip will be one for resting and refreshment or some other relaxing activity. Young children may not be immediately ready to recall their experiences and may be too fatigued to react. Sometime later you can provide for follow-up activities, which increase the value of a field trip. It is through these activities that children can reconstruct their experiences, use their memory, relate events to ideas, use language and creative expression, and become involved in dramatic play with others.

Discussions.   Some discussion of the trip can take place. The children should have the opportunity to tell about their impressions of the trip and to raise ques-tions. They might dictate a thank-you letter or a story about the trip. You can use this time to help them clarify their ideas and concepts and recall their experience. "What do you think the scale was for?" "Why did the people wear uniforms?" "How many types of beans did we see?"

Play.   Following a trip, you will want to add props to the housekeeping or play corner that will help the children to act out their experiences. Pieces of hose after a trip to the fire station, gardening tools and equipment following a trip to the florist, various hats and uniforms—all encourage children to replay the trip.

Additional Experiences.   Additional experiences can be structured to reinforce the goals and purposes of the trip. Often the trip is the stimulus for a unit or more com-plete study of a concept. Vicarious experiences such as reading stories, seeing movies, listening to a resource person, and viewing slides have more meaning after a trip.

Creative Expression.   You can provide opportunities for creative expression after a trip. Blocks can be made available for constructing, and paints, clay, and other materials for creating can be given to the children. Music, dance, and dramatics are also encouraged.

Increasing Knowledge.   Depending on the type of field trip taken and the goals of the trip, you can structure activities that will enable you to determine the effectiveness of the trip and to increase the children's knowledge.

- ❑ A discussion of near and nearer, left and right, far and farthest will help children understand time-space relationships.
- ❑ You might construct bingo games using the words children have noted on the trip.
- ❑ You and the children can use riddles: "I'm thinking of something we saw on the trip. It was made of metal and was red and white."
- ❑ Absurdity games can be played: "I put my mail in the supermarket. What is wrong?"
- ❑ Follow the trip route on a map, using a toy car or model of a person.
- ❑ Give the children pictures of houses, stores, workers, or whatever was seen on the trip to play with and sort into categories.

SUMMARY

The entire world is available for children's learning. Become an astute observer of the environment and use all the resources you can find to foster children's learning. The children and their parents, as well as the school staff, can serve as resources for the social studies. The school building and classroom provide children many opportunities to learn social studies concepts.

The classroom should contain a quiet space for each child, sand and water, and centers of interest. There should be centers for blocks, dramatic play, housekeeping, a library, and writing, and a varied selection of art materials.

Others materials are also useful. You can select textbooks, children's literature, reference materials, audiovisual resources, computer programs, and pictures to foster specific concepts. Real objects aid in re-creation of the natural environment and are vital to the social studies; things for children's manipulation and experimentation are best. You can also use bulletin boards, learning stations, and other commercial materials as resources.

The field trip is the cornerstone of the social studies. You can plan several different types of field trips for the year. Children learn best through actual experiences, and these trips offer a rich resource for the social studies.

PROJECTS

1.   Walk in and around a school building. Make a list of all of the possible resources for children's social studies found within the building and the block around it.

2. Make a floor plan of a primary classroom designed for children's learning. Include as many interest centers as space allows, but plan carefully for the arrangements of each.

3. Observe during activity or work time in kindergarten and primary classrooms designed for open education. How do the activities differ in the kindergarten and primary room? List the social studies experiences the children are having during this time. How many skills, attitudes, and concepts do you see children using or reflecting?

4. Make a card file of children's literature that relates to history, geography, economics, or international education.

5. Begin a resource collection of your own. Include pictures and reference materials for yourself and for use by children. Begin to collect posters, photographs, and other materials you believe would be useful for teaching social studies.

RESOURCES

Professional books offer teachers many ideas for integrated learning through the use of resources. Among these are

Art-Another Language for Learning (1995) by Cohen and Gainer. Elaine Cohen offers many suggestions for incorporating art into the social studies curriculum.

Joan Moyer's *Selecting Educational Equipment and Materials: For School and Home* (1995), Association for Childhood Education, offers excellent suggestions for equipping classrooms.

Whole Language Across the Curriculum: Grades 1, 2, & 3 (1995), edited by Shirley Raines and published by Teachers College Press, gives suggestions for planning an integrated learning environment.

Catherine Loughlin's and Joseph Suina's books on preparing the learning environment, *The Learning Environment,* and *The Literacy Environment,* both from Teachers College Press, are the most valuable texts available for planning a learning environment.

REFERENCES

Anselmo, S., & Zinck, R. A. (1987). Computers for young children? *Young Children, 42*(3), 22–28.
Bakst, K., & Essa, E. L. (1990). The writing table: Emergent writers and editors. *Childhood Education, 66*(3), 145.
Barbour, N., Webster, T., & Drosdeck, S. (1987). Sand: a resource for the language arts. *Young Children, 42*(2), 20–26.
Bennett, L. (1995). Wide world of breads in children's literature. *Young Children, 50*(3), 64–70.
Cartwright, S. (1990). Learning with blocks. *Young Children, 45*(3), 38–42.

Clay, P. L. (1980). *The schools and single parents: Accessibility is the key*. Reston, VA: National Association of Single Parents.

Crosser, S. (1994). Making the most of water play. *Young Children, 49*(3), 28–33.

Curry, N. (1974). Dramatic play as a curriculum tool. In D. Spoonseller (Ed.), *Play as a learning media* (pp. 60–69). Washington, DC: National Association for the Education of Young Children.

Dixon, G. T., & Chalmers, F. G. (1990). The expressive arts in education. *Childhood Education, 67*(1), 12–18.

Elkind, D. (1981). Child development and the social science curriculum of the elementary school. *Social Education, 45*, 435–437.

Fromberg. D. (1995). *The full-day kindergarten*. New York: Teachers College Press.

Hirsch, E. S. (1984). *The block book*. Washington, DC: National Association for the Education of Young Children.

Lanser, S., & McDonnell, L. (1991). Creating quality curriculum yet not buying out the store. *Young Children, 47*(3), 4–11.

Loughlin, C. E., & Martin, M. D. (1987). *Supporting literacy: Developing effective learning environments*. New York: Teachers College Press.

Mitchell, L. S. (1934). *Young geographers*. New York: Bank Street College.

Noori, K.K. (1995). Understanding others through stories. *Childhood Education, 71*, 134–137.

Nuffield mathematics project. (1967). New York: Wiley.

Ragasto, M. (1982). Computer-assisted instruction. *ETS Developments, 24*, 3–4.

Schickedanz, J. (1986). *More than the ABC's*. Washington, DC: National Association for the Education of Young Children.

Schuman, J. M. (1981). *Arts from many hands*. Upper Saddle River, NJ: Prentice Hall.

Seefeldt, C. (1993). Learning for freedom. *Young Children, 48*(3), 4–10.

Seefeldt, C. (1995). Art-A serious work. *Young Children, 50*(3), 39–66.

Vergeront, J. (1996). *Places and spaces for preschool and primary (indoors)*. Washington, D.C.: National Association for the Education of Young Children.

Vukelich, C. (1990). Where's the paper? Literacy during dramatic play. *Childhood Education, 66*(4), 205–210.

Wright, J. & Shade, D. (Eds.). (1995). *Young children: Active learners in a technological age*. Washington, DC: National Association for the Education of Young Children.

PART TWO

The Processes of Social Studies

❑ **Chapter 4:** Social Skills
❑ **Chapter 5:** Attitudes and Values
❑ **Chapter 6:** Thinking and Concept Formation

Chapter 4

Social Skills

*A successful social studies program will produce a citizen who is informed,
skilled in the process of a free society, committed to democratic values, and who
feels obligated to participate in social, economic, and political processes.*

J. Brophy, 1990, p. 374

Children learn what they live. The skills, attitudes, and values of a democratic society are learned only as children experience living in a democracy. The small democracy of the early childhood program supports and fosters the processes and skills children need, not only to participate in democracy, but to continue to work to change and improve that democracy in the future.

In the democratic society of the classroom, social skills are fostered daily as teachers plan opportunities for children to interact with one another, to lead and follow, to select leaders, vote, and resolve their own conflicts.

Valued and respected within the democracy of an early childhood program, children, in turn, are able to respect others, both those who are similar to themselves and those who differ. The rights of the individual are continually balanced with those of the group. Freedom of speech and thought are fostered. Dissenting voices, even when in the minority, are respected. Children are expected and taught to assume responsibility for themselves and to participate to the fullest extent possible in the working of the group.

Actually, the entire early childhood program and curriculum are designed to foster children's social skills, but the skills that enhance children's "abilities to learn, to make decisions, and to develop as competent, self-directed citizens are more meaningful and useful when developed within the context of the social studies" (NCSS, 1989, p. 16).

Through the social studies, children form the foundation of a healthy self-concept, developing the skills of communicating, sharing, cooperating, and participating in a social group.

SOCIAL SKILLS

Thumb in mouth, Shawn stands watching Scott, Allen, and Tim build with the blocks. Taking his thumb from his mouth, he asks, "Can I play?" "NO! Only us can build with blocks." Shawn sighs, then sits at a table and watches a group of girls paste pictures in scrapbooks.

"I'm the mother," Claress informs the group playing in the housekeeping corner. She then proceeds to direct the children in their play until, one by one, they leave and find something else to do.

"Andrea, Andrea," the girls call, "come and play store with us." Smiling and nodding, Andrea takes Marcia by the hand and joins the others, saying, "Marcia's going to play with us too, OK?"

In any one group, there will be great differences in children's social skills. Some, as Andrea, seem to naturally attract other children to play with them and seem sensitive to the needs of others. Other children, such as Shawn and Claress, seem to have limited social skills or understanding of how to get along with others.

Differences in the ability to relate with others depend in part on children's maturity. Although most 3- and 4-year-olds are moving from parallel play to beginning associative play and are able to manage one playmate at a time, others

A wide range of social skills will be present in any classroom.

prefer solitary play and are not yet ready to relate to others. By age 5, children generally have developed a special friend and will be able to visit this friend on their own. By the time children are 6 or 7, most will be able to take turns, negotiate, and cooperate to keep play going, and they begin to form peer groups.

Theories of Socialization

Children enter the preschool-primary classroom with a wide range of social development and skills. Researchers have advanced a number of theories to explain why children differ in their ability to relate effectively with others. Among these are behavioral theories, those based on Freudian psychology, and the more current social-cognitive theories.

Behavioral Theories

Behavioral theory has its roots in the philosophy of John Locke, who viewed children as arriving in the world as a blank slate. The slate would be written on by those educating a child through a series of rewards and punishments.

Historically, behaviorists have believed that learning comes about because a person receives a reward, or reinforcement, for an action or a correct response (Skinner, 1974). Children are conditioned by a series of stimuli and responses, and learning results from the conditioning provided by adults and the environment. They learn from having their needs satisfied—or not satisfied—by another person or environmental factors. When a child's behavior is followed by something pleasant or some type of reward or reinforcement, the child will repeat the behavior. If a child's behavior is followed by something unpleasant or ignored, the behavior will eventually disappear.

Using the idea that social behaviors that are reinforced will increase, teachers make certain that children's interactions with other children are positive and rewarding. The room is arranged with sufficient materials to enable children to interact pleasantly, without being frustrated by lack of space or materials. Children are praised and reinforced for prosocial behaviors. A child who shares or cooperates and is praised will continue to share and cooperate.

On the other hand, behaviors can be extinguished. Inappropriate or undesirable social behaviors can be eliminated simply by ignoring them, though sometimes it is difficult to do so. For example, a lot of 4-year-old children like to spit. The child who is spit upon screams and cries; the adults admonish or punish the spitter. This serves the same function as attention; thus the child will spit again. When teachers ignore the spitter and focus their attention on the child who received the abuse, the possibility of eliminating antisocial behavior will occur.

Not all social behaviors are learned through a series of stimuli and responses. Behaviorists' studies have shown that children also learn social and antisocial behaviors by observing models. The models may be their teachers or parents, as well as the media. By observing people, cartoon characters, or actors receiving rewards for aggressive behaviors, children will model and repeat these behaviors. When prosocial behaviors are observed, these too will be modeled and imitated by children.

By studying the theories and practices of behaviorists, teachers can learn to reinforce children's positive social skills and foster their development. On the other hand, behaviorist techniques are useful in eliminating undesired behaviors. Teachers using these techniques, however, must realize that they are controlling children externally, and children still will need to develop their own internal controls for their behavior.

Freudian Theory

Freud's theories were basically concerned with emotion, motivation, and personality development (1949). He viewed children as possessing human sexual energy, and believed this energy is invested in different ways as they grow and develop.

Freud stated that the three basic drives the infant possesses are the sexual drive, survival instincts, and the drive of destructiveness. He defined three structures to explain a person's personality: The *id* is the instinctive structure that infants possess and that drives them to seek satisfaction. As they come in conflict with reality, as they grow and develop, the *ego,* or rational part of the being, emerges. Finally, the *superego,* or moral or ethical part of the being, is developed.

Freud (1949) believed that children go through distinct developmental stages. The particular stages called psychosexual stages reflect the development of gratification zones. The *oral stage* (first year of life) reflects the infant's need for gratification from the mouth. An infant's eating, sucking, spitting, and chewing are not only a need to satisfy hunger, but also provide pleasure. The *anal stage* (second to third year) reflects the toddler's need of gratification from the rectal area. The *phallic stage* (fourth and fifth years) reflects the preschooler's source of gratification from the genital area. The *latency stage* (middle childhood) reflects a repression of sexuality ending during the preadolescent years at the start of puberty. During the *genital stage* (teenage years), the adolescent develops a mature sexuality and love relationship, which derives its primary source of pleasure from the genital area.

As the needs at each stage are gratified, the child moves on to the next developmental stage. Freud maintained that if too much or too little gratification occurs at any stage, the person becomes fixated at that stage. He asserted that the reasons for different personality problems such as alcoholism, depression, compulsiveness, overaggression, and promiscuity are the result of a person's fixation at one of the stages.

Erik Erikson's Theory

A follower of Freud, Erikson focuses his theory on the ego and what it means for human development. Erikson (1963), as Freud, believes that each stage of life is characterized by a central problem. Unlike Freud, he sees these crises as psychosocial rather than psychosexual. The stages result from social interaction instead of being the product of conflict between inner drives and the need to develop a superego.

Erikson theorizes that there are eight psychosocial stages, each of which has a negative and a positive trait:

Erikson taught us that each stage of life is necessary for a child to move on to the next.

1. basic trust vs. basic mistrust

2. autonomy vs. shame and doubt

3. initiative vs. guilt

4. industry vs. inferiority

5. identity vs. role confusion

6. intimacy vs. isolation

7. generativity vs. stagnation

8. ego integrity vs. despair

Each of the eight positive psychosocial strengths exists at all eight stages and is related to the others. However, each strength has a critical period for development and there is a proper sequence to the eight stages. For a child to develop in a normal pattern of behavior, the positive attribute of the stage needs to be satisfied at the critical period before the next stage is developed. The person's development from a trusting infant to an old man or woman with ego integrity depends on the successful integration of all the stages.

The stages most pertinent for early childhood educators are basic trust vs. mistrust, autonomy vs. shame, initiative vs. guilt, and industry vs. inferiority.

Basic Trust.   For basic trust to develop, the infant between birth and 18 months of age must gradually develop a sense of "inner goodness" because she has determined that there is an "outer predictability." The environment has provided consistency, continuity, and sameness of experiences (Clarke-Stewart & Koch, 1983).

Without this, the child will develop a basic mistrust and hostility toward others and the world.

Autonomy.   Between 19 months and 3 years of age, toddlers develop a sense of autonomy. As they start to walk they develop a desire to let go, as well as a need to hold on. Children begin to develop a sense of self and pride in their achievements. If they are shamed because of their attempts at letting go and their experiments with the world, they will develop a sense of shame about themselves and self-doubt as they function in the world.

Initiative.   At the age of 3 or 4, a new stage, initiative, unfolds. At this stage the child is able to undertake and plan her own activities and do them in cooperation with other children. If the adult world does not offer proper regulations, the child may undertake more than she can achieve, which develops into a sense of guilt or failure. On the other hand, if the adult world doesn't permit practicing developing skills, children live with a sense of failure.

Industry.   From 6 years of age until puberty, children develop a sense of industry. At this stage they become producers of things and users of tools, not the least being reading, writing, and mathematics. Children become socially adept as they work beside and with others. One problem that can occur in this stage is that children may develop a sense of inadequacy in using the "tools" of their world, or see themselves as inferior to others. Another danger is overworking so the child becomes a "conformist or thoughtless slave of his technique" (Erikson, 1963, p. 247).

Social-Cognitive Theories

Children are whole beings. They cannot be divided into parts for physical, intellectual, social, or emotional growth. Social-cognitive theories recognize this wholeness. Its adherents see social-emotional growth parallel to, or even the same as, intellectual growth.

A basic principle of social-cognitive theories is that what happens in one area of growth or development affects other areas. Children who can't make friends, cooperate, or share have difficulty in a group. Unable to relate with others, to make friends, these children may also have difficulty focusing on schoolwork. Likewise, children who have trouble learning may also have difficulty in developing social skills. And it's well accepted that emotional problems—perhaps anxiety, learned helplessness, or insecurities—can affect children's ability to learn and achieve.

A child's social behavior is considered within the context of cognitive maturity. A 3-year-old scribbling away on a piece of paper continues scribbling with the marker on a neighbor child. The child is not punished because a 3-year-old cannot yet cognitively differentiate that others are not objects and have feelings. Rather the teacher attempts to teach the child, saying, "Color on your paper," showing her the paper and saying, "Color here. Do not color on other children." By evaluating children's social behavior in terms of cognition, teachers have a better understanding of what they can and cannot expect children to do at any given age.

Another principle of social cognition is the idea that the individual is in charge of his or her own learning. Although growth stems from the interaction of maturation and experience, the individual must construct social knowledge. Stimulating children to think about social relations, and offering them suggestions to enable them to construct knowledge of social skills, are viewed as important.

With this framework, teachers guide children to talk about social situations or problems and come up with their own solutions. Instead of offering solutions to a child who grabs a toy from another by saying, "Use your words instead of grabbing and she'll know what you want," or offering alternative solutions by saying, "Give her a turn now," the idea is to develop children's skills of thinking of solutions for themselves. There is no recrimination. Shaming or blaming children for behavior isn't acceptable in a democratic classroom.

Spivack and Shure (1978) developed the Cognitive Approach to Interpersonal Problem Solving. Inherent in this approach is the assumption that the ability to think clearly paves the way for emotional relief and healthy social adjustment. When children have problems relating socially, teachers are supposed to ask them what happened, how they felt in the situation, what they did, and what other ways they could act in similar situations. In addition to the scripted learning experiences that comprise their program, Spivack and Shure (1978) continue to maintain that the dialogues teachers have with children informally and in connection with ongoing events are even more important in developing children's social skills.

Factors Affecting Social Development

Children's development of social skills is affected by the nature of their family and early educational experiences. Most children begin their life in some sort of family. Whether in a nuclear, blended, or extended family, a communal arrangement, or a single-parent family, the child learns social patterns and skills within the context of this family. Children find love and security and form attachments with people who protect and care for them.

In the family, children become socialized through interactions with parents, siblings, relatives, and neighbors; once in a school setting, they need new ways of acting, relating, and socializing. Children who have had a strong attachment to a nurturing figure and who see themselves as separate from this nurturing figure are ready for a group situation. Children who have not fully developed strong attachments to another person may have a more difficult time adjusting to the complexity of the social system of the school.

The Family

Children who experience the security of loving parents and have strong attachments to their parents are better able to reach out to relate with others. According to attachment theory, children who enjoy a secure attachment relationship with their mothers use this relationship as a support to venture out and explore their environment. They reach out to others, return to the mother for support, and venture out again, going further into the world of social relationships (Ainsworth, Belhar, Waters, & Wall, 1978). "As the child confidently wanders out to test the social waters, he gains an enlarged social world, expanded social contacts, and greater opportunity to learn from experience in social interaction" (Kemple, 1991, p. 51).

Parents who are social themselves serve as models for their children. Children may be able to use the image of their parents interacting with others in their own attempts to make and be friends with other children, or to cooperate and share. Socially competent parents may affect their children's social skill development in another way. Parents who are secure and competent offer children a model of security from which to build their own social skills.

The nature of parent-child interactions is also related to a child's development of social skills. Children who are raised in democratic families, where reasons are given along with the rules, are more likely to be socially active and open minded. Parents who explain, "No hitting. If you ask her for the truck instead of hitting, she'll give it to you," or, "We always say thank you to someone who does something for you," or, "In church, we sit quietly during the sermon so others can hear. If you want to, you can write in your notebook, or take a puzzle with you so you don't disturb the other worshippers" are more likely to have children who cooperate, share, and initiate social activities.

On the other hand, parents who are more authoritarian, who demand obedient, conforming, and dependent offspring, may have children who are never really comfortable exploring the world for themselves. Often, these children fail to develop the ability to relate effectively with others throughout their life.

Gender differences play a role as well. Fathers' interactions with their children rated as authoritarian, commanding, and directing were related to lower popularity of both boys and girls while mothers' directiveness was related to greater popularity of girls (MacDonald & Parke, 1984). MacDonald (1987) concluded that popular boys had fathers who engaged in emotionally arousing, physical play. Rejected boys did not engage in physical play with their fathers.

Sex-role stereotypes that continue to pervade our society affect how children develop socially. If girls are expected to be retiring, submissive, and quiet and to follow instead of lead, they develop along these lines. On the other hand, if boys are supposed to be assertive, aggressive, and in command and to lead, they develop social skills that relate to these traits.

Role of the Community

The characteristics of the community also affect children's developing social skills (Wallach, 1995). Teachers who take the time to observe and know the community in which children live are better able to build on its strengths or work to mediate potential negative effects the community might have on children's social development.

Children who live in violent or unsafe communities may be fearful and withdrawn when in the classroom. For children exposed to domestic abuse, gang violence, petty or not-so-petty criminals, "feelings of being safe and secure do not exist" (Wallach, 1995, p. 4). Their feelings of insecurity will interfere with their total development, especially social skills development.

Children who experience violence in their community will need to find the following in the preschool/primary classrooms:

- ❑ meaningful relationships with caring and knowledgeable adults
- ❑ schedules and environment that are as consistent as possible
- ❑ structure and very clear expectations and limits
- ❑ many opportunities to express themselves safely in play, art, and stories and story telling (Wallach, 1995)

Even children who live in relatively safe environments are exposed to a great deal of violence. "Children's experience with violence is by no means limited to the inner city. Throughout American cities, suburbs, and rural areas, young children often experience high levels of violence as victims of family violence and non-family assaults, witnesses of family and community violence and viewers of media violence" (Slaby, Roedell, Arezzo, & Hendrix, 1995, p. 1). Each day the effects of observing violence, whether in their community or through the media, are present in the classroom.

Teachers have found a number of ways to help children and their parents cope with the prevalence of violence in children's lives. Teachers and parents discuss the problems of children's viewing violence that the media presents, and work to change the media. They also work with children to

- ❑ develop the concept of real and not real by informing children which stories, movies, and television shows are "real" and which are not. They then ask children to determine which shows or movies are factual and which are fantasy.
- ❑ develop critical viewing skills for evaluating media violence.
- ❑ reduce television viewing.
- ❑ watch more prosocial television programs (Slaby, Roedell, Arezzo, & Hendrix, 1995).

The Role of the School

Once children are in a school setting, other factors affect their social development. The teacher, in addition to a child's parents and family, becomes an agent of socialization. Now the teacher, and perhaps the principal, set the rules, limits, and standards for behavior. Other children, as well, become models, setting new or different standards for social behaviors.

Entrance into the school society can be difficult for young children. Leaving home, unsure of how to manage interacting with this new socializer and with other children, preschool-primary students can find beginning school a miserable experience. Many transition techniques have been designed and implemented to ease children's entrance into school. Some schools encourage parents to stay with their children part or all of the first few days, to let the children know they are not being totally deserted. Some schools begin by inviting a small group of children on the first day, adding another four or five each day until the total group has been integrated. This allows children to get used to relating to small groups and to become familiar with the school and new social situation before the total group is in attendance. Home visits by the teacher or visits to the school by parent and child help ease some of the possible stress.

The dichotomy of socialization—developing a strong sense of individuality while learning to become a member of a group—is ever present in the school situation. Children must retain their individuality, yet they must give it up by putting the welfare and interest of the group before their own. At school, they find they must share not only materials, toys, and time, but also the attention of the teacher. Here they learn to cooperate, to see others' viewpoints, and to work together for the common welfare.

The school's role during these early years is twofold. First, school experiences must focus on strengthening the child's self-concept and feelings of individuality. Children who feel good about themselves can make the difficult, complex adjustments necessary for group living. Having aided the child's development of self-esteem, the school must use this strong sense of self as the base for guiding children into positive group experiences where they can learn the skills required to live in a society.

In the school, the focus on social skill development is threefold, revolving around the development of

1. the self-concept. Children's feelings about themselves are the foundation from which they learn to relate to, and communicate with, others.
2. prosocial skills. Being able to cooperate and share are necessary for forming solid relationships with others.
3. the making and keeping of friends. Children who relate to and communicate with others, sharing and cooperating, are those who receive acceptance from their peers and can make and keep friends.

The Self-Concept

"I'm not big now, but I'm growing. I can ride a bike and run and jump and skip, and next year I'll learn to read, too," answers Domingo when asked to tell about himself. Domingo's answer reveals his attitude about himself—not very big, but growing, an "I can do" attitude, and an attitude that says, "I will grow, I will learn, I can do it!"

Self-esteem, self-identity, and self-concept—educators use these terms to denote the totality of meanings, feelings, and attitudes children maintain about themselves. *Self-concept* refers to cognitive activity—children's awareness of their own characteristics and of likenesses and differences between themselves and others. *Self-esteem* refers to children's regard for and feelings about themselves. *Self-identity* has a social connotation—it brings awareness of group membership.

Whatever the definition or terminology used, scholars have long recognized the importance of feelings of self-esteem in human behavior. As a theoretical construct, the "self" has been an object of interest since the 17th century, when Descartes first discussed the "cogito," or "self," as a thinking substance. Throughout the ages, prominent theorists and researchers have recognized the importance of feelings of self-esteem in human behavior. Theories of Freud (1949), Rogers (1961), Maslow (1969), and others have been directed toward understanding the conduct of human beings by examining the feelings and beliefs an individual holds about herself or himself.

The theories of these scholars differ greatly. However, amid the diversity, there appear to be two assumptions that are basic to all theories of self. One assumption is that self-esteem begins to be established early in life and is modified and shaped by the children's succession of experiences with significant people in their environment. The other assumption present in all theories of self is that self-esteem has a predictable effect on behavior.

The school situation can foster children's self-esteem and build the foundation for future relationships with others. Teachers can structure the classroom and respond to children in ways that contribute to their feelings of worth (Greenberg, 1989).

Names

People's names make them unique. The use of children's names in the classroom fosters a sense of esteem in children. When you use a child's name, you are saying, "I know you and I respect you." Teachers may encourage children not only to call one another by name, but also to use the names of the teachers, volunteers,

Social studies experiences provide a point of departure for children's writing.

and assistants. In this way, children learn that each person is an important individual and that each is different from the other (Perez, 1994).

"I can't say my last name, but I can show it to you," says Michael, leading the teacher to a piece of plaid fabric, mounted and framed. "My last name begins with *Mc,* and that's my sign." First names come naturally to the children and teacher, yet you do not want to neglect children's family names. Children might, as Michael did, find out the history of their last names, the places on the map where the names originated, or what they mean.

Very young children might be encouraged to learn their parents' first names. Understanding that mother and father have their own names helps children see their parents as people in their own right. In the classroom, you might

❏ use children's names in songs and substitute their names in stories, poems, and games.

❏ write the children's names on objects that belong to them.

❏ make up news stories using the children's names: "Susan has new shoes. They are brown."

❏ purchase a stamp pad and rubber stamps with the children's names individually imprinted on each. Children just learning to read their names enjoy these stamps.

❏ place two stacks of name cards on the game table for the children to play with. Children could sort through these and find the name that belongs to them, all the names they can read, or any names that are alike and, depending on their age, could classify them according to boys, girls, friends, or initial or final sounds.

❏ take snapshots of the children and mount them on cards with their names. As the children become familiar with the pictures and names, the names are cut from the card and the children can match the names with the pictures.

❏ make bulletin boards using children's names. One might be, "We are in kindergarten. There are 15 children," with the children's self-portraits and names below.

The Physical Self

Children, being physical beings, have attitudes about themselves involving their physical body. How that body moves and interacts with objects, how children think they look, the kinds of skills their bodies can do—all influence self-esteem. Self-awareness is thought to originate when infants begin to discover themselves and their environment by flinging their hands about and learning what is part of their bodies and what is not. Sensations of cold, hunger, and warmth all work together to help infants learn about body and self. During the entire sensorimotor period, children use their bodies to learn about themselves and their world.

Recognizing the importance of children's physical self to the development of self-esteem, you might

Do's

1. Recognize the differences in names among Vietnamese, Cambodian, Hmong, and Laotian.

2. Learn to pronounce their names clearly, correctly, and in the Southeast Asian way. For example, Ngu-yen Van Thu is pronounced Wen Van Tu (Vietnamese). Sok Phoung is pronounced Sawk Poong (Cambodian).

3. Teach children to write their names in the American way.

4. Respect the "special" quality of given names.

5. Recognize that the family name is placed first as an emphasis of a person's roots.

6. Determine if the family has chosen to "Americanize" the use of the family name. If so, call the child by his or her preferred name.

7. Respect the child's choice of name.

Don'ts

1. Assume all Southeast Asian names are used in the same way.

2. Call a child "Nguyen," "Chan," or "Sourivong," as it is improper to address a child by the family name.

3. Neglect to show children the differences in writing names in the American and Southeast Asian ways.

4. Treat names as unimportant.

5. Minimize the importance placed on the family's roots.

6. Assume that all Southeast Asians will prefer the use of their given name only. Instead of being called Mr. Van, the father may want to be called Mr. Nguyen.

7. Change the name in an effort to Anglicize it. For example, don't call Vinh Vinnie or Nhung Nancy.

Box 4.1

What's in a Southeast Asian Name?

From "What's in a Name? In Particular, a Southeast Asian Name?" by Robert D. Morrow, 1991, *Young Children*, *44*(6), p. 23. Copyright 1991 by National Association for the Education of Young Children. Reprinted by permission.

❑ take many photos of children for scrapbooks, bulletin boards, or gifts.

❑ provide all kinds of mirrors for children to use—full length, hand, magnifying—and give children feedback as they look at themselves: "You have dark brown eyes." "Look at your shoulders." "Where are your eyebrows?"

❑ keep records of children's height and weight. Cash register tapes or long strips of paper, exactly the heights of the children, help them see how tall they are. Make certain you are sensitive to children who are taller or smaller than others.

❑ measure other parts of the body, such as hands, feet, ear, thumbs, and noses, with arbitrary measures.

❑ play games that emphasize body parts—Looby Loo, or Simon Says.

❑ provide large and small muscle equipment for children to climb in, through, over, or under, and to manipulate with their fingers and hands.

❑ make booklets or charts of things children can do. A booklet called *I Can Run* could begin with the main sentence "I can run" serving as the base for other pages in the book, beginning with "I can run quickly, I can run slowly, . . . angrily, . . . happily," and so forth. Children can illustrate each page. Other similar books could be titled *I Can Jump, . . . Bend, . . . Climb, . . . Stretch, . . .* and *. . . Hop.*

A vital part of the child's physical self is sex. As children mature, they become aware of sexual differences. This awareness is often apparent in frank discussions while using the bathroom or in detailed drawings of self. A confident and aware teacher treats discussions and questions with respect and is ready to help clear up misconceptions.

"Teachers and parents must recognize the importance of sexuality and its relationship to children's positive or negative feelings about themselves" (Atwood & Williams, 1983, p. 58). Atwood and Williams recommended that adults working with children use proper names for genitals, talk frankly about the differences between boys and girls, and encourage taking on the roles and feelings of others during sociodramatic play.

Adult attitudes toward sexuality are important to children's self-esteem.

> For many of us, the topic of sexuality produces guilt and anxiety as well as positive feelings. Adults who infer in subtle ways that certain behaviors are bad may create anxiety or shame in the child. Positive feelings are aided by a teacher who understands and accepts the child's sexuality. (Atwood & Williams, 1983, p. 56)

Sex awareness also deals with sex role and requires you, the teacher, to examine your values and prejudices. Women's movements have made our nation aware of society's part in assigning rigid sex roles early in life. For example, the statement "He's all boy" reinforces behavior in boys that would not be tolerated in girls. You can help children become aware of their own sexuality without assigning them stereotyped sex roles. You can

❑ be certain that the block, woodworking, and wheel toy areas do not become boys' centers, and the housekeeping area a girls' center.

❑ dismiss, or call together, children with red shoes, blue socks, buckle shoes, zipper jackets, green eyes, and so forth, rather than dividing the group by boys and girls.

❑ provide male and female models in a variety of job situations.

❑ ask the boys' help in cleaning up, cooking, washing tables, and other tasks often stereotyped as women's work.

❑ find stories to read portraying men and women in various occupations not assigned by sex role.

❑ challenge children when they make statements such as "Boys can't do that," "That's not for girls," by giving information and facts to correct their stereotyped thinking.

Academic Self-Esteem

Crucial to children's self-esteem is the acquisition of skills and knowledge. Success in learning imparts confidence. Children who can read, write, climb trees, and put puzzles together feel they are competent, worthy persons. In a school for young children, there are many opportunities for them to experiment with ideas and materials, and there is time to gain some kind of mastery.

You can help children perceive themselves as learners and enhance their self-esteem by

❑ providing toddlers and very young children with equipment they can handle by themselves. Low coat hooks and small tables and chairs permit the youngest child to achieve some sense of mastery over self and the world. Juice can be prepared in small pitchers so 3-year-olds can fill their own glasses. In the bathroom, small fixtures and towels and soap placed within children's reach permit children to be in control. Children feel they are competent when they can care for their own needs (Weitz, Quickle, Pejchi, & Wilson, 1991).

❑ allowing kindergarten and primary grade children to continue developing a sense of mastery and self-control by encouraging them to master mechanical things, including the record player, slide projector, or filmstrip projector. Learning to use the computer could also foster children's sense of competence.

❑ expanding primary grade children's understanding of the world. Knowledge of their immediate environment, obtained through field trips and direct experiences, is expanded to gaining knowledge of the larger community and the world as children learn to read and gain information through books and other written materials.

Assessing Self-Esteem

As with any other skill, you will want to assess children's growing self-esteem. Standardized tests designed to assess self-concept are available. Even if you use a standardized measure, you will still want to assess children's growth through:

1. *Observation.* Observing children, you can record how well they are (a) working with others, (b) entering into group play, (c) trying new activities, and (d) growing in their overall ability to relate to others.

2. *Interview.* Children enjoy talking about themselves. A few questions, such as "What makes you smile?" "How do you feel when . . . ?" "Who are your best friends?" "What makes you angry?" "What will you do when you grow up?" "What do you do when you can do anything you want to?" will give you insight into children's self-concepts.

3. *Self-reports.* Helping children make self-evaluations is another way of estimating self-concept. You might help children make booklets of *Things I Learned in Kindergarten, Things I Need to Learn, My Best Subjects Are, I Need to Work Harder On.* Other booklets or creative writing might be *My Three Wishes, Things I Do Not Like, My Angry Book, A Book of Me,* or *My Family.*

Prosocial Skills

Relating With Others

With a strong sense of self, children are ready to learn to live within a group. Basic to living with others is the ability to communicate.

> Men live in a community in virtue of the things they have in common and communication is the way in which they come to possess things in common. Without communication to insure the participants in a common understanding to secure similar emotional and intellectual dispositions, there could be no community, no group with which to relate. (Dewey, 1944, p. 4)

Certainly the ability to communicate, verbally or nonverbally, is essential before children can learn the social skills required of them to live in a group. Dewey believed that social life was identical to communication.

Social skills are grounded in a strong sense of self.

Communicating

Not all communication is verbal. Just like adults, young children are quick to read the meaning of touching, gestures, smiles, sounds, facial expressions, and ways of moving. "Don't be scared," one kindergartner told another on the way to the engineer's room. No one had said a word about being frightened of the experience, yet one child sensed fear of a new experience in the other by reading nonverbal signals.

Communication, however, is not always easy. A young child, with limited language ability and background of experiences, has trouble communicating verbally. Communication also demands the ability to put one's self in the role of another. Effective communication, and hence social relationships, depends on the child's ability to see how another person feels and to take into account the other's needs.

Flavell (1979) has studied children's ability to take on the view of others. His work suggests that role-taking ability first requires (a) an understanding that there is a perspective other than one's own, that not everyone sees, thinks, or feels alike; (b) a realization that an analysis of the other's perspective might be useful; (c) possession of the ability to carry out the analysis needed; (d) a way of keeping in mind what is learned from the analysis; and (e) knowledge of how to translate the results of analysis into effective social behavior; that is, in terms of getting along better with the person whose viewpoint is under consideration.

Role-taking ability begins as children participate in dramatic play, which involves children taking on the roles of others. Everyone familiar with young children has observed them acting as parents, doctors, teachers, horses, babies, or fire fighters. This type of play is particularly valuable. It helps children to understand their world, to sort out the roles they observe, and to understand how they fit into the scheme of things. Dramatic play that occurs spontaneously and without interference from an adult is perhaps the best way children can learn to see the viewpoints of others, eventually learning to take on the roles of others.

Dramatic play is a highly cognitive activity. In taking on the roles of others, children become less egocentric. They use language and symbols and hold images in their minds for long periods of time, acting as if the blocks were trucks; the boards, streets; or the boxes, tables. Dramatic play's involvement of other children makes it a valuable strengthener of social skills.

Creative dramatics offers children yet another opportunity to learn the skills involved in taking on the roles of others (Ishee & Goldhaber, 1990). In creative dramatics, children act out, by themselves or with others, the role of another person, animal, or thing. In the preschool-primary classroom, creative dramatics begins with rhythmic activities—children acting like leaves or snowflakes or moving like animals. Pantomime is another beginning step in creative dramatics and role playing. Without using words, children can show the group how to do something they do at home, at the beach, in a store, or at school and let the group decide what the action represents.

With rhythmic and pantomime activities serving as a base, children can be asked to act out nursery rhymes or entire stories. Younger children need something that has parts for all. "Humpty-Dumpty," "Jack and Jill," or "Little Nancy

Etticoat" are excellent for beginners: One child can be Humpty-Dumpty, and all the others can be the king's horses and the king's men; all the children can act out the parts of either Jack or Jill while the rhyme is being read; and all can become Nancy Etticoat.

Children in kindergarten or the primary grades can wait to take turns or act as the audience. The folktales "Three Billy Goats Gruff," "Goldilocks," and "The Three Pigs" are good beginners for creative dramatics, but there are many other appropriate stories that children can act out. Eventually, children learn the process of taking on the role of another as they mature and grow.

Children's growth in role-taking ability is related to their cognitive growth and general maturity. Direct teaching of role taking is not effective for preschool-primary children. But children can be given experiences that will provide them with opportunities to practice and develop role-playing skills. You can help children grow in taking roles of others by

❑ asking them to imagine how someone else feels; to speculate: "How do you think Roberto felt when you called him that?" "How would you feel?" "Have you ever had someone say something to you that hurt you?"

❑ helping children to connect their own feelings with the things they are involved in; with things that happen to them. You can ask: "How did you feel when . . . ?" "Why were you angry?" "Did it make you feel good when . . . ?"

❑ communicating to the children your understanding of the context of children's experiences, what children are feeling and the reasons for it: "You feel very angry now because you didn't get to paint." "You're happy because

---

Teachers Nell Ishee and Jeanne Goldhaber have a special bin for books that lend themselves to acting out. In this bin, kept near the area where children act out stories, are

Assorted Versions of Traditional Folk Stories

"Three Little Pigs"

"Three Billy Goats Gruff"

"Stone Soup"

"Old Mother Hubbard"

Other Books

Caps for Sale

The Carrot Seed

In the Night Kitchen

The Runaway Bunny

Box 4.2
Stories for Reenactment

your block building is tall and sturdy." "You feel sad because they didn't ask you to help them with the house."

Role play is a technique that can be used to help children take on the view of another. As children role-play, they have a chance to gain insights into the feelings of others, think about alternatives for action, and explore consequences of their actions.

Children can be given "what if" problems and situations to act out. Young children have great difficulty placing themselves in unfamiliar roles or in roles of others. Their egocentricity does not allow them to see another's point of view; therefore, all "what if" problems should be real and related to children's own experiences. You might say: "Nancy, what if Steve took your car while you were looking for a place to park it? Steve, you pretend to take the car; Nancy, what would you do? What other ways could you act?"

Some other kinds of questions you might ask children about real situations are: "What if you are waiting for your turn on the slide and someone pushes ahead of you?" "What if you want to play in the housekeeping area, but children there say no, you can't come in?" "What if there is only one wagon, but two children want to ride in it?"

Effective communication demands the ability to receive and produce language. Once children have some verbal skills, communication becomes easier. Parents and teachers of young children often remark on how much easier and pleasanter it is to work and live with preschool children once they are able to express their needs, wants, and ideas verbally and to understand the language spoken to them. Once children have language, they no longer need to hit, bite, scream, or cry to communicate with others. Once they can express ideas and communicate through language, many frustrations are eliminated. Language is a useful, safe, and effective way to communicate feelings, ideas, and thoughts (Kuebli, 1994).

Listening and Speaking.   Listening is a major way children learn language. Listening skills, so essential to learning to communicate with others, are critical for all learning. Once children can listen to others, they can begin to see others' viewpoints, learn from others, and expand their world.

Young children have short attention spans and should not be asked to listen for long periods of time. Asking children to sit still and listen to another child, teacher, or visitor just helps children develop tuning-out techniques. Most often, young children's listening experiences will result from their interactions with others, based on their activities and mutual explorations. If children are asked to listen to others, make certain they are comfortable, that outside distractions are kept to a minimum, and that the activity or speech is interesting to listen to.

Almost every school experience involves listening. In relation to social studies, children will listen to records, stories, and visitors to the class, as well as to one another.

There will be occasions for individual children to speak in front of a group. When a 5-year-old loses a tooth, is leaving to move to another school, or creates a lovely painting, that child will want to tell the entire group about the experience. These speaking and listening experiences gradually evolve into group discussions.

Group discussions are not easy for young children. Their ability to listen and attend to a topic while in a group, and then offer their opinions about the topic, cannot be rushed. Gradually, children will learn the process of holding and continuing a group discussion. Teachers can help children develop this ability by using statements that guide discussion:

❑ "Sekai, we are talking about the crane operator now. Can you save your book till later?" or something similar to keep the discussion focused on a topic.

❑ "Roberta, you were talking about your trip; next you can tell us what you did at Betty's house," to prompt children to keep track of what they were talking about.

❑ "Let Bettina finish what she is saying, then we'll listen to you," to encourage children to listen.

❑ "Speak a bit louder so everyone can hear you," or, "Tell us again what you saw on your trip," to help the child who is speaking to hold the attention of the audience.

Perhaps the most pleasant listening and speaking experiences revolve around children's literature. Listening to a good book read by the teacher, a parent, or an older child is one of the most pleasurable experiences a child can have, and one that can teach children social skills (Luke & Myers, 1995). There are many social studies books available, some beautifully illustrated, that tell children about the past, places far away, or their personal lives and experiences. It would be difficult not to find books specifically suited for any group of children.

When you read books to individual children or small groups, you have opportunities to recognize the ideas of each child, to talk about the illustrations, to ask and answer questions, to go back and read that page one more time, or even to skip "that part" and go on. Children can chime in, singing the repetitive phrases, reciting the last line, or telling their version of the ending. You can use stories to stimulate children's interest in a topic; for information; or for summing up a topic or unit. They can be read before nap, after lunch, during activity time, or during a regularly scheduled story time that is planned each day and occurs without fail. During this time, children, stretched out on the floor or clustered around the teacher, enjoy the group experience of listening to a story. One teacher calls this time "belly and book time" as his group of 4-year-olds usually stretches out on their stomachs rather than sit on their bottoms.

Reading and Writing.   Just as social studies provides ample opportunities that promote children's listening and speaking skills, it also provides a medium for children's reading and writing. Once children have gained experience in listening and speaking, they find they need, and can use, the written word.

Children need writing to label their paintings, to let others know their building blocks are the gas station, and to record their experiences. Working with preschool-primary children, the teacher often acts more like a secretary than a teacher, recording the children's spoken language. You begin the process by saying, "The way you said that was good. Let me write it down so we won't forget

Social studies provides many opportunities for reading and writing.

it," or, "Why don't you write that in your journal so you won't forget." In this and in many other ways, you let children see their spoken words being recorded and, once recorded, read by others. When a 4-year-old asks, "Do you have time to write down my story before I forget it?" you can be certain the child has conceptualized the processes of listening, speaking, reading, and writing and has a sophisticated knowledge of the purposes of language.

There are hundreds of ways children can use writing and reading in connection with social studies. Children 4 years old or under can

- ❑ practice writing as a part of dramatic play. Provide crayons, receipt books, calendars, note pads, and envelopes for children's play. Watch children's play interests. If they are interested in travel play, add tickets and luggage tags. If they play store, add grocery lists, play money, and checkbooks with markers.
- ❑ be encouraged to talk about their work and watch as their words are recorded.
- ❑ have many opportunities to draw. Drawing is probably the most important single activity that assists both writing and reading development as well as fostering understanding of others (McWhinnie, 1992; Schiller, 1995).

Those 4 and 5 years old can

- ❑ dictate booklets and stories and illustrate them.
- ❑ tell about their paintings and drawings, watching as the teacher writes their words.
- ❑ dictate letters to the fire fighter or other community workers, either asking questions or thanking them for permitting them to visit.
- ❑ ask the teacher for labels for their buildings, gardens, or other group projects.
- ❑ dictate and record plans for a party or other celebration.

❑ dictate their thoughts, ideas, or concerns about some current news event.

Above the age of 5, children could use reading and writing to

❑ follow the news.

❑ plan and produce their own class newsletter.

❑ vote for the name to be given the hamster, the foods that will be shared at a party, or what games will be played.

❑ write their own history books and read the books and writings of others about the present and past.

Sharing

Learning to communicate is, in part, learning to share. To communicate, children must share their ideas, take turns talking and listening, and share their time and interest. Learning to share is an important goal of preschool-primary education; the welfare of society depends on the willingness of its members to share.

Children do need to share resources—toys, blocks, materials, equipment—in the preschool-primary classroom. They also need to share the teacher's attention. As children mature, they begin to share in the life of the school—planting gardens, cleaning up the playground, putting on a school play, or decorating the hallway. All these activities encourage children's development of group social responsibilities—resulting in later participation in voting, government, and the concerns of the community and the world.

Learning to share and to take turns begins early in life.

Everyone finds sharing a little difficult and uncomfortable at first, for each must give up some personal ideas, material, or time, sacrificing something for the good of others. Children have shared with their family and with those in the neighborhood, but once in school they find they must participate in many other types of sharing and share on a larger scale. When children are a part of very large groups, it sometimes seems as if they are called on to share constantly and are never able to have their own needs or desires fulfilled. Their ability to share is closely tied to children's total development; as they mature, the ability to share increases. In fact, sharing is a sign of maturity in our culture.

Sharing depends in part on the ability to assume the role of another. Selman (1980) identified five levels in the development of cognitive role taking:

> *Level 0* (about age 3–7)—Children are aware that other people think differently, but either insist "I can't read his mind" or blithely assume that people in the same situation have the same point of view.
>
> *Level 1* (about age 6–8)—Children realize that two people may see the same situation differently. They become increasingly interested in other people's inner, psychological life.
>
> *Level 2* (about age 7–12)—Now children realize that another person can think about what they are thinking and "tune in" on their thought processes.
>
> *Level 3* (about age 10–15)—The child is able to think about two different viewpoints simultaneously and sees how one influences the other. Children can step back from a two-person relationship and watch how they and another person interact from the viewpoint of a third party.
>
> *Level 4* (ages 12–15)—Children understand the role of society and the usefulness of social conventions.

The ability to share does depend on the development of role taking, but it also involves being able to read other people's emotions. Children have to learn the difference between joy and sadness, anger and happiness, and pain and pleasure in others.

Children seem better able to identify others' emotions in familiar situations than unfamiliar (Shantz, 1983). For instance, children are better able to identify happiness or unhappiness of children at a birthday party than emotions of people at a summit meeting.

As a rule, children under the age of 4 do not understand motives or intentional acts. They assume all behavior is intentional, even the actions of inanimate objects. Between the ages of 5 and 6, children will begin to distinguish between unintended and intended acts. They gradually are able to differentiate between intentional acts and accidents.

Up to the age of 7, children focus on the concrete, observable characteristics, and by the age of 8, they can begin to focus on abstract traits such as emotions, personality, or abilities.

Fostering Sharing Behaviors.   More sharing takes place in classrooms where there is a feeling of security, a model present who shares, an abundance of materials and equipment, and where sharing is taught.

Security.   If children feel secure, and if they have enough for themselves, they are better able to share with others. Thus, you need to establish a classroom atmosphere of security. Insecure children are not ready to accept the social techniques of sharing. With young children, small groups with high teacher or adult ratios seem to foster children's ability to share. Small groups allow for

- ❏ more teacher-child interaction. Teachers who have too many children to interact with are frustrated and short-tempered, and do not have time to give children the personal attention that says, "You're valued and respected" and "I care for you."
- ❏ increased recognition. Children can share their ideas and thoughts more readily; they have more opportunities to take lunch money to the cafeteria, carry the flag, have their story read, play the game the way they want to, or lead the entire group in a song.
- ❏ feelings of social adequacy. Young children just learning to relate to others can find handling relationships with many other children a monumental task. But when there are only a small number of others, children feel more adequate and competent in their ability to relate (Furman, 1995).

Models.   Children who observe models sharing appear to be better able to share, and the teacher is the best model. Where the teacher is noticeably spontaneous, warm, and responsive to the children, there are many more sympathetic responses than in a group where the teacher tends to be hard-boiled and unsympathetic to children in distress. Teachers who deliberately try to develop warm friendships with children and who respond freely and openly to children's needs have children who participate more freely in group activities, who have higher leadership scores, and who show more evidence of sharing than do teachers who make little or no effort to work closely with individuals and who participate as little as possible in the activities of the group (Prescott, Jones, & Kritchevsky, 1967; Wittmer & Honig, 1994).

Physical Environment.   Children confined in small play spaces, with limited equipment and toys, are more frequently observed fighting than those in larger play spaces with an adequate number of materials. With plenty of space and equipment, sharing becomes easier (Curry & Arnaud, 1995).

You can arrange an environment conducive to sharing even if space is not available. Placing the equipment so that it is readily accessible to children, selecting some things to place on tables, and providing other materials on open shelves invite children to use and share the available materials rather than focusing on a single piece of equipment or having to hunt for toys.

Direct Teaching.   Teachers teach, and among the things they teach children are the social skills involved in sharing. You can use direct teaching in connection with children's play and social interactions. Children can be taught skills by directed doll play, by practice in solving conflicts over toys, or through direct statements made as they are playing: "We do it this way in school," or, "Take two more turns, and then it's Aletha's turn" (Curry & Arnaud, 1995; Curry & Johnson, 1990).

Explicit coaching may be helpful. Successful coaching techniques include the following:

- ❑ Clarify the concepts and behaviors that need to be addressed, such as the idea that hitting is not going to solve the problem.
- ❑ Discuss the idea and behavior with children and ask them to think about alternative ways for relating with others.
- ❑ Practice social skills through role play with others.
- ❑ Coach children in the use of concepts and behaviors in real situations (Asher & Hymel, 1981).

Books are also useful when teaching children prosocial behaviors (Wittmer & Honig, 1994). Reading Aliki's *We are Best Friends,* in which a boy makes new friends, can be followed with discussions of how children could make new friends. One second-grade teacher asked each child to write a personal letter to a friend.

It's George, by Miriam Cohen—the story of a boy who is not appreciated by other first graders until he becomes a hero—illustrates a number of ways to make friends. Elizabeth Winthrop's *Lizzie and Harold* shows children that friends can be older or younger than oneself and of the opposite sex. After reading the book, teachers of first and second graders can discuss who can be a friend, list games friends play together, and even put children in pairs to learn to play Cat's Cradle and The Mattress, as described in the book.

Cooperating

Cooperating is another skill useful for living in a society. Children, in order to cooperate, must sometimes give up or share something and become less egocentric, less concerned about themselves, and more concerned about the welfare of the group. That cooperation is a necessity for the welfare of any society is understood. But guidance and support in learning to cooperate are also necessary, especially for young children, who must learn to balance the task of developing a strong sense of self with that of learning to become a member of a group.

Cooperative behaviors, like sharing behaviors, develop as children mature. The more social experiences children have had, the better their ability to cooperate. Research suggests the same kinds of factors that influence sharing behaviors also influence children's ability to cooperate.

Reinforcement.   Children will be more cooperative when they are rewarded. Weingold and Webster (1964) asked two groups of children to work on a mural

Cooperation is a skill developed in the small democracy of the classroom.

project. In one group, each child was rewarded for the group product, but in the other group, children were told that only the child doing the best job would receive a reward. In the first group, there was an increase in friendly, cooperative behavior and peer interest. This group's product was also judged to be complete and creative. In the latter group, there was less work on the product and more boasting and depreciating behaviors. Weingold and Webster reinforced cooperative behaviors in children and found they continued on; but cooperating behaviors decreased in those who were punished or ignored.

School Size.   The size of the group influences the type of cooperative behavior children exhibit. In child-care centers of medium size, there were more incidents of social and cooperative behavior on the part of both teachers and children than in larger centers. In large centers, there was more need for control, scheduled routines, and greater rigidity on the part of adults. Teachers in the larger centers were less free to foster the warm, accepting relationships among children so necessary for both cooperation and sharing.

Competition.   Cooperation is the opposite of competition. In many classrooms, competition is fostered because of the belief that it is good for children and consistent with the life in our society. Competition is natural, and teachers could not avoid it if they tried; nevertheless, competition destroys group cooperation and is especially damaging to young children's self-identity within the group. To encourage cooperation, you need to reduce competition by (a) playing games that do not have winners and losers; (b) remembering that children are individuals; (c) asking all children to take part in special tasks; and (d) complimenting all the children frequently.

Making and Having Friends

"What was the best thing that ever happened to you?" a counselor asked a group of disabled teenagers. "One time," replied one of the young women, "I had a friend."

Everyone wants and needs to have a friend. For young children, having friends and being accepted by peers are critical to their development of a positive self-concept and prosocial skills, and are related to academic achievement.

Children who have friends

- ❏ are accepted by their peers.
- ❏ seem to adjust more easily to school (Ladd, 1990).
- ❏ have fewer adjustment difficulties when teenagers (Parker & Asher, 1987).
- ❏ are better adjusted emotionally and have fewer mental health problems (Cowen, Pederson, Babigian, Izzo, & Trost, 1973).

Making friends is related to other social skills. It's hard to say which comes first, social skills or friends; nevertheless, children who are able to cooperate and share and who are able to communicate effectively with others seem to be able to make and keep friends. Children who are able to cooperate seem to be better accepted by their peers, and those who argue and fight are often rejected by others (Ladd, Price, & Hart, 1988). In one study, children who were able to communicate effectively with others were better liked. These children made it clear to whom they were talking, either by saying the other child's name, establishing eye contact, or touching the child to whom they were talking (Kemple, 1991). They also spoke to one another and were more likely than other children to give a reason for their actions. Instead of just saying, "No, I don't want to play," they would explain, "No, I don't want to play house. Let's play office instead—you can be the secretary, I'll be the boss."

Teachers do play a role in helping children to make and be friends. Kemple (1991) suggests that teachers begin by observing children who have difficulty making friends. In observing, try to answer these questions:

1. How does the disliked child interact with others?
2. How does the child interact with individual children, small groups, or larger groups?
3. Does the child misinterpret the intentions and cues of other children?
4. Does the child resort to aggression as a means of solving problems?
5. When rejecting another, does the child give a reason or an alternative suggestion?
6. Does the child make irrelevant responses to playmates' communications?

"One time I had a friend," said a disabled child when asked to recall a happy time, demonstrating that friendships are critical.

Observing children who have trouble being a friend or making friends helps to pinpoint their problems. Once you identify why children have difficulty, you can choose from a wide variety of approaches to help them (Kemple, 1991). The same or similar techniques used to help children develop prosocial skills can be used. In addition, Kemple (1991) suggests the following:

❏ Organize special play sessions, grouping children lacking in social skills with those who are more competent (Rogers & Ross, 1986).

❏ Pair an isolated child with a younger child (Furman, Rahe, & Hartup, 1979).

❏ With an aggressive child, suggest and teach alternative means of resolving conflicts (Schickedanz, Schickedanz, & Forsyth, 1982).

❏ Use role play to help children develop alternative solutions to difficult social situations.

❏ Assist children who have difficulty becoming part of a group ("Wendy, you can be cashier").

❏ Provide on-the-spot guidance ("Tell him what you want, Scott").

❏ Use skits, puppet activities, or group discussions in which children are presented with a hypothetical situation (e.g., two puppets want to use the same fire truck) and are encouraged to suggest and evaluate a wide range of potential solutions.

❑ Steer a child who has trouble entering a social group to smaller or more accepting groups of children. Rather than suggesting that a child attempt to enter ongoing play by asking, "Can I play?" a teacher can help the child observe a group, try to figure out the theme, and then think of a role that would contribute to that theme (Hazen, Black, & Fleming-Johnson, 1984).

You can also help children make friends by enabling them to achieve recognition and prestige when in a group:

❑ Children feel honored and gain recognition from the group when the class makes them a get-well or birthday book consisting of a collection of pictures and stories by the other children.

❑ Prestige is the reward for children who can explain to others how to make a clay dinosaur, how to find the way to the principal's office, or how to care for the hammer and saws.

❑ Friends are made as the teacher encourages children to work on group projects. Singing songs and playing games together, such as The Farmer in the

---

Jacob's presence in our classroom has made life more difficult for all of us. We have had to slow down our pace, think more about the needs of others, and spend more time meeting them. Is this bad? (Heitz, 1989, p. 14).

Special attention to social skills is given when children with disabilities are mainstreamed into the classroom. Teachers have found the following methods helpful:

❑ Observe the mainstreamed children to identify strengths, weaknesses, and how they relate to the others and how the others interact with them, and talk with the children's parents. Both steps provide an indication of the children's uniqueness and what types of strategies will be useful in helping them to gain social skills and become involved with the group.

❑ Provide materials that encourage social interaction among children, matching toys and materials to the developmental level of both the disabled children and the others.

❑ Teach social techniques to the children. Children can be taught to persist when interacting with disabled children, for instance, asking a hearing-impaired child a question more than once or persisting in asking the child to play and work with them.

❑ Encourage individual children to regularly spend time with the special-needs children. Recognize and reinforce their social interactions.

❑ Give children time to adjust to special-needs children and accept their individual differences. Heitz (1989) reports that when Jacob, a child with cerebral palsy, was mainstreamed, a very small 5-year-old girl was careful *not* to take his hand when playing games or for any other reason. Doing so meant that if Jacob fell, she would too, whereas a larger girl could take his hand and share her strength with Jacob.

Box 4.3
Helping Disabled Children Make Friends

Dell, Ring Around the Rosie, and other simple games, (really a remarkable accomplishment for young children) help them to feel a part of a group.

❏ Structuring activities that require more than one child to be successfully completed is helpful. You might arrange for children to plant and maintain a garden, make soup or pudding, bake bread or cookies, create and put on a puppet show, construct a playhouse, paint a mural, or play board games.

Books, as well, can be used. Reading Leo Lionni's *Swimmy,* in which a little, lonely fish teaches others how to work together to scare the big fish away, can be followed by children making a mural of *Swimmy,* creating a big fish from many little fish each child draws and cuts out. Margaret Miller's *Whose Hat?* shows adult groups, many of which provide services, and *Fire Fighters,* by Robert Mass, offers children a view of the daily lives of fire fighters who live and work together.

SUMMARY

Although young children bring to the classroom a number of skills—walking, talking, relating—it is the school's responsibility to ensure the continuation of skill development. The social studies teaches map reading, graphing, and learning cardinal directions; other skills are shared responsibilities with all the school subjects.

The skills most important for the preschool-primary classroom are the social skills and thinking skills. The social skills of learning who you are and developing self-esteem are prerequisites to learning about others. All children's group activities are social by nature, yet teachers need to plan specific activities and experiences to foster cooperation and encourage social interactions.

Teaching children prosocial behavior involves helping them learn to relate to each other, as well as the communicative skills of listening, speaking, reading and writing, and the skills of learning to share and cooperate. Because making and having friends is so integral to children's success in school and life, teachers also plan ways for children to make and have friends.

PROJECTS

1. Observe 4-, 5-, and 6-year-olds at play. What evidences of cooperation and sharing do you note? How do the ages of the children relate to any differences in their play behaviors?

2. Plan a lesson for developing social skills in a group of young children. Write a complete plan designed to foster the development of the social skill you have selected. If possible, try your plan out with a group of children.

3. Interview several teachers. How important do they consider social skills in their total program? What types of planning do they do to foster social skills?

4. Watch children's cartoon shows for an entire Saturday morning and record instances of violence. Then observe children playing at home or school and

record the nature and the number of instances of violence in their play. Analyze your observations, comparing the amount and degree of violence in the cartoons with that of the children's play. Did you observe similarities?

RESOURCES

Early Violence Prevention: Tools for Teachers of Young Children (1995) by Slaby, Roedell, Arezzo, and Hendrix, published by the National Association for the Education of Young Children. A must for teachers who want to foster children's social skills development.

Kelso's choice: Conflict management for children (1994) by Glass and O'Neill, (published by Rhinestone Press, P.O. Box 30, Winchester, OR 97495.) A curriculum kit designed to teach children social skills, including sharing and cooperating, walking away, and cooling off.

Skill-streaming in early childhood: Teaching prosocial skills to the preschool and kindergarten children (1990) by McGinnis; published by Research Press, Champaign, IL. Designed for children who lack prosocial skills.

REFERENCES

Ainsworth, M. D., Belhar, M., Waters, E., & Wall, S. (1978). *Patterns of attachment.* Hillsdale, NJ: Erlbaum.

Asher, S. R., & Hymel, S. (1981). Children's social competence in peer relations: Sociometric and behavioral assessment. In J. D. Wine & M. D. Syme (Eds.), *Social competence.* New York: Guilford Press.

Atwood, M. E., & Williams, J. (1983). Human sexuality: An important aspect of self-image. *Young Children, 38*(2), 56–61.

Brophy, J. (1990). Teaching social studies for understanding and higher-order applications. *The Elementary School Journal, 90,* 351–419.

Clarke-Stewart, A., & Koch, J. B. (1983). *Children: Development through adolescence.* New York: Wiley.

Cowen, E. L., Pederson, A., Babigian, H., Izzo, L. D., & Trost, M.A. (1973). Long-term follow-up of early detected vulnerable children. *Journal of Consulting and Clinical Psychology, 41,* 438–446.

Curry, N. E., & Arnaud, S. (1995). Personality difficulties in preschool children as revealed through play themes and styles. *Young Children, 50*(4), 4–10.

Curry, N. E., & Johnson, C. N. (1990). *Beyond self-esteem: Developing a genuine sense of human value.* Washington, DC: National Association for the Education of Young Children.

Dewey, J. (1944). *Democracy and education.* New York: The Free Press.

Erikson, E. (1963). *Childhood and society.* New York: W. W. Norton.

Flavell, J. H. (1979). Metacognition and cognitive monitoring. *American Psychologist, 34,* 906–911.

Freud, S. (1949). *An outline of psychoanalysis.* New York: W. W. Norton.

Furman, R. A. (1995). Helping children cope with stress and deal with feelings. *Young Children, 50*(2), 33–41.

Furman, W., Rahe, D., & Hartup, W. W. (1979). Rehabilitation of socially withdrawn preschool children through mixed-age and same-age socialization. *Child Development, 50,* 915–922.

Greenberg, P. (1989). Ideas that work with young children. Learning self-esteem and self-discipline through play. *Young Children, 44*(2), 28–32.

Hazen, N. L., Black, B., & Fleming-Johnson, F. (1984). Social acceptance: Strategies children use and how teachers can help children learn them. *Young Children, 39*(6), 26–36.

Heitz, T. (1989). How do I help Jacob? *Young Children, 45*(1), 11–16.

Ishee, N., & Goldhaber, J. (1990). Story re-enactment: Let the play begin! *Young Children, 45*(3), 70–75.

Kemple, K. M. (1991). Preschool children's peer acceptance and social interaction. *Young Children, 46*(3), 47–56.

Kuebli, J. (1994). Young children's understanding of everyday emotions. *Young Children, 49*(3), 36–46.

Ladd, G. W. (1990). Having friends, keeping friends, making friends and being liked by peers in the classroom: Predictors of children's early school adjustment. *Child Development, 61,* 1081–1100.

Ladd, G. W., Price, J. M., & Hart, C. H. (1988). Predicting preschoolers' peer status from their playground behaviors. *Child Development, 59,* 986–992.

Luke, J. L., & Myers, C. M. (1995). Toward peace: Using literature to aid conflict resolution. *Childhood Education, 79.*

MacDonald, K. (1987). Parent-child physical play with rejected, neglected, and popular boys. *Developmental Psychology, 23,* 705–711.

MacDonald, K., & Parke, R. D. (1984). Bridging the gap: Parent-child play interaction and peer interactive competence. *Child Development, 55,* 1265–1277.

Maslow, A. (1969). *Toward a psychology of being.* New York: Van Nostrand.

McWhinnie, H. (1992). Art for young children. In C. Seefeldt (Ed.), *The early childhood curriculum: A review of current research* (2nd ed.). New York: Teachers College Press.

Morrow, R. D. (1991). What's in a name? In particular, a Southeast Asian name? *Young Children, 44*(6), 23–29.

National Council for the Social Studies. (1989). *Position statements: Social studies for early childhood and elementary school children: Preparing for the 21st century.* Washington, DC: Author.

Parker, J. G., & Asher, S. R. (1987). Peer relations and later personal adjustment: Are low accepted children at risk? *Psychological Bulletin, 10,* 357–389.

Perez, S. A. (1994). Responding differently to diversity. *Childhood Education, 70,* 137–142.

Prescott, E., Jones, E., & Kritchevsky, S. (1967). *Group day care as a child rearing environment.* Pasadena, CA: Pacific Oaks College.

Rogers, C. (1961). *On becoming a person.* Boston: Houghton Mifflin.

Rogers, D. L., & Ross, D. D. (1986). Encouraging positive social interaction among young children. *Young Children, 41*(3), 12–17.

Schickedanz, J. A., Schickedanz, D. L., & Forsyth, P. D. (1982). *Toward understanding children.* Boston: Little, Brown.

Schiller, M. (1995). An emergent art curriculum that fosters understanding. *Young Children, 50*(3), 33–39.

Selman, R. (1980). *The growth of interpersonal understanding.* New York: Academic Press.

Shantz, C. W. (1983). Social cognition. In P. H. Mussen (Ed.), *Handbook of child psychology* (4th ed.) (pp. 495–554). New York: Wiley.

Skinner, B. F. (1974). *About* behaviorism. New York: Knopf.

Slaby, R. G., Roedell, W. C., Arezzo, D., & Hendrix, K. (1995). *Early violence prevention: Tools for teachers of young children.* Washington, DC: National Association for the Education of Young Children.

Spivack, G., & Shure, M. (1978). *Social adjustment of young children: A cognitive approach to solving real-life problems.* San Francisco: Jossey-Bass.

Wallach, L. R. (1995). Helping children cope with violence. *Young Children, 48*(4), 4–12.

Weingold, H., & Webster, R. (1964). Effects of punishment on cooperative behavior in children. *Child Development, 35,* 12–16.

Weitz, L., Quickle, G., Pejchi, L., & Wilson, S. (1991). Building self-esteem? Try real accomplishments. *Young Children, 46*(3), 39.

Wittmer, D. S., & Honig, A. S. (1994). Encouraging positive social development in young children. *Young Children, 49*(5), 4–13.

Chapter 5

Attitudes and Values

Democratic values should be taught in the classroom, in the curriculum, and in the daily life of the school.

California State Department of Education, 1987, p. 6.

Social studies educators are virtually unanimous in stressing the importance of addressing democratic values in the classroom, not only as objects of study, but as considerations to be taken into account when making decisions (Brophy, 1990). Nevertheless, because attitudes and values, which represent the worth or merit people place on things, excite feelings and expression, and predispose people to behavior and action, there is less agreement about how these values, or even which ones, should be taught.

The controversy over what values should be taught and how stems from the nature of attitudes and values themselves. An opinion is a verbal expression of a belief, but values and attitudes imply an emotional liking or disliking attached to the belief. Values do not exist in and of themselves; they are not things, but are reflected in specific value judgments or claims that individuals make.

Listen to and observe children or adults talking about people, society, their government, or religion. Adults yell and argue, and children hit, kick, and call one another names as they defend their attitudes and values. It's clear that attitudes and values are emotionally laden, personal, and deeply ingrained.

Because values and attitudes deal with feelings and personal beliefs, many believe that children should learn these in their own home or church. The family and church, some claim, should have the sole responsibility for teaching values and attitudes; the school, and those who teach, should not be responsible for teaching other people's children what to value or believe.

In a way, there can be no discussion about whether schools and teachers should be involved in teaching children attitudes and values. Even though the development of attitudes and values does occur primarily outside the classroom (NCSS, 1989), the transmission of attitudes and values to young children in any early childhood program is, in fact, unavoidable.

There actually is nothing that occurs in a preschool or primary grade that is not bound up in, and influenced by, values and attitudes. Just the fact of going to school and learning to read is value bound in the belief in our culture that school is good and all should be literate. The social studies, however—those studies that introduce children to the different ideas, beliefs, and values of other people and cultures—are even more directly related to teaching children values and attitudes. Social studies "should provide a setting for children to acquire knowledge of history and the social sciences and to be exposed to a broad variety of opinions, facilitating the formulation, reassessment, and affirmation of their beliefs" (NCSS, 1989, p. 15).

Prerequisite to understanding the role of attitudes and values in the social studies is knowledge of (a) how attitudes and values are learned; (b) current methods and strategies of teaching attitudes and values; and (c) which attitudes and values should be taught in schools for young children.

HOW CHILDREN LEARN ATTITUDES AND VALUES

Research suggests that attitudes and values are learned in much the same way knowledge and skills are gained. There are at least three theoretical views of attitude and value formation: (a) values and attitudes are modeled, (b) they are reinforced, and (c) they are learned.

Values and Attitudes Are Modeled

Young children take on the values and attitudes of those close to them. Because they love their parents and need their parents to love and care for them, young children want to be like their parents in every way. They will model the attitudes and values of their parents.

Parents aren't the only significant others in young children's lives, however; teachers are very important to young children, as well. They hold their teachers in high regard and have strong emotional ties to them. Because the teacher is an authority figure, one who cares for, protects, and loves them, they are likely to model the teacher's attitudes and values. In addition, children may model the attitudes and values of movie or TV stars, or of others who hold high prestige in our culture.

The expectations of any society or group of people—family, school group, peers—all influence an individual's values. When children enter a new group, they are brought face to face with a new set of values, new ways of behaving, and new sources to identify with and model. Using this theory, teachers would strive to model attitudes and values consistent with our democratic society. They would model

❑ valuing the dignity of each individual.
❑ allowing universal participation in rule setting and rule establishing.
❑ permitting each person freedom of speech, opportunities to express ideas and feelings.
❑ reinforcing the rights of each individual for protection and happiness.

❑ seeing that everyone has a part in the school society and that everyone has some responsibility to others.

❑ cooperating and accepting responsibility in the school and community.

Teachers would provide other exemplary models in the media of the school. Choosing storybooks that provide a balance of genders and race, ethnic, and religious groups in a variety of roles and situations, teachers would consciously provide role models consistent with the values of a democracy.

Values and Attitudes Are Reinforced

Reinforcement theory is used to explain how children learn attitudes and values. Behaviorists claim that children learn their attitudes through reinforcement, as do adults. When children behave in certain ways, and their behaviors are reinforced with attention or some type of reward, the behavior will appear again. Responses and behaviors that are rewarded will be repeated. The same process of conditioning is applicable to attitude and value learning. Children who behave in ways consistent with their beliefs and who are reinforced will have the belief strengthened. Using this theoretical approach, teachers would be careful to reinforce

The value and dignity of each child are respected when a variety of materials is available.

democratic attitudes and values. Beliefs incongruent with that of a democracy would be ignored. Eventually these would diminish and be extinguished.

Values and Attitudes Are Learned

Cognitive theory is another view of attitude and value formation. Cognitive theory suggests principles of cognitive growth and development, and cognitive structures influence the formation of children's attitudes. This view sees humans as striving after goals. Thus, humans acquire attitudes and values consistent with these goals.

Cognitive theories of learning moral development are stage theories. Piaget suggested that children's attitude and values are consistent with their thought processes.

In Piaget's first stage, children obey rules because they feel obligated to. Piaget called this stage moral realism, or the morality of constraint, because children obey rules as if they were sacred and unalterable. Right and wrong are simply what authorities tell them, and they believe everyone views things the same way. They judge the rightness or wrongness of an act on the basis of the magnitude of its consequences, the extent to which it conforms to rules, or whether or not the action is punished. If they disobey, they believe their actions will be followed by some misfortune willed by God or some inanimate object.

The next stage, called autonomous morality, appears around age 7 or 8. Children view rules as established, but maintained through reciprocal agreement and able to be modified when needed. The child's judgments of right and wrong take into consideration intentions as well as punishments. Conforming to peer expectations, considering other people's feelings, expressing thanks, and putting oneself in the place of others guide behavior.

When formal thought develops, around adolescence, children reach the understanding of right and wrong and the place of rules. They can make new rules, understand the purpose of rules, and understand all the consequences that arise from accepting or rejecting the attitudes, values, and rules of a society.

Piaget believed children's learning of moral values involves maturation and interactions with others. Children's immature cognitive development, or egocentric thought, limits their ability to see things from the perspective of others, and their dependence makes them feel obligated to comply with the demands of others. Moral development requires that children give up egocentric thought as well as their feeling of being obligated to obey adults or the will of others.

Through social experiences, children are challenged to give up some of their egocentrism. Further, as children interact with peers, they find they must reciprocate, which facilitates the awareness of the internal states that underlie the actions of others and contributes to the tendency to take other people's intentions into account.

Through these interactions, each person constructs individual moral values. Just as with the construction of intelligence, the child only comes to know moral values after experiencing, manipulating, examining and exploring them in many ways over time. Moral values can only come from repeated encounters in which the child is an active participant in making sense of the information.

Riley (1984) believes that these repeated encounters should permit children to make choices. By making choices as they interact with others, children are able to construct a sense of right and wrong. "Learning from choosing: to achieve a reliable sense of right and wrong, children must make choices; it is the task of the parents and school to make this possible" (Riley, 1984, p. 5). Teachers can provide children with many opportunities to choose and to experience the consequences of their choices. Initially, children might choose what they will play, with whom they will play, and when they will change their play. For children in the primary grades, choices become increasingly more complex and numerous, and the choices adults make for them decrease (Riley, 1984).

Which Theory?

Each of these theories is used to support an approach to the teaching of attitudes and values. Historically, reinforcement theory was used to support teaching values and attitudes to the young through indoctrination. During the 1970s and 1980s, other approaches became popular. Raths, Harmin, and Simon (1978) advanced the idea that children should not be indoctrinated into the values of our nation, but rather should be taught to clarify their own attitudes and values by reflecting on the consequences of their actions and searching for consistency between their feelings and actions. Others advocated that children learn by reasoning about morals and analyzing values.

Indoctrination

Direct instruction in values has been and remains dominant in classrooms (Brophy, 1990). Children are exposed to stories and historical accounts exemplifying what are seen as basic United States values and behaviors, and then are rewarded and reinforced for expressing and behaving in ways that are consistent with these values.

Some educators believe that attitudes and values should be indoctrinated. The authors of the national civics standards, *National Standards for Civics and Government* (CCE, 1994), suggest that children memorize numerous isolated facts, understands abstract concepts, and become indoctrinated in the values of democracy. Given unlimited amounts of time to spend in drill and practice, it may be possible to train children to recite the numerous civics standards. However, by memorizing instead of learning, children would become like parrots in a circus— able to recite the three branches of government, explain the consequences of absence of government, or name the people representing them at the local, state, and national levels, but comprehend very little.

The ability to recite the numerous facts in the civics performance standards has nothing to do with becoming a productive member of a democracy. Research shows that children who have been indoctrinated in civics fail to understand the basic obligations of citizenship in a democratic society; therefore, the standards negate their very purpose. Learning through indoctrination, children are more likely to be unable to accept social responsibility as adults or participate in social criticism, and would be more willing to follow whoever is in power without question (Torney, Oppenheim, & Farnen, 1975). It seems wiser and more democratic to respect young children by teaching them to value their flag, their country, and democracy in ways that are congruent with their development and learning.

Value Clarification

Believing that values are something an individual chooses, prizes, and then acts upon, teachers plan ways for children to explore their own feelings, reactions, and values within a safe and secure environment. Teachers can:

❑ encourage children to make choices freely. Many choices and child-initiated activities would be planned. Young children would be given information and helped to uncover and then examine alternative choices. For instance, a teacher of 5-year-olds might tell them the choices they have for activity time. "Today you can build with blocks, paint at the tables or the easel, work with clay, or play in the airplane. Think about what you want to begin with." A teacher of primary children could ask them to select a book from those on a particular shelf, develop a project from three choices, or decide whether they would like to draw, construct a replica, or make a slide-tape show for a report.

❑ ask the children to weigh alternative choices thoughtfully. "If you decide to build with blocks, will you still have time to make your desert garden?" Primary children could be asked to weigh the consequences of actions. "Is this really important to you?" "What might happen if you use that idea?" "What other choices do you have?" "When might you use that idea?" "What would be good and bad about the idea?"

❑ encourage children to consider what they prize and cherish. "Would other children believe that?" "Is that important to you?" "Should everyone go along with your idea?" "Did you do it yourself?" "Are you glad you feel that way?" "Have you felt this way for some time?" "Is this idea so good everyone should feel that way?" "Who else feels that way?" (Raths et al., 1978, p. 35).

❑ help children to act on their beliefs, giving opportunities for them to express their own ideas, to develop repeated behaviors or patterns in their life.

Raths (1962) believed that a secure classroom atmosphere would be necessary for teachers to lead children to develop and understand their own values and attitudes. Children cannot make free choices or express their values in words and actions unless they feel secure and comfortable. School must be a place where children can feel psychologically safe to talk about their feelings and beliefs. Teachers need to listen to children expressing their beliefs and ask questions to help them clarify these. Teachers must respond nonjudgmentally to children's ideas, questions, and responses. "Clarifying values dignifies the child as an individual, while at the same time encouraging him or her to more consistently and maturely deal with one's feelings, attitudes, and values" (Schug, 1987, p. 223).

Value Analysis

Through value analysis, teachers attempt to develop students' ability to make rational and logically defensible moral judgments by teaching the processes of reasoning about moral or value questions (Brophy, 1990). Value analysis is based on the idea that although moral judgments can vary widely in the extent to which they are rational and logical, the goal of value education should be to help individuals learn to make rationally and logically defensible moral judgments. To achieve this, students are taught a set of skills essential to reasoning about moral/value questions (Leming, 1985) that will help them to understand the consequences of particular values, the conflicts that may occur among two or more values, and the reasons for particular value choices.

Emphasizing thinking, value analysis is primarily a cognitive strategy (Banks, 1979; Taba, Durkin, Fraenkel, & McNaughton, 1971). The process, which begins with identification of the problem or issue, is similar to Dewey's description of thinking and problem solving.

1. *Identifying values.*   In a given situation, students are asked to identify the values people in that situation hold. The situation may be something that has happened to the children, or may be a story or problem posed by them.

A teacher read a story to the children.

Susan is in trouble. She was supposed to complete all her math problems and give them to her second-grade teacher before recess. Instead of working on her problems, she chose to paint. When she realized her time was gone, she asked Freddy if she could copy his paper. What should Freddy do?

To guide the children in value analysis, the teacher might ask, "What problem are Freddy and Susan facing?"

2. *Comparing and contrasting values.*   Pupils can identify the similarities and differences in different people's value choices. They are asked to determine values of the same individual in different situations or to determine values of different individuals in the same situation.

Continuing, the teacher would ask, "What does Susan think about the problem? What does Freddy think? What does Susan's behavior tell us about what she values? What does Freddy's behavior tell us about what he values?"

3. *Exploring feelings.*   By talking about their own feelings, identifying with the feelings of others, and experiencing situations in which new feelings are aroused, children can understand the strong emotional component of their own values and those of others.

"Why do you think Freddy feels the way he does? Why does Susan feel the way she does? How would you feel?"

4. *Analyzing value judgments.*   Children are able to provide evidence to support or refute a particular value judgment.

"What would happen if Freddy helped Susan? What if Freddy refuses to help? Is there some other alternative?"

5. *Analyzing value conflict.*   Presented with value dilemmas, pupils are able to determine what the conflicts are, what alternatives are possible, the consequences of each, and what alternative might be the best outcome and why.

"What do you think Susan and Freddy should do? Why do you think so? What do you think the outcome will be?"

Testing is the final phase in value analysis. Testing includes four steps: (a) role exchange (willingness to exchange positions with the least advantaged person in the agreement); (b) universal consequences (If everyone followed the course of action, would the consequences be acceptable?); (c) new cases (Are the consequences of the action acceptable in new but similar situations?); and (d) subsumption (Does the principle follow from a higher acceptable principle?).

WHAT VALUES SHOULD BE TAUGHT?

Because attitudes and values deal with the "shoulds"—what people *should* do, the standards they *should* live by, or the things they *should* value, endorse, live up to, or maintain—the question of what values to teach is controversial. One person's standards for behavior differ from another's, and conflicts arise. Each would want their children to learn a different set of values.

Obviously teachers will not teach children what religion they should believe in, or what political party they should vote for. Teaching children what religious beliefs to hold and which political party is of higher value than another, among other values, is up to the family. No teacher can tell a child or parent that the values they hold are wrong. On the other hand, teachers who do not raise questions about values, ask children to examine their own feelings, nor promote the values inherent in our democracy may perform a disservice to our democracy by avoiding these topics. If teachers do not actively promote the values of our society, children learn nothing about democracy; rather, they learn that they can do whatever they wish.

The values that do matter, and are worthwhile and even necessary, are those that are consistent with the values of democracy. In schools for young children, the universal attitudes and values consistent with the rights and responsibilities of living in a democracy are those that are taught. Stemming from the Declaration of Independence and the Bill of Rights, these attitudes and values have been described in various ways by the different commissions on the social studies.

The California State Department of Education's *History-Social Science Framework* maintains that

> the curriculum places a continuing emphasis on democratic values in the relations between citizens and the state. Whether studying United States history or world history, students should be aware of the presence or absence of the rights of the individual, the rights of minorities, the right of the citizens to participate in government, the right to speak or publish freely without government coercion, the right to freedom of religion, the right to trial by jury, the right to form trade unions, and other basic democratic rights. (1987, pp. 6–7)

Similarly, the National Council for the Social Studies suggests that, within the context of the social studies, children learn "positive attitudes toward knowledge and learning and develop a spirit of inquiry that will enhance their understanding of their world so that they will become rational, humane, participating, effective members of a democratic society" (1989, p. 17).

Agreeing, the National Commission on Social Studies in the Schools believes that what it calls "civic virtue"—United States democratic traditions and political institution, ideals, human values and achievements, and the understanding and transmission of citizenship—"is not just a matter of the observance of outward forms, transmitted from the old to the young, but also a matter of reasoned conviction, the end result of people thinking for themselves" (1989, p. xi).

By focusing on those values that (a) are congruent with our democracy, (b) are necessary for children to become participatory members of a democratic society, and (c) predispose children to learning to learn, the social studies can meet the intent of the three commissions on the social studies.

Democratic Values

In an early childhood program, children are not just preparing to become members of a democratic society but actually *are* citizens of a democracy. Within the democratic environment of an early childhood program, children practice principles of democracy. Daily they contribute to building and fostering a democratic society, and daily they receive the benefits of belonging to this society.

Through every experience in the program, young children learn that they are worthy, valued, and respected. They know that their individual needs and wants will be met, and that their rights to freedom of speech, and pursuit of happiness and other rights will always be protected. At the same time, however, they are learning to expand their concerns and give up some of their egocentrism. As members of a democratic community, children develop a sense of shared concern, recognizing that their interests overlap with the interests of others, and that their welfare is inextricably entwined with the welfare of others.

It is the teacher who establishes and maintains the basic principles of democracy in the classroom. The way the teacher establishes control, deals with individual children and their interactions with one another, and teaches sends a powerful message to children about the values of a democracy. Although there is no one right or wrong way for a teacher to do this, when observing in a democratic classroom, one immediately becomes aware of how teachers actively support individual worth and dignity while at the same time protecting and nurturing the welfare of the total group. In a democratic group, certain tenets are consistently followed.

1. *Teachers share control.*   Teachers do not give orders and expect children to blindly follow their directions. Rather than emphasizing the task or the skill to be learned, teachers focus on how children are feeling, reacting, and interacting with one another.

> A second-grade group was working in the computer room with the computer teacher. One child had difficulty with the program and did not seem to know what to do with the computer or how to solve the math problems. His neighbor turned to him and began to help. "Stop talking now!" said the teacher firmly, writing both children's names on a box on the board, which meant each child might later lose some

Teachers share control with children by encouraging them to lead and follow.

favored activity or reward. "It's not time for social talk; it's time to do your math drill." The teacher ignored both the fact that one child had no clue of what to do or how to use the computer to practice this particular math drill and the fact that the other child was offering to help.

2. *Children make choices.*   Instead of the teacher prescribing work to be done, how, and under what time constraints, children make choices about what they will learn, how, and with whom. Cookbook approaches, filling in the blanks, and following prescribed lesson plans are replaced with centers of interest, learning stations, and other materials for learning. Rather than solo learning, group work is fostered.

> "Here are some plastic containers," said a teacher to the first graders who had been grouped into committees. She gave each group a box of different-sized and different-shaped clear plastic containers. "Your group's task is to decide which container holds the most sand, and which the least. You may use the scale, the tape measure, or any other materials in the sand or water tables. Report to me when you have reached a decision."

3. *Discipline is firm and consistent, but does not revolve around force, coercion, or threat.*   Already believing that rules come from authority and that being good means following orders, children need to participate in setting and following rules and begin the long process of separating intent from action.

> Jennifer, a rambunctious 5-year-old, always seemed to be the cause of some trouble with the other kindergarten children. She jumped from one group to another, often upsetting what the others were doing. She never seemed to sit still or simply walk

from one place to another, but jiggled, jumped, and ran around, a real perpetual motion machine in action. One day she knocked Sean down as she darted across the room. The teacher took her aside and began again the process of identifying and labeling for Jennifer her actions and their results.

"You are a very active girl. You need to move about a great deal. When you do so, you hurt others. How do you think we can arrange for you to move about without disturbing the other children?"

4. *Freedom of thought and speech are fostered.*   Children are expected to have opinions and express them. This expectation governs every area of the curriculum. Instead of children getting sheets of paper on which to color or patterns to trace around for art activities, they are asked to express their own ideas, thoughts, and feelings in drawings, paintings, or their constructions. In language arts, they are asked to discuss, write, and express what they know and feel and to make choices about how they will learn math and science skills.

A kindergarten teacher, picking up on the children's interest in dinosaurs, asked them to draw their favorite dinosaur. Clifford drew a large scribble, added some legs and horns, and called it a "monster" dinosaur. Judy laughed at him, saying, "That's not a dinosaur. That's not real, that's just a scribble." The teacher said, "Judy, this is the way Clifford draws a dinosaur. It's his pretend monster dinosaur. Your dinosaur is a picture of a stegosaurus, Roberta's is a green dinosaur, and Alice didn't draw a dinosaur at all but drew the forest in which they might have lived." Thus the teacher demonstrated for the children that, although they have different ideas and express them in different ways, each individual's expression is valid.

5. *Children are never overwhelmed by the power of others.*   Teachers are not power figures in the classroom, nor do they permit children to govern through power assertions, bullying, or threats.

In a kindergarten, two boys had gained control of the class. They threatened the others with physical violence, took smaller children's milk money, and had on more than one occasion overwhelmed children in the bathrooms, taking their pants off. As a result, the other children refused to go to the bathroom and began giving the two their money and following their demands. Knowing these behaviors could not be permitted to continue, the teacher began a behavior management program with the class and the two boys. She taught the other children how to ignore the boys, and some skills for coping with them. At the same time, she began rewarding the two boys for cooperative behavior. She channeled their needs for power in constructive ways by asking them to lead a song, take charge of the blocks, and become monitors. The behavioral techniques didn't solve the problem, but they gave the teacher and the other children a way to regain control without being overwhelmed with emotions. As a result, she was then able to work with the boys on the cause of their behaviors.

6. *A sense of community is built.*   A classroom is a group of individuals. The teacher develops this group into a community by helping them share goals. Even young children can begin to see that they are a part of, and share in, the common goals of their family, their own group of friends, the class, and the school. Not only are children encouraged to see themselves within the context of the total group, but small groups within the total group are fostered (Au & Kawakami, 1991).

Common shared experiences lead to common goals. A trip to the zoo leads to deciding on group rules for the trip, which questions will be answered, and which exhibits will be visited. After such a trip, one second-grade teacher arranged for the total group to complete a mural of their experiences. Knowing that a sense of community develops as children work together, the teacher then divided up the group by their interest in birds, reptiles, fish, and mammals, and had each group complete a project and then report to the total group. Throughout the process, the teacher helped the children recognize both their own identity and the needs of the group.

7. *Teachers model respect for others.* A teacher who cares about and respects each child in the group, and each adult who works with the children serves as a model for the children. Teachers model and encourage mutual respect. They let the children know in a number of very explicit ways that each is respected and cared for.

"Let me know when you want me to help you with your math." "You be the judge. It's up to you whether you want to keep this in your book report or not," a second-grade teacher was heard to say to the children. A teacher of 4-year-olds fostered the idea that it is all right not to be competent in everything. Talking privately to a child who couldn't walk the balance beam, she said, "It's OK not to be able to balance— you'll be able to do so as you grow. You do know how to dress yourself, draw, and sing." Overhearing one child laughing at another's sandwich of shrimp and catsup a

A sense of community is built when children are asked to work together.

kindergarten teacher, said, "When you laugh at Sallie's lunch, it upsets her. It's OK if you don't like it, or even if you'd like to try it, but you cannot make fun of what other people like."

8. *Teachers elicit respectful, caring behaviors from the children.*   Teachers are powerful models for children. They not only model respectful, caring behavior, but they explain what they are doing and find other ways to demonstrate respect.

> Kathy, a 5-year-old with spina bifida, was mainstreamed in the kindergarten. The teacher not only modeled caring behaviors for the children, but was explicit in gaining their respect for Kathy. At times, the teacher would casually ask a child to help Kathy with her coat or chair, or to reach something. Other times, she would pair Kathy with a partner for necessary help.
>
> To enable Kathy to be a responsible member of the group, the teacher found a carpenter's apron with lots of pockets that could be filled with toys and materials. This permitted Kathy to assume some responsibility in cleaning up. At the same time, the teacher provided the same kind of apron for the other children so, even though Kathy was different, all the children could take advantage of cleaning up with an apron.

Participation in a Democratic Society

It is from the base of social interactions within the democracy of the preschool-primary classroom that political awareness grows. "From this, children develop behaviors that are or are not consistent with the democratic process, positive and nonaggressive conflict resolution or the opposite, awareness of or respect for authority or the lack thereof" (Allen, Freeman, & Osborne, 1989, p. 57).

When teachers follow the principles of a democratic society, children daily experience political concepts. They understand that some people are in authority and know that these people make and enforce rules in their homes, schools, and communities. The child's peer group, family, school, and community relations serve as initial exposures to the core of politics, which is power and its use. Children directly experience rules and limitations as given and behavior as good or bad as it conforms to the rules (Fromberg, 1995).

Furthermore, even very young children are aware of politics beyond their classroom. Researchers note that children are increasingly more politically aware and can talk about many topics from the field of political science, even though their range of knowledge about any one topic is narrow (Adrian, 1971; Connell, 1971). Even 4-year-olds were able to identify and accurately label pictures of political symbols, such as the flag and the president and his wife.

Connell (1971) noted that before the age of 5, children's political concepts are made up of bits and pieces of information collected from home, school, and the media. These concepts, according to Connell, typically reflect young children's lack of ability to synthesize information, as well as their lack of cognitive development. Their political concepts are "full of political figures, cartoon characters, familiar figures of fact and legend that jostle each other with splendid promiscuity" (p. 11). At age 5, children seem to have concepts that reflect their personal knowledge of political symbols such as the flag and certain songs and stories.

Around the age of 5 or 6, children understand that the world has two groups of people—special and nonspecial—with those in power being considered special. The special people in power are also viewed with benevolence. Greenstein (1968) concluded that children see authority figures as benevolent people who will care for each of them personally either as a result of the children's cognitive ability or from their emotional needs for safety and security.

In their study of children's political understanding, Hess and Torney (1967) support these findings. They found that young children's involvement with politics begins early, with strong emotional attachment to the president. Children seem to think of the president personally, as someone who would help them if they telephoned him or went to him in person with a request.

By age 7, children's political concepts, partially as a result of changes in their cognitive abilities, also seem to change. Concepts are now more accurate, and a political consciousness develops. Children can now construct a simple idea of government and the political world. They seem to have a store of ideas, but continue to draw randomly from it. They do not yet distinguish among levels of government; when asked what political figures such as mayors, congress people, and presidents do, they say, "All those people do the same thing."

Connell (1971) concluded that children, even by age 7, do not reproduce the communications that reach them from the adult world; they work them over, detach them from their original context, and assemble them into a general concept of what government is all about. However inaccurate and incomplete children's political concepts are, they form the base for children's later development.

From the research on children's political learning, the following conclusions can be reached:

1. Concepts of politics begin in early childhood and the process of development is continual.
2. Basic attachments and identifications are among the first political concepts acquired.
3. Children view political authority figures as positive, benevolent and personal.
4. Feelings and affection develop before knowledge.
5. It isn't until late childhood that children can distinguish between different political roles and acquire basic factual information needed to map out their political world (Parker & Kaltsounis, 1986, p. 18).

Teaching Political Concepts

Political concepts, typically based on children's own experiences, are introduced to children informally. Most children are acquainted with the flag, patriotic songs, the Pledge of Allegiance, laws, and rules; you can use these to introduce political concepts. In addition, the voting process, as well as daily life in the political groups of the family and classroom, provides opportunities to foster children's understanding of political concepts.

Flags as Symbols.   Children see the flag as something belonging to a class of objects, such as stars, and do not think of it in connection with a country until around 12 years of age (Hess & Torney, 1967). You can help children develop a concept of the flag by

❑ asking the Veterans of Foreign Wars, American Legion, or other patriotic group to demonstrate the proper ways of handling and caring for the flag.

❑ arranging for the children to participate in displaying the flag.

❑ encouraging children to design flags for the classroom. They could design flags that mean time to come in, time to clean up, or story time, or a class flag can be designed, with the children deciding on design, color, and meaning.

❑ asking children where they see the flag. Have them construct a booklet called "I See the Flag," drawing pictures and stories of the flags they see in their neighborhood and community.

❑ reading stories of Betsy Ross and the history of the flag. A book for older children is *The Flag of the United States* by D. Jeffries.

Political Attitudes and the Pledge of Allegiance.   Written in 1892 by Francis Bellamy, associate editor of *The Youth's Companion* and vice president of the Society for Christian Socialists, the Pledge of Allegiance was created to celebrate the 400th anniversary of America's discovery. Since public school children first recited it in 1892, the question of whether or not students should be required to recite the pledge in school has been a continuing issue (Seefeldt, 1989).

From 1937 to 1943, there was constant litigation, with rulings both upholding and then rejecting the constitutionality of requiring students to salute the flag and recite the Pledge of Allegiance. In 1940, the United States Supreme Court ruled that the state could require all children to salute the flag. The Court reversed itself in 1943 and held that the flag salute required by state law violated the religious beliefs of Jehovah's Witnesses and could not be compelled.

This holding remains today, and no one, whether child or adult, may be compelled to salute the flag. Requiring children to recite the pledge, therefore, is a violation of fundamental constitutional rights and freedoms. Totalitarian countries impose political orthodoxy upon their citizens by mandating displays of allegiance; the United States does not.

Recital of the pledge may be opposed for other reasons as well. For most children, the ritual of the pledge is meaningless, done without thought. As such, it does not foster love of country or patriotic attitudes and values.

Just as Connell (1971) said they do with other political concepts, children construct their own knowledge of the pledge by putting things they know together with the unknown, in splendid capriciousness. Thus they recite, "one nation on the windowsill," "with liberty and jelly for all," and "I pledge allegiance to the flag, of the United States of American, and to the Publix [the name of a food store chain in the South] for which it stands."

Further, children have no clear idea of what the pledge is (Easton & Dennis, 1969). "It's like a song I guess," explains a 7-year-old. "No, I think it's a prayer," said another child. Asked what they think about when they say the pledge, a great many children confess, "I think about going out to play" or "about sitting down" (Seefeldt, 1989).

Because the pledge holds little meaning, reciting it is more an act of indoctrination than patriotism. "These rituals establish an emotional orientation toward country and flag even though an understanding of the meaning of the words and actions has not been developed. These seem to be indoctrinating acts that cure and reinforce feelings of loyalty and patriotism" (Hess & Torney, 1967, p. 124).

Ritual acts of indoctrination do not promote patriotism; rather, they have the opposite effect (Hess, 1968). In fact, frequent participation in patriotic rituals has been associated with lower scores on knowledge of civics and less support for democratic values (Torney, Oppenheim, & Farnen, 1975).

Rather than using the pledge as a form of nonsensical indoctrination, try introducing children to its meaning:

❑ Reserve saying the pledge for special days—Earth Day; Lincoln's, Washington's, or Martin Luther King's birthday; Flag Day or other holidays—so that children learn that the pledge has a special meaning and importance.

❑ Invite a scout troop to class to demonstrate their flag ceremony and recite the Pledge of Allegiance. The scouts might explain the meaning of their actions and tell what the flag means to them.

❑ Sing patriotic songs, or read poems or stories about the flag that may be more meaningful to young children. "This Land is Your Land," "Yankee Doodle," and "Flag of America" are examples of songs children can enjoy and can understand.

Patriotism.   Patriotism involves much more than daily recitation of the pledge, or even recitation of the pledge on special occasions. Children must first learn who they are and how they fit into their own immediate community. Only after children develop individually, in relation to family, school, neighborhood, and community, can they begin to gain an understanding of their country.

Explorations into the school community might be a first step. Children develop pride in being members of the school community. They share in caring for the school, keeping it clean as well as decorating its halls with artwork, or participating in events such as picnics or parties. Children can also observe the work of the many people who serve the school. The diversity of jobs, the variety of people, and the need for mutual cooperation can be observed by the children.

From this base of understanding how a community works, children can then take neighborhood field trips and explore the larger community. Here, too, they observe how people are interdependent and begin to see that they and their school are small parts of a larger world.

You can't take children on a field trip through the nation, but you can give children experiences that will enable them to begin to comprehend its size, magnificence, and diversity. Some of these experiences will necessarily be vicarious, but many can be concrete, with each one planned to help children develop knowledge of their country.

The pleasurable, sensory experience of eating is one way to acquaint children with their country. When children eat oranges from Florida, they can locate Florida on a map and learn something about why oranges grow in Florida and not in Chicago. Or they could eat avocados from California, peaches from Georgia, potatoes from Maine, cherries from Michigan, or pineapples from Hawaii. It is also fun for children to plant the seeds from the foods. Then they can make comparisons between distant places and their own community (Seefeldt, 1982).

The best resources are the children themselves. They can find out where they were born and where their parents and grandparents were born and lived. Primary children can locate these places on a map or they can bring photos or props illustrating life in different areas of the United States.

Value Participation

The ability to be responsible for oneself and to participate fully in the welfare of the group is an asset in any society, but in a democratic society, it is a requirement for citizenship. The disposition to work for the common good, to participate in joint efforts, begins early in life.

For young children under the age of 7 or 8, participation begins as they assume responsibility for themselves. Rooms for 3- and 4-year-olds are arranged not only to permit but to promote children taking responsibility for their own dressing, toileting, and washing. These very young children may begin to assume responsibility for others and the group by joining in small groups for brief discussions, to dictate thank-you notes or other letters, or to listen to stories and sing songs. With adult assistance, 3- and 4-year-olds can participate in setting tables, serving food, cleaning up after play and work, or caring for plants and animals that belong to the group.

Early on, children learn to participate in enabling children with special needs to function fully in the group. In one group of 4-year-olds, the children casually and regularly helped Kathy, the girl with spina bifida, by handing her her crutches, helping her on with her coat, carrying things for her, and waiting patiently for her as they played.

Over age 5 or 6, children participate in other types of group activities. They can plan together and divide up responsibilities. Sharing ideas, children in the primary grades are able to solve problems and make plans for their own learning. Children who are given responsibilities they can fulfill within the group are learning to participate in a democratic society. Experiences with voting and following the will of the majority give children opportunities to experience democracy in action. With very young children, everyone can have her or his own way. For example, children can vote to make either Jell-O or pudding, with each group being allowed to make what they choose. Or the class may be divided for games, those voting for Simon Says playing in one area of the room, and those for Lobby Loo in another area. After a number of experiences with voting, the entire class may follow the will of the majority.

Learning to live and participate within a group means setting rules and following them. Children should take part in establishing rules in the class. They can contribute to the rules for woodworking, block building, use of the bathrooms and water tables, and so forth. Other rules are made for them. All must participate in a fire drill, and, because there is little opportunity for them to contribute to the rules of the drill, they can use this occasion to discuss why it is important to follow certain rules, why rules are made, who makes them, and how they are made. Children can also become aware of other rules they must follow: the traffic laws, rules for riding the bus, and rules at home. These questions might be discussed: "What would happen if no one followed the rules?" "Do you think everyone should obey traffic rules?" "Why?"

Experiencing rules and discussing the purposes for them can help children realize that rules are made to protect them and others. Children should also realize that they have the responsibility to follow the rules, to make rules that are needed for living within a group, to change rules that no longer function to protect them and others, and to adjust the rules to fit changing situations.

Children's ideas should continually be moving toward conventional knowledge. Children should be moving from

- ❏ perceiving rules as coming from "on high."
- ❏ thinking of rules as unchanging.
- ❏ perceiving people as powerless before the law.
- ❏ being egocentric, self-centered, and indifferent to others.

They should be moving to

Children have opportunities to be responsible for their own classroom.

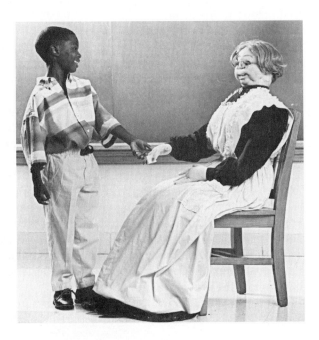

❑ knowing that rules and laws are established by people.

❑ realizing that rules and laws are always changing.

❑ understanding that they have control over their own lives.

❑ being empathetic, socially responsible, and considerate of others (Hickey, 1990).

The values of participating in a democratic society extend to the wider community as well as to the classroom. Even very young children can be introduced to the idea of serving others.

"I don't want to go," a 4-year old said when asked if he wanted to go visit the elders in a nearby nursing home. "But I'm going! You see," he said, "sometimes it's good to do things for other people. I don't like it, but I'm going because the old people like to see us little kids."

Serving others is a part of being a productive member of a society. Even though a primary developmental task of young children is to feel secure and safe, and to know that adults and their community will protect and serve them, young children can be introduced to the concept of serving others. Within the family, children are taught to care for siblings and to help their parents. Two-year-olds are able to fold diapers, entertain the baby, and help with setting the table. Three- and 4-year-olds assume more of their own care by helping their parents put their toys away—and even their laundry. They can also accompany their parents to visit elderly or ill neighbors, or to bring food.

Once in preschool, children are taught to serve their peers as well. Some learning occurs as children model their teachers who demonstrate how to care for other children, or they may be asked to do so directly: "Ask Cassidy to join you" or "Hold Bryan's hand while we're on the trip."

Children may also learn to serve the adults who care for them. "Help Ms. Jones (the aide) to set the tables" or "Ms. Jones needs two helpers to mix paints." "Who will sweep up the sawdust, wash the clay off the tables, or pick up the scraps on the floor?" teachers ask, adding, "We want to help Ms. Smith, the custodian, so she won't have as much work to do." Other times children may cook something for the lunchroom workers, or present a painting or thank you note to the director or principal of the school.

Knowledge of the community is necessary to expand children's serving of others in the broader community. Children can interview community workers to find out how they can help with their jobs. Fire fighters, police officers, and other community helpers are more than willing to involve children in serving the community. One fire fighter, during a visit to a first-grade class, told the children that they could help by asking their parents to check their smoke alarms each Halloween. By doing so they would help keep their family safe, the fire fighter explained, which would help fire fighters do their jobs. Several parents reported to the teacher how grateful they were for this instruction; when they checked their smoke detectors they found the batteries dead.

Once in the primary grades, children like the 4-year-old who articulated his good feelings from doing something for others can serve others in their community. Depending on the community, neighbors who need help, or the agencies and associations serving others, children can be involved in a number of ways. One primary group took on the task of picking up trash from an elderly neighbor's yard next to the school. Another group made name tags from old greeting cards for a community organization. Others have written get-well letters, read their favorite stories on tape to give to hospitalized children, and selected books to give to Ukranian children learning to speak English.

Five-year-olds in one community wrote joke books and distributed them to children in waiting rooms of nearby medical facilities and doctors' offices. Parents and children waiting to see the healthcare provider found the books relaxing, and the 5-year-old helpers learned that "the process of helping others gives the helper a lasting sense of pride and satisfaction" (Patchin, 1994, p. 21).

SUMMARY

Democratic attitudes and values are taught in the preschool-primary classroom. Children gain attitudes and values through modeling, reinforcement, and learning and have been taught through indoctrination, programs of value clarification, and value analysis.

Each preschool-primary classroom serves as a small laboratory of democracy in which children live the values of democracy. In a democratic classroom, teachers share control, children make choices, freedom of speech and thought are fostered, children's rights are respected and they are not overwhelmed by the power of others, a sense of community is built, and teachers serve as models of respect for others. Through their interactions with others within a democracy, children will also learn political values, especially those of patriotism, participating in a democracy, and learning to learn.

PROJECTS

1. Teaching attitudes and values means you must first understand your own belief system. As an individual, take some time to consciously scrutinize your own attitudes and values. Next, within your class, engage in a full and open discussion of values and attitudes. You might begin with one of the following topics:

    a. Competition is a part of our society, and children should be taught to compete as early as possible.

    b. Every child needs two parents to develop his or her own full potential.

    c. War toys should be banned from preschools.

    d. Boys should be encouraged to play with dolls.

2. Observe in a classroom. Record any observations of teachers modeling democratic values. What instances can you find of teachers sharing control with children, respecting each child, encouraging children to speak freely

and have opinions, and fostering children's willingness to participate in the workings of the group?

3. The fact that you are in college suggests that you have developed an attitude of learning to learn. How did you develop the attitude of learning to learn? Who did you model after? When do you think this attitude developed? Did any of your experiences in early childhood education foster this attitude?

RESOURCES

The best resources for teaching young children the attitudes and values congruent with those of our democratic society are

Greenberg, P. (1991). *Character development: Encouraging self-esteem & self-discipline in infants, toddlers, & two-year-olds.* Washington DC: National Association for the Education of Young Children.

Riley, S. S. (1984). *How to generate values in young children.* Washington, DC: National Association for the Education of Young Children.

Seefeldt, C. (1993). Teaching for freedom. In *Young Children, 48*(3), 4–10.

REFERENCES

Adrian, C. (1971). *Children and civic awareness.* Upper Saddle River, NJ: Merrill/Prentice Hall.

Allen, J., Freeman, P., & Osborne, S. (1989). Children's political knowledge and attitudes. *Young Children, 44*, 57–60.

Au, K. H., & Kawakami, A. J. (1991). Culture and ownership: Schooling of minority students. *Childhood Education, 67*, 280–292.

Banks, J. (1979). *Teaching strategies for the social studies: Inquiry, valuing and decision-making* (3rd ed.). New York: Longman.

Brophy, J. (1990). Teaching social studies for understanding and higher-order applications. *Elementary School Journal, 90*, 351–419.

California State Department of Education. (1987). *History-social science framework.* Sacramento, CA: Author.

Center for Civics Education (1994). *National Standards for civics education.* Calabasa, CA: Center for Civics Education.

Connell, R. (1971). *The child's construction of politics.* Melbourne, Australia: University Press.

Easton, D., & Dennis, J. (1969). *Children in the political system.* New York: McGraw-Hill.

Fromberg, D. (1995). *The full-day kindergarten program* (2nd ed.). New York: Teachers College Press.

Greenstein, F. (1968). The benevolent leaders. *Political Science Review, 50*, 934–943.

Hess, R. D. (1968). Political socialization in the school. *Harvard Educational Review, 38*, 528–536.

Hess, R. D., & Torney, J. V. (1967). *The development of political attitudes in children.* New York: Anchor Books-Doubleday.

Hickey, M. C. (1990). . . . and justice for all. *The Social Studies, 81*, 77–80.

Leming, J. (1985). Research on social studies curriculum and instruction: Interventions and outcomes in the social-moral domain. In W. Stanley (Ed.), *Review of research in social studies education: 1976–1985* (pp. 123–213). Washington, DC: National Council for the Social Studies.

National Commission on Social Studies in the Schools. (1989). *Charting a c ourse: Social studies for the 21st century.* New York: Author.

Parker, W., & Kaltsounis, T. (1986). Citizenship and law-related education. In F. Atwood (Ed.), *Elementary school social studies: Research a guide to practice.* (NCSS Bulletin No. 79, pp. 14–33). Washington, DC: National Council for the Social Studies.

Patchin, S. H. (1994). Community service for five-year-olds. *Young Children, 49*(2), 20–21.

Raths, J. (1962). Clarifying children's values. *The National Elementary Principal, 42,* 34–39.

Raths, J., Harmin, M., & Simon, S. (1978). *Values and teaching.* Upper Saddle River, NJ: Merrill/Prentice Hall.

Riley, S. S. (1984). *How to generate values in young children.* Washington, DC: National Association for the Education of Young Children.

Schug, M. C. (1987). *Teaching the social studies* Glenview, IL: Scott, Foresman.

Seefeldt, C. (1982). I pledge. *Childhood Education, 58*(5), 308–311.

Seefeldt, C. (1989). Perspectives on the pledge of allegiance. *Childhood Education, 65,* 131–133.

Taba, H., Durkin, M., Fraenkel, J., & McNaughton, A. (1971). *A teacher's handbook to elementary social studies* (2nd ed.). Reading, MA: Addison-Wesley.

Torney, J., Oppenheim, A. N., & Farnen, R. F. (1975). *Civic education in ten countries: An empirical study.* New York: Wiley.

Chapter 6

Thinking and Concept Formation

"Thinking is a way of learning."

Dewey, 1933, p. 15

After you read this chapter, you should be prepared to respond to the following questions:

❑ What processes are involved in thinking and how do teachers foster these?

❑ What is concept formation and why is it an important part of social studies?

❑ What are key concepts?

❑ How do teachers nurture concept formation?

W hat educational goal is more important than the development of children's thinking skills? The survival and growth of a democracy are possible only when its members are able to think, solve problems, and continue to learn.

At one time it was believed that critical thinking was possible only for older students or an exceptionally bright younger child. Today, however, we know that young children use all the same processes involved in adult thinking. They question and sense problems, locate information, see relationships between ideas and things, organize and summarize information, and reach conclusions.

Observe children at play and you will find that they can independently

question and sense problems. Children question constantly and, according to researchers, this questioning is the initial step in thinking. If the goal is to teach children to think, then teachers should encourage them to question and to identify a problem—one that is their own, not the teacher's.

locate and collect information. Children younger than age 4 locate and collect information in connection with their play. "I found a feather," squeals a delighted child. Another looks up into the tree and asks,

"Which bird lost the feather?" Back in the classroom they try to find a reference book on birds to identify the one that the feather came from.

see relationships between ideas and things and begin to generalize. "This paint is just like mud—it slips around." By 4 years of age children can relate an experience to something that has happened before or that will occur in the future. Over the age of 5, children begin to relate their ideas to the ideas of others by listening and through books and other media. From a simple generalization that mud is like paint, children increase their ability to draw generalizations about the things in their world, connecting one fact or concept to others.

organize information. Children begin to classify their world during infancy. They learn that some things are to suck, other things are not. Some are food, others are not. By the time children are toddlers, they use words as a means of categorizing their world.

infer, solve problems, and reach conclusions. The ability to infer, solve problems, and reach conclusions is one of the highest forms of thinking. Children four years old and younger solve problems daily. "Sit up on the seesaw. Then we can make it go up and down." By 5 years of age, problem solving extends beyond personal experiences into the classroom, school, and community.

ROLE OF THE TEACHER

Teachers can foster children's thinking in the preschool and primary classroom (Metz, 1995) by providing children with meaningful, integrated, and interesting experiences.

Planning Experiences

Planning experiences that foster children's thinking begins with identifying resources and arranging centers of interest. Effective teachers take the time and care to identify resources the families, community, and the children have to offer because these resources represent meaningful experiences.

Experiences that stem from children's here-and-now world promote thinking because they:

1. *are first-hand.*   The younger the child the greater the need for first-hand, sensory experiences. Through the primary grades, children must find plenty of opportunities to touch, taste, move about, take apart, and put together again. It is through these sensory experiences that children absorb information about the nature of their world, and develop perceptions of heavy/light, smooth/rough, soft/hard. Raw materials like paints, blocks, sand, and water provide children with the opportunity to solve problems, make decisions, and think.

The younger the child the greater the need for sensory experiences.

Dewey (1944) called for more "stuff" in schools and encouraged teachers to use raw materials so children could develop the ability to think. He believed that raw materials, such as wood, clay, and paints—without any predetermined end or goal for their use—push children into thinking. Given blocks, sand, water, and boxes, children must figure out what to do with the materials, how they will do it, and when they have achieved their goals. They will have to monitor their own thinking and doing. When children are failing to achieve a goal, they must decide whether to adjust their actions and change their plans. When they reach their goal, determined only by them, they experience the joy of achievement and the satisfaction that comes from thinking.

2. *involve others.*   Experiences to foster thinking must involve others. Throughout the day, while working in centers, arguing on the play yard, or discussing a story in the classroom, children are expected to interact freely—talking, discussing, arguing, and negotiating. Through these naturally occurring interchanges, children are challenged to adjust their egocentric thought, assimilating and accommodating different points of view. If they are to get along at all, children must consider the ideas, thinking, and wishes of others (Dyson, 1988). Through this type of informal give-and-take, children are forced to deal with the perspectives of others and build a foundation of understanding that there are different ways of looking at the world.

Vygotsky maintained that this type of social activity is the generator of thought. He believed that individual consciousness is built from outside through relations with others. "The mechanism of social behavior and the mechanism of consciousness are the same" (1986, p. ii). Whether working with others in centers or playing outside, children have an opportunity to build this social consciousness.

3. *are covered with language.*   Experiences make the need for language real and necessary. "Children not only speak about what they are doing, their speech and action are part of one and the same complex psychological function" (Vygotsky, 1986, p. 43). Through talking, arguing, discussing, listening, reading, and writing, children clarify and expand on their experiences.

Experiences and activities give children something to talk about. When children are given the freedom to talk, their informal conversations and interactions "contribute substantially to intellectual development in general, and literacy growth in particular" (Dyson, 1988, p. 535). Children converse informally as they work together on a puzzle, rotate the eggs in an incubator, or build with blocks. More formal conversations take place during group times. Teachers encourage children to tell how they completed a project, how they found their way to the

Working together with manipulatives gives children something to talk about.

nurse's office, or why they think the fish died. Plans for the day or the party next week may be discussed. As children talk, listen, and discuss shared experiences, they gain insights into one another's perceptions of the experiences, how others view the world.

Writing is also used to communicate. Invitations and thank-you notes may be written or dictated in regard to children's experiences. Notes can be written for another class, and letters might be dictated and sent to siblings, grandparents, and parents.

Experiences demand expression. Langer (1942) believed that humans were born with an urgent physiological need to express the meaning of their experiences in symbolic form—a need no other living creature has. As children think about their experiences, they develop images, feelings, and ideas about them. Expression of these can take any number of forms. Children may draw or paint a picture about their experience or describe it in dance or tell about it, or they may dictate or write about their ideas.

Literature and reference books are used to extend and expand firsthand experiences so children have a richer mental model of their world and the vocabulary to describe it (Snow, 1983). Stories may be read aloud several times a day. The entire range of literature, from poetry and folktales to the encyclopedia, serves to help children sum up and clarify their ideas gained through firsthand experiences.

FOSTERING THINKING PROCESSES

Setting the stage for thinking is necessary, but teachers also need to recognize and foster the processes involved in thinking: questioning and sensing problems, locating information, organizing information, interpreting, reaching conclusions, and making generalizations.

Questioning and Sensing Problems

Children are full of questions, at least when they are outside of school. The same type of questioning should abound in preschool–primary classrooms. This is not the old-fashioned kind of questioning where teachers asked children to recite the "right" answers or questioned them to "test" their knowledge. Rather, thinking begins when children themselves sense a problem and pose a question to try to understand reality.

It is not always easy to think of a question. Think back to your own experiences, perhaps after a professor ended a lecture by asking, "Are there any questions?" only to be met with silence. In this situation there were no questions because no one in the class had an idea, understanding, or knowledge of content. Without knowledge or understanding, there was nothing to question. Then too, suppose you had a question about the lecture, but felt uncomfortable asking it because everyone would know of your ignorance and might laugh at you.

Children, as well, must have some knowledge, information, or content to sense a problem or ask a question. In a classroom filled with materials for learning—sand, water, blocks—and a teacher who uses the child's here-and-now world in the broader community as a resource for learning, questions will arise. Rooms should be arranged with centers of interest, and materials within the centers juxtaposed to challenge students to ask "Why?" "How?" "What if?"

It is not enough to have a rich environment to stimulate questioning. A psychologically safe environment is also necessary. A child may have a question or sense a problem, but may not feel free to ask it. Children's questions must be accepted and not seen as frivolous or attempts to challenge authority. In classrooms in which children are respected and teachers themselves question and ponder, children feel safe and are free to question.

Locating Information

Young children learn about their world and themselves through observation; nearly every social studies activity includes observing. By encouraging children to use all their senses, you can strengthen their observation skills.

Field trips are especially useful in fostering observation skills. Whether a trip is within the school building, school yard, or immediate community, children

Is there something in the classroom for children to think about and question?

have opportunities to gather information through the senses. You might plan different types of field trips to make children aware of the information they can gain through the senses:

1. *A feeling trip.* Plan a trip to discover the different textures in the school building or schoolroom, or outside the school. Children can take large pieces of newsprint and blunt, chunky crayons with the paper removed to make "rub overs" of the textures they find. Placing the paper over the texture of a tree trunk, sidewalk, screen grating, or concrete block, children rub over the paper with the side of their crayon, actually feeling the differences between rough and smooth, and observe the texture appearing on the paper. Back in the classroom, children could discuss the textures they noted, observe other textures in the room with their hands and eyes, and try to incorporate roughness and smoothness in their drawings and paintings.

Children can use feeling-observation skills for collecting information on other field trips. You might ask children to feel the smoothness of the fire truck or the roughness of the truck's tires on a trip to the fire station or to observe textures of the environment on a trip to a farm. Trips within the school building, the immediate neighborhood, or the larger community become more meaningful when children are aware of the information they can obtain through the sense of touch.

2. *A smelling trip.* Children could take a trip to notice how useful the sense of smell is in gathering information. Smells of the office, cafeteria, gym, outdoors, street, or different stores could be observed and discussed. On the trip, children could be helped to distinguish between observations and inferences; "What do you smell?" "Now, what do you think that smell means?" "What are the cooks making?" "You think you smell bread, but can you be sure that it is unless you see it for yourself?" Children can complete their observations and test their inferences by seeing and tasting the bread.

The sense of smell could be used to make continual observations about, and gain information from, the environment. As they try foods from other cultures, children could be asked to smell the food before tasting it or to use smell to identify plant life in the neighborhood.

3. *A looking trip.* Children can take other trips to strengthen the sense of sight. Ask children to look for different colors, shapes, and sizes they notice within the school building or even a room of the building. Encourage them to describe specifically, naming things as tall, thin, wide, narrow, shiny, low, bright, or tiny, instead of the usual big or small.

4. *A hearing trip.* You could arrange a field trip just for listening. "What sounds do you hear in the room? In the hallway? In the cafeteria? In the gym? On the street? In the supermarket?" Take along a tape recorder to capture some of the sounds. Have the children listen for information by asking them to stand still, close their eyes, and name the things they hear. Back in the classroom, children can listen to the tape and recall the sounds they heard. They might draw pictures of the sounds they heard or tell about other things that make similar sounds. They could compile booklets of the sounds of home, school, cafeteria, or office.

Observation is a process that continues throughout the day. Teachers use every opportunity to help children locate information by observing. Look for ways to challenge children as they observe. Questions such as "What else do you see? Is it larger than . . . ? Smaller than . . . ? How does it feel?" and such statements as "Look at this part," "Find another one just like it," "It's green just like . . ." "Look at the dots on it," help children collect information through close observation of the environment.

You can provide additional activities to check children's observing ability and foster their observation skills. The following suggestions make good transition experiences between activities:

1. Three or four children face the class in a line. Ask the other children to observe them closely and then close their eyes. When eyes are closed, rearrange the children in the line. Then ask the other children to open their eyes and describe what has changed. As children show an increased ability to observe and describe changes, have the children in the line change or remove something they are wearing—eyeglasses, a pin, scarf, or headband—then ask the others to tell what is different.

2. Put a few objects on a tray. Ask the children to look closely, then close their eyes. While their eyes are closed, remove one of the objects or change positions of the objects on the tray. Then ask children to tell what is missing or what has changed.

3. Make sounds behind a screen, using a piece of cardboard or large box as the screen. Crumple some paper, whirl an egg beater, hit wood blocks, ring bells, and make other sounds, asking children to identify each. "What do you hear?" "What do you think made the sound?"

4. Cut up an apple, turnip, radish, pear, potato, or other white fruits and vegetables. Cut all in identical sizes and shapes, removing the outer skin or coloring. Ask children to taste the cubes and describe their observations. "What does it taste like?" "How does it feel?" Children can describe what they observe through taste, touch, and sight; then ask if they can guess what they are tasting and name the fruit or vegetable. With any tasting projects, children must be mature enough to be aware of the dangers of identifying unknown substances by tasting them. Without frightening them, caution children against ever trying to find out about some strange material by tasting it. Tell children to always ask an adult before tasting, smelling, or feeling something they do not know about.

Kindergarten and primary-age children will want to begin to locate information through references and resource materials. Locating information through the library and media does not take the place of direct observation but is used in addition to it. When children ask, "Where does the garbage go after it's in the truck?" "Why did the orange tree die?" "How does the telephone work?" you can reply, "I don't know, but let's find out." In this way, children can use prints, photographs, pamphlets, magazines, newspapers, maps, and other reference materials to collect information.

Organizing and Interpreting Information

Once children have collected information, they must organize it. The process of concept formation serves to organize information; children become aware of the need to classify, compare and contrast, summarize, and interpret the information, ideas, and questions that arise from their observations.

Classifying.   Classification, the process of arranging information into categories, is basic to concept formation. Classification is used to impose order on a collection of objects or events, to identify objects or events, and to show similarities and differences, as well as interrelationships, between them. Children classify without direction from adults. They sort, group, and regroup buttons, sticks, acorns, rocks, and toys as they play with them. Given any group of objects, one of the first things children begin doing is to sort them by placing them into groups and categories. Children's ability to classify follows a set pattern of developmental stages.

> *Stage One*—Children sort objects according to a single property that is perceptually obvious, such as color, size, or shape. Or they may classify according to some category they cannot communicate or are not really aware of themselves. They change their categories frequently, beginning again. When asked why she put all the buttons in this pile, a child might shrug and say, "I don't know," or, "All of those are like my mother's."

> *Stage Two*—True classification refers to abstracting a common property in a group of objects and finding the same property in other objects in that group. All of the red buttons, and so forth, are grouped together, and children can identify how they have classified the objects.

> *Stage Three*—Multiple classification refers to objects grouped on the basis of more than one common property. Multiple classification entails a recognition that any given object could belong to a number of different classes at the same time. For example, children will group all the large, red buttons together.

> *Stage Four*—All/some relationships appear at this level. *All/some* refer to children's being able to recognize a distinction among classes on the basis of a property that belongs to all members of the class, and one that belongs only to some members of a class. For instance, in a display of red squares, red triangles, and red circles, understanding all/some relationships would enable a child to recognize that all the shapes are red, but only some of them are squares, circles, or triangles.

> *Stage Five*—Class inclusion relationships refer to children's ability to form subclasses of objects or events while including all subclasses within a larger class. For instance, in a container of plastic chips, some

red and some blue, there is a subclass of red chips and one of blue,
both of which belong to the class of plastic chips.

By age 5, children can usually classify in terms of one characteristic; later, by
two. Classification by the function that is performed develops even later. Children's first experiences with classification should be completely exploratory in
nature, without adult interference. Later, you might ask them why they put all
the objects together; if there are any other ways they could think of to group the
objects; and to name the groups. Children can classify people at work or play,
tools used by workers, or happy or sad faces.

Comparing and Contrasting.   Comparing, the process of noting similarities
between things, and contrasting, noting differences, are used as children classify
and sort things into categories. Comparing and contrasting mean that children
observe details and features of things and mentally sort them into categories of
likenesses and differences. Comparing and contrasting are used to form concepts
and are considered basic to thinking. You can use any experience to help children
see likenesses and differences among objects or events. A kitten wandering onto
the playground can lead children to wonder how the kitten is like them and different from them. Determining likenesses is difficult for young children, but with
help, they can see the kitten eats, sleeps, and has two eyes and two ears. Children
can compare and contrast themselves, animals they raise, jobs their parents do,
pictures they see, books they read, movies they watch, or stores they visit.

Critical thinking might be part of comparing and contrasting. As children
see how things are alike and different, you could ask them to state their preferences for one or the other. When they make selections about the way they like to
sing a song, hear a story, or play a game, you might ask why they made the selection: "What parts of it do you like?" "How does it make you feel?" "Why do you
like it?" and "Why didn't you choose something else?"

Having collected, compared, classified, and contrasted information, children
need to summarize it. In connection with unit topics, lessons, or something of
interest they have experienced, children can summarize their findings by

- ❑ reporting to the class, either by speaking, writing, or dictating to the teacher, who then reports to the others.
- ❑ drawing, painting, or modeling something that describes their findings.
- ❑ acting out of skit, play, or story telling all about the topic.
- ❑ making charts, tables, records, or graphs of their experiences.

Graphing.   There are many ways of presenting information and conveying
ideas. Charts, graphs, sketches, cartoons, and pictures are useful in summarizing
and presenting information in simplified form. Graphs, one way of presenting
information in summary form, can be used by young children, especially if the
children construct them. They should be closely related to children's experiences
and based on their interests.

"Amy has the most brothers in her family; see—she has more boys on our family graph than anybody else," pointed out Cannala, aged 4, to the visitor, demonstrating that, although she was only 4 years old, she could interpret pictures in the form of a graph and gather useful information. Graphing—portraying information in pictorial form—is usually introduced to children in the fourth grade. However, when children graph their own experiences, they appear to grasp readily the relationships and information the graphs illustrate.

The skill of interpreting graphs and being able to present information in the form of a graph is becoming increasingly important in our technological society. A graph condenses numerous facts and bits of information into an easy-to-see, easy-to-read pictorial form and is an efficient way of communicating information.

Several different types of graphs can be introduced to young children. The picture graph, which uses symbols or pictures instead of bars or lines, is usually introduced first. The bar graph is introduced after children have become familiar with the picture graph. Line graphs, made by drawing lines at right angles to each other, may be too abstract for the youngest children, but could be introduced to primary children who have had many previous experiences with picture and bar graphs.

Children learn how to interpret graphs by making their own graphs to illustrate relationships they have experienced. You must introduce graphing with concrete materials and experiences, gradually progressing to abstractions.

> For example, two pupils working together may each take a few handfuls of colored cubes, counters or other suitable objects from a box. After counting up, say all of the yellow ones taken, it could be that Jack has five such cubes and Tom has two. These cubes are then placed vertically or horizontally so that each can see how many yellow ones were collected. (Lovell, 1971, p. 132)

Following discussion of this experience, the number of colored blocks each child collected can be represented using colored paper squares, the same color as the blocks, pasted to another paper. Later, any kind of information—types of leaves, number of children with brown eyes, types of bottle caps, sizes of acorns found, or number of pets—can be collected and recorded. Lovell cautions, "Much experience needs to be given pupils using either squares of paper or through drawing some other symbol, and there should be no hurry in moving the child on to the use of squared paper" (p. 158).

Robison and Spodek (1965) described a graphing experience with kindergarten children that takes children from the concrete to the abstract. Children, discussing family similarities and differences, lined up in front of a mark on the board that represented their family type and composition. To make the children conscious of the need to record information, the teacher asked them if they could stay in their lines for a week or more, so they could talk about family size. When the children protested that they would get sleepy, hungry, or tired, the teacher asked if they could use something else in the line instead of themselves. Having rejected the use of cats, who would run away, and pianos, which were too big and expensive, blocks were decided on and the children replaced themselves in the line with blocks. The next problem was to find a substitute for the blocks, which had to be put away. A flannel board, with felt squares representing the children, was the final abstraction.

Once children have had experiences making graphs with concrete objects, they can illustrate other experiences. Some experiences that can be illustrated graphically might arise spontaneously; you can structure others.

One class, newly integrated and riding buses for the first time, became nervous and anxious as the time neared to return home. Several began asking the teacher what bus they rode on, worrying that they would get on the wrong bus. The teacher quickly drew a graph on the board showing which children rode which bus. As the principal announced each bus, the teacher was able to point to the graph and read the names of the children riding that bus. The children readily saw the relationship illustrated by this graph and, the next day, constructed it on a bulletin board. They consulted it for several weeks, and the children were reassured that they would catch the right bus. Several of the children pointed out that bus 70 was an empty set, for none of the children in their room rode on that bus.

A kindergarten class visited a farm where the farmer told them that the pony they had ridden on was 13 hands high. Using her hand, she showed them

On a field trip children learned that the farmer measured her horse with her hands. Back in the classroom, children measured things with their hands.

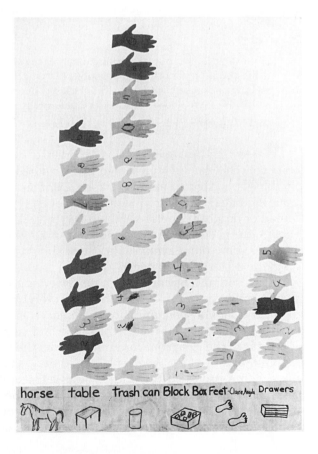

how ponies are measured. Returning to the classroom the teacher noted the children's interest in measuring objects in their room using their hands. As the children traveled around the room measuring everything in sight, the teacher began transferring their observations to a graph. Later, the graph was constructed by the entire class. Each child in the class, when asked, was able to point to the trash can, the tallest thing measured in the class, and feet, the shortest thing measured.

A graph illustrating how many states each child had visited was constructed in a first-grade classroom in a city in Florida, which is heavily populated with families from every state in the nation. The teacher suggested and structured this graph to initiate a discussion of where the children had lived and to acquaint them with the states of the nation.

You might suggest graphs showing the number of children who have a birthday during each month; the number of sunny, rainy, or cloudy days of the month; or the number of children with the same color hair. As the children play with sand or water, you could ask them to graph how many cups each of their containers holds. Children's weight and height also lend themselves to graphical representation.

"The pupil needs to be questioned about the information which can be obtained from the pictorial representation, especially that which is concerned with relationships between the variables, and the deductions, however simple, which can be made from the representation" (Lovell, 1971, p. 159). You might ask children to show which has the most, the least, more than, less than, or fewer than, and you can encourage them to discuss the representations of the graph.

Seeing Relationships and Beginning to Generalize

Generalizations are relationships between two ideas or two or more concepts usually expressed as declarative, highly abstract statements such as "the earth is constantly changing" or "we are all interdependent."

Because generalizations are highly abstract, it was once believed that teaching them in the preschool or primary classroom was inappropriate. Today it is recognized that generalizing, the process of connecting one idea with another, cannot be taught but can only be learned through experiences.

The child who said "mud and paint are the same, they both feel slippery," could not have done so without experiencing both paint and mud. The child who generalized that everyone has a home could not have done so without first observing the homes of rabbits, birds, and classmates. Both children could have collected information from various media and then reflected on, organized, and analyzed this information.

Skillful, reflective teachers can plan experiences that are presented as a continuous whole instead of isolated activities. A thread of meaning should run through them with one experience building upon another.

A group of 4-year-old children took a walking field trip around their school to collect fall leaves. After the trip the teacher asked the children to look through the leaves they collected and find three different types of leaves—maple, oak, and sweet gum. A graph of the three types of leaves was made by the children and the leaves were placed on a chart board. The teacher then read a book about trees. On a windy day the children again went outside to watch leaves fall from trees. They talked about how the leaves twirled and swirled as they fell. Back in the classroom, the children danced as falling leaves while the teacher played the piano, matching the music to their motions. Throughout the experiences, the teacher took photographs which, when organized on a wall chart and in a photo album, helped children reflect on their experiences and reach generalizations about trees and leaves.

A first-grade group decided to study animals, beginning with cats. They first observed their own cats and wrote stories about them. The children sorted and classified pictures of cats roaming freely in the world, and those in zoos and homes. Next the class visited a veterinarian who described how cats and dogs grow, showed them pictures, and let them see the skeleton of a cat. After this experience, one group of children decided to study bones and another continued to expand their knowledge of cats by consulting books and other media. Both groups wrote stories, painted, and drew pictures. To culminate the experience, the groups presented their findings to each other. These experiences, presented as a continuous whole, gave the children the opportunity to develop conceptual relationships and generalizations between and among concepts from biology, mathematics, language, and science.

Planning continuity in field trips is another way teachers can foster children's ability to reach generalizations. First field trips for 3-, 4-, and 5-year-old children who are just beginning to master relationships within their immediate environment should be walking field trips in or around the school. Taking children away from their familiar environment may confuse them rather than clarify their thinking and enable them to make associations. By the primary grades, however, children have gained sufficient knowledge of their world, as well as the necessary cognitive maturity, to recall past experiences and relate these to the new.

To be able to generalize, children must first have a solid understanding of the concepts to which the trips are related. Thus, some field trips and experiences should be repeated to give children the opportunity to grasp and understand the concepts embedded in the trip or experience.

Thoughtful questions and comments by teachers aid children in seeing associations. For instance, the teacher who had the children classify leaves might have asked them "What other leaves have points like this one?" or "How are these alike and how are they different?" During the study of cats, the teacher asked questions such as "Can you give another example of that?" "How is this cat like the one in the zoo?" "Where else did you see this?"

Interpreting, Reflecting, and Reaching Conclusions

When you ask children about the meaning of an experience, you are asking them to interpret. Children can discuss their experiences with others, sharing their ideas and perceptions of some event: Following a field trip, a visit from a police officer, or the experience of sitting on the fire truck, children can tell each other how they felt, the part that frightened them, and generally give their interpreta-tions of the event. When all children are encouraged to contribute, either for-mally or in spontaneous discussions, they begin to see how each person brings a different perspective to the same idea or experience. Through vicarious experi-ences, children can also use the skill of interpreting—telling about their impres-sions of a picture or photograph; dancing and moving to a record; drawing, painting, or illustrating in some other way their interpretation of a book or movie.

Real problems that need solving also require children's interpretations. Chil-dren must observe all the information present in the situation, understand the meaning of the events, and interpret these events to come up with a solution. In these kinds of situations, Dewey's (1933) requirement for thinking—seeing some-thing ahead instead of something behind—is present.

You can use any problem that presents itself for children to interpret:

❑ Why are these blocks left out? How can we arrange things so it won't happen again?

❑ Why have the plants died? How can we find out, and what can we do about it?

❑ The bathroom toilet is always stopped up and overflows. The janitor said it's because of all of the paper towels in the toilet. What should we do?

❑ Too many children want to paint at the easel at the same time. How can we solve the problem?

❑ How many different ways can you use these materials?

You can focus children's attention on the problem to be solved by asking, "Why did it happen?" "How can we keep it from happening again?" "Where did it go?" "What should we do?" These questions might help children predict, sug-gest hypotheses, and evaluate their interpretations to solve the problem.

An experience is not complete unless children reflect on that experience and think about it. Young children are generally not as attuned to their own cognitive processes as older children are. Adults can help children to think about their own thinking. During the preschool-primary grades, children can be introduced to the idea that at times they will be confused and not have clear ideas, but by thinking about things, they can reach a better sense of what to think and do.

The process of thinking about thinking might begin by helping children dis-tinguish between understanding and not understanding things. Teachers help children to think about their thinking in other ways. By organizing their ideas through graphing, classifying, or sorting materials into categories, children will be thinking about their own thinking. Other opportunities to reflect and think about their own thinking are formally planned. Teachers can

❑ ask children to stop working on a problem or project, to pull away and think again about what they want to accomplish, what they have done so far to achieve this goal, and what they still have to do.

❑ help children organize their ideas. Either group or individual activities enable children to do so. They many dictate or write a story, create a book or chart, or write a poem. Journal writing, keeping a diary, or writing "My History in First Grade" are other ways for children to organize their ideas.

❑ have children present their ideas to others. They might describe and discuss how they completed their project, found a solution to some problem, or put on a play. One kindergarten class became intrigued with different bears in the stories they had enjoyed. Comparing the bears in *Winnie the Pooh* by A. A. Milne, *The Three Bears,* and *Little Bear* by Else Holmeluna Minarik, the children put on plays about the different bears. One group created a display for the room of stuffed bears and books about bears, and still others made a bulletin board and mural illustrating what they had learned about bears.

CONCEPT FORMATION

Good teaching invariably concerns itself with conceptual understanding, for concepts are the ingredients for thinking. In Jean Auel's *Clan of the Cave Bear* (1980), the members of the clan had no word or gesture to represent tree. With brains limited to memorization only, the clan members had to name and think about each kind of tree separately. They were unable to conceptualize or categorize

Holding show and tell after work time permits children to describe their accomplishments.

trees into a singular concept or idea. Thus they were limited in their ability to think and to solve problems.

With the ability to group things into categories or to think in terms of concepts, we are freed from focusing on each isolated fact. When children have an idea or concept, they have knowledge of how facts and pieces of information are related and interrelated. They understand something and because they've organized the information into a concept, it holds meaning to them.

Memorizing a lot of facts as isolated bits of data is without meaning. With enough drill and practice and perhaps a lot of reinforcement, children can memorize a great number of facts. Unfortunately, children who are taught social studies facts by rote are rather like parrots who have been taught to recite. Neither parrot nor child has any idea or concept of what has been memorized. "A teacher who tries to do this usually accomplishes nothing by empty verbalism, a parrot-like repetition of words by the child, simulating a knowledge of the corresponding concepts but actually covering up a vacuum" (Vygotsky, 1986).

Teaching for concept formation leads to more learning, as learning concepts is never complete. This incompleteness leads children and learners of any age to continue to want to learn still more in an attempt to complete their understanding. Hence, unlike a compilation of isolated facts, a store of concepts motivates a child to continue to learn more (Prawatt, 1989).

Not only do concepts foster learning, they make it easier. Concepts are like mental filing cabinets. Children can use concepts to organize and categorize their experiences into meaningful wholes. Even the youngest children begin to understand the world by sorting the things they see, smell, taste, and hear into categories. Infants learn broad categories first—things to suck on that produce food, things to suck that give no food; things that are painful, those that are pleasurable; faces that are familiar, those that are not.

Toddlers build broader categories of concepts. For example, they first construct the idea of things that are dogs and not dogs. As they experience dogs and have the names of different dogs labeled for them, they begin to construct an idea.

Thus the social studies is organized around concepts key to each process and discipline content area. Just as Dewey advised as long ago as 1916, the National Council for Social Studies today advocates organizing social studies around teaching concepts, not isolated facts. By organizing social studies around key concepts or ideas, conceptual themes, and units, children will be able to make sense of abstract ideas and facts, and begin the lifelong process of acquiring knowledge (NCSS, 1989).

Key Concepts

Meaningful and conducive to future learning, the concepts considered key in each social science discipline organize children's learning experiences. In *The Process of Education* (1960), Bruner pointed out that each subject, every discipline, has its own structure. This structure is identified through concepts that are key and that define the discipline. These key concepts or ideas are used by the

Children think and solve problems, categorizing the things in their world.

teacher to organize and direct their interactions with the children. When teachers think about and internalize concepts that are key to any social studies discipline, they then have a way to think about content, the way children understand this, and set about to organize the children's experiences in the school setting.

The key concepts that relate and connect isolated facts into a unified whole also enable teachers to organize a whole, unified, and integrated curriculum. When the focus is on big ideas, teachers are not able to teach isolated facts, but only the connection between facts. Thus the wholeness of the child, and of knowledge, is honored.

Long before Bruner wrote *The Process of Education* (1960), Lucy Sprague Mitchell demonstrated how teachers bring children and social studies together by organizing their interactions with children around key ideas from geography. Before she wrote *Young Geographers* (1934), the social studies curriculum was based on isolated facts that children memorized. Mitchell called this curriculum "Pops and Caps" because for children to memorize the names of the 48 states and their populations and capitals (pops and caps to some children) was considered a worthy achievement.

Decrying this sterile and meaningless curriculum, Mitchell, in *Young Geographers*, designed a continual, meaningful curriculum revolving around key concepts in geography. She matched the key ideas from the field of geography with the interest drives, orientation, and tools of children from infancy through adolescence. She observed how the infant, before walking and talking, attends to and experiences the qualities of things, and how the understanding of the relationship of self to not-self develops. The tools of the infant are the use of the senses and muscles in direct exploration; the content of geography is the direct experience of the immediate environment. Mitchell specified a continual geography curriculum for each stage of a child's life, ending with the 12-year-old who has adult interests and orientations to anything three dimensional, the use of a wide variety of tools, and the capacity for abstract thought.

Continuing today, the social science disciplines of history, geography, economics, global education, and others are organized around key concepts. This text is organized around the concepts considered key in each of the social science disciplines. It describes what is known of how children understand these, and it offers suggestions for expanding children's embryonic concepts into fully developed, complete, and accurate ideas. Using key concepts of any given discipline, teachers can nurture children's concept formation.

Concept Development

The process of learning concepts takes place from the moment of birth. Entering the world without a store of knowledge, infants cannot think because they have nothing to think about. They have not yet constructed any ideas or knowledge. Infants, however, are very efficient learners and at birth immediately begin their lifelong pursuit of constructing concepts.

Hearing, smelling, tasting, and seeing, infants start to organize and categorize their experiences, continually seeking out and responding to their environment. The initial instincts with which infants were born—seeing, grasping, sucking—become more complex, more coordinated, and, eventually, more purposeful. This process is called adaptation. Assimilation and accommodation are the processes that make adaptation possible (Lefrancois, 1992; Piaget, 1959).

Assimilation and Accommodation

Assimilation is the term Piaget gave to mean *taking in.* Assimilation is absorbing new material into an already-existing idea or schema. An infant sucks and has a sucking schema. Infants suck on nipples and get milk, but this same sucking gets no milk when used on finger, toes, or mother's hair; they have to accommodate, or change their sucking schema, to make it fit things that are not nipples. A child was given a whole orange for the first time and bit into it as she would an apple. She had an idea or construct of apples—whole fruits that were bitten into—but no construct of fruit that needed peeling. She was assimilating the orange into an already-existing pattern, idea, or schema for fruit. The next time she was given an orange, she peeled it, changing her pattern of thought to accommodate the new information gained through experience.

Adaptation

Assimilation and accommodation are not separate or independent, but take place at the same time. Piaget calls this interaction assimilation and accommodation, and adaptation. Through their interactions and experiences, children construct ways of thinking that are more effective in enabling them to deal with their environment. As they gain more experiences, they acquire more structures and thus can adapt to more and more complex situations.

Early Concepts

Every day, children spontaneously form and use concepts that they construct through the processes of assimilation and accommodation. These ideas, or ways of thinking about the world, develop without schooling, without any type of instruction. Piaget calls these spontaneous concepts (1959).

These first concepts are embryonic in nature. Children's early concepts "stand in the same relationship to true concepts as the embryo to the fully formed organism" (Vygotsky, 1986, p. 58). Everyday, spontaneous concepts are pseudo-concepts, often based on the way things look, or seem to be, rather than on scientific fact. Although inaccurate, incomplete, and vague, children's early concepts are sufficient to permit them to make simple classifications of things in their world. They recognize a man, but frequently cannot distinguish among different individuals belonging to the same class.

Children's incomplete concepts are full of misconceptions, which sometimes get them in trouble. A 4-year-old has a concept of car as something that has life and intent. A car, alive with headlights that are eyes that can see, will obviously stop upon seeing the child in the street. Children may see a toy or candy in the store that they desire and simply take it. They have no concept of purchasing, of exchanging money for goods.

As children mature, so do their concepts. Their ability to see, hear, and feel increases. They can attend to and perceive more and more of their environment, and gradually recall and remember the things they have seen, heard, felt, and tasted.

Nurturing Concept Formation

Concepts cannot be taught; they can only be constructed by each individual. Teachers can, however, nurture children's embryonic concepts by providing a rich environment and conditions that will foster the development of fully formed, accurate, and complete concepts of social studies. Such conditions of teaching must be matched to the readiness of each child.

The Problem of the Match

"The task of teaching a subject to a child at any particular age is one of representing the structure of that subject in terms of the child's way of viewing things" (Bruner, 1966, p. 33). This is the problem of the match—of matching what we want to teach the young child with the child's prior knowledge, ways of knowing, and abilities to learn.

In a way, matching teaching to the child is similar to the old concept of readiness, of waiting to instruct until the child is ready. Yet Bruner wrote that this concept of readiness isn't what he meant: "Readiness is a mischievous half-truth. It is a half-truth largely because it turns out that one teaches readiness or provides opportunities for its nurture, one does not simply wait for it" (1966, p. 76).

Vygotsky (1986) calls this teaching to the zone of proximal development. The problem is for the teacher to understand the zone of proximal development, which means to understand a child's current mental age and the level that individual reaches in solving problems with assistance. Vygotsky (1986) maintains that good teachers do not wait for this to develop but "march ahead of development and lead it" (p. 104). Instruction "must be aimed not so much at the ripe as at the ripening functions" (p. 104). Teachers must try to determine the lowest threshold at which instruction can begin, as well as the upper threshold, and then lead children to what they cannot yet do.

If this were easy to do, all children would be successful learners. Obviously, it is not. Even if teachers had all the time and assistance in the world to uncover each child's zone of proximal development and match instruction in every content area to it, they would have difficulties.

First, concepts are unique to each child, developed through personal experiences and constructed by each individual. No two people hold the same idea or concept of something. Ask a group of people to describe their concept of beauty, truth, or loyalty, and no two will have the same idea. Beauty is an abstract concept, but even concrete concepts, such as dog and cat, are individual to each child and influenced by experience, temperament, and environment.

Then too, children may have fairly accurate concepts but be unable to verbalize these. Children probably do have fairly accurate concepts of cooperation, family, and neighborhood—after all, they do cooperate and live in a family and neighborhood—but are unable to tell us about these concepts. On the other hand, children may tell us all about something, like space travel or gravity, and have no concept of it whatsoever.

Still, teachers must try to discern children's understanding of concepts. If they do not have this discernment, they cannot match their instruction or the experiences they plan to the maturation level of the child, and failure will result. Missing a child's level by offering some experience the child has already mastered, teachers can turn children off to schooling. Without some challenge, children are bored and find school a useless, meaningless activity. Conversely, the greatest failure results when teachers try to introduce children to some concept beyond their capabilities and understanding. Not only do children find this instruction meaningless, but they sense their failure to achieve and feel less able or willing to take the risks involved in learning something new. When the school reinforces this sense of failure through grouping or retention practices, children know they are failures and will try to distance themselves from the source of failure—the school—in the future.

By analyzing children's responses and behaviors, teachers will have a better understanding of children's existing concepts. This understanding permits them to better match content to children, bringing the social studies and young children together with meaning. (See Box 6.1.)

The Problem of the Match

Chapter 2 offers a number of suggestions you can use to gain a better understanding of a child and his cultural background. Additionally, you might try these techniques to uncover the child's level of concept learning.

Try to get children to tell you all they know about something. Talk with a child, or a small group of children, and ask

❑   What can you tell us about . . . ?

❑   What can you draw or write about . . . ?

❑   What can you do to show us about . . . ?

Get children to dig into their past experiences by asking them to give an example of what they are saying, draw an illustration of what they mean, or act out a "for instance."

Then too, you can observe children, asking yourself,

❑   What does the child do in this situation?

❑   How does she work with the materials confronting her?

❑   What does she choose to do and say in this instance?

❑   What did the child choose to do and say in a previous instance?

Ask children to think through their actions, guiding them with questions such as

❑   How did you get your answer?

❑   Why do you say that?

❑   Why do you suppose this is so?

❑   What do you think would happen if you did that?

Analyze the children's responses and your observations, asking yourself,

❑   Are the child's errors consistent?

❑   Is there a pattern to them?

❑   Are they logical?

Box 6.1
Uncovering children's concepts
From *Research: Children's Concepts* by H. F. Darrow, 1964, Washington, DC: Association for Childhood Education International.

Guidelines for Concept Formation

Another aid to matching social studies content and children's understanding is for teachers to recall the universal characteristics of children at a given age or stage. "Research on the intellectual development of the child highlights the fact that at each stage of development the child has a characteristic way of viewing the world and explaining it to himself" (Bruner, 1960, p. 33).

This is what the National Association for the Education of Young Children's (NAEYC) *Developmentally Appropriate Practices: Serving Children from Birth through Age 8 (DAP)* (Bredekamp, 1986) is all about. By identifying the characteristics of children at a given age, and describing the teaching practices that match them, this book insures instruction appropriate for children of a given age.

Guidelines for Appropriate Curriculum Content and Assessment in Programs Serving Children Ages 3 Through 8 (NAEYC, 1991) uses the broad parameters of stages in children's concept formation as a base for making decisions about appropriate curriculum content. At first, children are only *aware* of events, objects, people, or concepts. Next they *explore* these ideas, beginning the process of figuring out the components or attributes of events, objects, people, or concepts. *Inquiry* is the

---

Guidelines for Appropriate Curriculum Content and Assessment in Programs Serving Children Ages 3 Through 8

What children do	What teachers do
Awareness	
Experience	Create the environment
Acquire an interest	Provide opportunities by introducing new objects, events, people
Recognize broad parameters	Invite interest by posing problems or questions
Attend	Respond to child's interest or shared experience
Perceive	Show interest, enthusiasm
Exploration	
Observe	Facilitate
Explore materials	Support and enhance exploration
Collect information	Provide opportunities for active exploration
Discover	Extend play
Create	Ask open-ended questions, "What else could you do?"
Figure out components	Describe child's activities
Construct own understanding	Respect child's thinking and rule system
Create personal meaning	Allow for constructive error

Box 6.2
Model of learning and teaching

What children do	What teachers do
Inquiry	
Examine	Help children refine understanding
Investigate	Guide children, focus attention
Propose explanations	Ask more focused questions, "What else works like this? What happens if . . . ?"
Focus	Provide information when requested, "How do you spell . . . ?"
Compare own thinking with that of others	Help children make connections
Generalize	
Relate to prior learning	
Adjust to conventional rule systems	
Utilization	
Use the learning in many ways; learning becomes functional	Create vehicles for application.
	Help children apply to new situations
Represent learning in various ways	Provide meaningful situations to use learning
Apply to new situations	
Formulate new hypotheses and repeat cycle	

Box 6.2 *(continued)*
From "Position Statement: Guidelines for Appropriate Curriculum Content and Assessment in Programs Serving Children Ages 3 through 8" by National Association for the Education of Young Children, 1991, *Young Children, 46*(3), p. 36. Adapted by permission.

next process of developing understanding of commonalities across events, objects, people, or concepts, and *utilization* is the functional level of learning, at which children can apply or make use of their understanding (NAEYC, 1991). "To learn something new, children must become aware, explore, inquire, use and apply. This process occurs over time and reflects movement from learning that is informal and incidental, spontaneous, concrete-referenced, and governed by the child's own rules to learning that is more formal, refined, extended, enriched, more removed in time and space from concrete references and more reflective of conventional rule systems," (NAEYC, 1991, p. 36). The process continues over and over throughout life and learning.

SUMMARY

Organizing the social studies around the skills of thinking and concept formation is essential. Thinking, a continuous process, begins when the curriculum is organized around children's experiences with the world and their play. It is through play that children sense problems and begin to question. These questions and problems are then used by teachers to encourage children to locate information, organize data, interpret data, and reach conclusions.

Teaching for thinking is also teaching for concept formation. Teachers identifying key ideas or concepts from each of the social science disciplines then use these to organize children's learning experiences. Knowledge of each child's level of understanding of the concepts is necessary to plan experiences that will foster children's thinking and concept formation.

PROJECTS

1. Observe children at play. Note and record their questions, the problems they sense, and how the problems are solved. Which of the other processes involved in thinking—locating information, organizing data, inferring, generalizing, and reaching conclusions—are observed?

2. What concepts do children have of social studies concepts? Ask children to tell you what a family is, or to give a definition for brother or sister. Are children's concepts everyday, spontaneous concepts or adult-like? Report your findings to the class.

3. Take a concept, such as family, and design a lesson plan that would take children from awareness to complete utilization of the concept.

RESOURCES

Every early childhood teacher should read the original writings of both Piaget and Vygotsky.

Piaget, J. (1959). *The language and thought of the child.* London: Routledge and Kegan Paul.

Vygotsky, L. (1986). *Thought and language.* (Newly Revised). Cambridge: MIT Press.

In addition, *Scaffolding children's learning* (1995) by Laura E. Berk and Adam Winsler is a must, as is Sue Bredekamp and Teresa Rosegrant's *Reaching potentials: Appropriate curriculum and assessment for young children* (1992). Both of these resources are published by the National Association for the Education of Young Children, Washington, DC.

REFERENCES

Bredekamp, S. (Ed.). (1986). *Developmentally appropriate practices: Serving children from birth through age 8.* Washington, DC: National Association for the Education of Young Children.

Bruner, J. (1966). *Toward a theory of instruction.* Cambridge, MA: Harvard University Press.

Bruner, J. (1960). *The process of education.* Cambridge, MA: Harvard University Press.

Dewey, J. (1933). *How we think.* Boston: D.C. Heath.

Dewey, J. (1944). *Democracy and education.* New York: Free Press.

Dyson, A.H. (1988). The value of time off tasks: Young children's spontaneous talk and deliberate text. *Harvard Educational Review, 57,* 534–564.

Langer, S. (1942). *Philosophy in a new key.* Cambridge, MA: Harvard University Press.

Lefrancois, G.R. (1992). *Of children* (7th ed.). Belmont, CA: Wadsworth.

Lovell, K. (1971). *The growth of understanding in mathematics.* New York: Holt, Rinehart and Winston.

Metz, K.E. (1995). Reassessment of developmental constraints in children's science construction. *Review of Educational Research, 65,* 93–129.

Mitchell, L.S. (1934). *Young geographers.* New York: Bank Street College.

National Association for the Education of Young Children. (1991). *Position statement: Guidelines for appropriate curriculum content and assessment in programs serving children ages 3 through 8.* Washington, DC: Author.

National Council for the Social Studies. (1989). *Social studies for early childhood and elementary school children: Preparing for the 21st century.* Washington, DC: Author.

Piaget, J. (1959). *The language and thought of the child.* London: Routledge and Kegan Paul.

Prawat, R.S. (1989). Promoting access to knowledge. *Review of Educational Research, 59,* 1–43.

Robison, H., & Spodek, B. (1965). *New directions in the kindergarten.* New York: Teachers College Press.

Snow, C.E. (1983). Literacy and language: Relationships during the preschool years. *Harvard Educational Review, 53,* 165–189.

Vygotsky, L. (1986). *Thought and language.* (Newly Revised). Cambridge, MA: MIT Press.

PART THREE

The Content of the Social Studies

❑ **Chapter 7:** History
❑ **Chapter 8:** Geography
❑ **Chapter 9:** Economics
❑ **Chapter 10:** Multicultural Education
❑ **Chapter 11:** Current Events

Chapter 7

History

After you read this chapter, you should be prepared to respond to the following questions:

- ❑ What concepts are key to the study of history?
- ❑ What concepts of time do young children have? How can time concepts be taught?
- ❑ How are concepts of change introduced to young children?
- ❑ Can holiday celebrations introduce children to the concept that there is continuity to human life? How? What other ways are children introduced to the idea that life has continuity?
- ❑ How are children introduced to the past?
- ❑ What are the methods of the historian and how do children use these?

Who hasn't heard a child appeal for "just one more story about the olden days, when I was really, really little." Young children are highly interested in their past. The stories of what they did yesterday appeals as nothing else does. Dewey (1966) recognized children's interest in the study of history, writing "Teaching history is not difficult because the child's interest in the way people lived, and how and why they lived as they did, what kinds of houses they had, what kinds of clothing they wore, and how they did business, that interest is endless and ceaseless" (p. 12).

Children's interest alone would be sufficient rationale for including history in the early childhood curriculum, for research confirms that interest in a topic is a prerequisite for learning (Hidi, 1990). But history is important for other reasons as well. Dewey (1966) pointed out that knowledge of history is "essential to gain in power to recognize human connections, and to enrich and liberate more direct and personal contacts of life by furnishing that context background and outlook" (p. 258).

Today, there is renewed interest in the study of history because theoreticians believe that without knowledge of the past transmitted through a common national memory of the study of history, children would be unable to identify with their nation and assume their civic responsibility as adults (CSDE, 1987).

"Without history, a society shares no common memory of where it has been, of what its core values are, or what decisions of the past account for present circumstances. Without history, one cannot undertake any sensible inquiry into the political, social, or moral issues in society" (NCHS, 1995, p. 1).

KEY CONCEPTS

The study of history has been defined as a time-oriented study that refers to what we do know about the past. It deals with the concepts of change and the continuity of human life and includes knowledge gained from a critical and systematic investigation of the past.

Using this definition, the concepts of time, change, continuity of human life, the past, and the methods of the historian can be identified as appropriate to introduce to young children:

❑ *Time.* The study of history is time oriented. As children do experience themselves in time, the introduction of this concept can be appropriate for young children.

❑ *Change.* A value inherent in the teaching of history is that it helps children to accept the inevitability of change. The concept that change is constant and not to be feared can be taught to children.

❑ *The continuity of human life.* The human connections Dewey (1966) writes about might be thought of as the continuity in human life. That life has a continuity can be taught to children through their own experiences.

❑ *The past.* Children do experience the immediate past. They can discuss and record it. Children can also handle objects and records from the more distant past and gain an understanding of life before their time.

❑ *The methods of the historian.* The goal of the study of history is not to make children into historians, yet it can help children to utilize the methods of the historian in order to make their lives more meaningful, richer, and fuller. Children can be taught to recognize problems; to observe, analyze, and infer from the data; and, finally, to reach conclusions.

The national history standards, *History for Grades K-4* (NCHS, 1995) recognizes the complexity and abstractness of the concepts considered key to the study of history. Still, the authors of the standards believe that children, even in the earliest grades, can begin to build historical understandings and perspectives, and begin to think historically. When history is presented to them in ways that are appropriate to their development, young children can

❑ learn to differentiate time present, time past, and time long, long ago.

❑ find history of interest and deep meaning when it is centered around their own lives, their families, and community.

❑ appreciate history when its study is embedded in myths, stories, legends, and biographies.

❑ get a firsthand glimpse into the lives of people who lived long ago with records of the past, artifacts, letters, diaries, family records, and photograph albums.

❑ begin to use the methods of the historian, learning to question, study, and reach conclusions. (NCHS, 1995, p. 3)

TIME

> What notion of time has our Tommy got? As he flattens his small palms and nose on the bathroom window and gazes out dreamily at the terrace and the mulberry tree? Does yesterday exist for him save as something very distant, vague and separate as were, a little while ago, his own toes and feet? (McMillan, 1921, p. 235)

Research illustrates children's concepts of time and how these develop. According to the research, children do not have a sense of time as adults know it, but like Tommy, they do have an intuitive sense of time.

Development of Time Concepts

Limited to their perception of the succession and duration of time, and to their ability to sequence and organize daily experiences, children's intuitive ideas of

What notion of time do children have?

Sensori-Motor 0–2	Preoperational 2–6/7	Concrete 6/7–10
observes, follows routines by 2, aware of day/night attends to environment	ideas of time are personal and subjective measures time with arbitrary units by 5, some understanding of time units such as day recalls past, plans for future by 5, can sequence events of a day and use time words	utilizes clocks, watches, to tell time ready for instruction in time concepts conventional concepts will not develop until formal operational period at age 12+

Box 7.1
Time Concepts Develop

time are subjective. This subjectivity leads to errors. Five-year-olds know that waiting for 10 minutes will be harder than waiting for 5, but they also conclude that it takes less time for a fast-turning wheel to spin for 5 minutes than it does for a faucet to drip for the same amount of time (Acredo & Schmid, 1981).

Intuitive time is distinct from operational time. Operational time involves the understanding of relations of succession and duration and is based on analogous operations in logic, which may be either qualitative or quantitative (Piaget, 1946). It is not until children enter formal operations, around the beginning of adolescence, that they are able to master operational time.

Perhaps because temporal sequencing requires only qualitative comparisons, such as little versus large, children as young as age 4 or 5 are able to demonstrate some understanding of the ability to sequence events. Four- to 6-year-olds are able to order actions in sequence to achieve a goal; they know that events happen in order, and are able to sequence their day around cyclically organizing daily occurrences (French, 1989; French & Nelson, 1985; Vukelich & Thornton, 1990). Four-year-olds can accurately judge temporal order at above-chance level, and by age 5 are able to judge the backward order of daily activities and the forward order from multiple reference points within the day, and to evaluate the lengths of intervals separating daily activities. By about age 7, children can also judge the backward order of events from multiple reference points.

Temporal sequencing concepts—such as before and after, tomorrow and yesterday, or those that require only that children "position" two points in time— are learned more readily than quantitative temporal relations. To understand quantitative temporal relations, a child must realize that the interval between say 1:00 and 2:00 is the same as that between 2:00 and 3:00. Children who understand only the sequence may not fully appreciate that the intervals are equal. Parenthetically, this same problem with equal intervals characterizes a child's initial mistakes in utilizing linear distance (Forman & Kaden, 1987).

By the time children reach kindergarten, they use terms involved in telling time with a clock. Although they have not internalized the concept of duration of an interval, such as hour and minute, they understand that these terms do have meaning (Elkind, 1981). Springer (1952) described how children between the ages of 4 and 6 gain concepts of clock time. Children first begin to associate activities with the regular daily class schedule; then they associate this schedule with time by the clock. Next, concepts of hour, half hour, and quarter hour develop.

Five-year-olds begin to understand temporal units of time—such as day, date, and calendar time, formulated on the temporal or sequential order of events—and can orient themselves in time, associating time with an external event: "It is day, the sun is shining," or, "It is night, the stars are out." Understanding calendar time includes the ability to identify time concepts such as first, last, next, later, sooner, before, and after. By age 5, children can tell what day it is, and will use general terms such as *wintertime* before they will use the general terms *today, before,* or *in a few days* (Ames, 1946). Children are first able to respond to a time word; next, they can use the word themselves; finally, they can use the time word to answer a question correctly. At ages 6, 7, and 8, children can begin to use conventional methods to orient themselves in time, and then clocks, watches, and calendars start to have some meaning (Patriarca & Alleman, 1987).

From an extensive review of the literature, Dunfee (1970) suggests that young children are receptive to planned instruction in time. This instruction, however, is based on the cyclical, recurring, and sequential events of a child's day and life. Although it would be inappropriate to ask children to memorize the names of the days or months in order to tell time or learn operational time concepts, it is appropriate for adults to give children labels for these things and to make certain their life has a routine. By experiencing routines, measuring time and its passage with arbitrary measures, children will gain initial concepts of time.

Routines That Teach Time

"I don't know what time it is, but my daddy always comes to take me home after my nap," states a 3-year-old in a child-care center. Based on the research of Piaget, it seems desirable to help children in their development of time concepts based on the routines that the day brings. In a school for young children, routines, or predictable procedures, can help develop understandings of time as well as feelings of security.

Even though schedules in the preschool and primary classroom are flexible, there are regular routines. "After breakfast, we play outside." "Before our snack, we wash." "Nap follows lunch, and outdoor play follows your nap." Later, in the primary grades, the children can chart their own routines and take more responsibility for scheduling their day according to their own desires.

Many books are available that deal with the routines of the child's day. The Kinder Owl books, *Good Morning, Good Night,* and *Daddy is Home,* Ezra Jack

Keats's *The Snowy Day,* and McCloskey's *One Morning in Maine* are examples of books that might help young children to understand the regular, timed routines of the day.

In addition to structuring regular routines and reading stories to the children that deal with concepts of time, teachers should take every opportunity to convey ideas about time to the children. They should give children the correct time words to connect their experiences, such as "today," "this morning," "next," "a little later," "this afternoon," "yesterday," and "last week."

Measuring Time

Children will not be able to measure time conventionally until after age 8 or 9. Rather than asking children to measure time with a clock in the preschool and primary classrooms, you can structure experiences using arbitrary measures. Using arbitrary measures gives the children meaningful experiences with the concepts of duration, sequence of events, and temporal order, which will prepare them to tell time in the traditional way later. Give the children

❑ a stopwatch for them to use independently or with activities structured by the teacher. The children can use the stopwatch to see how long it takes them to put

Box 7.2
Experience with Time in the Integrated Curriculum

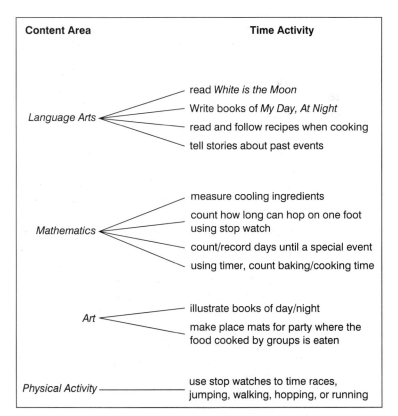

Content Area	Time Activity
Language Arts	read *White is the Moon*
	Write books of *My Day, At Night*
	read and follow recipes when cooking
	tell stories about past events
Mathematics	measure cooling ingredients
	count how long can hop on one foot using stop watch
	count/record days until a special event
	using timer, count baking/cooking time
Art	illustrate books of day/night
	make place mats for party where the food cooked by groups is eaten
Physical Activity	use stop watches to time races, jumping, walking, hopping, or running

away the blocks, hang up their coats, put five pegs in a pegboard, or hop across the room. You might help them record things such as how long they can bounce a ball, hop on one foot, or jump or run in place. Four-year-olds and younger children enjoy playing with the watch and using watches as props for their play.

❑ an hourglass to use to see if they can wash the tables, pick up all the art scraps, put the doll clothes away, or get ready to go home—all before the sand empties into the other half of the glass.

❑ a cooking timer that buzzes when the set time has ended. Children enjoy keeping track of the time with a cooking timer. They might use the timer to determine when the bread should be taken from the oven, when the cookies will be finished, or when the vegetables have simmered for 5 minutes. Or they might see if they can complete some task before the buzzer sounds.

❑ an old alarm clock to play with. They can turn the hands, take it apart, or set the alarm. These clocks, purchased at a local thrift shop or donated to the classroom, can give the children another opportunity to take an active part in measuring time.

The Passage of Time

Learning about history requires that children develop a sense of the passage of time. "What did you do today?" you can ask the 2-year-old, as you help him into his coat before going home. The teacher of primary children asks, "Do you remember what we did for the Halloween party?" "What things should we include in our Valentine's party?" Using the children's actual experiences, these questions can help them to develop a sense of the passage of time.

Kinds of questions that might help children recall the immediate past and foster an understanding of the passage of time include the following:

For the very young—"What did you like best about today?" "What did we have for lunch today?" "What did you like best about our walk in the rain?"

For the kindergarten child—"How many days has it been since Karl's birthday?" "What did we have for lunch yesterday?" "What did we do last week?" "What did you like best about kindergarten this week?"

For the primary child—"How many sunny, rainy, and snowy days did we have last month?" "How many days has it been since our Thanksgiving party?" "What can you do this year that you could not do last year?"

Nothing is more interesting to the young child than her or his own life. Help the child to understand the passage of time by capitalizing on this egocentrism. In the beginning of the year, you might start a history booklet for each child. Snapshots taken throughout the year, pieces of work the child has completed, paintings or stories dictated or written, records of weight and height, and some of the interesting things said can all be recorded in a history book. At the end of the year, the children will have individual life booklets that will give them a meaningful understanding of the passage of time.

CHANGE

The study of history, in many respects, is the study of change. Some changes have represented progress; others have not. Nevertheless, change is part of living, and adapting to change is crucial to living fully. Rather than fearing change, children can be taught to accept the inevitability of change and can learn ways to adapt to the changes they experience.

Surrounding the children with opportunities to experience change, the immediate environment offers many learning tools. From the school, neighborhood, nature study, and themselves, children can learn that (a) change is continuous and always present, (b) change affects their lives in different ways, and (c) change can be recorded, and these records can help others to understand the things that have changed.

In School

Whether in a child-care center, kindergarten, or primary classroom, things are constantly changing. The children may help rearrange the furniture for some special activity or for more efficient use of space. Painting the school classrooms or some other redecorating activity is a change that occurs often. Animals or plants in the classroom offer opportunities for the children to observe changes.

Changes also occur in the school building. Rooms are decorated for holidays, the building is readied for winter with plastic runners in the hallways, snow fences, or storm doors. Older primary children can study the changes that have occurred in the school building. They might be able to find pictures of the building before it was remodeled or discover records of what once stood where the school is located. How the school got its name, who it was named for and why, how many people have been principals, and the backgrounds of the teachers in the school are all possible topics for study.

Second or third graders might make a time line for their school that can help make history come alive (Tiene, 1986). A good time line might begin with the date the school was built, include its naming and dedication and any renovations or changes, and end with the present.

In the Neighborhood

Leaving the school building and yard helps the children to recognize the many changes in their immediate neighborhood: New neighbors move in, a house goes up, a building is torn down, the street is repaired, or a park is built. You can use the changes around the school to foster children's awareness of the continuous nature of change.

Older children may make a record of the history of the changes that have occurred in the neighborhood by (a) interviewing the residents to find out what changes have taken place, (b) finding records of the past in the city clerk's or newspaper office, or (c) reconstructing the past with models.

In Nature

Watching an apple tree change outside the window can provide a class with a year's activity involving the concept of change. In the fall, the children can collect and count the leaves and sort them according to size, color, and shape. They can gather apples, cut them open, eat them for a snack, and make applesauce. The class could make a booklet of the changes that occurred to the tree during the winter. The children might pose questions about the life of the tree during the winter: "Is it dead?" "Will it ever have leaves again?" "What will happen to it?" When the first buds appear in the spring, the class will conclude that the tree did not die.

This activity, although not an everyday one, can continue throughout the year as the teacher asks questions and focuses the children's attention on the tree. The outdoors yields still other changes; it may be possible for children to observe changes in caterpillars, tadpoles, or other living things.

In Children

"Accordingly, if you want to do some beginning historical work in the early grades, set children to uncovering their personal histories" (Elkind, 1981, p. 436). Children change—they grow, learn new skills, lose teeth, get their hair cut. Children's study of history can begin with the study of children themselves. Focusing on how children change, you might

❑ celebrate their birthdays. You can make a badge or sign for the birthday child to wear. Put a large age numeral on the badge. Let children decorate cookies or cupcakes using cream cheese frosting, raisins, nuts, or pieces of fruit. Suggest they use the same numbers of candles, fruit, or decorations as their years of age.

❑ have the children find out how much they weighed when they were born. Fill a bag with sand so that it weights about the same as their birth weight. Let the children weigh the sandbag on a bathroom scale. Holding a bag of 6 or 8 pounds of sand, children gain a concept of how small they were when they were born. Weigh the children, record their current weight, and compare it to the birth weight. This experience is not to measure exactly sand and birth weight, but to give children a concrete example of how they have changed since they were born.

❑ let the children taste a bit of strained baby food, perhaps some green beans; then let them taste whole, cooked green beans. Ask the children: "Why did you need the strained food when you were babies?" "What can you eat now that you couldn't eat when you were babies?" "How have you changed?"

Box 7.3
Change in the Integrated Curriculum

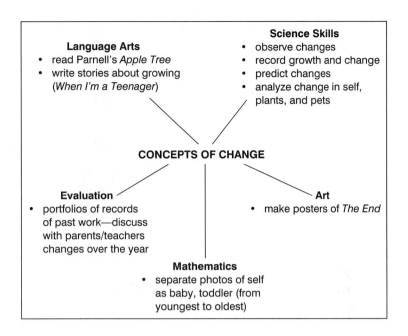

Language Arts
- read Parnell's *Apple Tree*
- write stories about growing
  (*When I'm a Teenager*)

Science Skills
- observe changes
- record growth and change
- predict changes
- analyze change in self,
  plants, and pets

CONCEPTS OF CHANGE

Evaluation
- portfolios of records
  of past work—discuss
  with parents/teachers
  changes over the year

Art
- make posters of *The End*

Mathematics
- separate photos of self
  as baby, toddler (from
  youngest to oldest)

❑ examine items of clothing they wore when they were smaller. Some children
may be able to bring diapers, baby shoes, sweaters, hats, or other items of
clothing they wore in the past. Encourage the children to compare these
items with similar articles of clothing they are wearing now.

❑ ask them to bring in snapshots that were taken of them in the past, when they
were infants, first began to walk, or learned to dress themselves. Comparing the
photographs with the way they look now, children can develop the understanding that they are still the same people, but they have changed. Ask them: "What
could you do when you were babies?" "What things couldn't you do?" "What will
you be able to do in the future when you get bigger?" "How will you change?"

Reading books to children can stimulate discussions about change. The
book *The Growing Story,* by Ruth Kraus motivates thinking. After reading the
book, you can ask children how they are like the boy in the story: "Have you ever
outgrown clothes?" "What did you do with them?"

The poem "The End" by A. A. Milne begins,

When I was one, I was just begun;
when I was two I was barely new,

and leads into making a mural on the theme of "Growing." On a large sheet of
wrapping paper, print the numerals 1, 2, 3, 4, and 5. Have the children draw pictures of something they could do at each age and paste these on the chart. Ask
the children how they have changed. Remind them that they are the same people, even though they, and the world about them, change.

The story of history begins with the children themselves.

Children will continue to change. First and second graders may think about the future. You can initiate a discussion of how they will change in the future, and what they will want, need, and be like when they are teenagers or adults. They could draw pictures of what they will look like when they are 14, 45, and 75. Or ask them to write or dictate a story about their life in the first, second, or third grade, with a parallel story that projects what their life will be like when they are in the fifth grade, high school, or college. Ask them: "What will you be learning?" "How will you learn it?" "What will you be like?"

You might take a field trip to another playground or school and let the children observe older children at work and play. Ask them to identify skills the older children are demonstrating that they cannot do. Ask them how they think they will learn the skill and what other skills they will learn in the future.

Children experience change as they adapt to modifications in daily routine. Routines always remain as stable points in the day, yet they are often changed by necessity, and these variations help children accept the inevitability of change. "Today our picnic is canceled because of the rain—what can we do instead?" "Ralph's grandmother was coming today, but she couldn't make it so she will come tomorrow." "Let's watch the custodian; we can have our juice later."

THE CONTINUITY OF HUMAN LIFE

Although life is constantly changing, there is a continuity to human experience. Exploring their family histories, children can gain a sense of this continuity. Celebrating holidays, as people have continually done, also gives children the feeling of connection among human experiences.

The Family

Each family has something unique from the past to give to its children. Margaret McMillan puts it this way:

> What is it to belong to an old family? Just this. It is belonging to people who are worth thinking about and being remembered for a long time, at least by their own children. At the bottom of this all, is a dim consciousness that life is not a trivial thing, not a mere scurrying across a stage and ending in utter darkness, but a play with some kind of relating and meaning to the acts. (McMillan, 1921, p. 235)

You can help parents see the value of talking to their children about the parents' own past. You may need to prepare the parents for the questions their children might be asking them about their past. Otherwise, some parents, faced with struggles and the problems of day-to-day living, might find the questions of their children rude or prying.

Intergenerational Contacts

"The continuity of all cultures depends on the living presence of at least three generations" (Mead, 1970, p. 3). In our culture it is not easy for three generations to share one another's living presence. Older people are separated from the young by physical and social distance. Rather than children and older persons developing informal relations in the family, church, or neighborhood, a process of separation of the ages is taking place. The connections between the young and old are broken. The natural ways the generations used to interact and relate are no longer available.

Recognizing that the ways the old and young used to establish continuity of life are no longer available, many are looking to intergenerational programs in school and nonschool settings to provide for the living presence of at least three generations. In these intergenerational programs, children, adults, and elders interact with one another, reestablishing the relationships of caring and continuity of life.

Today an estimated one hundred thousand older persons are involved as volunteers in schools working with young children. Programs are in day-care centers, nursery schools, grade and high schools, as well as the Head Start and Follow Through programs, libraries, parks, recreation centers, museums, 4-H Clubs, and many other community agencies. These programs, sponsored by pri-

Intergenerational contacts foster the idea that there is continuity to the human experience.

vate organizations and federal agencies, often have as their primary goal reestablishing linkages between young and old.

The programs build on the love and affection the young and old in our country have for one another. Children do have a feeling of affection for older persons, calling elders "friendly, good, rich, and wonderful" (Seefeldt & Warman, 1990). Children believed it would be fun to play checkers, cards, and other games with older persons. But at the same time, these children saw old people as sick, tired, sad, bossy, wrinkled, crippled, and ugly. Further, they indicated that they themselves would never grow old. They feared and dreaded their own eventual aging and death. It is important to note that the children in this study reported few contacts with older people either inside or outside the family unit.

Perhaps if these children had contact with older people who were healthy, happy, active, and fulfilled, they would not be able to classify the old as tired and sick, nor would they dread their own aging. If children could share the love of an older person and do things with elders that were of interest in their own schools, it might be more difficult for them to accept the stereotypical ideas of age and aging.

Older people also report enjoying the company of children. In a study by Seefeldt and Jantz (1982), older persons reported that children would be fun to do things with and would make good friends for older people. They thought children were very interested in learning new things and were "the hope of the future."

Intergenerational programs in the school can provide a way for children and elders to enjoy one another's company, to learn from one another, to share feelings of affection, and to provide children with a concrete example of life's continuity.

To initiate a program in your school, you might first locate organizations that sponsor intergenerational programs. The Retired Senior Volunteer Program, ACTION, and National School Volunteer Program are examples of programs that may offer services in your area. If these are not available, you might contact any of the following agencies to obtain materials on initiating an intergenerational program in your school:

Administration on Aging

American Association of Retired Persons/National Retired Teachers Association

National Council on Aging

Administration on Children, Youth and Families

You can invite older neighbors, people on the school staff, or children's grandparents or older relatives to visit the class frequently. Just letting your community—the churches, civic organizations, Senior Citizens, and other groups—know you would like elders to work with children in your school puts you in contact with volunteers.

Once the children and the older volunteers are comfortable with one another, the older persons might

❑ read stories to one or two of the children at a time, holding them close.
❑ take part in a birthday party for a child. The volunteers could tell the children how many candles their cakes would need or recall some of their early birthdays.
❑ play with the children, helping them informally with their activities.
❑ help the children prepare a special treat—making peanut butter or baking cookies.
❑ talk with the children about the olden days and the things they like to do with their own grandchildren.

For the children, the benefits of intergenerational contact are great. They sense the continuity of life, learn about the past, and have the attention of one more adult. But the rewards are just as important for elders (Sears & Bidlake, 1991).

> For the elderly residents, this is a journey into usefulness. Their visits to the center let them again be an active part of the younger community. They participate in whatever activity is planned for that day: creative art activities, story time, or music may be part of the visit. The lap that holds only a cover in the wheelchair now holds a child eager to hear a book being read. Holidays bring back fond memories for the residents through the children's special activities: Halloween costumes, valentine giving, and Christmas caroling. Plans are always in the making for other events such as dinners and parties between elders and children. (Mitchell & Schachel, 1979, p. 30)

Holiday Celebrations

Celebrating holidays helps children see the rich cultural heritage of their past and the continuity of life (Vygotsky, 1986). Holiday celebrations with young children can be pure fun and relaxation; at the same time, they can impart historical knowledge in an accurate and authentic manner. "Holidays can serve as occasions for projects that will acquaint pupils with social studies concepts and information . . . they are occasions for teaching students about important ideas and customs that co-exist with one another in our country and in the world" (NCSSS, 1989, p. 9).

On the other hand, when poorly planned or thought out, holiday celebrations are disasters, and only serve to perpetuate myths and stereotypes or to indoctrinate the children (NCSSS, 1989). When social studies revolves around the celebration of holidays or the focus is on a "tourist curriculum" (Derman-Sparks, 1989), then "children visit a culture by participating in a few activities and they go home to their regular classroom life which leads to stereotyping and trivializing a culture—all people do is dance, wear special clothes, and eat" (Derman-Sparks, 1989, p. 86).

Holiday celebrations, planned around the children's activities and experiences, can be meaningful and enjoyable when

❑ *the routines of the regular school day are preserved.* Any dramatic change in routine is upsetting to young children. Missing a nap or changing lunchtime might be disastrous for 4-year-olds. Eliminating work time for primary children is unnecessary; instead of reading from a basal text or doing the usual seatwork, primary children might research library books about the holidays or solve puzzles with holiday words. In preschool, work time might include special materials associated with the holiday—orange and black paper and paint for Halloween, or scrap papers in pink, red, and white, plus glitter, for Valentine's Day.

❑ *parents or other members of the community are involved to ensure sensitivity to the culture of the children.* Involving parents or members of the community in planning the holiday celebration assures, at least in part, that the culture and ethnic diversity of the children, their families, and the community will be respected. Some celebrations, such as Halloween, Valentine's Day, or others, may be offensive to some ethnic groups. Parents can also add meaning to the celebrations by telling stories of their celebrations in another country or the history and meaning of specific holidays.

❑ *the children are fully involved in planning the celebration.* Children grow as they assume responsibility for their own lives. Planning holiday celebrations is an ideal opportunity for them to assume this responsibility. Young children have simple wants and are pleased when they can plan their own activities. They usually plan for very simple, manageable celebrations. "Let's play Simon Says and make cupcakes," and "We'll sing 'Flag of America' and hear the record of 'Daniel Boone' again," were suggested as party activities in one kindergarten.

❑ *the activities are kept simple and low-keyed.* Celebration of major holidays such as Christmas, Halloween, and Valentine's Day may result in tears of frustration and fatigue if children are overexcited and stimulated. A simple snack, perhaps something the children have planned and prepared themselves, can be added to the usual milk or juice break. Games familiar to the children can be played with some variation added. Rather than playing Simon Says at Halloween, the children can play Witch Says; Doggie, Doggie, Who Has Your Bone might become Steven, Steven, Who Has Your Valentine for a Valentine's Day celebration.

❑ *a few key concepts are selected for development.* Focusing on only one or two of the main ideas of the holiday, you can plan relevant activities. A discussion of some of the key concepts inherent in major holidays follows.

Columbus Day

By concentrating on the ideas of courage, vision, discovery, and inquiry that characterize Columbus and other explorers, young children can commemorate Columbus Day with integrity (Ahern & Moir, 1986). Kindergarten children could explore their school, neighborhood, or community with the goal of finding something that is new to them. First and second graders might make a dream for their own lives or draw or write about a vision they have for their own future. They could also define the word *courage* and read about others who have used courage to make discoveries or do things for people.

Some teachers have celebrated the day by focusing on sailing ships, on different forms of water travel, or on floating and sinking. One teacher, who wanted to make the point that Columbus didn't discover America because one can't discover a place already inhabited by many peoples, brought items to the class that were given to Columbus by Native Americans. Over a number of weeks, the children tasted chocolate, peeled and cooked potatoes, and shelled cobs of popcorn, which were later popped and eaten. Another teacher focused the day around spices, asking children to find out where spices grow and why Columbus was searching for new spices. They then cooked apple slices with and without spices and determined which they liked the best.

Halloween

Halloween is truly a child's holiday—it gives children a number of opportunities to be in control. First, by dressing up as a witch, a monster, or some other scary character, children become in charge, bigger than life. Just the fact of seeing other children dressed as monsters, and being able to control their own fears, gives children a great deal of satisfaction. The best part of Halloween is being in control of adults who, fearful of a trick, will on demand give children a treat.

However, unable to understand that they and others who dress up stay the same person, even though changed in appearance, very young children may find the holiday frightening. For children under the age of 4, activities should be low-key, and depending on the group of children, you may not want to include masks. Since this is a time of pretending to be frightened, one teacher used Halloween to discuss fears. In this kindergarten, the children listed their fears, found stories that included the theme of being frightened, interviewed adults to find out what they were afraid of, and dictated a class report about the nature of fear.

Thanksgiving

Thanksgiving is a time for people to be together and share their thankfulness. Children could thank all of the people in the school or in their homes and community who help them. Thank-you notes or booklets might be appropriate. Perhaps the children could prepare cookies, roast some nuts, or make applesauce or some other gift to share with another class in the school or to give to others as a symbol of their thankfulness.

The typical celebration of Thanksgiving often includes a great many stereotypes about Native Americans. Derman-Sparks (1989) proposes that, rather than perpetuating the myths about native peoples, "Thanksgiving be a time for appreciating Native American peoples as they were and as they are, not as either the Pilgrims or their descendants might wish them to be" (p. 88). She suggests

❑ starting by asking children what they know about Native Americans.
❑ teaching something of the daily contemporary life of specific Native American groups.
❑ for children in the kindergarten and primary grades, comparing the differences between daily life and ceremonial activities, comparing the past with the present, and comparing folktales of different Native American peoples.

Hanukkah

A happy holiday in the Jewish religion, Hanukkah is also a time to gather with friends and family. Meaningful observances of the holiday can be planned by parents or experts. Children enjoy hearing the story of the Maccabees, lighting the menorah candles, playing with a dreidel, and eating potato pancakes as they relive the traditions of Jewish families. Because Hanukkah falls close to Christmas, teachers must be cautious about distorting its meaning. Hanukkah does not have the same significance to Judaism that Christmas has to Christianity (Gelb, 1987). Other more important Jewish holidays might be observed—Rosh Hashanah and Yom Kippur in the fall, and Passover in the spring.

Christmas

Christmas is often overdone, and loses any real significance. Celebrations in preschools or the primary grades often serve to reinforce the commercialism that has become deeply connected with North American observance of the holiday (Gelb, 1987). The celebration of Christmas in nonreligiously affiliated schools and centers can also contribute to the development of ethnocentrism in majority children and isolate those of minority faiths.

Celebrations of Christmas could be associated with charity and compassion and with peace on earth and good will toward others as the major themes. Gelb (1987) suggests

- ❑ limiting Christmas activities to 2 or 3 days.
- ❑ emphasizing the giving aspects of the holiday rather than the getting of presents.
- ❑ asking parents to communicate their beliefs to children.
- ❑ becoming aware of the important celebrations of other religions.
- ❑ maintaining professional judgment in the face of pressures of the holiday season.

Derman-Sparks (1989) suggests that the celebration of Christmas be incorporated with December holidays from several cultural groups. Depending on the culture of the children, you might celebrate Kwanzaa (an Afro-American holiday) or the winter solstice (a Native American tradition), as well as Hanukkah.

Patriotic Days

Lincoln's and Washington's birthdays might serve to stimulate concern for our nation. You can focus on ecological concepts and the things we must all do to protect our land. Rather than relating myths of Lincoln and Washington, you can use patriotic days to encourage children's interest in the flag or the Pledge of Allegiance, or you might take the class to visit some historical spot in their city dedicated to great people of the past.

The historic struggle for freedom, self-determination, justice, and peace is an appropriate theme for patriotic days. Children in the kindergarten and primary grades might listen to historically accurate stories about the American Revolution and the Civil War, or even something about the two world wars, to explore our nation's quest for freedom. They could also explore the ideas of freedom and justice within their own group, school, and neighborhood.

Valentine's Day

Valentine's Day lends itself to a study of the mail system. Children can send letters through the mail to a friend, their parents, other relatives, or neighbors. Pictures drawn by 4-year-olds and placed in envelopes addressed to themselves are received with wonder and great joy, and stimulate a great deal of discussion among the children, their parents, and teachers.

Teachers in the kindergarten or primary grades could read books about Benjamin Franklin's life before and during the study of the post office. Second graders could easily trace the history of the post office and speculate on how we would communicate without it.

Today, Valentine's Day is a day of love. In one school, Valentine's Day was just one of the days observed during the school's Month of Love celebration that took place throughout February. Children discussed the concept of love. Groups wrote stories about love and read what others had written about the subject. One class of second graders collected all the LOVE stamps they could find. Then in small groups, they designed their own LOVE stamps and forwarded these designs to the post office for consideration.

Best of all, however, were the songs of love the children learned. Each group within the school selected their favorite such song to present to the entire student body. During lunchtime, individual tables of children selected a favorite song of love, and then stood and sang it.

Other Holidays

Lesser known holidays can also receive attention in preschool and primary classrooms. Earth Day, a time to care for the earth, to clean the classroom, plant something in the playground, or do something for the community, can be a meaningful day for young children. United Nations Day, with its focus on what the United Nations is, how it functions, and what it represents, can be informative as well as enjoyable. Martin Luther King's birthday provides an excellent opportunity for children to become acquainted with the life of an important black leader and his contribution to our nation.

THE PAST

Children are intensely interested in both the immediate and the distant past. Helping children understand and explore the past does not mean you must teach them a true historic sense of time. In helping children to gain a concept of the past, Wann, Dorn, and Liddle stated that

> adults must shuttle back and forth with children from the present to the past as they react to the ever present urge to understand what has gone before. This dipping into the past without concern for a logical development of chronology from the past to the present does not violate basic principles of learning. To wait until they can handle true chronology is to deprive children of one of the most important learnings of early childhood. (1962, p. 58)

Even though the past is untouchable and far away, vicarious experiences with the past are possible for young children. Many resources are available to help young children understand the past.

People

Parents, grandparents, the school staff, and neighbors are all resources for helping children understand the past. You can invite these people to the school to tell the children about the "olden days." The grandmother who tells children how her grandmother taught her to crochet, and then shows the children how to crochet a simple chain, or the grandfather who tells his story of marching out of northern Korea at the end of the Korean war, give children a vicarious sense of the past.

Objects

Children can compare hand eggbeaters, wooden cookie cutters, rolling pins, and kettles from the past with the newer versions. Children are fascinated by the differences among beating an egg with an old-fashioned beater (without ball bearings), with a new hand eggbeater, and with an electric mixer.

Other antiques that cannot be handled by the children can still be shared in the classroom. Parents and friends often have interesting and valuable items from the past that they are willing to demonstrate to the class (Braun & Sabin, 1987).

Almost every community has some type of museum to preserve the traces of the past. The local library, fire station, or church may house relics that children can observe. If only large museums are available in the community, you might select one room or section for the children to visit. Children also enjoy visiting older homes and buildings that have been renovated and restored.

Children are interested in toys and models that depict things from the past. Cars, boats, and planes, modeled after those no longer in use, give the children

---

History becomes especially accessible and interesting to children when approached through stories, myths, legends, and biographies that capture children's imaginations and immerse them in times and cultures of the recent and long-ago past (National Center for History in the Schools, 1995).

Adler, D.A. (1996). *One yellow daffodil: A Hanukkah story*. New York: Harcourt Brace Jovanovich.
    Children invite a shop keeper, Morris, to celebrate Hanukkah with them in their home. Morris confronts his past and once again celebrates the traditions of his childhood.

Anno, M. (1983). *Anno's USA*. New York: Philomel.
    A wordless picture book illustrating historic sites and places meaningful to Anno.

Bullock, K. (1993). *She'll be comin' round the mountain*. New York: Simon and Schuster.
    The beloved American folk-song, fun to sing and read, informs children about the long ago in America.

Cherry, L. (1992). *A river runs wild*. San Diego, CA: Harcourt Brace Jovanovich.
    This environmental history is the true story of the Nashua River Valley in Massachusetts from the beginning of human life to the present.

Clymer, E. (1980). *A search for two bad mice*. New York: Macmillan.
    An American family visits Hill Top, the home of Beatrix Potter.

Cooney, B. (1988). *Island boy*. New York: Viking.
    A record of the life of Matthias Tibbets, this picture book sets its scene on a rugged island off the coast of Maine during the 19th century.

Coerr, E. (1986). *The Josefina story quilt*. New York: HarperCollins.
    A simple introduction to the westward expansion.

dePaola, T. (1988). *The legend of the Indian paintbrush*. New York: Putnam.
    A gorgeous retelling of a Native American folktale about the origin of Wyoming's state flower.

Box 7.4
History and Children's Literature

Fitz, J. (1973). *And then what happened, Paul Revere?* New York: Coward-McCann.
   The story of Paul Revere. Appropriate for primary children.

Fitz, J. (1980). *Where do you think you're going, Christopher Columbus?* New York: Putnam.
   The story of the voyage of Columbus for primary children.

Guback, G. (1994). *Luka's quilt.* New York: Greenwillow.
   A story of Luka's grandmother's beautiful, traditional Hawaiian quilt.

Hamilton, V., Dillon, L., & Dillon, D. (1995). *Her stories: African American folktales, and true tales*. New York: The Blue Sky Press.
   For children ages 6 and up. "Her story" is about real and imagined African American women.

Lyndon, K. R. (1989). *A birthday for Blue.* New York: Whiteman.
   A pioneer boy spends his seventh birthday traveling in a covered wagon along the Cumberland Road.

Myers, W. D. (1993). *Brown angels: An album of pictures and verse.* New York: HarperCollins.
   A book of photos of children in many different places and many different times, accompanied by beautiful poetry.

Sneve, F. D. H. (1994). *The Nez Perce: A first Americans book.* New York: Holliday.
   The social life, customs, and interactions with white culture of the Nez Perce tribe.

Steptoe, J. (1987). *Mufaro's beautiful daughters: An African tale.* New York: Lothrop.
   A traditional African folktale beautifully told.

Van Lann, N., & Desimini, L. (1995). *In a circle long ago.* New York: Apple Soup Books, Alfred A. Knopf.
   From Inuit stories to Pueblo legends, this read-aloud treasury of tales, poems, and songs will be enjoyed by children ages 3 and up.

Ziefert, H. (1986). *A new coat for Anna.* New York: Knopf.
   Finding materials to make a coat in post-World War II Europe.

Box 7.4 *(continued)*

an opportunity to make comparisons between the things they know and use today and things from the past. Scrapbooks of old-fashioned cars, trains, or toys might interest children of kindergarten age; primary children might classify models according to use or age and could make charts sequencing the models from the oldest to the newest.

With any objects from the past, you need to initiate discussion to help extend and clarify children's concepts: "Why do you think the train was made like this?" "Who do you think used this?" "How do you know it was used a long time ago?" "How is it just like the one we use today?"

People also record the past in writing. Well-chosen biographies and engaging accounts of the past—such as Rylant's *When I Was Young in the Mountains,* Little's *Children of Long Ago,* or Johnson's *Tell Me A Story, Mama* can bring a meaningful awareness of the past to even the youngest of children. Books used to promote awareness of the historic past should be factual and truthful (Danielson, 1991; James & Zarrillo, 1991). If myth or fictionalized accounts of the past are used to teach historic time, then children might learn to distrust teachers, who, after all, are supposed to be truthful (Brophy, 1990).

The drama recorded in time lines of children's own history is also enjoyed. One teacher posted large calendars in a hallway on which the events of each day, week, and month were recorded. The children frequently referred to these, recalling their immediate past and telling one another their interpretation of the days, weeks, and months that had passed. In the process of telling their own narrative of the past, these children developed the realization that history is the story of people, recorded by people like them, and that they were "right now making the future" (NCSSS, 1989, p. xi).

METHODS OF THE HISTORIAN

Right from the start children can begin developing the skills of the historian. To do so requires that children be engaged in active questioning and learning and not in the passive absorption of facts, names, and dates. Real historical understanding requires that students engage in historical reasoning, think about cause-effect relationships, analyze records of the past, and reach conclusions.

Throughout their early educational experiences, children can be encouraged to

❑ *identify the problem.* Children must be able to identify their own problems; at the least, they must perceive the problem as their own (Russell, 1956). When you determine the problem and present it to the children for solving, it

Play with objects introduces children to the past.

becomes an exercise for them, rather than a problem. Problems that arise spontaneously in the classroom, school, home, or immediate community are real to the children.

❏ *gather information.*   To solve a problem, children must gather information. They might examine traces of the past to solve historical problems. They can also examine library books, interview older people, visit museums, or locate relics from the past.

❏ *observe the data.*   Having gathered the necessary information, children need to observe carefully. You can foster children's skills in learning to observe as you ask them to describe what they see, feel, taste, touch, and hear throughout the day.

❏ *analyze the information.*   Once children have gathered and observed the information, they can analyze it and make inferences from it. Historians, having gathered data from the past, observe them and make inferences about life— what it was like, how people lived, what they did, and what they believed in.

❏ *draw conclusions.*   Just as historians do, children reach conclusions about the past based on the available data. They may reach conclusions that are incomplete because (a) the traces of the past may be incomplete, (b) there is no one to interpret their discoveries of the past, or (c) their inferences are less than accurate. A group of children, after a visit to Mt. Vernon, might conclude that people in those days were very short because the beds were so small. When encouraging problem-solving skills in children, you need not be as concerned about their reaching the correct conclusion as about their ability to use the historian's method of solving problems.

The methods of the historian are developed in children as they are taught to observe their world.

SUMMARY

Children do have a sense of the past and are interested in studying their personal history. From these beginnings, you can foster concepts of history through the regular activities of the preschool-primary classroom. Focusing on the key concepts of time, change, the continuity of life, the past, and the methods of the historian, children can begin to develop an understanding of history.

It is true, however, that children's experiences in history must be as concrete as possible and vitally relevant to the child. Learning about their own pasts, experiencing the passage of time, interacting with older volunteers, studying the immediate past (what did we do today), and using the methods of the historian—all must be based on children's activities and experiences.

PROJECTS

1. Start personal history books for children in the class. You might ask the children to bring baby pictures to include in their books, and compare them with current photographs. Other items you could include are a graph of each child's height and weight and a discussion on the things each likes or does not like to do. Leave several blank pages in the book to fill with the same information at the end of the year. Children can then discuss the changes that have occurred in themselves during the school year.

2. Invite older persons to the class to discuss the things they remember about life when they were young boys or girls. Ask each one to bring a childhood photograph or an object that they used as a child.

3. Begin your own family history book by starting a family tree tracing your heritage.

4. Have the class make a history book of their school. They can find out when the school was built, what was on the land before it was built, who the school was named for, and how many people have been principals of the school.

RESOURCES

These associations offer teachers a variety of resources for teaching history.

National Center for History in the Schools
University of California, Los Angeles
10880 Wilshire Blvd., Suite 761
Los Angeles, CA 90024-4108

National Council for History Education, Inc.
26915 Westwood Rd., Suite B-2
Westlake, OH 44145-4656

Some useful resources include:

Nearby History: Exploring the Past Around You (1983) by D. Kyvig and M. Marty, Nashville: American Association for State and Local History. This reference book describes how to find and use local articles, and visual sources for teaching history.

National Standards: History for Grades K-4 (1995) is an excellent resource for teachers of young children. Numerous highly useful suggestions and ideas for introducing history to young children are included. National Center for History in the Schools.

REFERENCES

Acredo, C., & Schmid, J. (1981). The understanding of relative speeds, distances, and durations of movement. *Developmental Psychology, 17,* 490–493.

Ahern, J. F., & Moir, H. (1986). Celebrating traditional holidays in the public schools: Books for basic values. *The Social Studies, 77,* 234–239.

Ames, L. (1946). The development of the sense of time in the young child. *Journal of Genetic Psychology, 18,* 97–125.

Braun, J. A., & Sabin, K. (1987). The class reunion: Celebrating elementary heritage. *The Social Studies, 77,* 156–158.

Brophy, J. (1990). Teaching social studies for understanding and higher-order applications. *The Elementary School Journal, 90,* 351–419.

California State Department of Education. (1987). *History-social science framework.* Sacramento: Author.

Danielson, K. E. (1991). Helping history come alive with literature. *The Social Studies, 80,* 65–70.

Derman-Sparks, L. (1989). *Anti-bias curriculum: Tools for empowering young children.* Washington, DC: National Association for the Education of Young Children.

Dewey, J. (1966). *Lectures on the philosophy of education.* New York: Reginald D. Archambault, Random House.

Dunfee, M. (1970). *Elementary social studies: A guide to current research.* Washington, DC: Association for Supervision and Curriculum Development.

Elkind, D. (1981). Child development and the social science curriculum of the elementary school. *Social Education, 45,* 435–437.

Forman, G., & Kaden, M. (1987). Research on science education for young children. In C. Seefeldt (Ed.), *The early childhood curriculum: A review of current research* (pp. 141–165). New York: Teachers College Press.

French, L. A. (1989). Young children's responses to "When" questions: Issues of directionality. *Child Development, 60,* 225–237.

French, L. A., & Nelson, K. (1985). Temporal knowledge expressed in preschoolers' description of familiar activities. *Papers and Reports on Child Language Development, 20,* 61–69.

Gelb, S. A. (1987). Christmas programming in schools: Unintended consequences. *Childhood Education, 64,* 9–19.

Hidi, S. (1990). Interest and its contribution as a mental resource for learning. *Review of Educational Research, 60,* 549–573.

James, M., & Zarrillo, J. (1991). Teaching history with children's literature. *The Social Studies, 80,* 153–160.

McMillan, M. (1921). *The nursery school.* London: Dent.

Mead, M. (1970). *Culture and commitment: A study of the generation gap.* New York: The American Museum of Natural History.

Mitchell, A., & Schachel, C. (1979). Journey in time: A foster grandparent program. *Young Children, 34,* 30–39.

National Center for History in the Schools. (1995). *National Standards: History for grades K-4.* Los Angeles, CA: Author.

National Commission on Social Studies in the Schools. (1989). *Charting a course: Social studies for the 21st century.* New York: Author.

Patriarca, L. A., & Alleman, J. (1987). Studying time: A cognitive approach. *The Social Studies, 77,* 273–277.

Piaget, J. (1946). The child's concept of space. In H. E. Gruber & J. J. Voneche (Eds.), *The essential Piaget* (pp. 576–645). London: Routledge & Kegan Paul.

Russell, D. (1956). *Children's thinking.* Waltham, MA: Blaisdell.

Sears, A., & Bidlake, G. (1991). The senior citizens tea: A connecting point for oral history in the elementary school. *The Social Studies, 82,* 133–136.

Seefeldt, C., & Jantz, R. K. (1982). Elderly persons' attitudes toward children. *Educational Gerontology, 8,* 433–494.

Seefeldt, C., & Warman, B. (1990). *Young and old together.* Washington, DC: National Association for the Education of Young Children.

Springer, D. (1952). The development and transformation of monetary meaning in the child. *American Sociological Review, 17,* 275–286.

Tiene, D. (1986). Making history come alive. *The Social Studies, 77,* 205–206.

Vukelich, R., & Thornton, S. J. (1990). Children's understanding of historical time: Implications for instruction. *Childhood Education, 66,* 22–25.

Vygotsky, L. (1986). *Thought and language.* Cambridge: MIT Press.

Wann, K., Dorn, M., & Liddle, E. (1962). *Fostering intellectual development in young children.* New York: Teachers College Press.

Chapter 8

Geography

Geography is for life in every sense of that expression: lifelong, life-sustaining, and life-enhancing.

GESP, 1994

After you read this chapter, you should be prepared to respond to the following questions:

- ❏ Can you give a definition of geography and describe the skills of the geographer that children can develop in the preschool/primary grades?
- ❏ What concepts are considered key to the study of geography?
- ❏ How do children develop concepts of direction and location and how do teachers foster these concepts?
- ❏ What mapping skills can young children develop?
- ❏ How would you best introduce children to concepts of relationships within places, spatial interactions, and regions?

Geography, the field of study that enables us to find answers to questions about the world around us—where things are and how and why they got there (GESP, 1994), begins with life itself, "unofficially at birth" (Mitchell, 1934, p. 21). This study isn't that of memorizing countries and their capitals, nor of locating them on a map. Children's study of geography is that of a social scientist. During the period of early childhood, children are geographers. Like geographers, they dig in the sand, pour water from one container to another, watch the rain fall on the school playground, and explore space around them, all in an attempt to find out about the nature of the world on which they live. Children, as social scientists, investigate the earth—they taste the grass, feel the differences in the surfaces of the earth under their feet, and, based on their explorations, begin to make connections between the bits of information they gather, discovering significant relationships.

Like geographers everywhere and at every age, children develop and use the four skills that "will allow the students to better understand the world around him or her, and will couple social studies to the continual process of the student's trying to determine just where he or she is in the world" (NCSSS, 1989, p. 44).

The national geography standards, *Geography for Life* (GESP, 1994), lists five skills that children are to begin developing during their preschool and primary years.

1. *Ask geographic questions.* Questioning comes naturally to young children. Toddlers, driven by their innate curiosity about the world in which they live, ask, "What's dis?" "What's dat?" By 2 years of age the "Why?" questions begin. Why questions extend to not just asking "Why?" but to asking why is it this way. "Why is the sky blue?" "Why did you do that?" "Why do I have to do this?" By the time children are in the primary grades, actual geographic questions are asked: "What caused the lake?" "What made this hill?" Later, speculation questions occur, i.e., "Does corn always grow in this field."

2. *Acquire geographic information.* Locating, collecting, and processing information from a variety of primary and secondary sources, including maps, comprises another set of skills. These skills begin early in life, perhaps at birth, as an infant begins observing by flailing its arms in space as if attempting to locate itself. Toddlers are able to collect information, process it, and make differentiations, i.e., "This is a chair, this is a sofa." In the preschool and primary grades children consult secondary sources, books, authorities, pictures, and maps as they build their geographic skills.

3. *Organize geographic information.* Children in the preschool and primary grades begin to develop the skills of organizing geographic information when they are preparing maps and displays, telling and writing stories, or constructing graphs.

4. *Analyze geographic information.* In the preschool and primary grades, children will learn to use maps to locate themselves in space, and to interpret graphs. Many kinds of text books, encyclopedias, and literature are used to study geographic relationships.

5. *Answer geographic questions.* Reaching conclusions, the final stage in the thinking/problem solving process, completes the geographic skills to be developed in the preschool and primary grades. Children can present their findings to the group, write a story, paint a mural, or construct a replica of a place to demonstrate how they draw conclusions and make generalizations.

KEY CONCEPTS

Planning to teach geography begins with a study of children's immediate physical environment and their ability and opportunity to observe, speculate about, analyze, and evaluate that environment. Both the environment and children's explorations within it are complex and complicated. To help teachers organize the possibilities for children's geographic learning within an environment, the Geography Education National Implementation Project (GENIP) (1987) and the national geography standards, *Geography for Life* (GESP, 1994), have identified major themes or key concepts. Believing that the study of geography is more than just place geography, the project designers call for integrating place geography with the study of human-environment relationships by structuring geographical studies around five main themes:

1. **The earth is the place in which we live.** It is covered with land and water and is a part of the solar system. The physical characteristics—landforms, water bodies, climate, soils, natural vegetation, and animal life—and the human ideas and actions that have shaped their character (GENIP, 1987) are included in the concept of place.

2. **Direction and location.** From birth, children start orienting themselves in space. Although they do not develop a complete sense of direction until after the age of 11 or 12, they can experience direction through their own movement. Being able to orient oneself in space also means being able to locate self in space. The ideas of distance and measurement are included in these concepts.

Maps are vital tools for locating self in space. Children begin developing mapping skills by making and using maps, rather than by reading them.

3. **Relationships within places.** Humans interact on the earth. People adapt and modify the natural environment in ways that reveal their cultural values. Human population density is spread unevenly across the earth. People live in different communities and interact with others by means of travel, communication, and the use of products and ideas that come from beyond their immediate environment.

4. **Spatial interactions.** There are patterns of movement of people, products, and information. People are scattered unevenly over the earth. How do they get from one place to another? What are the patterns of movement of people, products, and information (Fromboluti, 1991)?

5. **Regions.** Regions are convenient and manageable units on which to build knowledge of the world and study current events. Children live in a region; its geographic description dictates how they live.

THE EARTH IS THE PLACE IN WHICH WE LIVE

"All stones have been made by builders out of the earth and the earth is broken stone." "Mountains made themselves so we can ski." These explanations of the nature of the earth were given in reply to questions posed by Piaget (1965, p. 207), and they aptly demonstrate young children's thinking on the nature of the earth. Piaget has labeled this stage of thinking as *artificialism,* the idea that children view things on the earth as for their own use, made for purposes (usually theirs), and also either made by themselves or by others—the mountains made themselves,

Sensori-Motor 0–2	Preoperational 2–6/7	Concrete 6/7–10
attends to qualities of things: self, earth, sky	moving on earth	8+, still having difficulty with left and right
moves in space	orients self in a given space (e.g., in a room)	still confused about relating directions
	represents world in buildings and drawings	12+, understands cardinal directions
	draws rough maps, can find treasures with rough map	
	begins orientation to distance	

Box 8.1
Geography Skills

the builders made the stones. Piaget, in attempting to determine where children obtained this line of thought, ruled out religious education or educational experiences of any nature. He stated: "Artificialistic thought may simply be a matter of never having considered the question before. Or it could arise from the powers parents, who appear to be godlike to children, have over them, leading children to believe that powerful people, like their parents, could crush stone to make the earth" (1965, p. 207).

Keeping in mind young children's thinking, you can help children build more accurate concepts of the earth by providing them with concrete, direct experiences structured around their immediate environment. In planning earth-study experiences, you need to ask yourself: "What have these children learned through their own experiences about the way the world functions?" "What have they learned about the natural phenomena—the action of earth forces, how water runs down a hill, the effects of the growth of plants and animals?" You can use the answers to plan experiences for children based on an identified key concept of geography, that of knowledge of the earth (Seefeldt, 1995).

Environment in Which We Live

We are alive and we live on the earth. What a simple idea. That is, unless you are a child under 6 or 7 years of age who believes that everything that moves is alive, and that even some things that do not move—like poison, which could have the intention to kill you (Piaget, 1965)—are also alive. To young children, cars, boats, clouds, rivers, and all sorts of things that move have life and consciousness.

As children are experiencing their environment, you can ask questions to help them sort living things from nonliving things. Ask them whether the objects or materials they are playing with are living or not living. Based on their answers, you can ask other questions or offer suggestions. Try to extend children's thinking by asking: "Do you think it's alive?" "Why do you think it's living?" "How can you tell?" "Are you living?" "What other things do you know that are alive?" "What things are not alive?"

After a walk outside, you could set up a table, bulletin board, or chart sectioned into *Living Things* and *Nonliving Things.* Children could place objects, or pictures representing things they have seen on their walk, into the appropriate sections. Rocks, sand, and pictures of houses might be placed in the *Nonliving* section, and pieces of plants and trees, and pictures of animals and birds, in the *Living* section. You might also help children make booklets or scrapbooks of living and nonliving things.

Other experiences can foster the concept that we live on the surface of the earth. When playing outdoors, children can classify things that live on the earth. You could use this activity to initiate a discussion of living and nonliving things.

The purpose of these experiences with living and nonliving things is not to change children's thinking, but to increase their awareness of the world around them. Piaget (1965) demonstrated that artificialistic thought is a stage that cannot be influenced by teaching. Thus, teachers are not concerned with trying to move children to the next stage of thought; rather, they want to provide children with experiences that will be useful when they reach the next stage of thinking. Talking with children about living and nonliving things, you can gain the understanding of their thought processes necessary for planning and evaluating the teaching-learning process.

The earth is the place in which we and other animals live. Some animals live in water; others on land.

Box 8.2
Geography—The Integrative
Power of a Field Trip

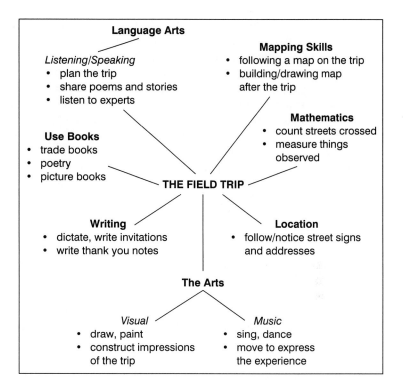

Land and Water

By experiencing their immediate environment, children can begin to make distinctions between the different surfaces covering their earth and the relationships between these surfaces and how they live. Children need time to play with, experiment with, and explore the nature of sand, water, and dirt—inside and outside—to learn the nature of the surfaces covering the earth. Digging in sand and dirt and playing with mud and water help children construct the physical knowledge of the earth on which they live that is so necessary for later formal thinking about the earth.

Within the school yard or immediate neighborhood, children can find different land surfaces. The playground may be grassy, paved with concrete or blacktop, or contain sand areas. Children can feel the different surfaces and classify them as hard, soft, rough, or smooth and discuss the purpose and use of each. Ask them: "Why is the street hard?" "What would happen if you fell on it?" "Have you ever fallen on the sidewalk?" "What happened?" "Ride your bike on the blacktop, on the grass, and then on the sand. Where is it easier to ride?" "Why?" Some of the surfaces may have been made by humans; others occur naturally. Kindergarten and primary-age children may be able to classify the surfaces.

Trips taken in the wider community allow children to observe different surfaces. One second-grade class in Boston took an overnight trip with their parents and their teacher, who had been with them since they entered school as 4- and 5-year-olds, to a ski resort to see, fall on, and actually experience mountains.

Even with field trips, children will not be able to actually experience all the earth's surfaces. "The schools' task is to furnish source materials" wrote Lucy Sprague Mitchell (1934, p. 31). Vicarious experiences with photographs, pictures, and reference or audiovisual materials may be used to help children develop an awareness of the different types of earth surfaces.

Depending on children's experiences with land and water, they could

❑ make a two-part mural, labeled *On Land, On Water,* and place pictures of things that live on land or in the water in the appropriate places.

❑ classify a group of pictures of land surfaces—hills, mountains, valleys, deserts—as *Land,* and another group of pictures of water surfaces—streams, waterfalls, lakes, oceans—as *Water.* Children could sort the two groups of pictures into appropriately labeled box lids.

❑ discuss and draw pictures of the kinds of activities that take place on land and in water, making a booklet or chart for the classroom. Swimming, fishing, and boating are classified as water activities; camping, playing ball, and gardening are classified as land activities.

A Nearly Round Sphere in a Solar System

How can young children, or any of us (except perhaps the astronauts), discover through personal experiences that the earth is round and a part of the solar system? These are two concepts that can only be taught through vicarious experiences. We do, in fact, learn about the roundness of the earth through photographs and books and by using globes.

Globes, however, are only appropriate for children over the ages of 6 or 7, and even then, when used in the primary classroom, they are only for the purpose of making children aware that the earth is round and can be represented as a sphere. The single value of using globes in primary classrooms is to provoke curiosity and a basic awareness of the shape of the earth.

Our Sun Is a Star (Martin, 1969) presents a simple yet accurate account of the earth as a part of the solar system. Primary children can read the book themselves, and 4- and 5-year-olds enjoy the beauty of the illustrations and the next when it is read to them.

Movement in Space

A complete and accurate understanding of the rotation of the earth on its axis and its revolution around the sun is not possible for young children. Yet, beginning experiences with the consequences of the earth's movement are possible and can form the foundation for later, more advanced understandings.

One effect of the earth's rotation is the appearance of night and day. Talk with the children about their day/night experiences. Ask if they can remember what they did at night after they went to sleep. Just as children believe all moving things are alive, they believe that dreams really happened. They will not believe an adult who tells them "It was just a dream." Nevertheless, discussing night dreams and day dreams and constructing murals or booklets of "Our Dreams" let children express their feelings about dreams.

You can encourage children to talk about what night looks like, how it feels, and how it differs from day. Ask them: "How is the sky at night different from the sky during the day?" Children could draw two different pictures, "My Room at Night" and "My Room by Day," or they could make night and day collages. Using two different pieces of construction paper—one black and one white—they can cut pictures from magazines and paste them on the appropriate piece of paper.

Day and night can also be represented in a circular format. Prepare construction paper circles by cutting a large half-circle out of black construction paper and another half-circle the same size out of white paper. Tape the two together to represent the two halves of our 24-hour day. Children can use white tempera to paint nighttime phenomena on the dark side, and colored tempera to draw daytime phenomena on the light side.

Playing with shadows can help children understand the earth's daily rotation. Some children may be able to figure out for themselves that the changes in a shadow's position, size, and shape are related to the time of day the shadow is made; other children are content to play. Some may want to know why there is no shadow at all at a particular time of day, or why the shadow is directly in front of the school building at one time of day, and off in another direction at another time. Other children may not relate the position of a shadow to the position of the sun at all. Children will absorb different depths of understanding from their experiences, and they need to be able to set their own pace with shadow play. You will want to respect children's individuality, for they are engaging in research as they explore and experiment with their shadows (Elementary Science Study, 1963).

You cannot plan just when children will be able to experiment with shadows but will have to take advantage of the weather conditions as they occur. You might want to explore shadows on sunny, cloudy, and windy days as well as at different times of the day and year. Children can

❑ find out what kinds of shadows they can make with their bodies.

❑ make shadows with different objects—umbrellas, boxes, or different kinds of toys.

❑ mark the shadows of a landmark—the school building, a tree, or the fence— at different times of the day.

❑ draw around shadows at different times of the day and compare the drawings.

❑ play shadow tag.

❑ play Simon Says with shadows. "Simon says: touch your shadow, stand with your shadow in front of you, hide in your shadow, step on someone's shadow." The children can take turns being leader.

Children's spontaneous play with shadows on a sunny day turned into an extensive exploration of the properties and magic of *l'ombra* (the shadow) in a child-care center in Reggio Emilia. Teachers used this natural response to the environment as the building block for a long-term investigation of shadows (New & Vecchi, 1995).

As children played with shadows, the teacher captured the event through photographs. The sharing of the photographs stimulated many more days of play with shadows. Children utilized a variety of objects to create shadow images, and the teacher followed their lead, providing other props, asking some questions, and suggesting experiments: "How many ways can you make a shadow of a pear?" (New & Vecchi, 1995).

After each experience, children were asked to draw their understanding of it or to answer the question, "How are shadows created?" with a drawing. Finally, the teacher added a provocation, placing a sticker "sun" on each child's paper and asking them to draw themselves and their shadow in relation to this sun.

Climate Conditions

Observing and recording climate conditions is the first step in understanding the revolution of the earth around the sun and the effects of this revolution on people. Many of these experiences will occur incidentally as children are working or playing; you can structure others.

You can use seasonal changes in weather to focus children's attention on the climate. Whether it is sunny and warm, cool and rainy, or cold and snowy, children can observe how weather changes throughout the year and draw conclusions about its effects on people's lives. Children can do the following:

1. Stand in the sun and then in the shade. What is different?
2. Stand in the wind and in a protected spot on the playground. What is different?
3. Discuss and examine different clothing worn in different weather conditions. Why are boots, hats, wool clothing, sun hats, snowsuits, or shorts worn?
4. Explore the nature of the wind. Go outside and blow soap bubbles: Give each child a paper cup halfway filled with soapy water, a straw to blow into the cup, or a pipe cleaner to swish through and make bubbles with.
5. Fly a kite.
6. Make pinwheels and take them outside to play with in the wind.
7. Take a walk in the wind. Walk with your back against it. How did it feel? Walk facing the wind; walk with the direction of the wind. Which way was it easier to walk?
8. Watch cloud formations and play "Do you see what I see?" Then go inside, make cloud pictures, and read a poem about clouds.
9. Wash some doll clothes or dress-up clothing. Dry these in the shade, sun, or wind. Where do they dry the quickest? Why?
10. Take a walk in a light rain. What happens to the surfaces of the playground in the rain?

11. Catch snowflakes on a piece of dark construction paper.

12. Read some poems about the weather. Act out some of these.

Kindergarten and primary children can begin long-term recording of weather conditions in the form of a time line with symbols for sunny, cloudy, cold, or warm days, and other seasonal weather conditions. Children can also make charts or booklets of "Things We Do in Winter," "Clothes We Wear in Summer," or "Food for Summer" to focus attention on how the seasons affect people and their activities.

DIRECTION AND LOCATION

Directionality is a projection of a sense of body sidedness (laterality) into objective space. As the child projects her body sidedness into space, she is constructing for herself, the coordinates of left-right, up-down, and front-back. Thus, through body movement, the child builds directional orientation" (Gerhardt, 1973, p. 23).

Young, active children learn directionality as they live and move. Human development takes place in space. By the time infants are a month or two old, they are exploring space around them by visual and tactile means. When children begin to walk, their investigations become more active and widespread. By 2 years of age, a child constructs what Piaget (1965) terms *sensori-motor space;* not the abstract representation of space an adult creates, but something bound up with the individual's sense of self and with motor activities (Sauvy & Simonne, 1974).

The young child's concept of space and directionality is developed from direct, active experiences moving through space. These initial concepts of space provide the basis for the subsequent formation of representational space. The child's discovery of space and of directionality within space will not be completed until the beginning of adolescence (Marzoff & DeLoache, 1994; Roberts & Aman, 1993).

Physically handicapped children have a special need to experience space. Children who cannot move for themselves still need to experience space, direction, and location. One teacher took the time to position children on tables in a circle to play games that other children experience. She believed these children, even though restricted to a table, needed to experience playing Looby Loo, Farmer in the Dell, and the other games that help children orient themselves in space. She also planned field trips into the community so the children could use maps, follow directions, and experience themselves in a larger space. Using two vans and a volunteer for each child, the group visited fast-food restaurants, doughnut shops, supermarkets, and the gas station—places visited by most children daily, but rarely available to the handicapped child.

Movement Exploration

A geography curriculum designed to help children orient themselves in space is a program of movement exploration. Movement exploration begins with the children becoming aware of their bodies and the things their bodies can do in space. It is based on elements first introduced by Laban in 1948. These elements are:

1. *Body Awareness*—the shape of the body in space, where the different body parts are, how the body moves and rests, the body's behavior when combined with other bodies, how the voice is a part of the body.

2. *Force and Time*—being limp, energetic, light, fluid, staccato, slow, or quick.

3. *Space*—where the body is in a room; the body's level: high (erect posture or in the air), middle (crawling or stooping), or low (on the floor); the body's direction (forward, backward, or sideways); body size (bigness or smallness); the body's path through space; and extensions of the body parts into space.

4. *Locomotion*—movement through space at various levels: lowest (wriggling, rolling, or scooting); middle (crawling, crouching, or using four limbs—ape walk); or highest (walking, running, skipping, galloping, sliding, leaping, hopping, and jumping).

5. *Weight*—relationship of body to the ground; ways to manage body weight in motion and in relation to others; body collapse; and body momentum.

6. *Working with Others*—collaborating with others to solve problems, develop trust, explore strength and sensitivity, and feel a sense of belonging.

7. *Isolations*—how individual body parts (head, shoulders, arms, hands, elbows, wrists, neck, back, upper torso, ribs, hips, legs, knees, ankles, feet) can move (swinging, jerking, twisting, shaking, lifting, tensing, relaxing, becoming fluid, pressing, gliding, floating, flicking, slashing, punching, and dabbing).

8. *Repetitions*—getting to know a movement and how it feels when repeated often; being able to repeat a shape or action. (Sullivan, 1982, pp. 3–4)

The teacher acts as a guide and offers children a challenge or a problem to solve. You might say: "Show how many different ways you can walk," "Make your body very tall; very small," or "How many different ways can you move across the room?" Children select their own level of participation and creativity as they respond. You can comment to help them analyze their movements and become aware of (a) their relationship to the physical environment; (b) their bodies and what they can do; and (c) the components of movement—speed, direction, and force.

To increase and clarify the concepts of directionality stemming from movement exploration, language-experience booklets or charts can be constructed. These can be called "I Can Move." They illustrate in writing and pictures the way children move: fast or slow; walk high, low, or sideways; with their hands touching the floor; on one or two feet; hop, skip, or slide; or move with someone else, and so forth.

Directional Terms

You can introduce games to help children develop concepts of up and down and other terms suggesting directionality. Ask a child to stand by any object in the room. Now ask another child to name a different object in the room. The first child must identify body position in relation to the named object; for example, in back of the desk, on the side of the workbench, in front of the window. Some kindergarten children can begin this game, but it is more appropriate for primary-age children. The more experienced children may be able to respond by saying, "The teacher's desk is on my right side," using directional terms.

Up and Down

To learn concepts of up and down, children can sing "The Noble Duke of York," acting it out as they sing and pretending to be mountain climbers, rain, snow, falling leaves, airplanes, kites, or floating dandelion seeds. Teachers can play other games to check children's growth in understanding directions by having individuals place a truck, doll, or block in positions that the teacher or another child suggests. You can say to a child: "Place Raggedy Ann on top; over; under; to the side of; behind; next to; or to the right of the sand table," using terms the children need to learn.

Left and Right

Concepts of left and right develop very gradually. A study in England revealed that even 8- and 9-year-old children could not accurately identify left and right in many cases. Learning the concept of left and right occurs as children move in space, grow, and mature. There is no place for a directed, highly structured program of teaching left and right. These concepts will develop with time and with many experiences of moving and exploring space (Roberts & Aman, 1993).

You can use the terms *left* and *right* incidentally, but always in connection with a real situation. You could ask the children to put the double blocks to the left of the cars when picking up blocks; to hold the bike with the left foot while reaching for something else; to park the wagon on the right; or to walk on the left side of the street on a field trip. Children can experience other left and right situations while playing Simon Says, Hokey Pokey, Looby Loo, or Follow the Leader.

There is no need to correct children when playing these games and learning left and right. The concept of left and right develops over time, and it is inappropriate to attempt to teach it directly. Nevertheless, you will want to introduce children to the concept of left and right and allow them opportunities to experience it.

Cardinal Directions

Children as old as 12 years of age do not appear to have an adequate grasp of cardinal directions. Lord (1941) demonstrated that children are not aware of cardinal directions until nearly reaching adulthood. Preston and Herman (1974) stated that "children in our present culture, with its abundant signs and guideposts, appear to have no pressing practical need to become direction conscious, and many of them, indeed, do not develop this awareness, yet the ability to orient oneself and to acquire a sense of direction is essential" (p. 424). To foster this ability, they suggested that all activities with cardinal directions be informal and used only as they apply to the actual experiences of young children.

One study by Howe (1969), however, demonstrated that direct teaching of cardinal directions to children in Grades 1, 2, and 3 was successful. Howe's teaching consisted of taking children outdoors around 8:45 a.m. to observe the position of the sun and telling the children that this was the eastern part of the sky. The same process, conducted from a new location, was repeated as weather conditions permitted. After the children mastered the concept that the sun was in that part of the sky called the east, Howe proceeded to the second step, asking children in what part of the sky the sun appeared in the morning.

Steps three and four were to help children acquire an association between the noon sun and the southern part of the sky. Leaving the school in advance of the usual 11:30 a.m. dismissal time, Howe established an association between south and east by asking the children where the sun had been in the morning. The fifth and sixth steps associated the later afternoon sun with the western part of the sky, and this direction, in turn, was associated with the others by reviewing where the sun was at noon and in the morning.

Howe next introduced a shadow stick, and more complex skills were developed. This apparatus was constructed of a square foot of board, with a 30-inch stick, not more than an inch wide, rising from the center of the board and perpendicular to it. The children took the shadow stick on field trips when they left the playground and used it to find the cardinal directions wherever they were.

Children learn directions as they experience themselves in space.

Even the youngest child can begin the lifelong practice of learning place vocabulary. Help children do this by identifying and naming for them

❑   places in their home, school, and community. ("This is the kitchen." "We play in the yard." "My school is on Ridgedale Way.")

❑   place names that will repeatedly occur in their lives. (They can locate community places: their home, their school, a hospital, the fire station, a park, a grocery store, all of which all are located in their city.

❑   their city, state, and nation.

Box 8.3
Learning about place
From "Place Geography" by B. A. Smith, 1990. *The Social Studies, 81*, pp. 221–226.

At the end of 10 weeks, Howe tested the children. Over 50% of the first graders could answer correctly all the questions pertaining to cardinal directions; 75% of the second and third graders were successful in answering all the questions. Howe concluded that young children, if taken outdoors, could be taught cardinal directions in relation to the sun, and that this teaching would later lead to the elimination of confusion over cardinal directions that many of us still have.

Relative Position

For developing concepts of relative position, second- or third-grade children can play a game called Who Is At My Side. Ask one child to stand before the group facing away from them. Ask another child to stand to the left or right of the first child. Give directions to the child standing on the side: "Stand in front of the child who is it; stand in back; stand facing; stand to the left." All the children can take turns with this game. This game is for second or third graders, not for kindergarten or younger children.

After children are familiar with the game, ask a group of three to stand in front of the class with their backs to the others. Ask the middle child to tell who is standing on the left or right. Then the other two children can each tell where the middle child is in relation to them.

Location

Concepts of location begin early in life. They develop from birth through age 14 months as infants explore and attend to the qualities of things in their environment, including their own bodies and visual and tactile senses. From age 14 months to age 3, children are able to distinguish between objects that are near and can be grasped and those farther away and to distinguish the space boundaries of their immediate environment, such as the bedroom or yard.

Initially, infants work out their own location and then go on to discern the whereabouts of other objects in their environment. With increasing visual skills and mobility, children expand their space boundaries. The greater the children's opportunities to roam and move about, the greater their ability to keep track of position and location (Stiles–Davis, Kritchevsky, & Bellugi, 1988).

By the early preschool years, there is an understanding of the spatial relationships between objects. Children express these concepts as they build with blocks, play with sand and water, and construct with other materials. Throughout the preschool and primary grades, their concepts of location continue to develop and are refined through children's direct exploration of their immediate neighborhood and community.

Many concepts of location can be developed through children's experiences in the school and community. Activities that foster concepts of location include the following:

- ❑ Ask the children to locate their classroom while on the playground or in front of the school building. Can they locate the office, lunchroom, and, walking around the building to another place, locate their room again?
- ❑ Take the children for a walk inside the school to find the signs that indicate location. Some schools may even have a map by the office door showing the school's floor plan. Other signs might include the exit and entrance, and signs over the stairs.
- ❑ Take the children outside to find street signs that indicate location: the sign that names the street the school is located on; the address of the school. Walk around the school with the children and ask them to tell how they would locate it if there were no street signs and addresses.
- ❑ Use the children's addresses to teach concepts of location. Ask them to draw a picture for, or write a letter to, their parents. Then, either dictate or write the children's addresses on their envelopes and mail them. Make a bulletin board of "Our Neighborhood"; the children can exhibit drawings of their houses and label them with their addresses.
- ❑ Make a class address book listing children's names, addresses, and phone numbers.
- ❑ Role play a "visitor" game. Have a child pretend to be new to the area. The other children will help the "visitor" locate a street or specific point in the neighborhood.

Concepts of location are, in part, concepts of direction, for being able to orient oneself in space means locating self in space. Concepts of location also include understanding distance.

Distance and Measurement

Watching children at play, you can see them use parts of their hands, feet, or sticks to measure off boundaries and distances. The concept of distance is important to the study of geography as well as for day-to-day living. It seems crucial, however, that experiences with the measurement of distance be informal, arbitrary, incidental, and based on actual experiences; for children who cannot conserve quantities cannot understand measurement. Piaget (1952) concluded that "there could be no more striking evidence that measurement is impossible without conservation of the quantities to be measured, for the very good reason that quantities that are not conserved cannot be composed" (p. 225).

The Nuffield Math Project (1968) suggested that teachers begin to introduce concepts of distance as children play by "considering the vocabulary which children use in their natural play. They all use the word big. In this context, our aim must be to refine the use of the word big so that high, low, far, near, deep, wide, tall, up, down, long are meaningful to them" (p. 68). Recognizing the importance of play, the Nuffield Project recommended that teachers use all the play situations they can to refine children's vocabulary. In addition, it is helpful to ask children to think of the largest, the deepest, the nearest, and the farthest thing they know. You can play a riddle game with the class: "I am thinking of something nearer than; I am thinking of something farther than, but not as far as."

Children can use arbitrary measures—hands, feet, lengths of string or ribbon—as well as standard measures to measure from one side of the room to the other, all the way around the desk, or to the top of the bookshelf. Preschool children play with rulers, tape measures, and yardsticks at the woodworking bench to simulate carpenter play, but do not use them as actual measuring tools.

Other materials children might use for measuring are

❑ trundle wheels to measure around the playground, the length of the hall, room, or school building. At least two children can use the wheel: one to push it and the other, or several others, to record the clicks.

❑ bamboo sticks or broom handles.

❑ odometers. Although preschool children will not use odometers as measuring tools, they can use one on a field trip to see that distance is measured in this way, too.

Maps and Globes

Maps are used to help people position themselves on the earth. Because maps are abstractions of reality, the skills needed to read and use them do not develop until children reach the age of 11 or 12. The ability to use maps requires understanding that

❑ the map is a representation. It is a small picture of a much larger place from a "bird's-eye view."

❑ symbols have meaning.

❑ the map is a way to orient oneself in space, which requires an understanding of location and direction.

For children to be able to conceptualize the total relationship of a map to the objects it represents or to infer information based on those relationships (Hatcher, 1983; Hawkins, 1979; Herman, 1980), they need a cognitive maturity not possible until early adolescence. But maturity is not enough. Without a foundation of spontaneous, playful and exploratory experiences with maps, children, no matter how mature cognitively, will not be successful map readers or users. The purpose of maps in the preschool and primary grades is to build this prior knowledge through children's play with, and use of, all types of maps (Miller, 1985).

Introducing Maps

When planning to introduce maps and map-reading concepts to young children, you might want to (a) survey the children to find out what their concepts are; (b) remember that all mapping must be done in connection with the children's own experiences; and (c) identify a few key concepts from the numerous skills involved in map reading.

Survey the Children.   Showing the children a map of their city or town, you ask them questions: "What is this used for?" "Have you ever seen one before?" "What do maps tell you?" "What do you know about maps?" "What are these lines for?" "What does this blue part stand for?" Other clues for questions arise as the children discuss their experiences with maps. Answers such as "It shows you where you live," or, "There's the ocean," give you an idea of the children's knowledge of maps and can direct lesson plans for extending this knowledge.

Young children seem to have a personal understanding of maps. Researchers have found that without any hesitation or need for prompting, children as young as age 3 interpreted aerial photographs and maps in geographical terms. They identified roads and decoded other environmental features. Although the children could not explain perspective, scale, or how the photos and maps were constructed, they did understand the concept of map (Muir & Cheek, 1991).

Research has not yet demonstrated the exact developmental sequence of children's understanding of maps; however, all experiences with maps in the preschool-primary classroom are simple, based on children's actual experiences, and for the purpose of acquainting children with maps and map reading in order to build a foundation they can use later, when they have the maturity to think abstractly, through the use of symbols (Miller, 1985; Mosenthal & Kirsch, 1991).

Use Firsthand Experiences.   Lucy Sprague Mitchell (1934) wrote: "Here again, I'm afraid of words with no images" (p. 18). Maps, already an abstraction, demand introduction to children in correlation with their actual experiences. Many concrete opportunities present themselves for introducing maps. A field trip to visit a neighbor finds the children consulting a map, while the arrival of a new student has the children locating the newcomer's neighborhood on a larger map.

Three- and four-year-olds play with small picture maps in the housekeeping/dramatic play area and with wheel toys, cars, and trucks. Board games such as Candy Land, Cherry Tree, Chutes and Ladders, and others are played.

Five-year-olds begin to use maps in connection with their experiences. Using personal knowledge, they are able to follow a map as they walk on a field trip, or find a hidden treasure on the playground. A map showing the school, where the children live, and the routes they follow to school is enjoyed.

Over the age of 5, children use maps as they build with blocks, and will make maps of their school and room. By the primary grades, maps will be a regular part of classroom activities, with children locating their homes and places far away from them on either maps or globes.

Develop Concepts.   Key concepts can help you plan for teaching map reading to young children. Before children are able to comprehend maps, they must understand the following:

1. **Representation.**   The concept that one object can represent another is not new to young children. They have looked at pictures representing cars, trucks, or animals and have seen photographs representing themselves. To fully understand maps, children must be able to understand that a map represents something else—a place.

2. **Symbolization.**   A map, itself a symbol for a place, uses other symbols. Colors symbolize land and water, lines symbolize roads and railroad tracks, and other symbols are used for houses, churches, or schools. Children are already

Children can build maps with blocks.

familiar with some symbols—letters for the sounds in their names, traffic signs— and can learn how other symbols are used in maps.

3. **Perspective.**   The concept that a map pictures a place as if you were looking at it from above is often difficult for young children to grasp. You must foster their understanding of a "bird's-eye view."

4. **Scale.**   Maps reduce the size of an actual place. Children can be introduced to the idea that a map is like the original place, except it is much smaller. Making maps small makes it easier for people to think about the place and to hold the map.

Representation

The idea that a map represents a place can be taught to children as they make their own maps. "Young children make maps before they read them" (Mitchell, 1934, p. 91). It may be that the children have already begun making maps as they work with blocks—laying out streets, shopping centers, and airports.

Blocks, which give the children a semiconcrete experience, are useful in map construction and in fostering the understanding that maps do represent some other thing. Using the blocks, you and the children can work together to make a map of their room or playground. When using the blocks to map the playground, classroom, or nearby neighborhood, you can help the children orient their building in the correct direction.

After children have become familiar with the idea of using blocks to represent a place that is familiar to them, they can transfer their map-making activities to paper. A walk around the block is an excellent time to draw a simple map of the area to consult during future walks.

Children learn about maps by making them.

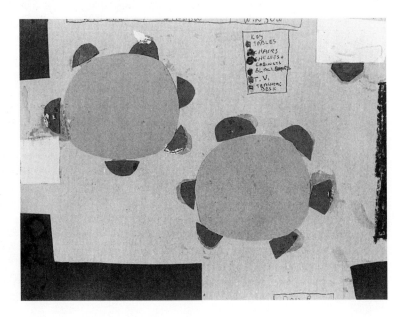

Figure 8.1
Continuum of mapping experiences

MAPPING OF THE	GRADE	MATERIAL
classroom	*2–3	blocks
school	K–3	boxes
playground	K–3	doll houses
house	K–3	sticks
route to school	K–3	paper
immediate neighborhood	1–3	drawing materials
wider community	1–3	

from the concrete to the abstract

*years of age (child care or preschool)

Rearranging furniture in a classroom provides additional opportunities for making maps. During informal work time, one teacher began to arrange different pieces of construction paper on a larger sheet. Curious children were asked to help "find a way to arrange the furniture." Telling them that this was a floor plan of their room, and that the red paper represented the piano, the blue paper the bookshelf, and the yellow papers the tables, the teacher and children moved the pieces around until they were satisfied with the arrangement. Later, the teacher and the children used this room map to place the furniture. Stimulated by this activity, the children brought in similar maps of their bedrooms, their houses, and their routes to school.

After traveling to someplace in the city or community, children often represent their trip by building the visited places with their blocks. Mitchell (1934), to foster mapping concepts, often added strips of blue oilcloth and long brown paper to the supplies of blocks. The children used these to lay out streets and to represent water as they constructed with the blocks, further extending their concept of representation.

One teacher in New York City created a floor map of Manhattan for children to use with their blocks (Davis, 1991). This map, about 10 ft × 20 ft, was constructed using brown wrapping paper and colored construction paper, which was covered with clear plastic. Using their personal experiences and ideas as a guide, the children erected buildings representing the Empire State Building, the World Trade Center, and Wall Street.

Other maps could be made from large pieces of linoleum, varnished wrapping paper, or canvas. When such maps are placed on the floor, 3- to 8-year-olds build small-scale buildings, bridges, and lighthouses on them, working out their own ideas of scale, direction, location, perspective, and orientation.

Mitchell (1934) called this type of map a tool-map. Tool-maps are not accurate maps. They are "rough maps which are not an end in themselves, but a means to better play and better thinking" (p. 28). Tool-maps, which can be made by the teacher or the children themselves, force children to actively work out relationships and organize their thinking.

All map play and map making designed to foster the development of the idea of representation should stem from children's own experiences and be on a continuum from the concrete to the abstract (see Figure 8.1).

Using incidental experiences and the children's interests, you can build further understandings of the concept of representation with maps. Children who are moving to another city or state, or who have entered the class from another state, can be shown on a map where they have come from or where they will be moving. You can help children route visits to grandparents, vacations, and other trips, showing them on a road map where they will travel. News stories of interest to the children are also occasions for you to use a map or globe to show the children where the event has taken place.

Play with maps may also foster children's understanding that maps represent places. You can put road maps near the bikes, in the housekeeping area, or near the wheel toys and blocks, encouraging children to use a map to "take a trip." Some commercial table-block games come equipped with maps for arranging trees, houses, buildings, and cars, giving children another experience in the representational nature of maps.

Symbolization

Fundamental to using maps is the understanding that a symbol represents a real thing. While constructing their own maps, children will often want to portray trees, playground equipment, cars, and other things in the environment. You can present these symbols in pictorial form during their initial experiences, and as their understanding of symbolization increases, you can introduce more abstract symbols.

To help children see the use of symbolization in maps, you might pin a small picture or cutout figure of each child to a map of the country to show each child's birthplace. Later, you can substitute a thumbtack or pin in place of the picture.

Color is used in a variety of ways on maps to symbolize different types of data. Young children can understand that the blue areas on the map generally represent water, and other areas—brown, green, or some other color—symbolize land.

You might introduce primary children to the use of a map's key and teach them how to use a map's legend. They might make their own maps, using colors to represent land and water, and lines to represent railroad tracks, highways, or boundaries.

Perspective

Perspective is a most difficult concept for young children, but you can introduce it. Children may not develop a complete understanding of looking down on the top of an object; yet you can expose them to the idea of a "bird's-eye view." Living in New York City gave Lucy Sprague Mitchell (1934) the opportunity to take her kindergartners to the top of a tall building to look down on the city. Following this trip, children's drawings indicated that they had gained the idea of perspective.

Preston and Herman (1974) had children stand on a chair and look down on a book on the floor in order to teach them the concept of perspective. You can provide other experiences, such as taking the children to various elevations to view the neighborhood. Photos depicting the same area from different points of view can help children gain experience with this concept. Some computer programs for children give them the opportunity to manipulate graphical perspective of objects and areas.

A block activity you might introduce in the primary grades involves asking children to select one block and trace around it on a piece of paper. Next, ask the children to see how many blocks of the same size and shape they can fit onto the form on the paper, piling one block on top of the other. This activity demonstrates to them that, no matter how high they build, the shape of the block on top remains the same as the shape drawn on their paper. This shape, which shows only the top of the block, represents the way that maps show only the tops of areas.

Experiences such as these may not fully develop the concept of perspective in young children, yet they will form a foundation on which you can build future learning (Okomoto, Case, Bleiker, & Henderson, 1996).

Scale

You can plan simple experiences with scale for young children. It will be years before they can interpret the scale of distance on a map, and yet they can understand the concept of scale—a map shows a real area made smaller (Liben & Downs, 1993).

Comparing the children's floor plans, block maps, or maps they used to find where they were born, you can continually point out that each is a map, just like the thing it represents, only smaller.

Photos of the children and pictures of familiar things are useful in demonstrating the concept of scale: "This is a picture of you. It's just like you, only you're much bigger, and this picture is very small." You can use model cars, boats, doll furniture, and dolls in the same manner, pointing out that there is a difference between the real object and the toy: "The toy is smaller; it's not real; it's a scale model." When Karl rushed into the classroom with a map of his bedroom, he told the other children, "It shows my bedroom just like it is, only this is much smaller." The teacher realized that Karl was beginning to grasp the concept of scale.

Research has not yet demonstrated the exact sequence of skills children develop in map reading. It does seem possible, though, to introduce children, through everyday experiences, to maps. However, beginning experiences with maps are simple and serve merely to acquaint the children with maps and map reading. These simple experiences build a foundation for their later map-reading and interpreting skills.

RELATIONSHIPS WITHIN PLACES

Geographers study how humans and environments are related, what advantages and disadvantages are present for human settlement, and how people modify and adapt to the environment. They try to find out why people live where they do, what the potentials are of this place or that, and how much of what is where.

Young children can be introduced to the ideas that humans have taken control of their environment, but at the same time, humans are also controlled by their environment. For example, to introduce children to the idea that they can control the nature of their world, they might

❑ look at the way they control their own environment. Children in kindergarten and the primary grades could work with you to arrange and rearrange their

A few examples of children's books that can stimulate explorations into the environment, introduce children to concepts of geography, and delight at the same time are:

Amos, W. H. (1981). *Life in ponds and streams.* Washington, DC: National Geography Association.
    Simple descriptions of pond life, plus outstanding photos.

Bains, R. (1982). *Wonders of rivers.* New York: Troll LB.
    An explanation of what rivers are and their role in our world.

Borden, L. (1989). *Caps, hats, socks, and mittens: A book of the four seasons.* New York: Scholastic.

Brown, C. (1995). Tractor. New York: Greenwillow.
    The passage of time is told through farm machinery and farm life in this picture book.

Centrars, B. (1982). *Shadows.* New York: Macmillan.
    This Caldecott Medal winner that explores the mysterious world of shadows.

dePaola, T. (1975). *The cloud book.* New York: Holiday.
    Ten of the most common clouds are identified in myths and story.

Dunbar, J. (1994). *The spring rabbit.* New York: Lothrop, Lee & Shepard.
    Rabbit who wants brothers and sisters is told by his mother to wait until spring.

Evans, L. (1995). *Rain song.* Boston: Houghton Mifflin.
    A book about thunderstorms presented as a song of rain.

First-grade students at R. T. Elementary School, Henderson, Nevada. (1994). *A day in the desert.* St. Petersburg, FL: Willowisp.
    The story, written by first graders, details a day in the Mojave Desert, home of the authors.

Fowler, S. G. (1992). *Fog.* New York: Greenwillow.
    A weather book with an intergenerational family.

Fowler, S. G. (1994). *I'll see you when the moon is full.* New York: Greenwillow.
    "When will you come back?" asks a child of his parent. "When the moon is full," answers the father.

Gans, R. (1984). *Rock collecting.* New York: Harper & Row.
    Primary children, just beginning to enjoy collecting, will find this book useful.

Hines, A. G. (1989). *Sky all around.* New York: Greenwillow.
    This book about things in the sky can lead to children looking at the sky to find the same things.

Hoban, T. (1984). *I walk and read.* New York: Greenwillow.
    This book of common signs encountered in various photographs leads to taking a walking field trip to identify signs in the school and neighborhoods.

Box 8.4
Children's Books for Geography

room or the play yard. Where should the new shelf be placed? If it's placed against the wall, how will children be able to reach it? Will placing it at an angle disrupt the flow of traffic to and from the bathrooms?

❑ take trips into the neighborhood to observe others changing the nature of their physical world. Children can observe people creating hills, ponds, and flat surfaces in order to build roads or make room for new buildings.

Jenkins, S. (1995). Looking down. New York: Houghton.
> This wordless picture book illustrates the perspective of astronauts viewing the earth from space.

Kinsey-Warmock, N. (1993). *When spring comes.* New York: Dutton.
> Set in the early years of the 20th century, this story shows readers the joyful pleasures of the coming of spring.

Loomis, C. (1994). *We're going on a trip.* New York: Morrow.
> Information and examples of travel that some children may not have experienced.

Lotz, K. E. (1993). *Snowsong whistling.* New York: Penguin.
> A lilting text following the seasons from fall to winter.

Morgan, S. (1995). *Triangles and pyramids and spirals.* New York: Thomson Learning.
> A delightful collection of triangles and pyramids embedded in the context of people's lives. After reading this book children can take their own trips in and around their school to find shapes.

Narahaski, K. (1987). *I have a friend.* New York: Macmillan.
> Shadows are the focus in this story of a boy who knows his shadow will return when the sun does.

Nixon, J. L. (1994). *When I am eight.* New York: Dial.
> A growing-up fantasy preschoolers will enjoy.

Possell, E. (1982). *Deserts.* New York: Childrens Press.
> Straightforward simple text and find color photographs are the highlights of this book.

Russo, M. (1994). *Time to wake up!* New York: Greenwillow.
> The youngest children will enjoy this simple story of morning routines.

Rydell, K. (1994). *Wind says good night.* Boston: Houghton Mifflin.
> Listen to the hushed sounds of night creatures as they hum their lullabies.

Schertte, A. & Lewis, E. B. (1995). *Down the road.* New York: Harcourt Brace Jovanovich.
> A child ventures toward independence following a dusty road.

Verdet, J. P. (1995). *Earth, sky, and beyond.* New York: Dutton.
> Even the youngest preschooler will be fascinated by this story of our universe.

Weiss, H. (1995). *MAPS: Getting from here to there.* Boston: Houghton Mifflin.
> This paperback presents exciting and meaningful ways for children over the age of 8 to learn map skills.

Box 8.4 *continued*

❑ control the environment around their school, perhaps planting a garden, flowers, or shrubs, or taking part in building a sand area.

❑ visit a private farm or a farm maintained by the city parks to acquaint children with farm life. At the farm, children can be introduced to the idea that people use soil, water, and sun to grow crops. They build fences to keep animals secured and use ponds or streams for their water (Fromboluti, 1991).

❑ observe how others have shaped their environment. Children in the primary grades might visit a bonsai garden or a reservoir, take a trip through a tunnel that goes under water or through a mountain, or observe a house being built on a hillside.

Humans respond to the environment. Although they will not explore why people settled where they did or how they used the resources of the land until they are in the middle grades, preschool and primary children can

❑ take a trip over a river and talk about why people built bridges *over* the water.

❑ go for a walk in the woods or go camping. "It is easy to understand why we wear long pants and shoes where there are rocks and brambles on the ground, and to realize the importance to early settlers of being near water when you no longer have the convenience of a faucet" (Fromboluti, 1991, p. 12).

❑ take a nature walk through a park or wildlife reserve to learn about local plants and wildlife and how natural features change over time.

❑ find out the name of the city they live in or the name of the city nearest to them. Third graders could take a trip to a nearby city and speculate on why people settled in an area.

SPATIAL INTERACTIONS

Regardless of where we live, we interact with others far from us. A part of the study of geography is understanding that people interact with others far from them. We depend on other places for food, clothes, and even items like pencils and paper. We also share information with each other using telephones, newspapers, radio, and television to bridge the distances (Fromboluti, 1991).

Children could

❑ take a trip to the local supermarket to observe the food delivery system. They could chart the types of trucks used to deliver the goods, find out where the goods came from, who grew the produce, and how many different types of preparation were required—picking, packing, canning—before the food got to the supermarket.

❑ make a graph of the transportation systems they have traveled on. They might graph the boats, buses, trains, or cars they have been in.

❑ find out how many different ways they can move on the surface of the earth. They might walk, run, hop, skip, jump, crawl, use a bike, a wagon, roller skates, and so forth.

❑ explore how animals move on, through, or above the earth or in the water.

❑ study the school's communication system, noting all of the machines used in the school for this purpose.

❑ use the mail system by writing and sending letters to one another or to their parents.

Play is the beginning of building an awareness of spatial interaction.

The booklet *Helping Your Child Learn Geography* (Fromboluti, 1991) lists other ways of fostering the idea of spatial interaction. These include

- ❑ giving children opportunities to travel by car, bus, bicycle, or on foot. Whenever possible, take other forms of transportation such as airplanes, trains, subways, ferries, barges, and horses and carriages.

- ❑ using a map to look at various routes you can take when you try different methods of transportation.

- ❑ watching travel videos and movies.

- ❑ having third graders play a license plate game, seeing as many different states' plates as they can and noting what each plate tells about the specific state. Children might look at the plates of parked cars.

- ❑ letting third graders walk around the school building and identify where things come from. They might even look at labels in their own clothing to determine where their clothes came from. At lunch, talk about where the foods were grown: Where is the nearest dairy? Where did the bananas and oranges come from? How did they get to the school?

- ❑ having primary children chart their family history by asking relatives where they came from. They could find these places on a map and make a chart of them, or make their own chart, mapping their own birthplace. They could discuss how and why they or their ancestors left this place or stayed.

- ❑ interviewing older people to find out what the neighborhood was like when they were young. Specifically ask about how they traveled, what they used for refrigeration, the foods they ate, the clothes they wore, and the schools they attended. How have things changed since the older people were children?

REGIONS

Concepts of region, which serve as symbols for individuals and society, are abstract and perhaps beyond the scope of young children. A *region* in geography is a place where the earth, space, and certain other characteristics are related. Regions on a map or globe are areas that are delimited as being different from others on the basis of certain characteristics. Regions are parts of the earth that have certain physical properties that direct the way people use the land, the way they live in societies, and the relationship of their societies to the earth.

All children live in a community of some kind. You can take the class on trips into a neighboring community to acquaint them with its characteristics. As children walk through the community, you can ask: "Why do people live near one another?" and "What do you think makes a neighborhood?" Back in the classroom, they could list all the things they found in the neighborhood.

Third graders might be asked to differentiate how geographic areas in their community are alike and different. Trips might be taken to a park, shopping center, and industrial area, and changes within these areas could be charted over the year. People living or working in the regions could be interviewed to find out how the changes affect their lives.

SUMMARY

Keeping in mind that children learn by doing, you can help preschool-primary children develop basic geography concepts. They can experience the earth on which they live, learning the names and qualities of its land and water surfaces. They can experience the rhythms of day and night, and of changing seasons.

Through movement exploration and other physical activities, children begin to understand the concept of direction. Learning their addresses, taking field trips, and locating themselves and objects in space, children learn the concept of location. They can explore the nature of geographical regions through field trips and vicarious experiences—movies, filmstrips, and other audiovisual aids.

Knowing how people interact, even though separated in space, helps children develop the concept of spatial interactions. And children are introduced to the idea of mapping their world as they draw and build their own maps.

When you teach young children geography concepts, it is important to keep in mind the directives of Lucy Sprague Mitchell (1934): Children learn by doing, through action, and with concrete experiences; we need not hurry them into the realm of the abstract.

RESOURCES

These associations offer free and inexpensive materials that can be used by teachers to plan social studies experiences as well as materials that may be used by children:

National Council for Social Studies
3501 Newark Street NW
Washington, DC 10016

National Geographic Society
17th and M Street NW
Washington, DC 20036

The booklet *Helping Your Child Learn Geography,* by Carol Sue Fromboluti, is available for 50 cents from

Geography
Consumer Information Center
Pueblo, CO 81009

REFERENCES

Davis, U. (1991, April). *The New York City Marathon: A social studies unit.* Paper presented at Hofstra's Annual Early Childhood Conference, Hempstead, NY.

Elementary Science Study. (1963). *Lights and shadows.* St. Louis, MO: Webster Division McGraw-Hill.

Fromboluti, C. S. (1991). *Helping your child learn geography.* Washington, DC: Department of Education.

Geography Education National Implementation Project. (1987). *K-6 geography: Themes, key ideas, and learning opportunities.* Macomb: Western Illinois University, National Council for Geographic Education: Washington, DC: U.S. Department of Education.

Hatcher, B. (1983). Putting young cartographers "On the Map." *Childhood Education, 59,* 311–315.

Hawkins, M. L. (1979). Teaching map skills in the elementary school. *Indiana Social Studies Quarterly, 32,* 33–37.

Herman, W. (1980). Toward a more adequate research base in social studies education. *Journal of Research and Development in Education, 13,* 24–35.

Howe, G. (1969). The teaching of directions in space. In W. Hermand (Ed.), *Current research in elementary school social studies* (pp. 31–43). Upper Saddle River, NJ: Merrill/Prentice Hall

Liben, L. S., & Downs, R. M. (1993). Understanding person-space-map relations: Cartographic and developmental perspective. *Child Development, 29,* 739–752.

Lord, F. (1941). A study of spatial orientation of children. *Journal of Educational Research, 34,* 481–505.

Martin, B. (1969). *Our sun is a star.* New York: Holt, Rinehart & Winston.

Marzoff, D. P., & DeLoache, J. S. (1994). Transfer in young children's understanding of spatial representations. *Child Development, 65,* 1–16.

Miller, J. (1985). Teaching map skills: Theory, research, and practice. *Social Education, 49,* 30–33.

Mitchell, L. S. (1934). *Young geographers.* New York: Bank Street College.

Mosenthal, P. B., & Kirsch, S. (1991). Understanding general reference maps. *Journal of Reading, 34*(1), 60–63.

Muir, S. P., & Cheek, H. N. (1991). Assessing spatial development: Implications for map skill instruction. *Social Education, 55,* 316–319.

National Commission on Social Studies in the Schools. (1989). *Charting a course: Social studies for the 21st century.* New York: Author.

New, R., & Vechhi, R. (1995). *Reggio Emilia: The project approach.* New York: Heineman.

Okomoto, Y., Case, R., Bleiker, C., & Henderson, B. (1996). Cross-cultural investigations. *Monographs of the Society for Research in Child Development, 61*(1–2, Serial No. 246).

Piaget, J. (1952). *The child's conception of number.* New York: Humanities Press.

Piaget, J. (1965). *The child's conception of the world.* Totowa, NJ: Littlefield Adams.

Preston, J., & Herman, W. (1974). *Teaching social studies in the elementary school* (4th ed.). New York: Holt, Rinehart & Winston.

Roberts, R., & Aman, C. J. (1993). Developmental differences in giving directions: Spatial frames of reference and metal rotation. *Child Development, 64,* 1258–1270.

Sauvy, J., & Simonne, D. (1974). *The child's discovery of space.* Baltimore, MD: Penguin Education.

Seefeldt, C. (1995). Transforming curriculum in social studies. In S. Bredekamp & R. Rosegrant (Eds.), *Reaching potentials: Transforming early childhood curriculum and assessment.* Vol. 2 (109–123). Washington, DC: National Association for the Education of Young Children.

Stiles-Davis, J., Kritchevsky, M., & Bellugi, B. (1988). *Spatial cognition: Brain bases and development.* New York: Lawrence Erlbaum.

Sullivan, M. (1982). *Feeling strong, feeling free: Movement exploration for young children.* Washington, DC: National Association for the Education of Young Children.

Chapter 9

Economics

The world facing students graduating in the year 2000 will be more crowded, the physical environment more threatened, and the global economy more competitive and interconnected. Understanding that world, that environment, and that economy will require high levels of competency.

National Geography Standards, 1995, p. 18

After you read this chapter, you should be prepared to respond to the following questions:

- ❑ How do children's economic concepts develop?
- ❑ What concepts are key to the study of economics?
- ❑ Why is introducing children to the concept of scarcity important, even in the preschool-primary grades?
- ❑ What economic decisions can young children make?
- ❑ How can you introduce young children to concepts of consumer and producer?

Economic literacy is believed essential for citizens of a democracy. According to the National Council for the Social Studies, all children "need useful and powerful economic knowledge and the formal development of critical-thinking skills" (1989, p. 16). If all people had everything they wanted, then knowledge of economic concepts would not be critical. But today there are major differences between what people need and what they can have, leading economists to state that an accurate and workable image of the social system in general, and the economic system in particular, is increasingly essential to human survival. The concept of scarcity—the difference between the unlimited wants of people and the limited goods, services, and materials available—is a major concern of economic education.

Economics is the study of how goods and services are produced and distributed and the activities of people who produce, save, spend, pay taxes, and perform personal services to satisfy their wants for food and shelter, their desire for new conveniences and comforts, and their collective wants for things such as education and national defense.

To become competent citizens, all children will need to be able to

❑ maintain sound personal finances.
❑ understand and appreciate the contribution of the many groups of workers who produce goods and services.
❑ interest themselves in the economic system and understand how it operates.
❑ think critically about economic problems and assume responsibility for them.

DEVELOPMENT OF ECONOMIC CONCEPTS

Children experience economic concepts daily. They observe parents exchanging money for goods, and they themselves participate in paying for some purchases. They receive money as gifts, sometimes saving it in a bank, or they may even participate in opening bank accounts. Advertising convinces children early in life that they need more than they can have. And children make decisions between the things they really need and those they only want.

In their play, children reveal some understanding of economic concepts. They use economic scripts as they play store, pretending to see and purchase goods, and they pretend to use money to obtain services (Pramling, 1991). Nevertheless, like geography and history concepts, children's economic concepts are far from fully developed. It is not until after age 9 that children understand the value of money, are able to compare coins, and comprehend the idea of credit or profit.

Following Piagetian theory, children's stages of economic understandings have been identified as (a) the unreflective and preoperational level, exemplified by a highly literal reasoning based on the physical characteristics of objects or processes; (b) the transitional or emerging reasoning level, exemplified by higher order reasoning and similar to Piaget's concrete operational stage; and (c) the reflective level of economic reasoning, based on children's ability to use abstract ideas and approximating Piaget's formal operations level (Kourilsky, 1985; Mugge, 1968; Schug & Birkey, 1985).

Researchers have found that 3-year-olds can distinguish between money and other objects but are unable to differentiate between types of coins. Until around 4½ years of age, children are generally unaware that money is needed to purchase things. Three-year-olds may take candy or toys from a store, totally unaware of the fact that money is exchanged for goods (Berti & Bombi, 1988). "They know that you can buy things in stores and recognize money and pretend to pay for things. They know the difference between 'yours' and 'mine' and identify adult activities as 'work'" (Berti & Bombi, 1988, p. 175).

Between ages 4 and 5, children are still unable to distinguish between and name coins, but they are aware that you need money to buy things. Scripts develop of pretending to ask for and get goods, to give and receive money, and to go to work, suggesting that children do have concepts of economic exchanges. They do not, however, understand the function of money in buying and selling but believe that shopkeepers give money to customers and that any type of coin is suitable for any type of purchase. No concept of production is present. At 4 or 5 years of age, children believe shopkeepers get their goods from some other shop, which gives these away without asking for money, and do not understand that shopkeepers are customers as well (Berti & Bombi, 1988).

Even though they understand that people go to work to get money, they do not understand the relationship between work and pay. To them, one works *and* one gets money, rather than one gets money *because* one works.

By age 6, children are progressing into concrete operations and have a clearer understanding of money; they can distinguish between and name the various denominations of coins and know which of them will buy more things. They continue to believe that the shopkeeper gives customers money, but are moving toward the idea that there is a manufacturer who produces goods for which the shopkeeper has to pay.

Around 6 and 7 years of age, children know that although you do not have to have the exact money to pay for a purchase, you do need enough. They are also moving toward some clarity of employer-employee relationships, but are far from a clear understanding of customer and producer concepts.

Seven-year-olds are able to compare coins and understand the value of money. They know that manufacturers are paid, as are employees, and that numerous persons and activities are necessary for the production and exchange of goods and money. Children no longer consider work as going someplace to get money, but begin to make a connection between the activity and the benefits (Berti & Bombi, 1988). They now have some idea of production and selling and can describe a few paid occupations that they can actually observe and with which they have direct experience, such as a police officer or a bus driver. They also now seem to understand that people are paid differently for different jobs, but they say that police officers make much more money than doctors or shopkeepers.

Children are consumers of goods, services, and materials, as well as food.

Between ages 7 and 10, preeconomic ideas are replaced with more accurate and conventional ideas. Nevertheless, it will not be until the period of formal operations that children are able to understand that the price of goods is based on the costs of production, which include the cost of labor. They do not understand that the materials necessary for production are not old or broken things, and they still confuse making something with mending something. Raw materials are not recognized as natural products.

KEY CONCEPTS

Using knowledge of children's awareness of economic concepts and their direct experiences, teachers can introduce preschool-primary children to essential economic principles. By organizing children's experiences around economic key concepts, teachers can introduce children to the main ideas of

- ❑ scarcity—the wants of people everywhere are unlimited but resources are limited.
- ❑ the necessity of decisions regarding the use of resources.
- ❑ the function of production, which is, to some extent, to meet the unlimited wants of consumers.
- ❑ the use of money and barter to purchase goods.

Scarcity

Basic to all economic understandings is the concept of scarcity. In every society—classroom, family, neighborhood, state, nation, and world—people have a wide variety of wants and desires. Everyone the world over always seems to need more food, clothing, things, and services than are available. The concept that everyone wants more goods and services than they can have can be introduced through experiences at school. Later, these experiences can be related to the children's families and to their neighborhoods.

Wants and Needs

"Daddy, I wanna. . . . " Every young child has wants and needs. Learning to distinguish between wants and needs, and how to conserve time, goods, and services, may help children develop concepts of scarcity.

1. Ask the children to pretend they can have anything they wish. Ask them to draw, tell, or dictate three wishes. Which of these things they've wished for do they think they will get? Which of them do they think they will not get? Why can't they have everything they wish?

2. Make a booklet or folder called *I Wanted, I Want, I Will Want.* Encourage children to discuss the things they have wanted in the past, whether they got

them or not, why they wanted them, and if they want them now. Draw or write about these things under the title "I Wanted." Ask them about things they want now and the things they think they will want in the future. Do the children think they will be able to have all of these things?

3. Make dream cloud pictures and have children illustrate things they want in the clouds as their dreams. Again, encourage discussion of the things the children say they want and those things they believe are realistic to have.

4. Tell folktales and stories about wanting things, such as *Cinderella, King Midas,* and *The Rabbit Who Wanted Wings,* and discuss the stories. Were these people or animals wise to want the things they did? Why? What things did they really need?

5. Make bulletin boards of "Things I Want for Summer," "Things I Want for Winter," and "When I Grow Up."

To make these activities meaningful for 4- and 5-year-old children, you might cut collections of pictures from catalogs or magazines so that the children can select pictures of the things that illustrate their ideas and paste them in scrapbooks or on a wall chart for the room. Older kindergarten children can draw their own pictures, and children in the primary grades could be encouraged to both illustrate and write their responses.

Experiences with the concept of scarcity can also arise from energy and energy conservation. Fry-Miller suggested the following activities to help children become more aware of energy waste, and to think of alternatives to waste:

❑ Make a list of energy-saving habits, such as turning off lights and appliances not in use, riding a bike or walking instead of using a car, limiting water use.

❑ Find something at home or in the classroom to recycle or repair, such as a toy or shelf.

❑ Work on a recycling project, such as collecting aluminum or newspapers from parents or other in the community. (1982, p. 10).

Many classroom experiences can be used to introduce the concept of scarcity. What things does the class as a group want? Which things do they need? It may be that supplies and materials are already limited by shrinking budgets, and it is an absolute necessity to conserve. Scraps can be saved for later use, brushes no longer useful at the easel may be washed and used outdoors for water paint, or junk can be collected with which the class can build sculptures.

It may be that the class can obtain some funding from the PTA or petty cash fund. Deciding how to spend this cash can be a group project. Make a list of pictures of the things all the children suggest. After the list is made, instruct each child to place a check by the things she thinks the class should try to get. The item with the most checks would then be purchased. You can then hold a discussion of the use of the items, how long they will last, how many ways they can be used, and how many children can use them at the same time.

The needs and wants of the school provide other experiences with the concept of scarcity. Kindergarten and primary children can take a walk though the school to identify the things the school needs, or they can interview the principal to find out what she considers important for the school to have. What things do the children think are possible for the school to obtain? What things are just dreams?

The playground can be explored, with the children naming all of the play equipment they would like to have. Later, in class, the list can be narrowed down to items that the children think are realistic additions, and efforts can be made to obtain these.

Time is another commodity that must be used wisely. Incidental experiences help children realize that they must make choices about the way they use their time. "If we clean up now, we can have time to. . . . " Children should make plans for the way they want to use their time. Even 4-year-olds can identify how they would like to begin their day and can list the things they think they will try to accomplish during the morning. When children make plans, they should be able to experience not having enough time to do all of the things they have planned. Recognizing the consequences of decisions is a true learning experience.

Families also have many needs, wants, and limited resources to obtain them. Ask the children to name all of the things their families need to live. The basic needs are shelter, food, and clothing. Experiences with the basic needs include

- ❑ asking children to draw a picture of the home they are living in. Classify these pictures as to type of home. Discuss the need for homes. Children age 5 and under could make scrapbooks using precut pictures.
- ❑ making booklets called *Things My Family Needs* and *Things My Family Would Like to Have.* Primary children could write as well as draw their ideas.
- ❑ having children discuss the foods they like to eat, why people eat food, what foods they would like to try, and what foods they eat only on special occasions.

Families also need clothing. The children can discuss all the types of clothing they need for the different seasons, in contrast to the clothing they would like to have. A lost-and-found box reinforces the idea of the importance of not having to replace clothing. What does it mean to the children if they lose an item of clothing?

Families also want things. Some want different kinds of recreational activities; other families want better housing and clothing, or pets. Charts and booklets of *Things My Family Wants* and *Things My Family Needs* help children clarify and distinguish needs from wants.

Decision Making

The ability to make wise decisions is an integral part of the study of scarcity. People cannot have everything they want—sometimes not everything they need. People must make decisions regarding which things they need and which things they want. Children who have had limited experiences in making decisions can find many opportunities for making choices within the classroom. Primary children, who have had little opportunity to make decisions about their lives—which

Sensori-Motor 0–2	Preoperational 2–6/7	Concrete 6/7–10
observes and attends to shape and size of coins	plays store, demonstrating initial concepts of consuming and purchasing	after 9, can compare coins, knows relative value of coins
observes shopping, consuming, and purchasing	counts more or less	understands that people work to make money
	recognizes coins/money	some clarity in understanding employer-employee relationship
	knows money is necessary to make purchases	

Box 9.1
Economics Concept Development

families they will have, the school or church they will go to, the neighborhood they will live in, or the clothes or food they use—need classrooms that are replete with opportunities to make choices and to experience the consequences of their choices. "Briefly we seek to give the young child the widest possible freedom to choose what to play with, how to play, how to make things, with a minimum of restrictive control" (Biber, 1964, p. 77).

It is also important for young children to be able to make decisions and experience the results of them in a secure classroom environment. Children must be able to experience the results of their decisions. According to Dewey (1944), there is no way to learn other than to experience the consequences of an action, yet children must have the right to make mistakes without the loss of self-esteem. As children experience the initial frustration of having made a wrong decision, they can learn how to live with the consequences of that decision and ways to decide more wisely next time.

Children can make decisions about which materials to use and how to use them; what to sing, play, or dance; where to plant the seeds; which group of children they want to work with; and even what things they want to learn. Other experiences with decision making that help children understand the concept of scarcity include the following:

1. Read the poem "The Animal Store" by Rachel Field. The children can act out the roles of pet store owner, the children purchasing pets, and all of the pets that might be found in the store. Discuss what they would buy if they had a hundred dollars to spend. Let the children make murals or pictures of the things they would buy.

2. Circle items in toy or other catalogs that they would like to have. Question the children: "Pick out the one toy you want. How did you decide on that toy?" Or, for older children: "You each have five dollars to spend. Shopping in this catalog, decide on a purchase. Why did you choose that instead of something else?"

3. Let the children decide what items to buy for a class project or party. Discuss what they want versus what they need, both in relation to what is available and how much money they have to buy it.

Children in the second or third grades may be ready to participate in discussions about decisions that affect the community. It may be that a new highway is being built, or that the school system must eliminate jobs. Your class may be interested enough in some of these issues to speculate on how they would respond if they were adults. Ask them: "Would you suggest to the school board that they cut music, art, or other special areas?" "Do you think they should combine classes and eliminate teachers' jobs?" "Should money be spent on the new highway or a new school building?"

Even though resources are scarce and choices must be made to provide for ever-expanding human needs, you can help children understand that most decisions do not involve a choice between all or nothing. "They do, however, require trade-offs among desirable alternatives or goals—that is, providing a little less of one thing in order to provide a little more of another" (Gilliard & Morton, 1981, p. 533).

Economic Production

Closely related to the concept of scarcity is the concept of production. The function of production, to some extent, is to try to meet the unlimited wants of consumers. In a democratic society, people choose the goods and services they consume and produce, although advertising and consumer demand influence both. The concept of exchange of money is related to economic production: Consumers use money to purchase goods and services. Children can develop concepts of (a) being a consumer, (b) the function of money, (c) the differences between goods and services, and (d) production.

Consumers

Even before children can walk or talk, they consume goods, use services, and express their wants and needs. As they mature, they will begin to choose what they buy. Their values influence the decisions they make; they will evaluate alternatives and select the best buy for their money and needs as well as act on their rights and responsibilities as consumers.

Throughout the school year, you can help children clarify their likes and dislikes. They might discuss and identify the stories they like or dislike, decide on materials they like, and explain why they did not select the alternative materials. Making lists, booklets, charts, or murals depicting favorite things at school, at home, or in the neighborhood will help children clarify their preferences. You can remind children to be honest and make decisions based on their likes rather than those of their parents, peers, or teacher (Waite, Smith, & Schug, 1991).

The best way to learn to become a wise consumer is to practice consuming. You need to provide as many opportunities as possible for children to make choices about purchases. In deciding on materials to purchase for the class or for

Children can experience concepts of producers and consumers.

themselves, children need to consider: "How long will it last?" "How many ways can it be used?" "Is it something I really need or just want?" "If I spend my money for this, will I have any left for other things?"

As consumers who watch 3 to 5 hours of television daily, children should be aware of advertising's influence on their decision making (Notar, 1989). Children do not distinguish between programs and advertisements and cannot understand that a commercial's intent is to sell something (Pramling, 1991). "Even worse, the advertisements are aimed at breaking down the resistance of rational adults" (Notar, 1989, p. 66).

Based on strong psychological research and theory, advertisements do affect consumer behavior. Teachers can begin introducing children to the idea that advertisements are designed to influence the purchase of goods and services. Children can begin to analyze ads. The language arts activity of writing ads about real or pretend products helps children to see how words are selected to influence purchases and to realize that commercials are written by people. If children do not have writing skills, the commercials can be dictated or orally presented to the class by a committee.

Children can send for an advertised cereal-box toy and, upon its receipt, compare the toy with its ad. Some questions you might ask the children include: "Does the toy do what the advertisement promised?" "What else could you have bought for the same amount of money?" "Would another purchase better fill your needs or wants?" "How else does the toy received differ from the advertised one?"

Primary children can also analyze ads for other toys. Ask the children to watch a particular ad on television, arrange to have it shown to the class, or bring in an ad from a current paper or magazine. Read the ad, then compare the claims with the product. The children can, if it is convenient, take a trip to the toy store, or the product can be made available in class. Have the children determine if the ad distorted the product. Typical questions might include: "Did the doll really move the way it did on television or the way the ad said it would?" "Did the car really move as fast as it appeared to in the television ad?" "Did any parts of the ad make you think something different about this toy? Which parts?" "Were all parts of the ad true?"

At times, certain advertising slogans become popular and can serve as another vehicle for analysis of ads. Any slogan that is popular can be tested by kindergarten or primary children: "Will this candy mint make your mouth feel fresher than another?" "Does this soap really clean the clothes better than another?" "Does this towel absorb better than another?" "Which soap makes your hands softer?" "Let's try it for ourselves."

To be truly effective, consumer education must involve parents. Let the parents know of the activities the children are involved in at school. Tell the parents how these activities will help children (a) weigh their purchases in terms of their goals, values, and resources; (b) make selections from the alternatives; and (c) accept the consequences and responsibilities that arise from their decisions. Inform the parents of the things they can do to reinforce children's abilities to analyze ads and make wise purchases. Parents can include children in their decisions about food purchases: "Would you like this box of cookies? It contains more cookies than this box, but the cookies in this box are made with real chocolate." Parents can also include children in discussions of making larger purchases: "We need a new carpet and a new washing machine; how can we decide which to buy?" You can invite parents to school to tell the children about their experiences as consumers, how they make decisions for purchases, or about the time an advertisement lured them into making a foolish purchase and how they felt about it.

Consumers have rights and responsibilities. Their rights are to choose which goods and services they will buy; to obtain accurate information about goods and services; to shop in safe places; and to be able to register complaints and seek redress of grievances. Consumers also need to respect the property and rights of others when shopping. You could take a shopping trip with the children to observe good and bad shopping manners. Children can make a list of all the things they think are improper shopping behaviors—running in the store, opening packages, or crowding at the checkout line. Ask them to add a list of proper shopping behaviors. Children might be able to role-play both good and bad behaviors.

Use of Money

People use money to buy goods and services. Children as young as 4 and 5 years of age are aware of the use of money. Through store play and actual trips to purchase goods, children learn the significance of money and prices. The cooperation of parents, who can involve children when making purchases, will help to extend and clarify children's concepts of money. You can plan a shopping trip to buy goods and materials. A small committee might make the trip. After the trip and purchase, the children can report to the class, telling how they made their decision, how much the purchase cost, and how much change they received.

Services

Children see the exchange of money when their parents purchase goods and materials, but they may never witness the exchange of money for services. The doctor and dentist are paid by check through the mail; the teacher, librarian, police officer, and postal employee are paid indirectly through taxes. You can focus children's attention on the services their families use by making charts of "Goods Our Families Consume" and "Services Our Families Use."

Other children can investigate the services that are supported by their parents' taxes and the taxes of others. Ask them: "Who pays for the school?" "Does the teacher get paid?" "Where does the money come from?" "What would happen if no one paid for the school building, the services of the janitor or teachers, or materials and supplies?"

You might arrange trips into the community to observe other services paid for by taxes. Children can observe the police officers, fire fighters, street cleaners, health workers, and other people whose services are paid for by tax money. On another trip, children can identify public property used by everyone—streets, parks, hydrants, fireboxes, street signs, lights, and sidewalks. Ask children to speculate about what would happen if people had to build their own streets or parks, or buy their own fire trucks. Bulletin boards, booklets, or murals labeled "Things Families Buy Together" and "Things Families Buy for Themselves" will reinforce and clarify the concept of using public services.

Production of Goods and Provision of Services

Although everyone is a consumer of goods and services, not all are producers. Interwoven with the concepts of scarcity, wants and needs, and consumers' responsible use of money is the concept of producer. Children can begin to develop the concept of producer by understanding the work they do at home and at school and the work their parents do.

Children can make charts as follows:

Work at School		Work at Home	
Goods	Services	Goods	Services
	Our Parents Produce		
	Goods	Services	

Goods children can produce at school include gifts for parents, greeting cards, books, garden products, and cookies. Question the children: "What things do you produce at home?" "What do your parents produce? Food? Clothing? Furniture?" "What services do you produce at school?" "What services do you produce at home?"

Specialization.   The concept of specialization—job diversification—arises from the identification of producers. Within the school building itself there are many specializations. There may be a building engineer, nurse, or lunchroom worker; there are teachers, a secretary, and a principal. Children can interview these different workers, finding out about their particular jobs—what they produce and how. Ask the children what would happen if each teacher were responsible for heating, cleaning the room, preparing the meals, repairing the windows, and answering the phone.

Children can experiment with diversity of jobs within the classroom. One day, instead of you preparing materials for the children, they can prepare their own paints, salt dough, and so forth. Discuss what happened. Ask the children which way was easier and more efficient. On another day, ask each child to prepare a snack, instead of the usual committee or teacher preparing for everyone. Children might time their preparation and clean-up and compare it to the time it takes when these jobs are divided and conducted by a few for the entire group.

Many Related Factors.   The study of producers leads into a study of the resources used in the production of goods. Production depends upon people, but also on natural resources, tools, machinery, and money. In the classroom, children can see that different materials are needed to produce a painting or to construct a playhouse. Children can make a chart of all of the tools within the classroom; they can take a trip through the school to identify the tools used by producers in the building. You

Through play, children explore the nature of different jobs and careers.

can initiate a discussion of the tools used at home or by the parents at work, or the tools, machines, and materials needed to keep the community functioning.

SUMMARY

The two major economics concepts that are appropriate for preschool-primary children are the concepts of scarcity and production. You introduce these concepts through children's experiences, both incidental and structured.

Daily, children experience the concept of scarcity. They must conserve materials and energy. They must consider their needs and wants in relation to available resources; they need to make responsible decisions and learn to live with the consequences of their decisions.

As consumers, children develop an understanding of the producer concept. Some produce services; others, goods. Money is required to pay for both services and goods. The diversity of producers' work leads children into a study of different kinds of jobs, as well as the resources producers use in their jobs.

Although research supports introducing young children to economic concepts, it is important to ground your teaching of concepts in children's concrete experiences. Children must be involved in experiencing for themselves, in doing and acting.

PROJECTS

1. With a small group of children, visit a supermarket or neighborhood store. What things are the children interested in that you could use to build economic concepts? List the ways you can extend these interests in the classroom.

2. Read chapter 8, "Economics—Explanations by Deduction," in *Social Science and Its Methods* by Peter R. Senn, or another economics text, to strengthen your own understanding of economics.

3. Select one concept from economics. Interview a group of children to determine their understanding of that concept. What experiences could you plan that might build more accurate, complete understandings of the concept?

RESOURCES

The Joint Council for Economic Education is the best source available for resources on teaching economics. Drop the council a postcard requesting a catalog and other free information.

The Joint Council on Economic Education
432 Park Avenue South
New York, NY 10016

REFERENCES

Berti, A. E., & Bombi, A. S. (1988). *The child's construction of economics.* Cambridge: Cambridge University Press.

Biber, B. (1964). *Some choices children can make.* New York: Bank Street College of Education.

Dewey, J. (1944). *Democracy and education.* New York: The Free Press.

Fry-Miller, K. M. (1982). Energy education: Responding to the nuclear power controversy. *Young Children, 37,* 3–14.

Gillard, J. V., & Norton, J. S. (1981). Economics: Scarcity and citizen decision making. *Social Education, 45*(7), 532–563.

Kourilsky, M. (1985). *Children's use of cost-benefit analysis: Developmental or nonexistent?* Paper presented at the annual meeting of the American Educational Research Association, Chicago, IL.

Mugge, D. (1968). Are young children ready to study the social sciences? *Elementary School Journal, 68,* 232–240.

National Council for the Social Studies. (1989). *Social studies for early childhood and elementary school children: Preparing for the 21st century.* Washington, DC: Author.

National Geography Standards. (1995). *Geography for life.* Washington, DC: U.S. Department of Education, The National Endowment for the Humanities, and The National Geography Association.

Notar, E. (1989). Children and TV commercials: Wave after wave of exploitation. *Childhood Education, 66,* 66–68.

Pramling, I. (1991). Learning about "The shop": An approach to learning in preschool. *Early Childhood Research Quarterly, 6,* 151–167.

Schug, M. C., & Birkey, C. J. (1985). *The development of children's economic reasoning.* Paper presented at the annual meeting of the American Educational Research Association, Chicago, IL.

Waite, P., Smith, S., & Schug, M. C. (1991). Integrating economics into the curriculum: Teaching ideas from England. *The Social Studies, 82,* 67–72.

Chapter 10

Multicultural Education

After you read this chapter, you should be prepared to respond to the following questions:

- ❑ How do children learn about others?
- ❑ Why is it important for teachers to know themselves, to examine their own attitudes and values toward other people?
- ❑ What concepts are key to teaching multicultural education?
- ❑ How can teachers resolve conflicts that occur between children in the classroom?

G eographic limitations no longer distance people from each other. Dewey might be surprised at how accessible the world is today. We can talk to almost in the world anyone in a matter of seconds and travel anywhere in a relatively small number of hours. With e-mail, the internet, and FAX machines, we are no longer apart from anyone in any nation.

Dewey might also marvel at the variety of cultures represented in today's schools. The current wave of immigrants from Asia, Central and South America, the Middle East, as well as Eastern Europe, has brought children of many cultures into schools for young children (Klein, 1995). "It's challenging, yet rewarding," explained a first-grade teacher. "In my class of 23 students, there are children from several Central American countries, two Hmongs, one Chinese, two Iranians, and two Romanians. And not one understands or speaks English."

The emphasis today must be on things that bind people together in cooperative human pursuits. All children must develop the attitudes, skills, and abilities to function in their own society and a worldwide society.

HOW CHILDREN LEARN OF OTHERS

Children's awareness of others begins early. Children as young as 2 years of age have been found to perceive similarities and differences among persons based on physical characteristics, clothing, language, and political orientation. By age 2½, "signs of pre-prejudice—of discomfort with physical differences—may appear and should be addressed" (Derman-Sparks, 1989). Others also document that children's ability to identify ethnic distinctions begins early and continues to manifest itself throughout life (Allport, 1952; Goodman, 1952; Lambert & Klineberg, 1967; Piaget & Weil, 1951).

Younger children seem more accepting of others than do older children. Second graders, for instance, recognize differences in people, but have little emotional reaction about it. By early puberty, however, rejection of others becomes pronounced.

Children in our nation express greater friendliness and open-mindedness to foreign people than children in other nations. Perhaps because of our immigrant heritage, or their greater exposure to television, books, films, and travel, children in the United States are more open and friendly toward foreign people than children in 10 other nations (Lambert & Klineberg, 1967; Pellowski, 1969).

Because ideas of others begin early, "it seems imperative to begin the development of world understanding during the early years, while the child is most impressionable and receptive. International understandings must begin with young children, while they are forming attitudes and points of view which will have an influence in their adult lives" (NAEYC, 1996).

A perception of how children learn attitudes toward others and the roles of self-concept and significant others in the development of children's views of others is a necessary foundation for teaching multi-cultural understanding.

1. The manner in which the concept of *own group* is taught to children, and ultimately learned by them, has important psychological consequences. The process of establishing the concept apparently produces an exaggerated and caricatured view of one's own nation and people. Thus, the stereotyping process itself appears to start in the early conceptions children develop of their own group; it is only much later, from 10 years of age on, that children start stereotyping foreign people.

2. Early training in national contrasts appears to mark certain foreign groups as outstanding examples of peoples who are different. The researchers noted a strong cross-national tendency for children, even the 6-year-olds, to refer spontaneously to the same foreign groups as people who are not like them.

3. The early training in contrasts appears to leave the impression with children that foreign people are different, strange, and unfriendly. Children stressed the differences of foreign people, which suggests that children's overall orientation is a suspicious one.

4. Early training in national contrasts also affects children's self-conceptions. Children in certain nations think of themselves in racial, religious, or national terms. Self-concepts of certain groups of children reflect what Lambert and Klineberg presume to be the culturally significant criteria used in their training to make distinctions between their own group and others.

5. It is made clear that parents and other significant people in the child's environment transfer their own emotionally toned view of other people

to the child by assigning specific attributes to members of particular groups during that very period of cognitive development when the child has not fully differentiated one group from another or his or her own group from others (Lambert & Klineberg, 1967).

What Are Your Attitudes?

Before teaching about another country, ask yourself what you really know and feel about the country. Because children will model after you and copy your attitudes and values, ask yourself the following:

1. What have I read from each country? Did this reading present an accurate point of view? Was it current? Was it written by someone of that nationality?
2. Am I familiar with any of the country's films or filmmakers? What do I know about the art of the country?
3. What do I know of the religious customs of the country? The government? The economy? Is my current information up to date? Is it free from stereotypes?
4. Are my background materials relevant to the culture as a whole, or do they just represent one minute portion of the people?
5. Have I talked to anyone who is a native of the country or who has lived in the country for some length of time?

In regard to personal teaching behavior—

Am I a world-minded citizen, concerned that my students become world-minded?

Am I constantly striving to gain more knowledge and increase my skills in human relations education? Am I planning and working cooperatively with parents to achieve the goals of human relations education?

In the classroom—

Do I convey an attitude of approaching human relationships with understanding and compassion, both in my verbal and nonverbal communication?

Is the point of view I present free from bias?

Do I create an atmosphere of warmth and acceptance? Do I provide freedom to create? Do I provide many opportunities for children to make choices and decisions on their level?

Do I encourage children to look at problems from various points of view? Is divergent thinking encouraged? (Pellowski, 1969, p. 3)

Teachers model understanding. It is clear that a teacher trained to promote cooperative learning, to value student opinion, to respect the rights and opinions of others, to encourage students to reflect upon their experience and play with new ideas, and to give students some responsibility for control over the learning process may foster many of the learning outcomes that are important in human rights education (Levin, 1994; Wardle, 1996).

Children bring to school values and attitudes developed early in life, values they have internalized directly from their parents. To survive, children must win their parents' approval by meeting their parents' expectations and by taking on their parents' attitudes and values. Teachers who plan to foster international understanding need to work closely with the children's families. Beginning with the attitudes and values of the home, you can add new experiences to extend understanding as well as provide additional information for parents and children.

To encourage multicultural understanding, you will want to include parents in their children's education at school. You can open the classroom to parents, welcoming them and their attitudes with respect and establishing a system of open communication. You might find these techniques useful:

1. Ask the parents to express their goals and objectives for their children: "What multicultural understandings do you want your children to learn this year?" "What do you think is important for them to know in the future?" "How do you think they should be taught these things?" "What do you want them to learn about people from other lands?"

2. As opportunities present themselves, you can help parents and the community explore their own attitudes and feelings about others through group discussions, meetings with resource persons, or individual conferences.

KEY CONCEPTS

Social scientists have identified several key concepts that contribute to children's multicultural understanding in the preschool-primary curriculum:

❑ *interdependency.* Social studies can emphasize the idea that the human experience is an increasingly globalized phenomenon in which people are influenced continually through their interactions with others.

❑ *multiculturalism.* The human experience is diverse and multicultural. Children's understanding and acceptance of cultures beyond their own begin during early childhood. Children are quick to recognize differences in people. It's more difficult for them to recognize that people everywhere have the same needs, feelings, and concerns.

❑ *conflict resolution.* Early on, children can learn to handle conflicts with others without aggression or violence. These early experiences can be extended to understanding how nations work together to settle differences without using force or violence.

INTERDEPENDENCY

We need to live with others, and others need to live with us. Young children will not be able to understand how our nation relies on other faraway nations for trade and commerce, and they certainly will not understand the political and cultural dependency of all nations. However, a basis for developing the concept that every part of the world is interdependent can be fostered in young children.

Interdependency begins early for humans because infants depend on their parents for their care. Parents, to be parents at all, depend on the infant. Within the context of the home, children experience the idea of interdependency. In the preschool-primary classroom, there are other opportunities to experience the concept of interdependency:

❑ Live pets, requiring food, care, and attention, give children concrete experiences with the interdependence of living things.

❑ Immediate classroom activities and happenings demonstrate to the children how important it is to be helpful and how they can help one another. They can return toys and materials to their proper places, leave the easels ready for

We are all interdependent.

the next painters, pick up coats that have fallen from hooks, or help one another button painting smocks.

❑ Each child can tell the class something she or he can do well or likes to do for the class. These statements could be recorded in a booklet or an experience chart.

❑ Children can take a trip through the school to see the relationships between the class and the school and the relationships among all the persons who work in the school.

❑ A pictorial chart, showing ways children can help one another, can be an ongoing project, with pictures added as new ways of helping are developed.

❑ Children can be involved in activities that require working together, such as setting a table, cooking simple foods, caring for a garden, or building a piece of large equipment. Each child can be responsible for a specific part of the group project.

Similarities

A focus on similarities, rather than differences, is recommended for a number of reasons. First, children are already able to identify differences and are more likely to concentrate on these rather than on how people everywhere are similar. Further, children begin stereotyping other groups by expressing distrust or fear of those who are different.

Focusing on similarities is not simplistic ("We have different color skins, but we're all alike"); instead, it is complicated and complex, and concentrates on the fact that humans everywhere share in the human experience. This shared "human experience and cultural diversity can be woven into all aspects of the curriculum. The emphasis on social and emotional development can be expanded to incorporate the enhancement of children's cultural identity and their awareness, concerns and respect for other people" (Ramsey, 1982, p. 24).

By illustrating that, regardless of group membership or geography, people are bound together by their similarities, the content of the social studies serves to unite people. Children who understand similarities among people are less likely to fear, distrust, and stereotype others. The world over, in all societies, people share the following commonalities:

❑ art forms
❑ group rules
❑ social organization
❑ basic needs
❑ language

Art Forms

Children who are encouraged to create their own poetry, paintings, dance, literature, or handicrafts can readily understand and appreciate the art of other countries (Schiller, 1995). Art from all nations can help children discover people's common heritage. Children can

❑ visit museums to observe the art of many cultures; you can display art from all over the world in the classroom.

❑ begin an exchange of their paintings, drawings, or creative writing with a school in some other land.

❑ invite foreign visitors to tell folktales from their nations; you can compare the folktales with those of the United States.

❑ listen to poetry from other lands—perhaps some haiku from Japan—and dictate their own poetry.

Group Rules

As children begin to realize that rules are necessary to live together effectively, they can understand how groups function more successfully when the rights of each group member are recognized. Children can

❑ establish their own rules for using playground equipment, allowing people in the housekeeping area, or walking to the cafeteria.

❑ use the rules of the school—walk in the hall, remain quiet while waiting for the bus—to illustrate the rules of a larger community. You can also help them compare classroom rules with their rules at home.

❑ explore the rules of the community such as the traffic rules. Do all communities have such rules? Why?

Performance Objective	Level of Self-Expression	Stimulus Questions
Identify family members and roles in Japanese families and describe jobs and responsibilities within the family.	Empathy	How do Japanese children feel?
Identify feelings and behaviors if child were in Japanese family.	Identification	How would you feel if you were him/her?
Identify/compare feelings, behaviors, and roles in own family.	Direct	How do you feel about your role in your family?

Box 10.1
An illustrative Sequence—Communities Around the World Share Similar Feelings (Grades 2–3)
From "Infusing human dignity into social studies" by S. F. Fagen, 1990, *The Social Studies, 81,* pp. 135–138.

❑ determine what rules the nation has and compare these rules to the laws of other lands.

Social Organization

Although the composition of families and social groups changes dramatically from place to place, all human beings live in some type of group or social organization. To comprehend the similarities among social groups, children in primary grades can

❑ graph their families' composition to show how many different kinds of family units are represented in their classroom. You will want to discuss with the children how these family units are the same.

❑ exchange letters with a family in some other nation to learn how it is like a family in this country.

❑ invite visitors from other countries to tell about their families, the things family members do together, and how they share work or celebrate holidays.

Basic Needs

Borrowing concepts from the field of economics, you can teach children that people the world over have the same basic needs for food, shelter, and clothing. Children might be able to

❑ taste food from other countries.

❑ examine different shelters from around the world. Ask them: "How are they just like our homes?" "How are they different?" "How many different kinds of homes do we live in?" "How are they alike?"

❑ compare the clothing of other nations. Question them: "How is it just like the clothing we wear?" "What things do we use that they do not?" One kindergartner, after comparing shoes from seven different countries, made the statement, "The shoes are different, but everybody has feet."

A unit on bread illustrates how people of different cultures, while having the same basic needs, meet these needs in different ways (Bennett, 1995). After reading the book *Bread, Bread, Bread* by Ann Morris, teachers asked children what kind of bread they ate at home. The names of the different breads were listed and discussed. Samples were brought to school, compared, and tasted. Children made bread and wrote stories about breads, learning that bread is a food all people have in common, even though the types may differ.

Language

People everywhere communicate both verbally and nonverbally. Verbal communication may involve many languages; nonverbal communication is useful when the verbal communication of others is not understood. Children can learn that both verbal and nonverbal communication skills are involved when they try to express feelings, ideas, attitudes, and knowledge. Children can

❑ be given many opportunities to communicate in the classroom on a one-to-one basis or in large or small groups. Methods might include using a telephone or tape recorder or dictating to you. You can draw children's attention to their use of nonverbal communication and extend the concept by introducing Indian sign language or the sign language used to communicate with the deaf, role playing, or dramatizations.

❑ read or listen to the story, *Children of the World Say Good Morning,* by Bill Martin, and learn how to say "good morning" in some language other than English.

❑ listen to someone speaking another language; you or a visitor might teach the children a few phrases in the language. You could teach a few simple songs and let the children listen to music from other countries.

One element common to communication is that people everywhere have feelings. If we saw our homes being destroyed, we would feel the way families in Iraq did when it happened to them; Biafran parents watching helplessly as their children starve feel as we would if our children were starving; Brazilian children feel the same way the children in the United States do when they can go to the beach and swim in the ocean.

Children learn to express their feelings positively in the classroom, without hurting others; they learn to recognize that all people have the same feelings. When reading stories of people from other lands, such as *The Story About Ping,* by Marjorie Flack, you can ask the children: "How do you think the boy felt when he fell into the water?" "How would you have felt?" "Did anything like that ever happen to you?"

One teacher, after reading Aliki's *The Two of Them,* asked children to talk about love. The children talked about love they receive from adults, how a cat loves her kittens, and so forth. In another lesson, two guinea pigs of different colors were used to demonstrate how things can be alike but different, which led to a discussion of how people can love others who may be different from them and can be friends with others who are different in skin color.

Other classroom experiences give children opportunities to clarify their feelings toward other people and understand the feelings of others. You can ask the children: "How did you feel when you hit him?" "How do you think he felt?" "How did it feel when they asked you to play with them?" "How did you feel when they called you a name?" You can also help children perceive the feelings of others: "What do you think she was telling you when she screamed at you?" "How do you think she felt?"

Resources for Learning About Others

While stereotypical cultural materials are not as prevalent as they once were, the most effective resources available for children's development of international

Bester, R. (1981). *Fire fighter Jim.* New York: Crown Books.
   A photographic introduction to an actual fire fighter.

Curtis, N. & Greenland, P. (1992). *How bread is made. How paper is made. How steel is made. How tires are made.* Minneapolis: Lerner.
   A series for young readers to find out how things are made. Encourages young children to ask how other things are made.

Dorros, A. (1993). *The radio man.* New York: HarperCollins.
   A split-page book in English and Spanish of migrant family workers.

Florian, D. (1983). *People working.* New York: HarperCollins.
   A variety of workers is introduced.

Harshman, M. (1993). *Uncle James.* New York: Dutton.
   A story of hard times on an Indiana farm, of interest to older primary children.

Jaspershon, W. (1994). *My hometown library.* Boston: Houghton MIfflin.
   Introduces children to people who work in service jobs.

Kimmelman, L. (1989). *Frannie's fruits.* New York: Greenwillow.
   A look at the seller's side of the fruit stand.

Machotka, H. (1992). *Pasta factory.* Boston: Houghton Mifflin.
   How pasta is made.

Maestro, B. (1988). *Dollars and cents for Harriet.* New York: Crown.
   A concept book in sizzling color about money.

Marston, H. I. (1993). *Big rigs.* New York: Dutton.
   Trucks and what they haul.

Mitchell, J. S. (1984). *My mommy makes money.* New York: Little & Brown.
   A story of several mothers who work outside of the home in a variety of occupations.

Ransom, C. (1993). *The big green pocketbook.* New York: HarperCollins.
   A child and her mother visit the bank and dry cleaner and complete other chores. The daughter puts all the mementos from the places visited in her big green pocketbook.

Rockville, A. (1984). *Our garage sale.* New York: Greenwillow.
   The planning and implementation of an American tradition, the garage sale, seen through the experiences of children.

Shulevitz, U. (1979). *The treasure.* New York: Farrar.
   A man's discovery that the most valuable things in life are usually found at home leads to discussing the differences between the things children want and those they really need.

Viorst, J. (1978). *Alexander, who used to be rich last Sunday.* New York: Macmillan.
   Alexander has great plans for the five-dollar gift he received from his grandparents.

Wellington, M. (1992). *Mr. cookie baker.* New York: Dutton.
   Follows a baker through the day.

Ziefert, H. (1986). *A new coat for Anna.* New York: Knopf.
   Finding materials to make a coat in post-World War II Europe.

Box 10.2
Books With an Economic Theme

Janice Hale suggests that teachers and parents use folktales to illustrate to African-American children the importance of faith and perseverance, including the body of literature that features heroes, from the mythical John Henry to Jack Johnson and Joe Louis. Literature that tells the stories of real-life African-American heroes and heroines, such as Jackie Robinson, Marian Anderson, and Booker T. Washington, transmits the message that quicksand and land mines characterize the road to becoming an African- American achiever in America and that it is possible to overcome these.

Some examples are

Abrahams, R. D. (1985). *Afro-American folktales.* New York: Random House.

Adoff, A. (1984). *Black is brown is tan.* New York: Harper.

Dumas, A. (1982). *Golden legacy.* Seattle: Baylor.

Giovanni, N. (1982). *Sing a soft black song.* New York: Hill and Wang.

Hudson, W. & Wilson-Wesley, V. (1988). *Book of black heroes from A to Z.* Orange, NJ: Just Us Books.

Musgrove, M. (1987). *Ashanti to Zulu: African traditions.* New York: Dial.

Box 10.3
Transmission of Cultural Values to Young African–American Children through Literature
From the "The Transmission of Cultural Values to Young African American Children" by Janice Hale, 1991, *Young Children*, 46(6), 7–16.

concepts are still the children themselves. Their heritage and backgrounds of experience provide a base from which you can build their knowledge.

Teachers, along with children and their families, can explore the ethnic heritage of the children in the class by making charts of the different nationalities represented, discussing the customs of different families, and participating in these customs.

Equally effective resources are people who have lived or visited in other countries, or who are citizens of other nations. As visitors to the class, they can illustrate how people everywhere are similar, yet they do things in different ways. "The mere presence of the resource persons, however, does not guarantee the development of positive attitudes and understandings of the people and countries being discussed" (Pellowski, 1969, p. 18). To ensure a positive experience for both visitor and children, you need to prepare for the resource visitor:

❑ Know something about the person to make sure that the individual has more than cursory knowledge of the country and is able to talk to children.

❑ Brief the visitor about the class and help plan the presentation. Young children become restless when asked only to listen. The visitor might be asked to include some concrete materials or props in the discussion to attract the children.

❑ Be certain that the children have sufficient understanding of the country. Visitors from Bombay or Rio de Janeiro are frequently appalled when children want to know whether they have refrigerators or automobiles.

Traditional values and customs are kept alive in the classroom.

❑ Prepare the children for possible differences in appearance or language before the visitor comes. Discuss with them how to behave in the presence of a guest. Plan with them to make the guest comfortable: "Who will take her coat? Where will she sit? How will we listen, ask questions, and thank her?"

❑ Have globes and maps available so that children can locate the country.

You can use other experiences to help children recognize cultural similarities. You might suggest specific television shows that offer children insight into other people's cultures, or bring in newspaper and magazine articles that clarify children's concepts of others. Reference books, travel posters, photographs, films, slides, and movies are also useful to compare people's similarities. Analyze these materials to make certain they

❑ reflect the many groups in our nation and world.

❑ do not omit, distort, or present with lack of sensitivity pictures of any group of people.

❑ reflect our pluralistic society.

Holiday activities can introduce children to pleasant and interesting aspects of other people's customs. Young children enjoy a Japanese Kite Day as they marvel at the Japanese custom of giving children a day off from school to fly kites. An egg tree for an Easter celebration helps children understand and appreciate Slovakian celebrations; baking and eating hot-cross buns may help children feel close to children in Great Britain.

Museums, historical societies, embassies—all offer children concrete experiences with other cultures. Each community will have some type of museum where children can view artifacts from other lands and compare their similarities.

Tasting a variety of foods derived from different ethnic cultures, discussing why people prepare the foods the way they do, and finding the countries on the map are all experiences that help children develop an awareness of other people's customs and similarities.

"Toys and play are universals in childhood and as such offer a bonding that serves as a natural basis for a global education curriculum" (Swiniarski, 1991, p. 161). Teachers can use toys and play to connect children with one another from all parts of the world. You can provide children with toys made in various countries, such as puzzles from Holland, blocks from Switzerland, dolls from Korea, or games originating in Africa, and children over age 6 or 7 can be introduced to games children in other nations play. In addition, teachers need to interact sensitively with children. They may point out that the differences in the dress of dolls reflect the variety of clothes people wear rather than being costumes or that steering wheels on cars are on *another* side of the car rather than on the *wrong* side (Swiniarski, 1991).

Other activities can take place. Kindergarten children can play with puppets and use these to retell stories. The variations in familiar folktales, such as the variety of ways people around the world tell the story of *Three Billy Goats Gruff* and the role of the troll, can be compared and acted out with puppets. First graders could compare toy catalogs from other nations, or draw and write their own (Swiniarski, 1991), and second graders might put on a toy fair in the school library.

CONFLICT RESOLUTION

"We're sharing" was the reply when two children, scuffling over the same bike, were asked what they were doing. Teachers of young children rarely experience a day without at least one conflict in the group. Whenever young children are together, there will be fighting and arguments. Conflict is healthy, and indeed necessary, for children's growth and development; it is the way they balance becoming individuals with learning to become a part of a group. Children's conflicts may arise

❑ *within themselves.* They cry over a puzzle that is beyond their ability; they wrestle with a decision to paint or work with clay; or, making the wrong decision, they go off to sulk, with thumb in mouth, alone with their conflict.

Culture is transmitted through stories, song, and art. The following are a sample of children's books transmitting culture.

Baden, R. (1990). *And Sunday makes seven.* New York: Whitman.
This rhythmic folktale is set in a village in Costa Rica.

Brusca, M. C. (1991). *On the pampas.* New York: Holt.
An Argentine ranch is the setting for the antics of two young cousins, both girls, who ride horses.

Dyan, S. (1994). *Under the moon.* New York: Dial.
The sensitive connection between past and present occurs when Jenny finds a Native American arrowhead in her backyard.

Gertz, S. E. (1991). *Hanukkah and Christmas at my house.* Middleton, OH: Willow & Laurel Press.
A holiday story that adds more understanding of diversity.

Grossman, V. & Long, S. (1991). *Ten little rabbits.* San Francisco: Chronicle Books.
With delightful surprise, this fable celebrates Native American traditions as it teaches young children to count from 1 to 10.

Gray, N. (1988). *A country far away.* New York: Orchard Books.
One single line of text separates top and bottom illustrations that tell the stories of a boy in an African village and another in a suburb of a Western nation.

Heide, F. P. (1990). *The day of Ahmed's secret.* New York: Lothrop.
An average day of a child in historic downtown Cairo.

Kimmel, E. A. (1994). *Anansi and the talking melon.* New York: Holiday House.
A folktale told in the tradition of West Africa and the Caribbean.

Oabinkaram, E. T. (1994). *The ancestor tree.* New York: Lodestar Books.
The children of the village teach the elders.

Pinkney, J. (1994). *John Henry.* New York: Dial.
The long-loved retelling of an African American folk tale.

Pomerantz, C. (1989). *The chalk doll.* New York: Lippincott.
A mother tells the story of her upbringing in Jamaica.

Rattigan, J. K. (1993). *Dumpling Soup.* Boston: Little.
A family celebrates the new year in Hawaii.

Sloat, T. & Sloat, R. (1993). *The hungry giant of the tundra.*
Traditional Ypik folktales.

Tafuri, N. (1993). *If I had a Puka: Poems in eleven languages.* New York: Mulberry Books.
Eleven short, beautifully illustrated poems in 11 languages.

William, M. (1994). *Zora Hurston and the Chinaberry tree.* New York: Lee & Low.
Children explore their town and listen to people tell stories.

Box 10.4
Multicultural Books

❑ *with others in the class.* Children fight with one another over toys or objects, in play, or about an idea.

❑ *outside their personal worlds.* Mother and father argue over who will take the car or how much money to spend; teacher and aide disagree about the best way to discipline or reward children; and children experience the conflict that occurs in the wider world as they watch strikes, fights, and wars in the movies and on television.

There are at least two effective ways to handle conflicts that occur when children are together. The first is to validate children's feelings and help them discover ways to express their feelings through nonaggression, and without hurting self or others. The second is to find ways to keep aggressive feelings from multiplying.

Minimizing Conflicts

You might minimize the normal conflicts within a classroom by

❑ helping children form close friendships and feel the security of friends. Children, feeling the support of friends, are able to react to frustrations with less aggression.

❑ making clear that aggressive acts are not allowed in the classroom, stopping them when and if they appear. Remember, however, that punishment can serve as a form of frustration and may only increase a child's need to act out aggressively.

❑ modeling for the children ways of meeting frustration without aggressive acts.

❑ establishing rules, in cooperation with the children, that protect the rights of each individual.

❑ removing potentially frustrating situations for the children by preparing the environment with sufficient equipment; by providing tasks children can succeed in; and by planning a balanced program with opportunities for choices, self-expression, and physical activity.

❑ helping children to deal with their feelings openly and to understand that people everywhere have feelings. The book *David Was Mad,* by Bill Martin, allows children to discuss their feelings of anger without guilt or fear of reprimand and to realize that everyone gets angry. The teacher might express personal feelings to the class—"I was really so angry that happened," or, "That makes me feel so happy inside"—and then demonstrate to the class positive ways of handling those feelings. When children begin to see that everyone has feelings, they are better able to relate openly to one another and to feel a oneness with all of the people of the world.

Even though classrooms are arranged to minimize frustration and conflict, accept the aggression that does occur as an opportunity for teaching. When fights occur, you can intervene and, if necessary, physically separate the children, taking each child by the hand and quietly calming them down. Then, after the children have settled down, follow up with a discussion of what happened, and a solution can be worked out. Rather than focusing on who started it or who said what and why or, worse yet, asking children to say they are sorry when they really want to hit harder, explain why the fight occurred and how to better handle the situation. You might explain why one child called another a name or took a toy: "He wanted to play with the wagon, and you wouldn't let him have it, so he hit you." "José, if you ask him for it, he might give it to you." "She called you a name because she wanted you to play with her, and you said no." Whatever you say to the children, it is important for you not to make them feel guilty, resentful, or more frustrated—all of which can lead to an increase in hostility and make peaceful settling of conflicts more difficult.

Teachers need to let children handle some conflicts without interference. As many conflicts are short, over before they have fully begun, children can handle them without help.

Redirecting children's anger or hostility gives them yet another way to deal with conflict and helps children know that they can be angry, but they must handle their anger in ways that will not be harmful to others. Words can help: "You really wanted to hit, spit, kick, or whatever, but you cannot hurt anyone here. Tell him how angry you are." Some teachers have found that anger can be dispelled by asking a child to run around the playground as fast as possible, to pound clay, to hammer nails into wood, or to draw or paint a picture.

Understanding War—Teaching Peace

Many children may be personally involved in wars because a parent, relative, or neighbor is serving or has served in the military, or because a relative or family friend is experiencing war. Even for children who are not personally involved in war, it is a part of their lives.

Television and the press bring war into children's homes. Even children's books revolve around the topic of war. When Dr. Seuss published *The Butter Battle Book* in 1984, it seemed as if children, their teachers, and parents would not be able to escape the topic of war (Carlsson-Paige & Levin, 1986).

Children's concepts of war develop early in life (Tolley, 1973; Torney-Purta, 1982). English children make their first coherent utterances about peace and war by the age of 6, and by the age of 7 or 8, they have fairly well-defined ideas of war and peace (Cooper, 1965). Easton and Hess (1961) wrote that the truly formative years of the maturing members of a political system would seem to be those years between the ages of 3 and 13.

You can't even think about teaching children about war and peace without first understanding children's thinking. Carlsson-Paige and Levin (1985) suggest the following strategies to uncover children's ideas of war and peace:

❑ Try to take the children's point of view when you listen to them talk about war.

❑ Consider the child's general cognitive development and understanding.

❑ Think about how children will transform what they hear about war in their own unique ways. (p. 6)

Because of their immature sense of social morality, young children seem to accept or favor war more than older children. According to Cooper (1965), girls are less likely to become interested in war, warlike games, or aggression than boys; boys, during interviews, referred to war more frequently. Tolley (1973) found no steady growth of either acceptance or repudiation of war in young children. He did note that 6-year-olds demonstrate a greater hostility to others than children of other ages, and that children in the third and fourth grades rate wars as more glamorous than do children of other ages. Children's concepts of peace, somewhat less tangible than concepts of war, are usually absent; when present, they are associated with interpersonal peace and absence of personal conflict.

Young children, perhaps since the beginning of time, have played war. Some behaviorists believe that young children who have little power or control over their lives play war as a means of feeling powerful and in control. By pretending to be a Power Ranger, Teen-Age Ninja Mutant Turtle, or whatever warlike action figure is popular at the time, children feel and experience the power they do not otherwise have. Others believe war play is a natural and safe way for children to express normal aggression and, as such, is necessary. Still others see war play as a way children can handle fear of war, or make sense of wars they observe in the media (Kuykendall, 1995).

Violence in the media is currently blamed for war play among children. Violent acts occurring in cartoons, movies, television shows, and computer games are observed and modeled (Greenberg, 1995). Violence marketed to children through the identity of television with compatible toys further channels children into imitating violence they have seen on the screen (Carlsson-Paige & Levin, 1995).

Just as children have always played war, teachers and parents have always struggled with how to respond to war play. Should teachers permit or ban war play? Should they redirect it—and how?

Obviously, any war play that intrudes on the rights and safety of others must be stopped. Even when war play is not out of hand, it can be redirected. Rather than focus on the game or the war toy, teachers might concentrate on children's feelings. "An openness to his own feelings, and an acceptance of feelings, might take a way the child's urgency for making use of war games" (Buettner, 1981, p. 104).

The end to war games, and ultimately wars, will come only when children and adults do not have to act out their "locked up feelings for a lifetime, when it is possible to succeed in setting their own feelings free, to reveal conflicts and openly resolve them. A beginning is made when parents and educators are learning appreciation of children and realizing their resistance to children's feelings" (Buettner, 1981, p. 104).

Believing children should learn alternatives to open violent behavior and actions that can stem from war toys in the school, Myers-Walls and Fry-Miller (1984) suggest banning war toys entirely. They suggest

❑ discussing with the children the reasons for banning war toys from the class-room.

❑ avoiding films, books, or games which glorify violence.

❑ stressing cooperative play.

❑ modeling positive, nonviolent behavior.

❑ providing toys and books that support peace. (p. 30)

If you think children are playing war as a means of handling their own fears of war, then you might try to

❑ consider and talk about fears. Respect that children are fearful and give them strategies for coping, but do not embellish their fears.

❑ give children accurate and appropriate information. Nothing is as bad as not knowing the truth. Know what and how much truth will help children at this point in time. Tell children in words they can understand.

❑ see that children develop mastery over self and their world; put them in con-trol as much as possible.

❑ emphasize cooperative play and positive, nonviolent behaviors.

SUMMARY

When teachers emphasize the things that bind people together and help children see the similarities among all people, regardless of culture, children are intro-duced to the multicultural nature of their world. As children learn about their own country, they also learn of other countries. A child's self-concept and the atti-tudes and values of significant others play an important role in developing multi-cultural understanding.

The fact that all people are dependent upon each other and that all people are similar is evident in the fact that all have language; families and other social groups; systems for provision of food, shelter, clothing, government and laws, religion and ethics; systems for explaining natural phenomena; rules regarding property; and art forms.

Some understanding of how to handle conflict is a part of multicultural edu-cation. Children can be made aware that they have conflicts within themselves, as well as with others. Some initial tools for settling conflicts can be introduced.

PROJECTS

1. Contact the embassies of different countries and request free materials that present current information about the country. Write to The Embassy of _____, Washington, DC. Some of the materials will be appro-

priate for use with young children; others will be useful in building your own understandings of other countries.

2. Begin a resource file of children's games from around the world. Teach one game to a small group of young children, explaining the origin of the game to them.

3. Read Dr. Seuss's *The Butter Battle Book.* As a class, discuss the uses and abuses in this story of two fictitious countries that disagree over which side their bread should be buttered on. Nancy Carlsson-Paige and Diane E. Levin's "The Butter Battle Book: Uses and Abuses With Young children" in *Young Children,* March 1986, could be used as a resource.

4. Collect magazine pictures portraying children in other countries. Think of several ways to use these pictures with young children.

5. Obtain a curriculum guide from your local school system or state department of education. Analyze the guide for stereotypic representations of other people.

6. Within your classroom or college, many nationalities and ethnic groups will be represented. Interview some of these people, asking them what elements of their culture they would want young children to understand.

RESOURCES

The National Association for the Education of Young Children's Position Paper, *NAEYC Position Statement: Responding to Linguistic and Cultural Diversity—Recommendations for Effective Early Childhood Education,* adopted 1995 and published in *Young Children,* January 1996, pp. 4–13, offers an excellent perspective on how teachers can learn to work effectively with cultural diversity.

A number of associations are devoted to fostering peace. These will have information and resources available for teachers:

Concerned Educators Allied for a Safe Environment (CEASE)
17 Gerry Street
Cambridge, MA 02138

Educators for Social Responsibility
23 Garden Street
Cambridge, MA 01238

University of Denver
Center for Teaching International Relations
Denver, CO 80208

Children in the primary grades will enjoy and benefit from having a pen pal. Even children in kindergarten can learn about others by exchanging pictures and dictated letters with other young children who live far from them. For help in setting up a pen pal program, contact

International Friendship League
40 Mount Vernon Street
Boston, MA 02108

League of Friendship, Inc.
PO Box 509
Charlottesville, VA 22905

Student Letter Exchange
Waseca, MN 56093

REFERENCES

Allport, G. (1952). *The nature of prejudice.* New York: Doubleday Anchor Books.

Bennett, L. (1995). Wide world of breads in children's literature. *Young Children, 50*(5), 64–70.

Buettner, C. (1981). War toys or the organization of hostility. *International Journal of Early Childhood, 13*(1), 104–112.

Carlsson-Paige, N., & Levin, D. (1985). *Helping young children understand peace, war, and the nuclear threat.* Washington, DC: National Association for the Education of Young Children.

Carlsson-Paige, N., & Levin, D. (1986). The butter battle book: Uses and abuses with young children. *Young Children, 50*(5), 62–63.

Carlsson-Paige, N., & Levin, D. (1995). Can teachers resolve the war-play dilemma? *Young Children, 50*(5), 62–63.

Cooper, P. (1965). The development of concepts of war. *Journal of Peace Research, 2,* 1–18.

Derman-Sparks, L. (1989). *Anti-bias curriculum: Tools for empowering young children.* Washington, DC: National Association for the Education of Young Children.

Easton, D., & Hess, R. (1961). Youth and the political system. In M. Lipset & L. Lowenthal (Eds.), *Culture and the social character of education.* New York: Free Press.

Goodman, M. (1952). *Race awareness in young children.* Reading, MA: Addison-Wesley.

Greenberg, J. (1995). Making friends with the power rangers. *Young Children, 50*(5), 60–61.

Klein, H.A. (1995). Urban Appalachian children in a Northern school: A study of diversity. *Young Children, 50*(3), 10–17.

Kuykendall, J. (1995). Is gun play ok here? *Young Children, 50*(5), 56–60.

Lambert, W., & Klineberg, O. (1967). *Children's views of foreign peoples: A cross cultural study.* New York: Appleton-Century Crofts.

Levin, D. E. (1994). Building a peaceable classroom: Helping young children feel safe in violent times. *Childhood Education, 70,* 66–70.

Myers-Wall, J.A., & Fry-Miller,K. M. (1984). Nuclear war: Helping children overcome fears. *Young Children, 39*(4), 27–32.

National Association for the Education of Young Children. (1996). NAEYC position statement: Responding to linguistic and cultural diversity—Recommendations for effective early childhood education. *Young Children, 51*(2), 4–13.

Pellowski, A. (1969). Learning about present-day children in other cultures. In *Children and International Education Portfolio No. 6.* Washington, DC: Association for Childhood Education International.

Piaget, J., & Weil, A. (1951). The development in children of the idea of the homeland and of relations with other countries. *International Social Science Bulletin, 3,* 66–73.

Ramsey, P. G. (1982). Multicultural education in early childhood. *Young Children, 37*(2), 13–25.

Schiller, M. (1995). An emergent art curriculum that fosters understanding. *Young Children, 50*(3), 33–39.

Swiniarski, L. B. (1991). Toys: Universals for teaching global education. *Childhood Education, 67,* 161–170.

Tolley, H. (1973). *Children and war.* New York: Teachers College Press.

Torney-Purta, J. (1982). *Research and evaluation in global education: The state of the art and priorities for the future.* Paper presented at the Conference on Priorities in Global Education, Easton, MD.

Wardle, F. (1996). Proposal: An anti-bias ecological model for multicultural education. *Childhood Education, 71*(3), 152–157.

Chapter 11

Current Topics

If the nation expects its adults to have an abiding interest in news and current developments and have a desire to keep informed, the groundwork for these attitudes, interests, and skills must be laid in their school.

John Jarolimek and Walter C. Parker, 1993, p. 204.

After you read this chapter, you should be prepared to respond to the following questions:

- ❑ How do children make and understand news?
- ❑ What skills and concepts can increase children's awareness of the need to care for their environment? How do children develop social consciousness?
- ❑ How can young children be taught to serve others?
- ❑ What concepts embedded in career awareness are meaningful to young children?

W ill the war come here, Mommy?" asks 3-year-old Shawn. Bombarded with information from the media, even young children are aware of current events and have some idea of what is going on in the world around them. They observe people working at various jobs and careers, and are aware of their own environment. "I've collected three bags of aluminum cans just in this one block," says Paul, full of pride because he is contributing to recycling efforts in the community. Then too, daily news events, both good and bad, affect young children. "I'm going to give my blanket to the homeless," announces 5-year-old Lavolia.

Because children do experience current events, teachers have the responsibility of including them in the social studies curriculum (Jarolimek & Parker, 1993). They can introduce children to the concept of news, and the main ideas of environmental education can foster awareness of careers.

From time to time, adding current topics that are of interest to children will help them make sense of the things that happen around them and gain feelings of competency and control over their lives. From this base of awareness, children will begin the long process of becoming informed citizens who are not only aware of worldwide events, but will participate in the whole of society.

Just because a topic is current, however, does not mean it should be introduced to young children. Before planning to include a current topic, ask yourself the following:

❑ Would this content help fulfill my fundamental goals for social studies?

❑ Is this content important in their individual lives?

❑ Can each child experience success with this content?

❑ Can this content be integrated with the rest of the curriculum of the preschool or primary grades?

❑ Is it suited to the developmental levels and abilities of the children?

❑ Does this content fit together with other topics from other school subjects?

❑ Can it be developed with the use of a variety of interesting and lively teaching strategies?

CURRENT EVENTS

For the young, the study of current events begins with themselves. They first become interested in current events by making their own news. From this base, teachers move to news events outside the children's immediate experiences so they may develop an awareness of life's problems, controversies, and achievements.

Making News

Instead of the tired and trite show-and-tell, many teachers have a news time. During this time, teachers and children share news. In addition to their own personal news, children in kindergarten and the primary grades are encouraged to share news items they find in the local paper or in news magazines.

Daily news sharing gives teachers the opportunity to help children clarify their ideas of news. Preschoolers often have the mistaken notion that sharing news means they must have something brand-*new* to share. It takes time and practice for children to learn that news does not mean new clothing or toys, but refers to events that happen in their school, community, and world.

In kindergarten, teachers may begin the day with a news story written on the board or an experience chart. This story is read to the children and should contain information of interest to them or that they need to know before they begin their work. As events that have happened, or will happen, to them or items of interest are shared in the news stories, kindergarten children will begin to pick out words they know in the stories and speculate about what the news for the day is. They will also begin to contribute items for the news story to be read to the group. By first grade, children will be able to write the daily news story.

Other news-sharing events can take place within the classroom. In some schools, a sharing time is scheduled at the end of the work period for children to tell about things they have done that day, show work they have completed, and evaluate their work. Children might tell how they made a particular item, how they worked on the block building, or what they read.

A news chart could be made in one area of the room. This chart could include photos of the children taken when they were working, on a field trip, or at play, with titles telling about the pictures. Children might bring items from home for the news chart, or you could display their news drawings, paintings, and dictated or written stories.

A simply written class newsletter duplicated by the teacher might be prepared. The objectives of the newsletter are to keep parents informed, to encourage children to develop concepts of news, and to develop children's understanding of the functions of a newspaper. Children can dictate or write news items for the newsletter. News notes might include interesting stories about the children: trips they have taken; their parent's jobs; and poems, songs, or stories the children enjoy and the things they have enjoyed during the year. Children can draw pictures directly on the master sheet to illustrate the newspaper.

Children become intimately involved with the processes of news making and reporting if they have the opportunity of actually seeing their pictures or reading stories about themselves in a newspaper. Many communities support small neighborhood newspapers, which will run human-interest stories of young children. A field trip to an apple orchard, celebration of a patriotic holiday, a class effort to clean up the school neighborhood, or a unit on safety might all be of interest to the local editor. Identify the issues and the kinds of events the community is interested in, plan to conduct these with the children, and place a call to the editor of the paper to arrange for a reporter and a photographer to cover the event.

Understanding News

When it is clear that the children understand what constitutes news, you can begin to present articles from newspapers or magazines to teach them to understand individual stories or items. Perhaps beginning with the news story and pictures carried in the local paper, the news chart or board can be expanded to include news of the broader community and environment. You or the children can clip a news item from the paper, tell the class about it, and put it on the board. It is best to begin with local news of interest to the children. A story and picture of storm damage, the new shopping center, street repairs, or a new baby at the zoo can arouse children's interest in looking through the newspaper.

You can bring newspapers to the classroom for children to find items to share. First graders might be interested in analyzing the parts of a newspaper. Using several old papers, children could cut out different elements—the headlines, news stories, news pictures, want ads, advertisements, weather maps, and comics.

Newspapers are not the only source of news for children. Television and radio are other major sources of news. To make television news useful for young children, you might

Children can listen to short segments of important speeches or the news.

❑ videotape a segment of a major news story to show to the children the next day. This lets them view and discuss current events that might not be available to them or might be too long to hold their interest. A brief segment from a presidential inauguration, space shot, or some event from another country would be interesting to children.

❑ use a television in the preschool or primary grades to watch a segment of some special news event.

❑ tape short portions of other events children could listen to. The Martin Luther King, Jr., "I Have a Dream" speech is an example.

As children become interested in the news and aware of current events, they will come into contact with controversial issues as well as tragic events. Some teachers omit all controversy or news of tragedies from the classroom, believing that young children are not mature enough to handle these. Others believe it not only impossible to protect children from these topics, but unfair. Nearly every child watches a plane crash or other disaster on TV over and over again and observes grieving families. It would be unfair and untruthful not to discuss this event with children or at least recognize that, having witnessed the event, they may need help in processing and understanding it. Either way, teachers need to approach controversial and tragic events with caution (Westmoreland, 1996).

Before including a topic for study, assure yourself that the children do have the ability to discuss and explore it. Ask yourself:

❑ Do these children have the mental maturity necessary to work on this topic?

❑ What in their backgrounds would enable them to respond to it and understand it?

❑ Is the issue of real significance to the children? Is their interest high?

You also must be certain that you understand the issue, know its history, and can objectively analyze your own values and attitudes toward the issue. In addition, you will want to inform the parents of your plans to handle the topic with the children. You might ask parents to serve as resources, sharing information they know about the issue. Controversial topics can provide children with a focus for research, encouraging them to find additional information, analyze it, and reach their own conclusions (Rohrer, 1996).

Watching television news shows and reading news magazines and newspapers allow children to begin to build a concept of the importance of being informed citizens. Children who have enjoyed making news and have seen the relationship between news events and their own lives look forward to daily news.

ENVIRONMENTAL EDUCATION

"It is particularly worrisome that children are being disconnected from what we call 'nature.' We ourselves are a part of nature, having evolved along with the other plants and animals. We ought to take more heed in our habitats, knowing their loss is a primary cause for species extinction" (Rivkin, 1995, p. 80).

Realizing we can no longer live this way, every individual, beginning with children, must be concerned with our diminishing natural resources, once thought inexhaustible. Each individual today must be concerned about the chain of life; the welfare of birds, insects, grass, and trees; and the conditions of the air, water, and land.

Any study of the environment and children's responsibility for protecting their world should be (a) ongoing, (b) interdisciplinary, (c) appropriate to the cognitive understandings of the children, (d) related to their everyday experiences, and (e) inclusive of information and concepts as well as attitudes and values.

You can integrate environmental education with children's other educational experiences as part of the total curriculum. Environmental education is based in several disciplines—biology, physics, government, politics, language, and mathematics are just a partial listing.

As in all your teaching of young children, you need to present environmental concepts built on children's experiences. Observation skills help children's understanding of interdependency, aesthetic awareness, and social consciousness—all parts of environmental education.

Observation Skills

We need to concentrate on allowing children to explore, to experience the marvels of nature themselves (Wardle, 1995). Encouraging children to become totally familiar with their environment is accomplished, in part, by teaching children to observe. As children observe and experience their environment, conceptual learning follows. "Eventually as the observations begin to form, learning comes naturally" (Kluge, 1971, p. 26).

Children can learn that they observe by looking. Have the children examine their eyes. Ask the children: "How many eyes do you have?" "What color are they?" "What parts of your eye can you see when you look in the mirror?" Give children the names for eyebrows, eyelashes, pupil, and eyelids.

You can relate children's learning about their eyes to the environment, discussing the nature of the eyes of fish, animals, birds, and reptiles that may live in the classroom. The children might identify differences between eyes of insects and mammals.

Help children identify the things they can see inside and outside their classroom, encouraging them to note colors, shapes, and sizes. Children can also explore what happens when they look through things, such as windows, magnifying lenses, and prisms, and what happens when they look into things, such as mirrors (Science 5/13, 1977).

As they observe, children use other senses. Observation experiences lead children to use their ears, and the senses of smell and touch as they explore their environment. They might discuss and chart the meanings of different sounds and smells.

Field trips within the school building, on the playground, and in the immediate neighborhood focus children's attention on the natural environment. You can encourage children to note the details of things around them. A class on a field trip around an inner-city block noted over 40 different types of plants growing between cracks in the sidewalks, in the street, and even between bricks of the row houses. It seemed impossible, when first looking at the cement and brick city, that so many plants could survive. The children not only observed their immediate environment but went on to classify the plants, noting their likenesses and differences and identifying the conditions that supported this life. To help them focus their observations, the children were given cardboard tubes from toweling to look through.

Another teacher asked second graders to look up and observe the sky. A flock of birds happened to catch the children's attention. Back in the classroom, the children identified the birds they had seen and planned ways they could provide for birds in their school. One group made birdhouses from empty milk cartons and hung these on trees around the school yard, and another located a large discarded plastic garbage can lid and made a birdbath. All the children took part in spreading peanut butter on pine cones and rolling these in birdseed to make feeders for their school and homes.

These activities were followed by the children observing and recording the birds that were attracted to their school and homes. The children found that some of the birds they observed had migrated miles to nest in their area. They marked the migration path of the birds on a map.

After interest in birds subsided, the teacher again took the children outside to observe, but this time she asked them to observe life on the ground. Turning over rocks, the children observed a variety of worm and insect life. Their observations led to finding a number of different insects, worms, and grubs. The children consulted books and found that worms are necessary to human life because they enrich the soil and that other insects are useful in cleaning up the environment. Leaving an apple core in a corner of the play yard, the class observed which insects ate the core and how many days it took before the core was completely gone.

Observations logically lead to other thinking processes. You can ask children to make inferences, predict outcomes, and suggest hypotheses: "Why do you think it's like this?" "What made the trees die?" "What would happen if . . . ?" "How can we find out?" Questions of this type can help children see connections between their observations and the protection of the environment. During field trips, you can point out the interrelatedness of land, water, air, plants, and animals.

Still, questions are used cautiously. Judith Dighe (1993) reminds us that some children can quickly be turned off by the what's-its-name? approach. "Surprising to me, the what-do-you-think . . . ? questions that teachers have been taught to ask can fall flat too" (Dighe, 1993, p. 59). Asking "What do you think made that hole in the acorn?" has "the effect of stopping a child's investigation when my intent was just the opposite." (p. 59). Dighe suggests that when children are observing and exploring their environment, it's best to take your cues from them—listening, watching, sharing interest and delight first, then ask questions that will help children further their own investigations (Dighe, 1993).

Interdependency

The concept of one form of life being dependent on another is basic to environmental education and stems from the biological and physical sciences. Through observations, children become aware of the chain of life around them and of their influence on that life. You can instill a reverence for life when you are cautious about picking wildflowers, tearing branches from trees, or removing a toad to place in a jar in the classroom. Your caution lets children know that the environment deserves respect.

Keeping a variety of living things in the classroom helps foster the concept of interdependency. The care of living things demonstrates to the children the precarious balance found in nature. Reptiles cannot live without insects; insects without plants; plants without sun, water, or soil; and the reptiles may become food for other living things. Keeping an aquarium in balance is sometimes difficult in a classroom, yet it teaches the importance of balance in maintaining life in one type of environment. You can stress children's interdependence with other living things. To live, children depend on and need to protect plants, animals, land, air, and water.

Aesthetic Awareness

Interwoven with the skills and concepts of environmental education is an aesthetic appreciation of the natural environment. As children learn to appreciate the beauty surrounding them, they become more aware of the chain of life and thus more concerned about protecting their environment.

Caring for animals fosters concepts of interdependency.

Aesthetic education is subtle: A classroom that is ordered, contains prints of famous paintings and growing plants, and is decorated with the work of the children leads them to appreciate the beauty of the environment. Dewey (1900) wrote, "If the eye is constantly greeted by harmonious objects, having elegance of form and color, a standard of taste naturally grows" (p. 307). You can point out the delicate construction of a spiderweb; the strong veins of a maple leaf; the smooth, shiny elegance of an eggplant; or the intricate parts of a wildflower. At times you may want to display a single perfect flower, a sculpture, a wood carving, or other object of beauty. In observing the beauty of the environment, encourage children to use all their senses: to look at the object from different perspectives; to notice shapes, sizes, smells, textures, and colors; and to share with one another the interesting things they find in their environment.

> Early childhood educators know that young children benefit from aesthetic experiences. Children are fascinated by beauty. They love nature, and enjoy creating, looking at, and talking about beauty. They express their feelings and ideas through succinct and picturesque language; song, sometimes boisterous and sometimes lyrical; and expressive movements—the essence of poetry, music, and dance. (Feeney & Moravick, 1987, p. 10)

Social Consciousness

Living in a democracy calls for the development of a strong social consciousness, which is basic to environmental education. It will demand that each individual enter into the process of assuming responsibility for environmental protection. If children have developed an awareness of the beauty of the natural environment and understand the concept of interdependence, then the development of a social consciousness—assuming individual responsibility for the common good—is the next step in environmental education.

Remember that the development of children's social consciousness, especially for the protection of the environment, may be a highly controversial goal. Parents and the community must be involved in formulating the objectives of an environmental education program. You will want their input into the kinds of activities you will provide to foster these goals. Many people believe that protecting the environment without concern for progress will destroy society; others, with vested interests in industry or production, might object for reasons specific to their interests.

Developing respect for the dignity and worth of life and sharing responsibility for the care of private and public property are part of developing social consciousness. Caring for their immediate environment leads children to concern for the wider environment.

To foster social consciousness, the three R's of being a good environmentalist can be introduced in the classroom. Children can be taught to (a) recycle, (b) reduce, and (c) reuse.

Recycle

Children who do not understand how goods get to a store, and will not understand concepts of manufacturing until nearly their adolescence, will have difficulty understanding the concepts involved in recycling. Regardless, even the youngest child can be taught the habit of recycling. They can learn to recycle glass bottles, jars, paper, and aluminum foil used in pie plates, TV dinner trays, and cans. Set up boxes to enable children to sort their trash, and arrange for them to take the containers to a recycling center. Parents can be involved and asked to purchase recycled notebook paper, stationery, and greeting cards.

A strong sense of social consciousness is built as children assume responsibility for the class.

Reduce

All of us, even the youngest, can begin to learn to reduce our use of materials, to cut down on what we consume. Children can

❑ learn to reduce their use of water. They can be taught to brush their teeth by first wetting their brush and then turning off the water, and to use water cooled in the refrigerator instead of letting the water run from the faucet to cool off. Teach children to remember to conserve water by saying, "Presto on! Presto off!"

❑ ask themselves if they really need a paper bag to carry a book home and if presents need fancy wrapping paper.

❑ conduct a "waste audit." First and second graders can conduct an inventory of the amount of waste in their school. They might focus on the cafeteria and observe the food placed in trash cans after lunch, or focus on their room alone, counting how much paper, electricity, water, or paint is being wasted. Or they might conduct a waste audit in their own homes. After the audits, they will report their findings to the class.

❑ get in the habit of using string bags or canvas totes to carry things.

❑ look for things to buy that are not wrapped in elaborate, unnecessary packaging. Even though they love individual pudding snacks or fruit juice containers, they might find other ways to have individual snacks that conserve packaging.

❑ use a lunch box instead of brown paper bags.

❑ learn to reduce the amount of art materials used.

Reuse

Children can be taught to reuse whatever possible. They can

❑ be shown how broken toys and other items can be fixed.

❑ save plastic bags to use again. If they're dirty, turn them inside out, rinse them, and hang them up to dry. A caution: Do not reuse plastic bags with printing or pictures on them, such as bread bags, in this way—the dye in the printing contains lead and can contaminate food.

❑ wash off aluminum foil, let it dry, and put it away.

❑ think of ways to use empty containers or other trash.

❑ cut up brown paper bags to use for wrapping packages for mailing or for drawing or painting.

❑ use computer paper for other projects.

❑ give books, toys, and materials they no longer use to someone else who can use them.

❑ use old greeting cards, catalogs, and magazines in their collages and other artwork.

❑ reuse empty milk cartons as plant containers.

One second-grade teacher initiated a unit on recycling. She first asked the children to predict the amount of material they would find in the trash cans from the school's office, their own room, and the duplicating room, where the copying machines and art and classroom supplies were kept. After the children charted their predictions, they collected the trash cans and sorted the trash into materials that really were trash and needed to be discarded, those that could be recycled, and those that could be reused. The final activity was following the trash collected in their own room on its path to the landfill. The group met with representatives from the sanitation department, mapped and followed the route of their trash, and observed a landfill. They speculated about what would happen to the trash when this specific landfill was full (Fernald & Allen, 1990).

The children formed groups to find out where and how materials could be recycled or reused. One group, after identifying how materials could be recycled, canvassed the entire school and gained the cooperation of all to institute a recycling program. Another group made toys from recycled materials, including rhythm instruments, a kaleidoscope, and milk-carton dollhouse furniture.

Following the interest of the children, the teacher broadened the unit to include concern for the wider environment. The children picked up trash around their school and learned how it was disposed. Awareness of waste processing can also be followed making or decorating trash cans for the playground and posters for the school on recycling, reducing, and reusing.

CAREER EDUCATION

Everyone needs a career—something that gives purpose and direction to life, something that is significant to the individual and useful to society at the same time. Without a career, without this purpose or direction to life, a person is aimless, capricious, and in danger of becoming a parasite (Dewey, 1900). Recognizing the critical need for each child to become a productive member of society, school systems, state departments of education, and the United States Office of Education have mandated beginning education for careers in the preschool and primary grades.

The idea of beginning career education in the preschool-primary classroom, of asking young children who are barely able to comprehend concepts of yesterday, today, or tomorrow to plan for a distant future, might seem inappropriate. Young children, intent on living each day fully, on developing skills, knowledge, and attitudes required for life in the present, have little real concern for a vague and distant future. Yet the preschool-primary class is the ideal place to begin education for a career; it is during these early years that children's attitudes, values, and essential skills are formed. These attitudes, values, and skills will remain with the children and serve to direct their entire lives. Career education seems much more a function of attitude, value, and skill of development than an artificial addition to the curriculum.

Attitudes and Values

Toward Self

Children must grow with a strong sense of self that will give them the confidence to shape their own destinies. Whether fostering career education or fulfilling the general goal of all education, you will want to plan for children to achieve all the self-confidence they need to go on growing and developing into socially responsible and constructive members of society.

Self-confidence is acquired as children are given jobs to fulfill in the classroom. Real responsibilities for preparing materials, cleaning up, and caring for pets, plants, and equipment help children feel successful, competent, and sure of their abilities to contribute to the welfare of the group and, later, to become productive members of society.

Toward Work

Attitudes toward future work are developed through programs designed to increase children's awareness of career opportunities. Children need to be aware of the choices they have and the things they can do.

Children can interview the workers in the school building, the neighborhood, or community to determine their attitudes toward work. Children can ask the following:

- What do you like about your job? Why?
- What do you dislike about it? Why?
- How did you decide to do it?
- What preparation did you need?
- Do you feel proud of your work? Why?
- Have you ever thought about changing jobs?

Help children think about the questions they will ask, perhaps listing them on a chart for reference. Children can compare the interview responses, exploring the different job choices available as well as discovering how people feel about their jobs.

Children can begin to speculate about the future. You might ask them: "What kinds of jobs do you think you might have when you grow up?" Remind them that they might be able to do several things, such as being a student, a parent, an engineer, or an interior designer. By asking children to think about the future, you increase their awareness of career choices and opportunities.

Toward Sex Roles

The question "What do you want to be when you grow up?" continues to be answered on the basis of sex. Despite the ever-increasing numbers of women who have entered the work force, "the occupational awareness, exploration, and decisions of boys and girls tend to remain stereotypical" (Jalongo, 1989, p. 108). Sex differences in attitudes toward careers and career aspirations begin during early childhood and persist into adolescence (Celkis, 1981; Jalongo, 1989). Boys know what their fathers do more often than girls, and are able to identify twice as many career options as girls.

The Women's Action Alliance suggests creating awareness of the role of women in the work force by taking trips into the community and other experiences. The focal point of the trips is to observe people working. Younger children may take trips a few blocks from the school building. You will want to emphasize the nonstereotypic jobs and workers the children observe on the trip. Older children can extend trips over a larger area. They can explore their city, suburb, or rural area by bus, car, or train. Children of all ages can photograph their observations. You will need to guide the children skillfully: seek out the unusual; challenge the stereotypes that are present; and point out the options that exist in career choices for all people, men and women.

Discussions follow each trip, or children can make a mural or booklet of jobs they have seen, jobs their parents hold, or jobs in one store. The emphasis should always be on people in the variety of roles in which they actually function rather than on the stereotypes found in books, the press, and other media.

Other experiences may be vicarious. Selecting books, photos, posters, and pictures showing women in a wide range of career options, both traditional and nontraditional, may be useful. Challenging children's stereotypical thinking is also recommended. When children announce, "You can't play here, only men can build houses," or, "You're the girl, you have to make the dinner," teachers can challenge them, saying, "Remember when we went to the construction sight? There were three women builders," or, "Men can make dinner as well as girls. At the fast-food restaurant, we saw only men making waffles."

Are there opportunities for boys and girls to work together?

Classroom

1. Are there the same number of pictures of girls as boys displayed around the room? _____

   ❑ If not, how many are pictures of girls _____ pictures of boys? _____

   ❑ Do the pictures of girls show girls involved in active play? _____

   ❑ Do the pictures of boys show boys in contemplative or caring roles? _____

   ❑ Do the pictures of girls show girls displaying "positive" behaviors, such as making decisions _____ , leading _____ , helping _____ , solving problems _____ and negative behaviors such as: crying _____ (or sad) _____ , hitting _____ , getting into trouble? _____

   ❑ Are there more pictures of one type than the other? _____ If yes, which type? _____

   ❑ Do the pictures of boys show boys displaying "positive" behaviors, such as making decisions _____ , leading _____ , helping _____ , solving problems _____ and negative behaviors such as: crying _____ (or sad) _____ , hitting _____ , getting into trouble? _____

   ❑ Are there more pictures of one type than the other? _____ If yes, which type? _____

2. In which areas of the room do you display pictures of both sexes involved in that area's activity? blocks _____ , dramatic play _____ , art _____ woodworking _____ , manipulative _____ , science _____ , other? _____

   ❑ Are all areas attractive, i.e., organized, clearly labeled, decorated with pictures of interesting items? dramatic play *Y N*, blocks *Y N*, science *Y N*, music *Y N*, woodworking *Y N*, cooking *Y N*, manipulative *Y N*, reading *Y N*.

   ❑ Are pictures of male and female adults engaged in comparable activities displayed? _____

   ❑ Which activity(ies) _____ ? Which sex(es) _____ ?

Box 11.1
Checklist for a non-sexist classroom

Essential Skills

Career education aids children's development of essential skills. One skill all children need is the ability to make wise decisions. You can incorporate decision making into the curriculum by telling children: "Do it your way," "You decide," or, "It's entirely up to you."

❑ Keep a record for one week (chosen randomly) of activities participated in by each sex:

	M	T	W	Th	F
Girls					
Boys					

Attitudes

1. Do girls and boys play in all areas of the classroom? _____ If not, in which areas don't girls play? _____ In which areas don't boys play? _____

   a. doll corner
      art
      cooking

   b. blocks
      woodworking

   c. sand/water
      reading

   ❑ Are there girls who play only in area A? _____ If yes, how would you characterize these girls?

   ❑ Are there girls who play only in areas A and C? _____ If yes, how would you characterize these girls?

   ❑ Are there boys who play only in area B? _____ If yes, how would you characterize these boys?

   ❑ Are there boys who play only in areas B and C? _____ If yes, how would you characterize these boys?

Box 11.1 *continued*

Skills in relating to people are essential to career education. Children who cannot relate to others are going to have a difficult time developing a career. Schools afford children the opportunity to learn to work with others and develop firm interpersonal relationships.

The essential skills of reading, writing, communicating, and learning to learn are basic to career education. But these skills must not be taught in isolation from the rest of children's lives, or the skills will have no meaning. Moreland

❑ Are there boys and girls who play in areas A, B, and C? _____ If yes, how would you characterize these children?

2. From the following list check those activities that you do not present to your class.
   woodworking _____ active games _____ sewing _____ cooking _____
   music _____ reading _____ electricity _____ dance _____.

   ❑ Why don't you?_____

   ❑ Do you plan a greater percent of noisy or quiet activities?

   ❑ Do you plan a greater percent of messy or neat activities?

   ❑ Do you disapprove of noisy girls? Noisy boys?

3. Check the statements which best describe your reaction to the children's appearance.

   Girls

   What a pretty dress.

   That's a good warm sweater to wear on a cold day.

   You came in like a big girl today.

   Linda is wearing ribbons.

   Those are good shoes for running.

   You look nice today.

   Short sleeves are comfortable on a warm day like today.

   Boys

   What a handsome suit.

   That's a good warm sweater to wear on a cold day.

   You came in like a good boy today.

   Mark has a part in his hair.

   Those are good shoes for running.

   You look nice today.

   Short sleeves are comfortable on a warm day like today.

Box 11.1 *continued*
From "Checklist for a non-sexist classroom" by F. George, 1990, *Young Children, 45,* pp. 10–11. Originally published by Barbara Sprung. Reprinted by permission.

(1973) wrote: "If there is a central message in our concept of career education it is to cry out against the absurd partitioning of the house of education, this separation of subject from subject, of class from class, this false and destructive distinction between subjects" (p. 501).

An integrated approach to the curriculum is essential. As Dewey (1900) suggested, teachers can relate mathematics to career education as children observe

The development of essential skills is a necessary part of career development.

carpenters using measuring devices. Then, teachers can help children to construct their own playhouse using measurements. Following a trip to the gas station to see what attendants and mechanics do, children can read to find out where gasoline comes from, how it is produced and refined, how it gets to the gas station, and perhaps how world politics is involved.

With attitudes of respect for self, work, and others, and the development of essential skills, children are prepared to find their places in a rapidly changing society where occupations appear and disappear. Children who have developed (a) respect for the dignity of people and the worth of occupations, (b) knowledge and understanding of the opportunities available, and (c) willingness to gain skills and an openness to learning throughout life are those who have been educated for careers.

SUMMARY

Today, topics once considered useful only to high school students and adults are part of the social studies curriculum for young children—the environment, current events, and career education.

Environmental education involves fostering children's observation skills, aesthetic sense, and concepts of interdependency and social consciousness.

Children first learn current events by making their own news. Newspapers, news stories, television shows, and other media can be introduced when the topic is relevant to children's lives.

Finally, career education begins in the preschool-primary classroom. There children experience decision making and learn about career choices.

PROJECTS

1. Review the reading, social studies, and mathematics textbooks used in a school system. How are genders portrayed? Record uses of sexist and non-sexist language. Are the words *fire fighter, police officer,* and other nonsexist language used?

2. Go through a local newspaper and a national news magazine. Clip those parts, stories, or pictures that might be of interest to young children. Find stories or parts that could be used to foster the goals for career development, environmental awareness, and political knowledge.

3. Using the yellow pages of a local telephone directory, identify associations or organizations that could be resources for fostering children's environmental awareness.

4. Explore the immediate neighborhood. What areas could be useful to point out the chain of life to young children? Which parts are examples of proper use of land? Are there any areas that could be used to illustrate careless use of the environment?

RESOURCES

Your local newspaper may offer resources for current events in your classroom. Try contacting them or the Newspapers Publishers Association for resources on news making.

Ranger Rick and *Your Big Backyard,* available from the National Wildlife Federation, 1412 Sixteenth Street, N.W., Washington, D.C. 20036-2266, are excellent resources for environmental education.

You might want to explore subscribing to children's newspapers. Some possibilities are

My Weekly Reader Grades K-6
245 Long Hill Road
P.O. Box 360
Middletown, CT 06457

Let's Find Out Grade K
Scholastic News Grades 1–6
Scholastic Magazines
902 Sylvan Avenue
Englewood Cliffs, NJ 07632

REFERENCES

Celkis, R. (1981). *Achievement motivation and the vocational development of adolescent women: A review of the application of achievement motivation research to vocational development theory.* (ERIC Document Reproduction Service No. ED 203244).

Dewey, J. (1900). *School and society.* Chicago: University of Chicago Press.

Dighe, J. (1993). Children and the earth. *Young Children, 50*(3), 58–63.

Feeney, S., & Moravick, E. (1987). A thing of beauty. *Young Children, 42*(6), 6–16.

Fernald, E. A., & Allen, R. F. (1990). Where is away? A geography concept. *The Social Studies, 81,* 29–32.

Jalongo, M. R. (1989). Career education. *Childhood Education, 66*(2), 108–115.

Jarolimek, J., & Parker, W. C. (1993). *Social studies in elementary education. (5th ed.)* Upper Saddle River, NJ: Merrill/Prentice Hall.

Kluge, J. (1971). What the world needs now: Environmental education for young children. *Young Children, 26*(5), 26–32.

Moreland, S. (1973). Career education, not job training. *Social Education, 37,* 501.

Rivkin, M. S. (1995). *The great outdoors: Restoring children's right to play outside.* Washington, DC: National Association for the Education of Young Children.

Rohrer, J. (1996). "We interrupt this program to show you a bombing." *Childhood Education, 71*(4), 201–205.

Science 5/13 (1977). *Early experiences.* London: Macdonald Education.

Wardle, F. (1995). Alternatives . . . Brudertof education outdoor school. *Young Children, 50*(3), 65–73.

Westmoreland, P. (1996). Coping with death: Helping children grieve. *Childhood Education, 72*(3), 157–167.

Do boys and girls participate in similar activities?

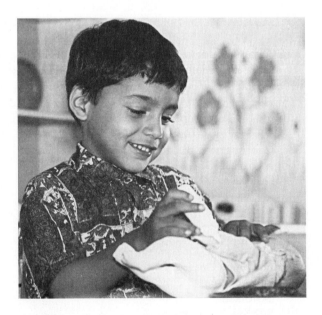

References

Acredo, C., & Schmid, J. (1981). The understanding of relative speeds, distances, and durations of movement. *Developmental Psychology, 17,* 490–493.

Adrian, C. (1971). *Children and civic awareness.* Upper Saddle River, NJ: Merrill/Prentice Hall.

Ahern, J. F., & Moir, H. (1986). Celebrating traditional holidays in the public schools: Books for basic values. *The Social Studies, 77,* 234–239.

Ainsworth, M. D., Belhar, M., Waters, E., & Wall, S. (1978). *Patterns of attachment.* Hillsdale, NJ: Erlbaum.

Allen, J., Freeman, P., & Osborne, S. (1989). Children's political knowledge and attitudes. *Young Children, 44,* 57–60.

Allport, G. (1952). *The nature of prejudice.* New York: Doubleday Anchor Books.

Ames, L. (1946). The development of the sense of time in the young child. *Journal of Genetic Psychology, 18,* 97–125.

Ames, L., & Ames, J. (1981). *Don't push your preschooler.* New York: Harper.

Anselmo, S., & Zinck, R. A. (1987). Computers for young children? *Young Children, 42*(3), 22–28.

Asher, S. R., & Hymel, S. (1981). Children's social competence in peer relations: Sociometric and behavioral assessment. In J. D. Wine & M. D. Syme (Eds.), *Social competence.* New York: Guilford Press.

Atwood, M. E., & Williams, J. (1983). Human sexuality: An important aspect of self-image. *Young Children, 38*(2), 56–61.

Au, K. H., & Kawakami, A. J. (1991). Culture and ownership: Schooling of minority students. *Childhood Education, 67,* 280–292.

Bakst, K., & Essa, E. L. (1990). The writing table: Emergent writers and editors. *Childhood Education, 66*(3), 145.

Banks, J. (1979). *Teaching strategies for the social studies: Inquiry, valuing and decision-making* (3rd ed.). New York: Longman.

Barbour, N., Webster, T., & Drosdeck, S. (1987). Sand: A resource for the language arts. *Young Children, 42*(2), 20–26.

Barclay, K. H., & Breheny, C. (1994). Letting the children take over more of their own learning: Collaborative research in the kindergarten classroom. *Young Children, 49*(6), 33–40.

Bennett, L. (1995). Wide world of breads in children's literature. *Young Children, 50*(5), 64–70.

Berti, A. E., & Bombi, A. S. (1988). *The child's construction of economics.* Cambridge: Cambridge University Press.

Biber, B. (1964). *Some choices children can make.* New York: Bank Street College of Education.

Bloom, B. (1963). *Stability and change in human characteristics.* New York: Wiley.

Braun, J. A., & Sabin, K. (1987). The class reunion: Celebrating elementary heritage. *The Social Studies, 77,* 156–158.

Bredekamp, S. (Ed.). (1986). *Developmentally appropriate practices. Serving children from birth through age 8.* Washington, DC: National Association for the Education of Young Children.

Bredekamp, S. (1987). *Developmentally appropriate practice in early childhood programs serving children from birth through age 8.* Washington, DC: National Association for the Education of Young Children.

Bredekamp, S. (1991). Redeveloping early childhood education: A response to Kessler. *Early Childhood Research Quarterly, 6*(2), 199–211.

Bredekamp, S., & Rosegrant, T. (1992). *Reaching potentials: Appropriate curriculum and assessment for young children. Vol. I.* Washington, DC: National Association for the Education of Young Children.

Brophy, J. (1990). Teaching social studies for understanding and higher-order applications. *The Elementary School Journal, 90,* 351–419.

Bruner, J. (1960). *The process of education.* Cambridge, MA: Harvard University Press.

Bruner, J. (1966). *Toward a theory of instruction.* Cambridge, MA: Belknap Press.

Buettner, C. (1981). War toys or the organization of hostility. *International Journal of Early Childhood, 13*(1), 104–112.

Burke, A. (1923). *A conduct curriculum for the kindergarten and first-grade.* New York: Scribner's.

California State Department of Education. (1987). *History-social science framework.* Sacramento, CA: Author.

Carlsson-Paige, N., & Levin, D. (1985). *Helping young children understand peace, war, and the nuclear threat.* Washington, DC: National Association for the Education of Young Children.

Carlsson-Paige, N., & Levin, D. (1986). The butter battle book: Uses and abuses with young children. *Young Children, 50*(5), 62–63.

Cartwright, S. (1990). Learning with blocks. *Young Children, 45*(3), 38–42.

Celkis, R. (1981). *Achievement motivation and the vocational development of adolescent women: A review of the application of achievement motivation research to vocational development theory.* (ERIC Document Reproduction Service No. ED 203244).

Center for Civics Education (1994). *National Standards for civics education.* Calabasa, CA: Center for Civics Education.

Clarke-Stewart, A., & Koch, J. B. (1983). *Children: Development through adolescence.* New York: Wiley.

Clay, P. L. (1980). *The schools and single parents: Accessibility is the key.* Reston, VA: National Association of Single Parents.

Connell, R. (1971). *The child's construction of politics.* Melbourne, Australia: University Press.

Cooper, P. (1965). The development of concepts of war. *Journal of Peace Research, 2,* 1–18.

Cowen, E. L., Pederson, A., Babigian, H., Izzo, L. D., & Trost, M.A. (1973). Long-term follow-up of early detected vulnerable children. *Journal of Consulting and Clinical Psychology, 41,* 438–446.

Crosser, S. (1994). Making the most of water play. *Young Children, 49*(3), 28–33.

Curry, N. (1974). Dramatic play as a curriculum tool. In D. Spoonseller (Ed.), *Play as a learning media* (pp. 60–69). Washington, DC: National Association for the Education of Young Children.

Curry, N. E., & Arnaud, S. (1995). Personality difficulties in preschool children as revealed through play themes and styles. *Young Children, 50*(4), 4–10.

Curry, N. E., & Johnson, C. N. (1990). *Beyond self-esteem: Developing a genuine sense of human value.* Washington, DC: National Association for the Education of Young Children.

Danielson, K. E. (1991). Helping history come alive with literature. *The Social Studies, 80,* 65–70.

Darrow, H. (1966). *Research: Children's concepts.* Washington, DC: Association for Childhood Education International.

Davis, U. (1991, April). *The New York City Marathon: A social studies unit.* Paper presented at Hofstra's Annual Early Childhood Conference, Hempstead, NY.

Derman-Sparks, L. (1989). *Anti-bias curriculum: Tools for empowering young children.* Washington, DC: National Association for the Education of Young Children.

Dewey, J. (1900). *School and society.* Chicago: University of Chicago Press.

Dewey, J. (1933). *How we think.* Boston: D.C. Health.

Dewey, J. (1944). *Democracy and education.* New York: Free Press.

Dewey, J. (1966). *Lectures on the philosophy of education.* New York: Reginald D. Archambault, Random House.

Dighe, J. (1993). Children and the earth. *Young Children, 50*(3), 58–63.

Dixon, G. T., & Chalmers, F. G. (1990). The expressive arts in education. *Childhood Education, 67*(1), 12–18.

Duffey, R. (1982). *Special days for special people.* Washington, DC: National Geographic Society.

Dunfee, M. (1970). *Elementary social studies: A guide to current research.* Washington, DC: Association for Supervision and Curriculum Development.

Dyson, A. H. (1988). The value of time off tasks: Young children's spontaneous talk and deliberate text. *Harvard Educational Review, 57,* 534–564.

Easton, D., & Dennis, J. (1969). *Children in the political system.* New York: McGraw-Hill.

Easton, D., & Hess, R. (1961). Youth and the political system. In M. Lipset, & L. Lowenthal (Eds.), *Culture and the social character of education.* New York: Free Press.

Elementary Science Study. (1963). *Lights and shadows.* St. Louis, MO: Webster Division McGraw–Hill.

Elkind, D. (1981). Child development and the social science curriculum of the elementary school. *Social Education, 45,* 435–437.

Erikson, E. (1963). *Childhood and society.* New York: W. W. Norton.

Fernald, E. A., & Allen, R. F. (1990). Where is away? A geography concept. *The Social Studies, 81,* 29–32.

Forman, G., & Kaden, M. (1987). Research on science education for young children. In C. Seefeldt (Ed.), *The early childhood curriculum: A review of current research* (pp. 141–165). New York: Teachers College Press.

Freeman, E. B., & Hatch, J. A. (1989). What schools expect young children to know and do: An analysis of kindergarten report cards. *The Elementary School Journal, 89,* 595–607.

French, L. A. (1989). Young children's responses to "When" questions: Issues of directionality. *Child Development, 60,* 225–237.

French, L. A., & Nelson, K. (1985). Temporal knowledge expressed in preschoolers' description of familiar activities. *Papers and Reports on Child Language Development, 20,* 61–69.

Freud, S. (1949). *An outline of psychoanalysis.* New York: W. W. Norton.

Fromberg, D. (1995). *The full-day kindergarten program* (2nd ed.). New York: Teachers College Press.

Fromboluti, C. S. (1991). *Helping your child learn geography.* Washington, DC: Department of Education.

Fry-Miller, K. M. (1982). Energy education: Responding to the nuclear power controversy. *Young Children, 37,* 3–14.

Furman, R. A. (1995). Helping children cope with stress and deal with feelings. *Young Children, 50*(2), 33–41.

Furman, W., Rahe, D., & Hartup, W. W. (1979). Rehabilitation of socially withdrawn preschool children through mixed–age and same–age socialization. *Child Development, 50,* 915–922.

Gargiulo, R. M., & Graves, S. B. (1991). Parental feelings: The forgotten component when working with parents of handicapped preschool children. *Childhood Education, 67*(3), 176–179.

Gelb, S. A. (1987). Christmas programming in schools: Unintended consequences. *Childhood Education, 64,* 9–19.

Genishi, C. (1992). *Ways of assessing children and curriculum: Stories of early childhood practice.* New York: Teachers College Press.

Geography Education National Implementation Project. (1987). *K-6 geography: Themes, key ideas, and learning opportunities.* Macomb: Western Illinois University, National Council for Geographic Education: Washington, DC: U.S. Department of Education.

Gillard, J. V., & Morton, J. S. (1981). Economics: Scarcity and citizen decision making. *Social Education, 45*(7), 532–563.

Goodman, M. (1952). *Race awareness in young children.* Reading, MA: Addison-Wesley.

Grace, F., & Shores, E. F. (1992). *The portfolio and its use: Developmentally appropriate assessment of young children.* Little Rock, AR: Southern Association for the Education of Young Children.

Greenberg, P. (1989). Ideas that work with young children. Learning self-esteem and self-discipline through play. *Young Children, 44*(2), 28–32.

Greenberg, J. (1995). Making friends with the power rangers. *Young Children, 50*(5), 60–61.

Greenberg, P. (1991). *Character development: Encouraging self-esteem & self-discipline in infants, toddlers, & two-year-olds.* Washington, DC: National Association for the Education of Young Children.

Greenstein, F. (1968). The benevolent leaders. *Political Science Review, 50,* 934–943.

Gullo, D. F. (1992). *Understanding assessment and evaluation in early childhood education.* New York: Teachers College Press.

Hatcher, B. (1983). Putting young cartographers "On the Map." *Childhood Education, 59,* 311–315.

Hawkins, M. L. (1979). Teaching map skills in the elementary school. *Indiana Social Studies Quarterly, 32,* 33–37.

Hazen, N. L., Black, B., & Fleming–Johnson, F. (1984). Social acceptance: Strategies children use and how teachers can help children learn them. *Young Children, 39*(6), 26–36.

Heitz, T. (1989). How do I help Jacob? *Young Children, 45*(1), 11–16.

Herman, W. (1980). Toward a more adequate research base in social studies education. *Journal of Research and Development in Education, 13,* 24–35.

Hess, R. D. (1968). Political socialization in the school. *Harvard Educational 38,* 528–536.

Hess, R. D., & Tornery, J. V. (1967). *The development of political attitudes in children.* New York: Anchor Books-Doubleday.

Hickey, M. C. (1990). . . . and justice for all. *The Social Studies, 81,* 77–80.

Hidi, S. (1990). Interest and its contribution as a mental resource for learning. *Review of Educational Research, 60,* 549–573.

Hill, P. S., (1923). Introduction. In A. Burke, *A conduct curriculum for the kindergarten and first grade* (pp. x–xix). New York: Scribner's.

Hirsch, E. S. (1984). *The block book.* Washington, DC: National Association for the Education of Young Children.

Howe, G. (1969). The teaching of directions in space. In W. Hermand (Ed.), *Current research in elementary school social studies* (pp. 31–43). Upper Saddle River, NJ: Merrill/Prentice Hall.

Hunt, J. (1961). *Intelligence and experience.* New York: Ronald Press.

Iran–Nejad, A., Mckeachie, W. J., & Berliner, D. C. (1990). The multisource nature of learning: An introduction. *Review of Educational Research, 60*(4), 509–517.

Ishee, N., & Goldhaber, J. (1990). Story re-enactment: Let the play begin! *Young Children, 45*(3), 70–75.

Jalongo, M. R. (1989). Career education. *Childhood Education, 66*(2), 108–115.

James, M., & Zarrillo, J. (1991). Teaching history with children's literature. *The Social Studies, 80,* 153–160.

Jarolimek, J., & Parker, W. C. (1993). *Social studies in elementary education. (5th ed.)* Upper Saddle River, NJ: Merrill/Prentice Hall.

Kemple, K. M. (1991). Preschool children's peer acceptance and social interaction. *Young Children, 46*(3), 47–56.

Kirst, M. W. (1991). Interview on assessment issues with Lorrie Shepard. *Educational Researcher, 20,* 21–24.

Klein, H.A. (1995). Urban Appalachian children in a Northern school: A study of diversity. *Young Children, 50*(3), 10–17.

Kluge, J. (1971). What the world needs now: Environmental education for young children. *Young Children, 26*(5), 26–32.

Kourilsky, M. (1985). *Children's use of cost-benefit analysis: Developmental or nonexistent?* Paper presented at the annual meeting of the American Educational Research Association, Chicago, IL.

Kozulin, A. (1986). *Vygotsky in context.* Introduction to L. Vygotsky, *Thought and Language.* Cambridge, MA: MIT Press.

Kuebli, J. (1994). Young children's understanding of everyday emotions. *Young Children, 49*(3), 36–46.

Kuykendall, J. (1995). Is gun play ok here? *Young Children, 50*(5), 56–60.

Ladd, G. W. (1990). Having friends, keeping friends, making friends and being liked by peers in the classroom: Predictors of children's early school adjustment. *Child Development, 61,* 1081–1100.

Ladd, G. W., Price, J. M., & Hart, C. H. (1988). Predicting preschoolers' peer status from their playground behaviors. *Child Development, 59,* 986–992.

Lambert, W., & Klineberg, O. (1967). *Children's views of foreign peoples: A cross cultural study.* New York: Appleton-Century Crofts.

Langer, S. (1942). *Philosophy in a new key.* Cambridge, MA: Harvard University Press.

Lanser, S., & McDonnell, L. (1991). Creating quality curriculum yet not buying out the store. *Young Children, 47*(3), 4–11.

Lazar, I., & Darlington, R. (1982). Lasting effects of early education: A report from the consortium for longitudinal studies. *Monographs of the Society for Research in Child Development, 47* (2–3, Serial No. 195).

Lee, F. Y. (1995). Asian parents as partners. *Young Children, 50*(3), 1–10.

Lefrancois, G. R. (1989). *Of children: An introduction to child development* (6th ed.). Belmont, CA: Wadsworth.

Lefrancois, G. R. (1992). *Of children* (7th ed.). Belmont, CA: Wadsworth.

Leming, J. (1985). Research on social studies curriculum and instruction: Interventions and outcomes in the social-moral domain. In W. Stanley (Ed.), *Review of research in social studies education: 1976–1985* (pp. 123–213). Washington, DC: National Council for the Social Studies.

Levin, D. E. (1994). Building a peaceable classroom: Helping young children feel safe in violent times. *Childhood Education, 70,* 267–271.

Liben, L. S., & Downs, R. M. (1993). Understanding person-space-map relations: Cartographic and developmental perspective. *Child Development, 29,* 739–752.

Lord, F. (1941). A study of spatial orientation of children. *Journal of Educational Research, 34,* 481–505.

Loughlin, C. E., & Martin, M. D. (1987). *Supporting literacy: Developing effective learning environment.* New York: Teachers College Press.

Lovell, K. (1971). *The growth of understanding in mathematics.* New York: Holt, Rinehart & Winston.

Luke, J. L., & Myers, C. M. (1995). Toward peace: Using literature to aid conflict resolution. *Childhood Education, 79,* 66–70.

MacDonald, K. (1987). Parent-child physical play with rejected, neglected, and popular boys. *Developmental Psychology, 23,* 705–711.

MacDonald, K., & Parke, R. D. (1984). Bridging the gap: Parent-child play interaction and peer interactive competence. *Child Development, 55,* 1265–1277.

Mager, R. (1962). *Preparing instructional objectives.* Palo Alto, CA: Fearon.

Martin, B. (1969). *Our sun is a star.* New York: Holt, Rinehart & Winston.

Martin, A. (1985). About teaching and teachers. *Harvard Educational Review, 55,* 396–420.

Marzoff, D. P., & DeLoache, J. S. (1994). Transfer in young children's understanding of spatial representations. *Child Development, 65,* 1–16.

Maslow, A. (1969). *Toward a psychology of being.* New York: Van Nostrand.

McAulay, J. (1961). What understanding do second grade children have of time relationships? *Journal of Educational Research, 54,* 312–314.

McMillan, M. (1921). *The nursery school.* London: Dent.

McWhinnie, H. (1992). Art for young children. In C. Seefeldt (Ed.), *The early childhood curriculum: A review of current research* (2nd ed.). New York: Teachers College Press.

Mead, M. (1970). *Culture and commitment: A study of the generation gap.* New York: The American Museum of Natural History.

Meisels, S., & Stelle, D. (1991). *The early childhood portfolio collection process.* Ann Arbor, MI: Center for Human Growth and Development, University of Michigan.

Metz, K. E. (1995). Reassessment of developmental constraints in children's science construction. *Review of Educational Research, 65,* 93–129.

Miller, J. (1985). Teaching map skills: Theory, research, and practice. *Social Education, 49,* 30–33.

Mitchell, A., & Schachel, C. (1979). Journey in time: A foster grandparent program. *Young Children, 34,* 30–39.

Mitchell, L. S. (1934). *Young geographers.* New York: Bank Street College.

Moreland, S. (1973). Career education, not job training. *Social Education, 37,* 501.

Morrow, R. D. (1991). What's in a name? In particular, a Southeast Asian name? *Young Children, 44*(6), 23–29.

Mosenthal, P. B., & Kirsch, S. (1990). Understanding general reference maps. *Journal of Reading, 34*(1), 60–63.

Mugge, D. (1968). Are young children ready to study the social sciences? *Elementary School Journal, 68,* 232–240.

Muir, S. P., & Cheek, H. N. (1991). Assessing spatial development: Implications for map skill instruction. *Social Education, 55,* 316–319.

Myers-Wall, J. A., & Fry-Miller, K. M. (1984). Nuclear war: Helping children overcome fears. *Young Children, 39*(4), 27–32.

National Association for the Education of Young Children. (1991). Position statement: Guidelines for appropriate curriculum content and assessment in programs serving children ages 3–8. *Young Children, 46*(3), 21–40.

National Association for the Education of Young Children. (1996). Position statement: Responding to linguistic and cultural diversity—Recommendations for effective early childhood education. *Young Children, 51*(2), 4–13.

National Center for History in the Schools. (1995). *National Standards: History for grades K-4.* Los Angeles, CA: Author.

National Commission on Social Studies in the Schools. (1989). *Charting a course: Social studies for the 21st century.* Washington, DC: Author.

National Council for the Social Studies. (1989). *Social studies for early childhood and elementary school children: Preparing for the 21st century.* Washington, DC: Author.

National Council for the Social Studies. (1989). *Position statements: Social studies for early childhood and elementary school children: Preparing for the 21st century.* Washington, DC: Author.

New, R. (1993). The integrated curriculum. In C. Seefeldt (Ed.), *The early childhood curriculum: A review of current research.* New York: Teachers College Press.

New, R., & Vechhi, R. (1995). *Reggio Emilia: The project approach.* New York: Heineman.

Newman, R. (1995). For parents particularly: The home-school connection. *Childhood Education, 71,* 296–298.

Noori, K. K. (1995). Understanding others through stories. *Childhood Education, 71,* 134–137.

Notar, E. (1989). Children and TV commercials: Wave after wave of exploitation. *Childhood Education, 66,* 66–68.

Nuffield mathematics project. (1967). New York: Wiley.

Ogle, D. M. (1989). K-W-L: A teaching model that develops active reading of expository text. *The Reading Teacher, 39,* 564–570.

Okomoto, Y., Case, R., Bleiker, C., & Henderson, B. (1996). Cross-cultural investigations. *Monographs of the Society for Research in Child Development, 61*(1–2, Serial No. 246).

Parker, J. G., & Asher, S. R. (1987). Peer relations and later personal adjustment: Are low accepted children at risk? *Psychological Bulletin, 10,* 357–389.

Parker, W., & Kaltsounis, T. (1986). Citizenship and law-related education. In F. Atwood (Ed.), *Elementary school social studies: Research a guide to practice.* (NCSS Bulletin No. 79, pp. 14–33). Washington, DC: National Council for the Social Studies.

Patchin, S. H. (1994). Community service for five-year-olds. *Young Children, 49*(2), 20–21.

Patriarca, L. A., & Alleman, J. (1987). Studying time: A cognitive approach. *The Social Studies, 77,* 273–277.

Pellowski, A. (1969). Learning about present-day children in other cultures. In *Children and International Education Portfolio No. 6.* Washington, DC: Association for Childhood Education International.

Perez, S. A. (1994). Responding differently to diversity. *Childhood Education, 70,* 137–142.

Piaget, J. (1946). The child's concept of space. In H. E. Gruber & J. J. Voneche (Eds.), *The essential Piaget* (pp. 576–645). London: Routledge & Kegan Paul.

Piaget, J. (1952). *The child's conception of number.* New York: Humanities Press.

Piaget, J. (1959). *The language and thought of the child.* London: Routledge and Kegan Paul.

Piaget, J. (1965). *The child's conception of the world.* Totowa, NJ: Littlefield Adams.

Piaget, J. (1969). *Science of education and the psychology of the child.* New York: Viking Press.

Piaget, J. (1969). *The psychology of the child.* New York: Basic Books.

Piaget, J., & Weil, A. (1951). The development in children of the idea of the homeland and of relations with other countries. *International Social Science Bulletin, 3,* 66–73.

Pramling, I. (1991). Learning about "The shop": An approach to learning in preschool. *Early Childhood Research Quarterly, 6,* 151–167.

Prawatt, R. S. (1989). Promoting access to knowledge. *Review of Educational Research, 59,* 1–43.

Prescott, E., Jones, E., & Kritchevsky, S. (1967). *Group day care as a child rearing environment.* Pasadena, CA: Pacific Oaks College.

Preston, J., & Herman, W. (1974). *Teaching social studies in the elementary school* (4th ed.). New York: Holt, Rinehart & Winston.

Ragasto, M. (1982). Computer-assisted instruction. *ETS Developments, 24,* 3–4.

Raines, S., & Canady, R. (1990). *The whole language kindergarten.* New York: Teachers College Press.

Ramsey, P. G. (1982). Multicultural education in early childhood. *Young Children, 37*(2), 13–25.

Raths, J. (1962). Clarifying children's values. *The National Elementary Principal, 42,* 34–39.

Raths, J., Harmin, M., & Simon, S. (1978). *Values and teaching.* Upper Saddle River, NJ: Merrill/Prentice Hall.

Ravitch, D. (1989). The revival of history: A response. *The Social Studies, 82,* 89–90.

Reynolds, M. C., & Birch, J. W. (1986). *Teaching exceptional children in all America's schools* (2nd ed.). Reston, VA: Council for Exceptional Children.

Riley, S. S. (1984). *How to generate values in young children.* Washington, DC: National Association for the Education of Young Children.

Rivkin, M. S., (1995). *The great outdoors: Restoring children's right to play outside.* Washington, DC: National Association for the Education of Young Children.

Roberts, R., & Aman, C. J. (1993). Developmental differences in giving directions: Spatial frames of reference and mental rotation. *Child Development, 64,* 1258–1270.

Robison, H., & Spodek, B. (1965). *New directions in the kindergarten.* New York: Teachers College Press.

Rogers, C. (1961). *On becoming a person.* Boston: Houghton Mifflin.

Rogers, D. L., & Ross, D. D. (1986). Encouraging positive social interaction among young children. *Young Children, 41*(3), 12–17.

Rohrer, J. (1996). "We interrupt this program to show you a bombing." *Childhood Education, 71*(4), 201–205.

Russell, D. (1956). *Children's thinking.* Waltham, MA: Blaisdell.

Sauvy, J., & Simonne, D. (1974). *The child's discovery of space.* Baltimore, MD: Penguin Education.

Schickedanz, J. (1986). *More than the ABC's.* Washington, DC: National Association for the Education of Young Children.

Schickedanz, J. A., Schickedanz, D. L., & Forsyth, P. D. (1982). *Toward understanding children.* Boston: Little, Brown.

Schiller, M. (1995). An emergent art curriculum that fosters understanding. *Young Children, 50*(3), 33–39.

Schug, M. C. (1987). *Teaching the social studies.* Glenview, IL: Scott, Foresman.

Schug, M. C., & Birkey, C. J. (1985). *The development of children's economic reasoning.* Paper presented at the annual meeting of the American Educational Research Association, Chicago, IL.

Schuman, J. M. (1981). *Arts from many hands.* Upper Saddle River, NJ: Prentice Hall.

Schweinhart, L. J., Weikart, D. P., & Larner, M. B. (1986). Consequences of three preschool curriculum models through age 15. *Early Childhood Research Quarterly, 1,* 15–45.

Science 5/13 (1977). *Early experiences.* London: Macdonald Educational.

Sears, A., & Bidlake, G. (1991). The senior citizens' tea: A connecting point for oral history in the elementary school. *The Social Studies, 82,* 133–136.

Seefeldt, C. (1982). I pledge. *Childhood Education, 58*(5), 308–311.

Seefeldt, C. (1989). Perspectives on the pledge of allegiance. *Childhood Education, 65,* 131–133.

Seefeldt, C. (1993). Learning for freedom. *Young Children, 48*(3), 4–10.

Seefeldt, C. (1995). Art—A serious work. *Young Children, 50*(3), 39–66.

Seefeldt, C. (1995). Transforming curriculum in social studies. In S. Bredekamp & R. Rosegrant (Eds.), *Reaching potentials: Transforming early childhood curriculum and assessment.* Vol. 2 (109–123). Washington, DC: National Association for the Education of Young Children.

Seefeldt, C., & Jantz, R. K. (1982). Elderly persons' attitudes toward children. *Educational Gerontology, 8,* 433–494.

Seefeldt, C., & Warman, B. (1990). *Young and old together.* Washington, DC: National Association for the Education of Young Children.

Selman, R. (1980). *The growth of interpersonal understanding.* New York: Academic Press.

Shantz, C. W. (1983). Social cognition. In P. H. Mussen (Ed.), *Handbook of child psychology* (4th ed.) (pp. 495–554). New York: Wiley.

Shuell, T. J. (1990). Phases of meaningful learning. *Review of Educational Research, 60,* 531–549.

Skeel, D. (1974). *The challenge of teaching social studies in the elementary school.* Pacific Palisades, CA: Goodyear.

Slaby, R. G., Roedell, W. C., Arezzo, D., & Hendrix, K. (1995). *Early violence prevention: Tools for teachers of young children.* Washington, DC: National Association for the Education of Young Children.

Snow, C. E. (1983). Literacy and language: Relationships during the preschool years. *Harvard Educational Review, 53,* 165–189.

Spivack, G., & Shure, M. (1978). *Social adjustment of young children: A cognitive approach to solving real-life problems.* San Francisco: Jossey-Bass.

Spodek, B., (1973). Needed: A new view of kindergarten education. *Young Children, 49,* 191–197.

Springer, D. (1952). The development and transformation of monetary meaning in the child. *American Sociological Review, 17,* 275–286.

Stiles-Davis, J., Kritchevsky, M., & Bellugi, B. (1988). *Spatial cognition: Brain bases and development.* New York: Lawrence Erlbaum.

Stone, L. (1986). International and multicultural education. In V. A. Atwood (Ed.), *Elementary school social studies: Research as a guide to practice* (pp. 133–145). Washington, DC: National Council for the Social Studies.

Sullivan, M. (1982). *Feeling strong, feeling free: Movement exploration for young children.* Washington, DC: National Association for the Education of Young Children.

Sund, R. B. (1976). *Piaget for educators: A multimedia program.* Upper Saddle River, NJ: Merrill/Prentice Hall.

Swiniarski, L. B. (1991). Toys: Universals for teaching global education. *Childhood Education, 67,* 161–170.

Taba, H., Durkin, M., Fraenkel, J., & McNaughton, A. (1971). *A teacher's handbook to elementary social studies* (2nd ed.). Reading, MA: Addison-Wesley.

Tiene, D. (1986). Making history come alive. *The Social Studies, 77,* 205–206.

Tolley, H. (1973). *Children and war.* New York: Teachers College Press.

Torney, J., Oppenheim, A. N., & Farnen, R. F. (1975). *Civic education in ten countries: An empirical study.* New York: Wiley.

Torney-Purta, J. (1982). *Research and evaluation in global education: The state of the art and priorities for the future.* Paper presented at the Conference on Priorities in Global Education, Easton, MD.

Vukelich, C. (1990). Where's the paper? Literacy during dramatic play. *Childhood Education, 66*(4), 205–210.

Vukelich, R., & Thornton, S. J. (1990). Children's understanding of historical time: Implications for instruction. *Childhood Education, 66,* 22–25.

Vygotsky, L. (1986). *Thought and Language.* Cambridge, MA: MIT Press.

Vygotsky, L. (1986). *Thought and language.* Cambridge, MA: Harvard University Press.

Waite, P., Smith, S., & Schug, M. C. (1991). Integrating economics into the curriculum: Teaching ideas from England. *The Social Studies, 82,* 67–72.

Wallach, L. R. (1995). Helping children cope with violence. *Young Children, 48*(4), 4–12.

Wann, K., Dorn, M., & Liddle, E. (1962). *Fostering intellectual development in young children.* New York: Teachers College Press.

Wardle, F. (1995). Alternatives . . . Bruderfof education outdoor school. *Young Children, 50*(3), 65–73.

Wardle, F. (1996). Proposal: An anti-bias ecological model for multicultural education. *Childhood Education, 71*(3), 152–157.

Weber, E. (1969). *The kindergarten: Its encounter with educational thought in America.* New York: Teachers College Press.

Webster, T. (1990). Projects as curriculum: Under what conditions? *Childhood Education, 67*(1), 2–4.

Weingold, H., & Webster, R. (1964). Effects of punishment on cooperative behavior in children. *Child Development, 35,* 12–16.

Weitz, L., Quickle, G., Pejchi, L., & Wilson, S. (1991). Building self-esteem? Try real accomplishments. *Young Children, 46*(3), 39.

Westmoreland, P. (1996). Coping with death: Helping children grieve. *Childhood Education, 72*(3), 157–167.

Winter, S. M. (1995). Special challenges in education-diversity: A program for all children. *Childhood Education, 71,* 91–96.

Wolery, M., & Wilbers, J. S. (1994). *Including children with special needs in early childhood programs.* Washington, DC: National Association for the Education of Young Children.

Wright, J. & Shade, D. (Eds.). (1995). *Young children: Active learners in a technological age.* Washington, DC: National Association for the Education of Young Children.

INDEX

A. B. C. Task Force, 30
Abilities of children, and curriculum planning, 26
Abrahams, R. D., 261
Abstract thinking
    concept formation and, 175
    graphing and, 165–166
    maps and, 223, 227
Academic self-esteem, 114
Accommodation, in concept development, 173
Acredo, C., 185
ACTION, 195
Active learners, children as, 24
Adaptation, in concept development, 173–174
Adler, D. A., 201
Administration for Children, Youth, and Families, 18, 195
Administration on Aging, 195
Adoff, A., 261
Adrian, C., 145
Advertising, and decision making, 245–246
Aesthetic awareness, and environmental education, 278–279
Afro-American Folktales (Abrahams), 261
Age appropriateness, and curriculum planning, 22
Ahern, J. F., 197
Ainsworth, M. D., 107
Alexander, Who Used To Be Rich Last Sunday (Viorst), 260
Aliki, 124, 259
Alleman, J., 186
Allen, J., 145
Allen, R. F., 282
Allport, G., 252
All/some relationships, 163
Aman, C. J., 217, 219
American Association of Retired Persons, 195
American Legion, 147

Ames, J., 7
Ames, L., 7, 186
Amos, W. H., 230
Anal stage, 103
Anansi and the Talking Melon (Kimmel), 264
Ancestor Tree, The (Oabinkaram), 264
And Sunday Makes Seven (Baden), 264
And Then What Happened, Paul Revere? (Fitz), 202
"Animal Store, The," 243
Anno, M., 201
Anno's USA (Anno), 201
Anselmo, S., 82
Arbitrary measures
    of distance, 223
    of time, 187
Arezzo, D., 108
Arnaud, S., 123, 124
Arranged environment, as unit introduction, 43
Art
    attitudes and values, 73
    change concepts in, 191
    children's literature and, 78
    field trips and, 73, 94–95
    geography and, 213
    as interest centers, 72–77
    learning experiences and, 45, 159
    movies/videos and, 79
    multicultural education and, 256–257
    past as concept and, 44
    social studies education and, 13
    time and, 187
Artificialism, and geography, 210–211, 212
Ashanti to Zulu: African Traditions (Musgrove), 261
Asher, S. R., 124, 126
Assimilation, in concept development, 173
Association for Childhood Education International, 18
Attachment theory, 106–107

Attitudes and values. *See also* Sex-role stereotypes; Stereotypes
    art and, 73
    career education and, 283–284
    of children, 254
    cultural knowledge and values, 31–32
    curriculum guidelines, 140–141
    democratic society participation, 145–152
    democratic values, 16, 133, 135, 140–145
    indoctrination theory of, 137
    interest centers and, 60
    learning process and, 134–140
    models of behavior, 134–135
    moral values, 136
    multicultural education and, 253–254
    of parents, 254
    projects and resources, 152–153
    reinforcement of, 135–136
    social studies education and, 16, 33
    of teachers, 134–135, 138, 253–254
    transmission of, 133–134
    value analysis theory, 138–140
    value clarification theory, 138
    value conflicts, 139
    value judgments, 139
    value participation, 149–152
Atwood, M. E., 113
Au, K. H., 143
Audiovisual resources, 43, 44, 77, 79–81
Auel, Jean, 170
Authoritarianism, in parents, 107
Autonomous morality stage, 136
Autonomy, as psychosocial stage, 105
Awareness, and concept formation, 177

Babigian, H., 126
Baden, R., 264
Bains, R., 230
Bakst, K., 72
Banks, J., 139
Barbour, N., 64
Barclay, K. H., 15
Bar graph, 165
Basic trust, as psychosocial stage, 104–105
Behavioral objectives, 38–40, 46
Behavioral theories, 102–103, 135
Behavior models. *See* Models of behavior
Belhar, M., 107
Bellamy, Francis, 147
Bellugi, B., 222

Benign neglect, and social-living curriculum, 6
Bennett, L., 60, 258
Berk, L. E., 10
Berliner, D. C., 12, 21
Berti, A. E., 238, 239
Bester, R., 260
Biber, B., 243
Bidlake, G., 195
Big Green Pocketbook, The (Ransom), 260
Big Rigs (Marston), 260
Bill of Rights, 140
Biology, and conceptual relationships, 168
Birch, J. W., 28
Birkey, C. J., 238
Birthday for Blue, A (Lyndon), 202
Black, B., 128
Black Is Brown Is Tan (Adoff), 261
Blocks
    as interest center, 65–66
    maps and, 226, 229
Bloom, B., 9
Body awareness, 218. *See also* Physical movement
Bombi, A. S., 238, 239
Book of Black Heroes from A to Z (Hudson and Wilson-Wesley), 261
Books. *See* Children's literature
Borden, L., 230
Braun, J. A., 201
Bread, Bread, Bread (Morris), 258
Bredekamp, S., 3, 13, 23, 30, 38, 177
Breheny, C., 15
Brophy, J., 3, 100, 133, 137, 138, 202
Brown, C., 230
Brown Angels: An Album of Pictures and Verse (Myers), 202
Bruner, J.
    cited, 32, 171, 172, 174–175, 176
    curriculum content and, 8
    key concepts and, 32, 171–172
    matching content to cognitive development, 174–175
Brusca, M. C., 264
Buettner, C., 267
Bulletin boards, 84–87
Bullock, K., 201
Burke, A., 5
Butter Battle Book, The (Seuss), 266, 269

California State Department of Education (CSDE), 17, 133, 140, 182

Canady, R., 40
Caps, Hats, Socks, and Mittens: A Book of the Four Seasons (Borden), 230
Cardinal directions, 219–221
Career education. *See also* Work
    attitudes and values, 283–284
    essential skills, 285–288
    purpose of, 282
Carlsson-Paige, N., 266, 267, 269
Cartwright, S., 66
CEASE (Concerned Educators Allied for a Safe Environment), 269
Celkis, R., 284
Center for Civic Education (CCE), 137
Centers of interest. *See* Interest centers
Centrars, B., 230
Chalk Doll, The (Pomerantz), 264
Chalmers, F. G., 73
Change concepts
    children and, 190–192
    in integrated social studies curriculum, 191
    as key concept, 183
    in nature, 190
    in neighborhoods, 189
    in school, 189
Charting a Course: Social Studies for the 21st Century (NCSSS), 17
Checklists, 51
Cheek, H. N., 224
Cherry, L., 201
Child choice, and high interest curriculum, 14–15
Children
    as active learners, 24
    attitudes and values of, 254
    change concepts and, 190–192
    child choice, 14–15
    cultural background of, 31–32
    curriculum planning decisions and, 22–30
    curriculum planning involvement of, 34–35, 196
    differences in, 25–26
    elderly and, 193–195
    evaluation and, 46
    experiences of, 3–4, 12, 25–26
    field trip planning and, 92
    as geographers, 208–209
    holiday celebration planning and, 196
    holistic view of, 6
    intelligence of, 9
    as models of behavior, 108
    multicultural education and, 251–254

    needs of, 23–24, 26–30, 41
    neighborhoods of, 31
    parent-child interactions, 107
    as resources, 56
    special needs children, 26–30, 41, 128, 149, 217
    stereotypes and, 256
    teacher-child interactions, 123
    teachers' knowledge of, 22–30
    time concepts of, 184–185
    universal characteristics of, 23–25
Children of Long Ago (Little), 202
Children of the World Say Good Morning (Martin), 259
Children's literature
    attitudes and values, 135
    change concepts in, 191
    as classroom materials, 78
    communication skills and, 117, 119–121
    conflict minimization and, 265
    economics and, 260
    friendship and, 129
    geography and, 213, 230–231
    history and, 201–202
    interest centers and, 71
    movies/videos and, 79
    multicultural education and, 259, 261, 264
    past concepts and, 202
    rotating of, 70
    sharing and, 124
    thinking skills and, 159
    time concepts and, 186–187
Choice
    attitudes and values, 136–137, 138, 142
    child choice, 14–15
    of interest centers, 61
Christmas, 198–199
Citizenship. *See also* Democratic society
    current topics and, 273
    economics and, 237
    education for, 5, 137, 141
    history and, 182
    political concepts and, 145–149
Civil rights, and social studies education, 8–9
Clan of the Cave Bear (Auel), 170
Clarke-Stewart, A., 104
Classification skills
    bulletin boards and, 84
    learning stations and, 88–89
    reflection skills and, 169
    thinking skills and, 163–164
Class inclusion relationships, 163–164

Classroom
  classroom materials as resources for, 77–89
  conflict resolution and, 263, 265
  current topics use, 272–273
  as democratic society, 3, 100, 141, 145
  discipline in, 142–143
  interdependency and, 255–256
  interest centers as resources for, 60–77
  living things in, 255, 278
  newsletters for, 57, 274
  non-sexist, 285–287
  scarcity concept and, 241
Classroom materials
  audiovisual resources, 79–81
  bulletin boards, 84–87
  children's literature, 78
  commercial materials, 85–87
  computers, 81–82
  learning stations, 86–89
  newspapers, 78–79, 274–275
  pictures, 83–84
  reference materials, 78–79
  vicarious experiences and, 77–78
Clay, P. L., 58
Climate conditions, 216–217
Clock time, 186
Cloud Book, The (dePaola), 230
Clymer, E., 201
Coaching, and sharing, 124
Coerr, E., 201
Cognitive Approach to Interpersonal Problem
  Solving, 106
Cognitive development
  classification skills and, 163–164
  concept formation and, 176–178
  matching content to, 13, 174–176
  Piaget's stages of, 9–10, 24–25, 136
  political concepts and, 145–146
  role taking ability and, 122
  social-cognitive theories and, 105–106
  Vygotsky and, 11
Cognitive skills, 6, 7, 109, 138–140
Cognitive theories
  attitudes and values, 136–137
  social-cognitive theories, 105–106
Cohen, Miriam, 124
Collage materials, 76
Columbus Day, 197
Commercial materials, 85–86
Communication skills

career education and, 286
  feelings and, 259
  friendships and, 126
  language and, 118
  nonverbal, 116, 258–259
  with parents of special needs children, 27
  as prosocial skills, 115–121
  role-taking ability and, 116–118
Community
  decision making and, 244
  democratic values and, 143–144
  environmental education and, 280
  holiday curriculum and, 7
  knowledge of, 30–33
  past as concept and, 44
  public services of, 247
  as resource, 44, 89–95, 160
  rules of, 257
  service to others and, 151
  social development and, 107–108
  survey of, 91–92
  violence in, 107–108
Comparing and contrasting, 164
Competence, and high interest curriculum, 14
Competition, and cooperation, 125–126
Computer-assisted instruction, 82
Computers, 81–82, 228
Concept boxes, 36
Concept development
  concept formation and, 173–174
  economic concepts and, 238–240, 243
  geography concepts and, 211
  political concepts and, 145–146
  time concepts and, 184–186
Concept formation. *See also* Thinking skills
  cognitive development stages and, 176–178
  concept development and, 173–174
  guidelines for, 176–178
  key concepts and, 171–173
  matching content to cognitive development,
    13, 174–176
  resources for, 179
  teaching and, 170–171, 175
Conceptual relationships, 168
Concerned Educators Allied for a Safe Environment (CEASE), 269
Conclusions
  historians' methods and, 204
  thinking skills and, 156, 168–170
Concrete experiences, 77, 165, 211

Concrete operational period
  as cognitive development stage, 10, 25
  economic concepts and, 238, 239, 243
  geography concepts and, 211
  time concepts and, 185
Concrete thinking, 175, 227
Conditioning, and behavioral theories, 102, 135
Conduct Curriculum for the Kindergarten, A (Burke), 5
Conflict resolution
  in classroom, 263, 265
  dramatic play and, 68
  as key concept, 254–255
  minimizing conflicts, 265–266
  value conflicts and, 139
  war and peace concepts and, 266–268
Connell, R., 145, 146, 147
Constructing
  children's literature and, 78
  as interest center, 74
Consumers, and economic production, 244–246
Content
  matching content to cognitive development,
    13, 174–176
  unit plans and, 42–43
Continuity of human life
  family and, 193
  holiday celebrations and, 196–200
  intergenerational contacts and, 193–195
  as key concept, 183
Contrasting and comparing, 164
Control, sharing of, 3, 141–142
Cooney, B., 201
Cooper, P., 266, 267
Cooperation, 124–126, 135
Country Far Away, A (Gray), 264
Cowen, E. L., 126
Critical thinking, 155, 164
Crosser, S., 64
CSDE (California State Department of Education), 17, 133, 140, 182
Cultures. *See also* Multicultural education
  art and, 73
  cultural knowledge and values, 12–13, 14,
    31–32
  holiday celebrations and, 7, 196
  modeling and, 76
  music and, 80
  sewing/weaving and, 74
  social studies education and, 12
Current events, 273–276

Current topics
  career education and, 282–288
  classroom use of, 272–273
  current events and, 273–276
  dramatic play and, 69
  environmental education and, 276–282
  projects and resources for, 289
Curriculum. *See also* Integrated social studies curriculum
  attitudes and values, 140–141
  civil rights and, 8–9
  here-and-now curriculum, 3–5, 11, 12, 59, 160
  high interest, 14–15, 21
  holiday curriculum, 7, 11, 196–200, 263
  key concepts of, 32, 172
  as meaningful, 13–14, 21
  Piaget and, 9–10
  relevance of, 40–41
  social-living curriculum, 5–7, 11
  social science discipline structure and, 8
  Sputnik's challenge to, 8
  tourist curriculum, 196
  Vygotsky and, 10–12
Curriculum planning
  child involvement in, 34–35, 196
  community knowledge, 30–33
  day-to-day lesson plans, 37–46
  evaluation and, 47–52
  field trips, 91–94
  knowledge of children, 22–30
  as meaningful, 21
  resources for, 33–34, 52–53
  short- and long-term, 33–37
  spontaneity and, 35–37
  thinking skills and, 156–159
  unit plans and, 40–46
Curry, N., 67
Curry, N. E., 123, 124
Curtis, N., 260
Cutting/pasting, 76

Daddy is Home, 186
Danielson, K. E., 202
Darlington, R., 9
Darrow, H., 49
Darrow, H. F., 176
David Was Mad (Martin), 265
Davis, U., 227
Day in the Desert, A (First-grade students at R. T. Elementary School, Henderson, Nevada), 230

Day/night experiences, 214–215
Day of Ahmed's Secret, The (Heide), 264
Decision making
    advertising and, 245–246
    career education and, 285
    consumers and, 244–246
    democratic values and, 133
    parent involvement in, 59
    scarcity concept and, 242–244
    social studies education and, 33
Declaration of Independence, 140
DeLoache, J. S., 217
Democratic society
    attitudes and values congruent with, 16, 133,
        135, 140–145
    classroom as, 3, 100, 141, 145
    economics and, 237, 244
    family as, 107
    indoctrination and, 137
    participation in, 145–152
    political concepts and, 145–149
    school organization and, 5
    social skills education and, 100
    social studies and, 2
    thinking skills and, 155
Democratic values, 16, 133, 135, 140–145
Dennis, J., 147
DePaola, T., 201, 230
Derman-Sparks, L.
    cited, 7, 30, 196, 198, 199, 252
    special needs children and, 30
Descartes, R., 110
Deserts (Possell), 231
Desimini, L., 202
*Developmentally Appropriate Practice in Early Child-
    hood Programs Serving Children from Birth
    Through Age 8* (Bredekamp), 13, 177
Dewey, J.
    career education and, 287–288
    cited, 115, 155, 157, 169, 182, 183, 243, 251, 279,
        282, 287
    communication skills and, 115
    concept formation and, 171
    decision making and, 243
    environmental education and, 279
    history and, 182
    problem solving and, 139
    progressive education movement of, 3
    thinking skills and, 157, 169
Dighe, J., 278

Dillon, D., 202
Dillon, L., 202
Directional terms, 219–221
Direction and location
    directional terms, 219–221
    distance and measurement, 222–223
    location, 213, 221–222
    maps and globes, 223–229
    movement exploration, 217–218
    relative position, 221
Direct teaching
    of attitudes and values, 137
    of cardinal directions, 220–221
    sharing and, 124
Disabled children. *See* Special needs children
Discipline, and democratic values, 142–143
Displays, 84–85
Dissenting voices, and social skills, 100
Distance and measurement, 222–223
Divergent thinking, 253
Diversity, value of, 3
Dixon, G. T., 73
Dollars and Cents for Harriet (Maestro), 260
Dorn, M., 200
Dorros, A., 260
Down, as directional term, 219
Downs, R. M., 229
Down the Road (Schertte and Lewis), 231
Dramatic play
    children's literature and, 78, 117
    current topics and, 69
    equipping, 67
    field trips and, 94
    friendships and, 127
    here-and-now curriculum and, 4
    history and, 67, 70
    as interest center, 66–68
    movies/videos and, 79
    role-taking ability and, 116
    writing and, 120
Drawing
    children's literature and, 78
    as interest center, 73–74
    writing and, 120
Drosdeck, S., 64
Duffey, R., 7
Dumas, A., 261
Dumpling Soup (Rattigan), 264
Dunbar, J., 230
Dunfee, M., 186

Duration, 187
Durkin, M., 139
Dyan, S., 264
Dyson, A. H., 157, 158

Earth
    artificialism and, 210–211
    environment and, 211–212
    land and water, 213–214
    movement in space, 214–216
    solar system and, 214–217
Earth, Sky, and Beyond (Verdet), 231
Earth Day, 200
Easton, D., 147, 266
Economic production
    concept development and, 239
    consumers and, 244–246
    money and, 246–247
    producer concept, 247–249
    services and, 247
Economics
    children's literature and, 260
    concept development, 238–240, 243
    definition of, 237
    economic production, 239, 244–249
    family and, 56
    housekeeping and, 67
    key concepts in, 173, 240–249
    learning stations and, 89
    multicultural education and, 258
    play and, 69–70, 238, 246
    projects and resources for, 248–249
    scarcity and, 237, 240–244
    sex-role stereotypes and, 113
Education, United States Office of, 282
Education of All Handicapped Children Act of
    1975, 27
Educators for Social Responsibility, 269
Ego, 103
Egocentrism, 136, 141, 188
Elderly, 193–195
Elementary Science Study, 215
Elementary-Secondary Education Act of 1965, 9
Elkind, D., 55, 186, 190
Embryonic concepts, 174
Emotional problems, 29
Employment. *See* Career education; Work
"End, The" (Milne), 191
Energy conservation, 241
Environment

arranged environment, 34
    complexities of, 4
    geography concepts and, 211–212
    least restrictive environment, 27
    relationships within places and, 229–232
    sharing and, 123
Environmental education
    aesthetic awareness and, 278–279
    interdependency and, 278
    observation skills and, 276–278
    social consciousness and, 279–282
Environmental Protection Agency, 276
ERIC Clearinghouse on Early Childhood Educa-
    tion, 52
Erikson, E.
    cited, 103, 105
    socialization theory of, 103–105
Essa, E. L., 72
Ethnicity, 252, 261. *See also* Cultures; Multicultural
    education
Evaluation
    authentic, 47
    checklists, 51
    children's participation in, 46
    informal interviews and, 49–50
    lesson plans and, 40
    observation and, 47–48
    Piagetian interview and, 10
    portfolios and, 48–49
    standardized tests and, 51–52
    structured interviews, 50–51
    time and, 187
    unit plans and, 46
Evans, L., 230
Experiences. *See also* First-hand sensory experiences
    art and, 73
    of children, 3–4, 12, 25–26
    concrete experiences, 77, 165, 211
    day/night experiences, 214–215
    as field trip preparation, 93
    generalizations and, 4, 167
    incidental experiences, 43
    learning experiences, 43–46, 159
    reflection skills and, 169–170
    thinking skills and, 156–159
    vicarious experiences, 77–78, 94, 148, 169, 214
Explicit coaching, 124
Exploration, and concept formation, 177

Facts

concentration of, 3
key concepts and, 172
memorization of, 171
Fagen, S. F., 257
Families. *See also* Parents
   attitudes and values, 133
   continuity of human life concept and, 193
   formal involvement of, 59
   holiday curriculum and, 7
   informal involvement of, 56–58
   integrated social studies curriculum and, 13
   as resource, 56–59
   social development and, 106–107
   spatial interactions and, 233
   wants and needs of, 240–241
Farnen, R. F., 137, 148
Federal Preschool Program and Early Intervention Program Act of 1986, 27
Feeling field trip, 161
Feelings
   attitudes and values, 139
   multicultural education and, 257, 259
   war play and, 267
Feeney, S., 279
Fernald, E. A., 282
Field, Rachel, 243
Field trips
   after the trip, 94–95
   art and, 73, 94–95
   career education and, 284
   change concepts and, 192
   as community resource, 89–90
   continuity in, 168
   curriculum planning and, 91–94
   economics and, 246, 247
   environmental education and, 277
   geography and, 213–214, 217, 223
   interpretation skills and, 168–169
   maps and, 90, 94, 217, 224
   observation and, 160–162
   types of, 90–91
Filmstrips, 80
Fire Fighter Jim (Bester), 260
First-grade students at R. T. Elementary School, Henderson, Nevada, 230
First-hand sensory experiences
   blocks and, 65
   curriculum and, 14, 21
   field trips and, 90
   importance of, 4
   learning and, 11–12

   maps and, 224–225
   thinking skills and, 156–157
Fitz, J., 202
Flack, Marjorie, 259
Flag of the United States, The (Jeffries), 147
Flags, 147, 199
Flavell, J. H., 116
Fleming-Johnson, F., 128
Florian, D., 260
Fog (Fowler), 230
Folktales, 80, 257, 261, 263
Follow Through program, 193
Foods
   food delivery systems, 232
   multicultural education and, 263
Force and time, 218
Formal thought
   attitudes and values, 136
   as cognitive development stage, 10, 25
   economic concepts and, 238
Forman, G., 186
Forsyth, P. D., 127
4-H Clubs, 193
Fowler, S. G., 230
Fraenkel, J., 139
Franklin, Benjamin, 199
Frannie's Fruits (Kimmelman), 260
Freedom of speech, 100, 134, 143
Freeman, E. B., 6
Freeman, P., 145
French, L. A., 185
Freud, S., 103, 110
Friendships, 126–129, 265
Froebel, F., 65
Fromberg, D., 43, 73, 145
Fromboluti, C. S., 210, 231, 232, 233
Fry-Miller, K. M., 241, 267
Furman, R. A., 123
Furman, W., 127

Gans, R., 230
Gargiulo, R. M., 27
Gelb, S. A., 198, 199
Gender issues, 107, 267. *See also* Sex-role stereotypes
Generalizations
   from experience, 4, 167
   thinking skills and, 156, 167–168
GENIP (Geography Education National Implementation Project), 210
Genishi, C., 52

Genital stage, 103
Geography. *See also* Direction and location; Earth
  children as geographers, 208–209
  definition of, 208
  families and, 56
  housekeeping/dramatic play and, 68
  key concepts in, 172, 173, 209–210
  land and water, 213–214
  learning stations and, 89
  regions, 234
  relationships within places, 229–232
  resources for, 235
  skills of, 209
  spatial interactions, 232–234
Geography Education National Implementation
    Project (GENIP), 210
Geography for Life (GESP), 209, 210
George, F., 287
Gerhardt, L., 217
Gert, S. E., 264
GESP, 208, 209, 210
Gifted children, 29–30
Gillard, J. V., 244
Giovanni, N., 261
Globes, 214, 223–229, 262
Gluback, G., 202
Golden Legacy (Dumas), 260
Goldhaber, J., 116, 117
Goodman, M., 252
Good Morning, Good Night, 186
Grace, F., 49
Graphing, 164–167, 169, 258
Graves, S. B., 27
Gray, N., 264
Greenberg, J., 267
Greenberg, P., 110, 153
Greenland, P., 260
Greenstein, F., 146
Grossman, V., 264
Groups
  group discussion, 43, 118–119, 127
  group meetings, 59
  group participation, 149
  group rights, 3, 100
  group rules, 257–258
  own group concept, 252
Growing Story, The (Kraus), 191
*Guidelines for Appropriate Curriculum Content and
    Assessment in Programs Serving Children Ages
    3 Through 8* (NAEYC), 177
Gullo, D. F., 52

Habits, and social-living curriculum, 5. *See also*
    Routines
Hale, Janice, 261
Halloween, 196, 197–198
Hamilton, V., 202
Hanukkah, 198, 199
Hanukkah and Christmas at My House (Gertz), 264
Harmin, M., 137
Harshman, M., 260
Hart, C. H., 126
Hartup, W. W., 127
Hatch, J. A., 6
Hatcher, B., 224
Hawkins, M. L., 224
Hazen, N. L., 128
Head Start Program, 9, 193
Hearing field trip, 161
Hearing impairments, 28–29
Heide, F. P., 264
Heitz, T., 128
Helping Your Child Learn Geography (Fromboluti), 233
Hendrix, K., 108
Here-and-now curriculum, 3–5, 11, 12, 59, 160
Herman, W., 219, 224, 228
*Her Stories: African American Folktales, and True
    Tales* (Hamilton, Dillon and Dillon), 202
Hess, R., 266
Hess, R. D., 146, 147, 148
Hidi, S., 14, 21, 182
High interest curriculum, 14–15, 21
Hill, Patty Smith, 5–7
Hines, A. G., 230
Hirsch, E. S., 66
Historians' methods, 183, 203–204
History
  attitudes and values, 134
  change concepts and, 189–192
  children's literature and, 201–202
  classification and, 88
  continuity of human life and, 183, 193–200
  families and, 56
  historians' methods, 183, 203–204
  housekeeping/dramatic play and, 67, 70
  importance of teaching, 182–183
  key concepts in, 173, 183–184
  past concepts and, 183, 200–203
  projects and resources for, 205–206
  of social studies education, 3–7, 11
  time and, 184–188
History for Grades K-4 (NCHS), 183
History-Social Science Framework (CSDE), 17, 140

Hoban, T., 230
Holiday curriculum. *See also specific holidays*
    continuity of human life and, 196–200
    multicultural education and, 263
    social studies education and, 7, 11
Honig, A. S., 123, 124
Housekeeping
    field trips and, 94
    history and, 67, 70
    as interest center, 66–68
How Bread Is Made (Curtis and Greenland), 260
Howe, G., 220
Hudson, W., 261
Hungry Giant of the Tundra, The (Sloat and Sloat), 264
Hunt, J. McVickers, 9, 13
Hymel, S., 124

Id, 103
If I Had a Puka: Poems in Eleven Languages (Tafuri), 264
I Have a Friend (Narahaski), 231
I'll See You When the Moon is Full (Fowler), 230
In a Circle Long Ago (Van Lann and Desmini), 202
Incidental experiences, 43
Inclusion, 30
Indians. *See* Native Americans
Individuality, and self-concept, 109
Individuals
    attitudes and values, 134
    individual appropriateness, 22–23
    individual rights, 3, 100, 134
    learning stations and, 87
    respect for, 3, 100, 144–145
    social-cognitive theories and, 106
Indoctrination, 137, 148
Industry, as psychosocial stage, 105
Inferences, 156
Informal conversations, and cultural knowledge
    and values, 31–32
Informal interviews, and evaluation, 49–50
Information
    acquiring, 204, 209
    analyzing, 204, 209
    gathering of, 204
    geographic, 209
    interpreting, 156, 163–167
    locating, 155–156, 160–163
    organizing, 156, 163–167, 209
Initiative, as psychosocial stage, 105
Inquiry, and concept formation, 177–178
Inservice activities, 32

Integrated social studies curriculum
    career education and, 287–288
    change concepts in, 191
    cultural background and, 12–13, 14
    geography and, 213
    key concepts and, 172
    time and, 187
    unit plans and, 40
Interdependency
    classroom activities and, 255–256
    environmental education and, 278
    here-and-now curriculum and, 4
    as key concept, 254
    multicultural education and, 255–263
    similarities and, 256–259
Interest centers
    art as, 72–77
    blocks as, 65–66
    children's literature and, 71
    choice of, 61
    floor plan of, 62
    housekeeping/dramatic play, 66–68
    introduction of, 61, 63
    learning centers distinguished from, 86
    library as, 70–72
    place of their own and, 63
    as resource, 60
    sand and water, 63–65
    special centers, 68–70
    types of, 63–77
    writing as, 72
Interests of children, and curriculum planning, 26
Intergenerational contacts, 193–195
Internalized action, 24
International Friendship League, 270
Interpretation skills
    learning stations and, 89
    thinking skills and, 168–170
    vicarious experiences and, 169
Interviews
    informal, 49–50
    Piagetian interview, 10, 49–50
    self-esteem assessment and, 114
    structured, 50–51
Introduction, to unit plans, 43
Intuitive time sense, 184–185
Iran-Nejad, A., 12, 21
Ishee, N., 116, 117
Island Boy (Cooney), 201
Isolations, and movement exploration, 218

It's George (Cohen), 124
I Walk and Read (Hoban), 230
Izzo, L. D., 126

Jalongo, M. R., 284
James, M., 202
Jantz, R. K., 194
Japanese Kite Day, 263
Jarolimek, J., 272
Jaspershon, W., 260
Jeffries, D., 147
Jehovah's Witnesses, 147
Jenkins, S., 231
Job diversification, 248
John Henry (Pinkney), 264
Johnson, Angela, 202
Johnson, C. N., 124
Johnson administration, 9
Joint Council on Economic Education, 249
Jones, E., 123
Josefina Story Quilt, The (Coerr), 201
Journal writing, 72

Kaden, M., 186
Kaltsounis, T., 146
Kawakami, A. J., 143
Keats, Ezra Jack, 186–187
Kemple, K. M., 107, 126, 127
Kimmel, E. A., 264
Kimmelman, L., 260
King, Martin Luther, Jr., 200, 275
Kinsey-Warmock, N., 231
Kirsch, S., 224
Kirst, M. W., 47
Klineberg, O., 252, 253
Kluge, J., 277
Knowledge
    art and, 73
    of children, 22–30
    of community, 30–33
    cultural knowledge and values, 31–32
    field trips and, 95
    questions and, 159
    of social skills, 33
    of social studies content, 16, 32–33
Koch, J. B., 104
Kodaly, Z., 80
Kourilsky, M., 237, 238
Kozulin, A., 11
Kraus, Ruth, 191

Kritchevsky, M., 222
Kritchevsky, S., 123
Kuebli, J., 118
Kuykendall, J., 267
Kwanzaa, 199
K-W-L chart, 36

Ladd, G. W., 126
Lambert, W., 252, 253
Land, 213–214
Langer, S., 159
Language. *See also* Communication skills
    behavioral objectives and, 39
    cognitive skills and, 7
    conceptual relationships and, 168
    curriculum for, 8
    freedom of speech and, 143
    language impairments, 29
    learning experiences and, 44
    multicultural education and, 258–259
    sign language, 259
    social studies education and, 13
    thinking skills and, 158–159
    Vygotsky and, 11
    writing and, 119–120
Language arts
    advertising and, 245
    change concepts in, 191
    conceptual relationships and, 168
    curriculum for, 8
    freedom of speech and, 143
    geography and, 213
    past as concept and, 44
    time and, 187
Lanser, S., 60
Larner, M. B., 9
Latency stage, 103
Laterality, 217
Laws
    education, 9
    special needs children and, 27
Lazar, I., 9
League of Friendship, Inc., 270
Learning
    active learning, 24
    attitudes and values, 134–140
    first-hand sensory experiences and, 11–12
    flexibility of, 41
    social interaction and, 12
Learning experiences

art and, 45, 159
   language and, 44
   unit plans and, 43–46
Learning resources. *See* Resources
Learning stations, 86–89
Least restrictive environment, 27
Lee, F. Y., 31
Lefrancois, G. R., 24, 173
Left, as directional term, 219
Legend of the Indian Paintbrush, The (dePaola), 201
Leming, J., 139
Lesson plans
   evaluation and, 40
   objectives and, 38–39
   preparation and, 37–38
   procedures and, 39–40
   spontaneity and, 36
Let's Find Out, 289
Levin, D., 266, 267, 269
Levin, D. E., 254
Lewis, E. B., 231
Liben, L. S., 229
Library
   as interest center, 70–72
   locating information and, 162
Liddle, E., 200
Life as concept, 211–212. *See also* Continuity of human life
Life in Ponds and Streams (Amos), 230
Line graphs, 165
Lioni, Leo, 129
Listening skills, 118–119
Little, Lessie, 202
Little Bear (Minarik), 170
Living things, in classroom, 255, 278
Lizzie and Harold (Winthrop), 124
Location. *See* Direction and location
Lock, J., 102
Locomotion, and movement exploration, 218
Long, S., 264
Long-term curriculum planning, 33–37
Long-term units, 40–46
Looking Down (Jenkins), 231
Looking field trip, 161
Loomis, C., 231
Lord, F., 219
Lotz, K. E., 231
Loughlin, C. E., 60
Lovell, K., 165, 167
Luka's Quilt (Guback), 202
Luke, J. L., 119

Lyndon, K. R., 202

MacDonald, K., 107
Machotka, H., 260
Maestro, B., 260
Mager, R., 39
Maps
   abstract thinking and, 223, 227
   environmental education and, 277
   field trips and, 90, 94, 217, 224
   geography and, 213
   introduction to, 224–226
   key concepts of, 225–226
   map reading skills, 33
   multicultural education and, 262
   perspective and, 226, 228–229
   representation and, 225, 226–228
   scale and, 226, 229
   spatial interactions and, 233
   symbolization and, 225–226, 228
MAPS: Getting From Here to There (Weiss), 231
Marston, H. I., 260
Martin, A., 26
Martin, B., 214
Martin, Bill, 259, 265
Martin, M. D., 60
Marzoff, D. P., 217
Maslow, A., 110
Mass, Robert, 129
Match the object, 88
Materials. *See* Classroom materials
Mathematics
   career education and, 287–288
   change concepts in, 191
   conceptual relationships and, 168
   curriculum for, 8
   freedom of speech and, 143
   geography and, 213
   learning experiences and, 45
   Nuffield Mathematics Project, 69, 223
   past concepts and, 44
   social studies education and, 13
   time and, 187
McAulay, J., 49
McCloskey, Robert, 187
McDonnell, L., 60
McKeachie, W. J., 12, 21
McMillan, M., 184, 193
McNaughton, A., 139
McWhinnie, H., 120
Mead, M., 193

Meaningful curriculum, 13–14, 21
Measurement
    distance and, 222–223
    of time, 187–188
Measurement and distance, 222–223
Media, 102, 108, 162
Meisels, S., 49
Memorization
    concept formation and, 171, 172
    indoctrination and, 137
Mental retardation, 29
Metz, K. E., 156
Miller, J., 224
Miller, Margaret, 129
Milne, A. A., 170, 191
Minarik, Else Holmeluna, 170
Mr. Cookie Baker (Wellington), 260
Mitchell, A., 195
Mitchell, J. S., 260
Mitchell, L. S.
    cited, 3, 4, 21, 30, 31, 90, 172, 208, 214, 224, 226,
        227, 228, 234
    curriculum planning guidelines of, 21
    here-and-now curriculum and, 3–5, 12
    key concepts and, 172–173
    maps and, 224, 227, 228
    resources and, 33–34, 59
    walking trips and, 90
Modeling (art), 76–77, 78
Models of behavior
    attitudes and values, 134–135
    behavioral theories and, 102
    children as, 108
    conflict minimization and, 265
    sex-role stereotypes and, 113
    sharing and, 123
    social development and, 107
    teachers as, 102, 123, 134–135, 144–145, 151, 265
Moir, H., 197
Money, use of, 246–247
Moral conduct, and social-living curriculum, 5
Moral realism stage, 136
Moral values, 136
Moravick, E., 279
Moreland, S., 286–287
Morgan, S., 231
Morris, Anne, 258
Morrow, R. D., 112
Mosenthal, P. B., 224
Movement exploration
    earth's movement in space, 214–216

physical movement and, 217–218
Movies, 79, 262
Moyer, J., 252
Mufaro's Beautiful Daughters: An African Tale (Step-
    toe), 202
Mugge, D., 238
Muir, S. P., 224
Multicultural education
    attitudes and values, 253–254
    children's awareness of others, 251–254
    children's literature and, 259, 261, 264
    conflict resolution and, 263, 265–268
    holiday curriculum, 263
    housekeeping and, 68
    interdependency and, 255–263
    key concepts in, 173, 254–255
    projects for, 268–269
    resources for, 259, 261–263, 269–270
    similarities and, 256–259
Multiculturalism, as key concept, 254
Multiple classification, 163
Murals, 76
Museums, 201, 257, 263
Musgrove, M., 261
Music, 13, 45, 79, 80
Myers, C. M., 119
Myers, W. D., 202
Myers-Wall, J. A., 267
My Hometown Library (Jaspershon), 260
My Mommy Makes Money (Mitchell), 260
Myths, and holiday curriculum, 7, 196
My Weekly Reader, 289

NAEYC (National Association for the Education
    of Young Children), 18, 41, 177, 178
Names, and self-concept, 110–111, 112
Narahaski, K., 231
National Association for the Education of Young
    Children (NAEYC), 18, 41, 177, 178
National Center for History in the Schools
    (NCHS), 7, 183, 184, 201, 205
National contrasts, 252
National Council for History Education, Inc., 205
National Council for Social Studies, 171, 235
National Council for the Social Studies (NCSS), 2,
    7, 15, 16, 17, 100, 133, 134, 140, 171, 237
National Council of Social Studies, 18
National Council on Aging, 195
National Geographic Society, 235
National Commission for Social Studies in the
    Schools (NCSSS), 17, 141, 196, 203, 209

National Retired Teachers Association, 195
National rules, 258
National School Volunteer Program, 195
National Standards for Civics and Government, 137
National Wildlife Federation, 289
Native Americans, 198, 199, 259
Nature, and change concepts, 190
NCHS (National Center for History in the
    Schools), 7, 183, 184, 201, 205
NCSS. *See* National Council for the Social Studies
    (NCSS)
NCSSS (National Commission for Social Studies
    in the Schools), 17, 141, 196, 203, 209
Needs
    basic needs, 258
    of children, 23–24, 26–30, 41
    scarcity concept and, 237, 240–242
    special needs children, 26–30, 41, 128, 149, 217
Neighborhoods
    change concepts and, 189
    environmental education and, 277
    here-and-now curriculum and, 3
    integrated social studies curriculum and, 13
    land surfaces of, 213
    relationships within places and, 230
    teacher's knowledge of, 31
Nelson, K., 185
New, R., 42, 216
New Coat for Anna, A (Ziefert), 202, 260
New Directions in the Kindergarten, 8
Newman, R., 32
News
    making of, 273–274
    understanding of, 274–276
Newsletters, for classroom, 57, 274
Newspaper Publishers Association, 289
Newspapers, as classroom materials, 78–79,
    274–275
Nez Perce, The: A First Americans Book, (Sneve), 202
Night/day experiences, 214–215
Nixon, J. L., 231
Non-sexist classroom, 285–287
Nonverbal communication, 116, 258–259
Noori, K. K., 78, 82
Norton, J. S., 244
Notar, E., 245
Nuffield Mathematics Project, 69, 223

Oabinkaram, E. T., 64
Objectives
    behavioral, 38–40, 46

evaluation and, 47
of field trips, 92
learning experiences and, 43–44
of lesson plans, 38–39
of unit plans, 42
Observation
    art and, 73
    of climate conditions, 216
    environmental education and, 276–278
    evaluation and, 47–48
    field trips and, 160–162
    friendships and, 126–127
    historians' methods and, 204
    learning stations and, 88
    self-esteem assessment and, 114
    thinking skills and, 160
Ogle, D. M., 35
Ohio, 6
One Morning in Maine (McCloskey), 187
One Yellow Daffodil: A Hanukkah Story (Adler), 201
Ongoing activities, as unit introduction, 43
On the Pampas (Brusca), 264
Open-door policy, 57
Operational time, 185
Oppenheim, A. N., 137, 148
Oral stage, 103
Osborne, S., 145
Our Garage Sale (Rockville), 260
Our Sun Is a Star (Martin), 214
Own group concept, 252

Painting, 73–74, 78
Pantomime, 116–117
Parents. *See also* Families
    artificialism and, 211
    attitudes and values of, 254
    consumer education and, 246
    current events and, 276
    environmental education and, 280
    evaluation and, 47
    field trips and, 90, 91, 92
    holiday celebrations and, 196
    involvement of, 58
    as model of behavior, 102
    multicultural education and, 252–254
    names and, 111
    parent-child interactions, 107
    past concepts and, 200
    recycling and, 280
    of special needs children, 27
    as volunteers, 59

Parke, R. D., 107
Parker, J. G., 126
Parker, W., 146
Parker, W. C., 272
Passover, 198
Pasta Factory (Machotka), 260
Past concepts
    integrated social studies curriculum and, 44
    as key concept, 183
    language arts and, 44
    objects and, 201–203
    people and, 200
Pasting/cutting, 76
Patchin, S. H., 152
Patriarca, L. A., 186
Patriotic Days, 199
Patriotism, 148–149
Pay, and work, 239
Peace concepts, 266–268
Pederson, A., 126
Pejchi, L., 114
Pellowski, A., 252, 253, 261
People Working (Florian), 260
Perception, and thinking skills, 25
Perez, S. A., 111
Personal space, in classroom, 63
Perspective, and maps, 226, 228–229
Pets, in classroom, 255, 278
Phallic stage, 103
Physical disabilities, 29, 217
Physical environment, and sharing, 123
Physical movement
    change concepts in, 191
    learning experiences and, 45
    movement exploration and, 217–218
    social studies education and, 13
Physical self, and social skills, 111–114
Piaget, J.
    artificialism and, 210–211, 212
    assimilation and, 173
    attitudes and values, 136
    cited, 4, 8, 9, 49, 173, 174, 185, 210, 211, 212, 217,
        223, 252
    cognitive development stages of, 9–10, 24–25, 136
    distance and measurement, 223
    economics concepts and, 238
    school as resource and, 59
    sensory-motor space and, 217
    social studies education and, 9–10, 12
    spontaneous concepts, 174
    time concepts and, 186

Vygotsky's views compared to, 11–12
Piagetian interview, 10, 49–50
Picture graph, 165
Pictures, as classroom materials, 83–84
Pinkney, J., 264
Place
    and geography, 221
    place of child's own, 63
    relationships within places, 229–232
Planning. *See* Curriculum planning
Play
    economics and, 69–70, 238, 246
    here-and-now curriculum and, 4
    with maps, 224, 228
    Piaget and, 12
    role play, 118, 127
    shadow play, 215–216
    Vygotsky and, 12
    war play, 267–268
Pledge of Allegiance, 147–148, 199
Political concepts, 145–149
Pomerantz, C., 264
Portfolios, and evaluation, 48–49
Possell, E., 231
Post office, 199, 232
Poverty cycle, 9
Power, and democratic values, 143, 145
Pramling, I., 238, 245
Pratt, Caroline, 65
Prawatt, R. S., 171
Prejudice, 251–252
Preoperational period
    as cognitive development stage, 10, 24–25
    economic concepts and, 238, 243
    geography concepts and, 211
    time concepts and, 185
Preparation, and lesson plans, 37–38
Prescott, E., 123
Preston, J., 219, 228
Price, J. M., 126
Problem solving
    interpreting and, 169
    problem identification, 155, 159–160, 203–204
    questions and, 155, 159–160
    thinking skills and, 139, 156
Procedures
    lesson plans and, 39–40
    unit plans and, 43–46
Process of Education, The (Bruner), 32, 171, 172
Producer concept, 247–249
Production, economic, 239, 244–249

Progressive education movement, 3
Projects
    for attitudes and values, 152–153
    for concept formation, 179
    for current topics, 289
    for economics, 249
    for history, 205
    for multicultural education, 268–269
    for resources development, 95–96
    for social skills, 129–130
    for social studies education, 16, 18
    for thinking skills, 179
Prosocial skills
    communication, 116–121
    cooperation, 124–126
    prosocial behavior as model, 102
    relating with others, 115
    sharing, 121–124
Proximal development, zone of, 11
Pseudo-concepts, 174
Psychoanalytic theory, and social-living curriculum, 6
Psychosocial stages, 103–105
Public Law 94-142, 27
Public Law 99-457, 27
Public services, 247

Quantitative temporal relations, 185–186
Questionnaires, for parents, 57
Questions
    concept formation and, 177–178
    geographic, 209
    problems and, 155, 159–160
Quickle, G., 114

Radio Man, The (Dorros), 260
Ragasto, M., 82
Rahe, D., 127
Raines, S., 40
Rain Song (Evans), 230
Ramsey, P. G., 256
Ranger Rick, 289
Ransom, C., 260
Raths, J., 137, 138
Rattigan, J. K., 264
Reaching Potentials: Appropriate Curriculum and Assessment for Young Children, Vol. 1 (Bredekamp and Rosegrant), 13
Reaching Potentials: Transforming Early Childhood and Assessment, Vol. 2 (Bredekamp and Rosegrant), 13

Readiness, 174
Reading skills, 119–121, 286
Realia, as classroom materials, 84
Recognition, 128–129
Record players, 80–81
Recycling, 280, 282
Reduce, 281
Reference materials
    as classroom materials, 78–79
    locating information and, 162–163
    multicultural education and, 262
    thinking skills and, 159
Reflection skills, 168–170
Regions, 234
Reinforcement
    of attitudes and values, 135–136
    behavioral theories and, 102
    of cooperation, 124–125
Relating with others, as prosocial skill, 115. See also Social interaction; Social skills
Relationships between ideas
    classification and, 163–164
    thinking skills and, 156, 167–168
Relationships within places, 229–232
Relationship thinking, and here-and-now curriculum, 4
Relative position, 221
Repeated field trips, 91
Repetitions, and movement exploration, 218
Report cards, 6
Representation, and maps, 225, 226–228
Resources. See also Children's literature
    for attitudes and values, 153
    children as, 56
    classroom materials as, 77–89
    community as, 44, 89–95, 160
    for concept formation, 179
    constraints on, 34
    cultural knowledge and values and, 31–32
    for curriculum planning, 33–34, 52–53
    economic concepts and, 248–249
    family as, 56–59
    field trips as, 89–95
    for geography, 235
    for history, 205–206
    interest centers as, 60–77
    in multicultural education, 259, 261–263, 269–270
    preparation and, 38
    projects and resources, 95–96

school as, 59–60
sharing of, 121
for social skills, 130
for social studies education, 18
teachers and, 55, 60
for thinking skills, 179
Retired Senior Volunteer Program, 195
Reuse, 281–282
Reynolds, M. C., 28
Rhythmic activities, 116–117
Right, as directional term, 219
Riley, S. S., 136, 137, 153
River Runs Wild, A (Cherry), 201
Roberts, R., 217, 219
Robison, H., 8, 165
Rock Collecting (Gans), 230
Rockville, A., 260
Roedell, W. C., 108
Rogers, C., 110
Rogers, D. L., 127
Role play, 118, 127
Role-taking ability, 116–118, 122
Rosegrant, T., 3, 13, 38
Rosh Hashanah, 198
Ross, D. D., 127
Routines
    change concepts and, 192
    holiday celebrations and, 196
    time concepts and, 186–187
Rules
    of community, 257
    democratic values and, 142–143, 145
    establishment of, 134, 149–150, 257, 265
    of field trips, 93, 94
    formal thought and, 136
    group rules, 257–258
    of interest centers, 63
    of nation, 258
    purposes of, 150–151
    of school, 257
Russell, D., 203
Russo, M., 231
Rydell, K., 231
Rylant, Cynthia, 202

Sabin, K., 201
Sand, as interest center, 63–65
Sauvy, J., 217
Scale, and maps, 226, 229
Scarcity concept, 237, 240–244
Schachel, C., 195

Schertte, A., 231
Schickedanz, D. L., 127
Schickedanz, J., 72
Schickedanz, J. A., 127
Schiller, M., 120, 257
Schmid, J., 185
Scholastic News, 289
Schools
    attitudes and values, 133–134
    change concepts and, 189
    democratic society and, 5
    environmental education and, 277
    integrated social studies curriculum and, 13
    land surfaces of, 213
    patriotism and, 148
    as resources, 59–60
    rules of, 257
    sharing and, 121
    size of, 125
    social development and, 108–109
    spatial interactions and, 232
    staff of, 59–60, 200, 248
    wants and needs of, 242
Schug, M. C., 138, 238, 244
Schuman, J. M., 73
Schweinhart, L. J., 9
Science
    conceptual relationships and, 168
    curriculum for, 8
    freedom of speech and, 143
    past as concept and, 44
    social studies education and, 13
    time and, 187
Science 5/13, 276, 277
Search for Two Bad Mice, A (Clymer), 201
Sears, A., 195
Security, and sharing, 123
See and find, 88
Seefeldt, C., 73, 80, 147, 148, 149, 153, 194
Self-choice, and high interest curriculum, 14–15
Self-concept
    academic self-esteem, 114
    assessing self-esteem, 114–115
    as cognitive skill, 109
    multicultural education and, 252
    names and, 110–111, 112
    physical self and, 111–114
Self-confidence, 283
Self-esteem, 109, 110, 113–115
Self-identity, 109
Self-reports, and self-esteem assessment, 114

Selman, R., 122

Senses, 161, 277, 279. *See also* First-hand sensory experiences

Sensorimotor period
 as cognitive development stage, 10
 economic concepts and, 243
 geography concepts and, 211
 time concepts and, 185

Sensory-motor space, 217

Sequence of events, 187

Sequencing, temporal, 185–186

Services, and economic production, 247

Service to others, 151

Seuss, Dr., 266, 269

Sewing, 74–75

Sex-role stereotypes
 career education and, 283–284
 non-sexist classroom, 285–287
 physical self and, 113–114
 social development and, 107

Sexuality, 113

Shade, D., 81, 82

Shadow play, 215–216

Shadows (Centrars), 230

Shantz, C. W., 122

Sharing skills, 3, 121–124, 126

She'll Be Coming 'Round the Mountain (Bullock), 201

Shop play, 69–70, 238, 246

Shores, E. F., 49

Short-term curriculum planning, 33–37

Shuell, T. J., 14

Shulevitz, U., 260

Shure, M., 106

Sign language, 259

Similarities, and multicultural education, 256–259

Simon, S., 137

Simonne, D., 217

Sing a Soft Black Song (Giovanni), 261

Skinner, B. F., 102

Sky All Around (Hines), 230

Slaby, R. G., 108

Slides, 80, 262

Sloat, R., 264

Sloat, T., 264

Smelling field trip, 161

Smith, B. A., 221

Smith, S., 244

Sneve, F. D. H., 202

Snow, C. E., 159

Snowsong Whistling (Lotz), 231

Snowy Day, The (Keats), 187

Social-cognitive theories, 105–106

Social consciousness, and environmental education, 279–282

Social development, factors affecting, 106–109

Social interaction. *See also* Social skills
 art and, 73
 Erikson's psychosocial stages and, 103–104
 high interest curriculum and, 14
 learning and, 12
 moral values and, 136
 thinking skills and, 157–158
 units and, 40

Socialization theories
 behavioral theories, 102–103, 135
 Erikson's theory, 103–105
 Freudian theory, 103
 social-cognitive theories, 105–106

Social-living curriculum, 5–7, 11

Social organization, 258

Social science disciplines
 integrated social studies curriculum and, 13
 key concepts of, 171–172
 structure of, 8
 teachers' knowledge of, 32–33

Social skills. *See also* Social interaction
 communication and, 116–121
 cooperation and, 124–126
 friendships and, 126–129
 interest centers and, 60
 learning experiences and, 45
 maturity and, 101–102
 projects and resources, 129–130
 prosocial skills, 115–126
 relating with others, 115
 report cards and, 6
 self-concept and, 109–115
 sharing and, 121–124
 social development factors and, 106–109
 socialization theories and, 102–106
 social-living curriculum and, 5
 social studies education and, 11, 15–16, 33, 100
 teachers' knowledge of, 33

Social studies education. *See also* Curriculum; Curriculum planning; Integrated social studies curriculum
 attitudes and values, 16, 33
 civil rights and, 8–9
 current approaches to, 12–16
 definition of, 2

here-and-now curriculum and, 3–5, 11
high interest nature of, 14–15, 21
history of, 3–7, 11
holiday curriculum and, 7, 11
key concepts and, 171–173
knowledge and, 16, 32–33
as meaningful, 13–14, 21
Piaget and, 9–10, 12
projects and resources, 16, 18
recent approaches to, 7–12
sand play and, 64
social-living curriculum, 5–7, 11
social skills and, 11, 15–16, 33, 100
Sputnik's challenge to, 8
teachers' knowledge of, 32–33
textbooks as resources, 78
Vygotsky and, 10–12
Social Studies for Early Childhood and Elementary School Children: Preparing for the 21st Century (NCSS), 17
Sociodramatic play. *See* Dramatic play
Solar system, 214–217
Some/all relationships, 163
Southeast Asian names, 112
Space, movement exploration of, 214–216, 218
Spatial interactions, 232–234
Speaking skills, 118–119
Special centers, as interest centers, 68–70
Specialization, and producers, 248
Special needs children. *See also specific impairments*
    friendships and, 128
    movement exploration and, 217
    types of, 26–30
    unit plans and, 41
    value participation and, 149
Specific-purpose field trips, 91
Speech, freedom of, 100, 134, 143
Speech impairments, 29
Spivack, G., 106
Split-group field trips, 90–91
Spodek, B., 8, 165
Spontaneity
    curriculum planning and, 35–37
    graphing and, 166
Spontaneous concepts, 174
Springer, D., 186
Spring Rabbit, The (Dunbar), 230
Sprung, Barbara, 287
Sputnik, 8
Standardized tests, 51–52, 114

Standard measures, 223
Standards
    for geography, 209, 210
    for history, 183
Stelle, D., 49
Steptoe, J., 202
Stereotypes. *See also* Sex-role stereotypes
    children and, 256
    family and, 58
    holiday curriculum and, 196
    multicultural education and, 259
    own group concept and, 252
    special needs children and, 30
    teachers and, 253
Stiles-Davis, J., 222
Story About Ping, The (Flack), 259
Structured interviews, 50–51
Student Letter Exchange, 270
Subjectivity, and time, 185
Sullivan, M., 218
Summarization skills, 89, 164
Summary, and unit plans, 46
Sund, R. B., 50
Superego, 103
Supreme Court, United States, 147
Swiniarski, L. B., 263
Symbolization, and maps, 225–226, 228

Taba, H., 139
Tafuri, N., 264
Tape recorders, 80–81
Teacher-initiated discussion, as unit introduction, 43
Teachers and teaching
    attitudes and values, 134–135, 138, 253–254
    blocks and, 65
    children's writing and, 119–120
    community knowledge of, 30–33
    concept formation and, 175
    curriculum planning and, 21–22, 33–37
    democratic classroom and, 141
    direct teaching, 124, 137, 220–221
    flexibility of, 41
    friendships and, 126–129
    knowledge of children and, 22–30
    as models of behavior, 102, 123, 134–135, 144–145, 151, 265
    parent involvement and, 58
    resources and, 55, 60
    respect for individual, 144–145
    sharing and, 121, 123, 124

social development and, 108
social studies knowledge of, 32–33
stereotypes and, 253
teacher-child interactions, 123
thinking skills and, 156–159
zone of proximal development and, 11
Television
    advertising and, 246
    as audiovisual resource, 80–81
    multicultural education and, 262
    as news source, 274–275
    violence and, 108
Tell Me a Story, Mama (Johnson), 202
Temporal order, 187
Temporal sequencing, 185–186
Temporal units of time, 186
Ten Little Rabbits (Grossman and Long), 264
Tests, standardized, 51–52, 114
Textbooks, 78
Thanksgiving, 198
Theories
    attachment theory, 106–107
    behavioral theories, 102–103, 135
    cognitive theories, 105–106, 136–137
    indoctrination theory, 137
    psychoanalytic theory, 6
    social-cognitive theories, 105–106
    socialization theories, 102–106
    value analysis theory, 138–140
    value clarification theory, 138
Thinking skills. *See also* Cognitive development;
        Concept formation
    abstract thinking, 165–166, 175, 227
    conclusions and, 156, 168–170
    concrete thinking, 175, 227
    critical thinking, 155, 164
    democratic society and, 155
    divergent thinking, 253
    generalizations and, 156, 167–168
    learning stations and, 88
    locating information and, 155–156, 160–163
    organizing and interpreting information,
        163–167
    perception and, 25
    picture reading and, 83
    problem solving and, 139, 156
    projects and resources, 179
    questioning and sensing problems, 155, 159–160
    reflection skills and, 168–170

relationships between ideas and, 156, 167–168
    social studies education and, 33
    teachers' role, 156–159
Thornton, S. J., 185
Three Bears, The, 170
Tiene, D., 189
Time concepts. *See also* Past concepts
    concept development and, 184–186
    force and time, 218
    in integrated curriculum, 187
    as key concept, 183
    measurement of, 187–188
    passage of, 188
    routines and, 186–187
    scarcity concept and, 242
Time to Wake Up! (Russo), 231
Tolley, H., 266, 267
Tool-maps, 227
Topics, and unit plans, 41–42
Torney, J., 137, 148
Torney, J. V., 146, 147, 148
Torney-Purta, J., 266
Touch and tell, 88
Tourist curriculum, 196
Toys, 201, 263
Tractor (Brown), 230
Tragic events, 275
Transition techniques, and social development,
        108–109
Transportation, 88, 232, 233
Treasure, The (Shulevitz), 260
Triangles and Pyramids and Spirals (Morgan), 231
Trost, M. A., 126
True classification, 163
Trust, basic, 104–105
Two of Them, The (Aliki), 259

Uncle James (Harshman), 260
Under the Moon (Dyan), 264
Unit blocks, 65
United Nations Day, 200
Unit plans
    advantages of, 40–41
    content and, 42–43
    objectives and, 42
    outline for family, 57
    procedures and, 43–46
    spontaneity and, 36
    topics and, 41–42

University of Denver's Center for Teaching International Relations, 269
University of Maryland's Center for Young Children, 35
Up, as directional term, 219
U.S.S.R., 8
Utilization, and concept formation, 178

Valentine's Day, 196, 199–200
Values. *See* Attitudes and values
Van Lann, N., 202
Vecchi, R., 216
Verdet, J. P., 231
Veterans of Foreign Wars, 147
Vicarious experiences
    classroom experiences and, 77–78
    classroom materials and, 77–78
    field trips and, 94
    geography and, 214
    interpretation skills and, 169
    political concepts and, 148
Videos, 79
Violence, 107–108, 267
Viorst, J., 260
Visual impairments, 28
Volunteers, 59, 193, 195
Voting, 149
Vukelich, C., 67
Vukelich, R., 185
Vygotsky, Lev Semenovich
    cited, 4, 7, 13, 40, 158, 171, 174, 175, 196
    matching content to cognitive maturity, 13, 175
    Piaget's views compared to, 11–12
    school as resource and, 59
    social interaction and, 40, 158
    social studies education and, 10–12

Waite, P., 244
Walking trips, 90, 168
Wall, S., 107
Wallach, L. R., 107, 108
Wann, K., 200
Wants and needs, 240–242
War concepts, 266–268
Warman, B., 194
War on Poverty, 9
War play, 267–268
Water
    geography concepts and, 213–214

    as interest center, 63–65
Waters, E., 107
We are Best Friends (Aliki), 124
Weaving, 74–75
Weber, E., 3
Webster, R., 124, 125
Webster, T., 42, 64
Weight, and movement exploration, 218
Weikart, D. P., 9
Weil, A., 252
Weingold, H., 124, 125
Weiss, H., 231
Weitz, L., 114
Wellington, M., 260
We're Going on a Trip (Loomis), 231
When I Am Eight (Nixon), 231
When I Was Young in the Mountains (Rylant), 202
When Spring Comes (Kinsey-Warmock), 231
Where Do You Think You're Going, Christopher Columbus? (Fitz), 202
Wholeness
    key concepts and, 172
    relationships between ideas and, 167–168
Wilbers, J. S., 27
Wild, R., 276
William, M., 264
Williams, J., 113
Wilson, S., 114
Wilson-Wesley, V., 261
Wind Says Good Night (Rydell), 231
Winnie the Pooh (Milne), 170 Winsler, A., 10
Winter, S. M., 25
Winter solstice, 199
Winthrop, Elizabeth, 124
Wittmer, D. S., 123, 124
Wolery, M., 27
Women's Action Alliance, 284
Wonders of Rivers (Bains), 230
Woodworking, 75–76
Work. *See also* Career education
    attitudes and values, 283
    job diversification, 248
    pay and, 239
Working with others, and movement exploration, 218
WOW trips, 91
Wright, J., 81, 82
Writing
    career education and, 286

communication and, 119–121
geography and, 213
as interest center, 72
thinking skills and, 159

Yom Kippur, 198
Young Children, 269
Young Geographers (Mitchell), 172

Your Big Backyard, 289
Youth's Companion, The, 148

Zarrillo, J., 202
Ziefert, H., 202, 260
Zinck, R. A., 82
Zone of proximal development, 11, 175
Zora Hurston and the Chinaberry Tree (William), 264